Contents

Program Practically – Introduction	13
Computer Program	13
Programming Languages	14
A computer program – can we compare it to a recipe used for baking or cooking?	15
Example code	16
Example code	17
The basic operations of a computer	18
Java program application formats	19
Format 1 - Console application	19
Format 2 - Window application (Swing)	20
Format 3 - Web application	22
The structure of a Java program	23
Import	27
Classes	28
Naming A Class (class identifiers)	30
Valid class identifier examples	30
Invalid class identifier examples	30
Module summary	32
Program Practically - Writing to and reading from the console	34
Input from the console	49
Code Review and summary	55
Program Practically - Commenting code for readability	60
Java Multiple line comments	70
Module summary	73
Program Practically - Data types, variables and conversion	75
Data Types	75
Conversion from one data type to another	77

Converting	77
Something a little different with our variables	94
Module Summary	108
Program Practically - Data types, variables, casting and parsing	110
Conversions using casting and parsing	110
Casting	110
Parsing	111
Module summary	125
Program Practically - Arithmetic Operations	127
Arithmetic in our business logic	127
Common arithmetical operators	129
Integer Division	129
Example	129
Example:	130
Plus Equals (+=)	148
Minus Equals (-=)	149
Multiply Equals (*=)	150
Divide Equals (/=)	151
Square root	152
Program Practically - Selection	157
Comparison Operators	158
The if construct	164
The if-else construct	170
The if else if construct	172
The Switch construct	178
Switch with strings	185
Switch with strings	191
Logical operators	200

Let's code some Java using AND operator	202
Let's code some Java using OR operator	206
Let's code some Java using NOT operator	210

Module Summary — 214

Program Practically - Iteration (Looping) — 217

Introduction to Iteration — 217

- For Loop — 218
  - Break Statement — 231
  - Continue Statement — 234
- While Loop — 239
- Break Statement — 246
  - Continue Statement — 248
- Do (While) loop — 252
  - Break Statement — 259
  - Continue Statement — 261
- Program Practically - Arrays — 267
- Single Dimensional Arrays — 270
  - Choice 1:
    - Declaring and creating an array in two stages — 273
  - Choice 2:
    - Declaring and creating an array in one stage — 274
  - Referencing the array elements — 276
- Exercise One - Declare and create string arrays in 2 stages with no initialisation — 277
  - foreach Loop — 286
- Exercise Two – Arrays and array errors — 289

Module summary — 299

Program Practically - Methods — 302

- Methods - concepts of methods and functions — 302
- Some points regarding methods — 303
- Now we will investigate the three types of method: — 306

Void Method	307
Exercise One – Create and use void methods	309
Value Method	323
Exercise One – Create and use value methods	325
Parameters Method	332
Method overloading is a form of Polymorphism (different forms of the same object).	341
Module Summary	345
Program Practically - Classes and Objects	349
A Class is a data structure	350
1. fields (sometimes called variables or members)	350
2. constants	352
3. methods	353
4. Accessors – also called getters and setters	355
5. constructor	358
Exercise One – Create a class without a main() method	368
Constructor	387
Additional Example for classes and objects	400
Exercise Two – Shapes and circle shapes formulae	400
Exercise Three – Shapes and rectangle shapes formulae	408
Module summary	417
Program Practically - String Handling	420
String Handling	420
Creating a String	421
String literal	421
Using New Keyword	423
String Methods	424
charAt(int index)	424
substring(startIndex, endIndex)	426
length()	428
startsWith(char)	429

startsWith(char, startIndex)	430
split (expression)	431
compareTo()	435
compareToIgnoreCase()	436
toUpperCase()	438
concat().	439
trim().	440
replace(old char, new char)	441
replaceFirst(regex, new string)	441
replaceAll(regex, new string)	441
Module summary	444
Program Practically - File Handling	447
An Overview of File Handling	447
Streaming – Old Java versus New Java	447
Writing to a file	448
Create a new package	448
Reading from a file	453
Module summary	457
Program Practically - Serialisation	460
Serialisation	460
De-serialisation	460
Access modifier - transient	460
Serialising the object	464
De-serialising the serialised the file back to an instance of the class	469
Access modifier - transient	474
Module summary	476
Program Practically - Module Labs	500
Module 2 Labs – Println()	501
Module 2 Labs – Possible solutions	502

Module 4 Labs – Data types 504

Module 4 Labs – Possible solutions 505

    Lab One - Possible Solution 505

    Lab Two – Possible Solution 506

    Lab Three – Possible Solution 507

Module 5 Labs – Data conversion and arithmetic 512

Module 5 Labs – Possible solutions 513

    Lab One - Possible Solution 513

    Lab Two – Possible Solution 515

Module 6 Labs - Arithmetic 516

    Lab One – Possible Solution 517

Module 7 Labs - Selection 519

    Lab One – Possible Solution 520

    Lab Two – Possible Solution 521

    Lab Three – Possible Solution 522

Module 8 Labs - Iteration 524

    Lab One – Possible Solution 526

    Lab Two – Possible Solution 527

    Lab Three – Possible Solution 529

    Lab Four – Possible Solution 531

Module 9 Labs - Arrays 533

    Lab One – Possible Solution 534

    Lab Two – Possible Solution 536

    Lab Three – Possible Solution 537

Module 10 Labs - Methods 539

    Lab One – Possible Solution 540

    Lab Two – Possible Solution 543

Module 11 Labs - Classes 546

    Lab One – Possible Solution 548

Module 12 Labs – String Handling 552
   Lab One – Possible Solution 553
   Lab Two – Possible Solution 554

Module 13 Labs – File Handling 556
   Lab One – Possible Solution 557
   Lab Two – Possible Solution 559

Module 14 Labs – Serialisation of a class 561
   Lab One – Possible Solution 563
   Lab Two – Possible Solution 567

© Gerard Byrne 2021

All rights reserved. No portion of this book may be reproduced, copied, distributed or adapted in any way, with the exception of certain activities permitted by applicable copyright laws, such as brief quotations in the context of a review or academic work. For permission to publish, distribute or otherwise reproduce this work, please contact the author.

About the author

Gerry currently works as a Senior Technical Trainer for a Forbes 100 company based in the US. Gerry's role includes upskilling and reskilling software engineers who develop business critical software applications, enhancing the programming skills of 'returners' to the workforce and introducing new graduates to the application of software development in the software industry.

His subject expertise has been developed over a forty-two-year career as a teacher, a lecturer and for the last 11 years, as a technical trainer in a corporate technology environment. Having delivered a range of courses on many varied computer languages and frameworks Gerry is well placed to understand how to teach skills and knowledge to a range of learners. His course delivery has included skilling people in the use of legacy technologies such as COBOL and JCL and more 'modern' technologies such as Java, C#, JavaScript, CSS, Bootstrap, HTML, React, Node.js, Spring Boot, Python, Android and Test-Driven Development.

Gerry, through his long career, has mastered teaching difficult concepts in a simple way that makes learning accessible and enjoyable. The textbooks and notes he produces follow the simple philosophy of keeping it simple, while making the instructions detailed. As an educator Gerry has taught other educators how to teach programming to their students and has provided materials that can be used by the teacher or pupil. Gerry is passionate about software development and believes we can all learn to write code if we are patient and understand the basic coding concepts.

Gerry's learning, development and teaching are driven by the current hot topics within the technology industry and for Gerry they are presently based around the:

- **back-end technologies of the Java programming language** and incorporating the **Spring Framework** to create API's
- **front-end technologies of HTML, CSS, JavaScript and React** because of the high demand for Full Stack Developers and the importance of being an 'all round' developer

About the book

The modules in this book will cover coding in Java using the Eclipse Integrated Development Environment. Other Integrated Development Environments exist such as NetBeans and IntelliJ IDEA Community Edition **see note below**. Whilst the step-by-step instructions and screenshots in the book are based around the Eclipse Integrated Development Environment they can still be used by those preferring a different IDE. All examples run in any IDE. The book is part of the 'Build your programming **muscle** series' by the same author.

The first module in the book is an introduction to programming, covering many of the concepts needed when developing Java code. In the next modules a wide range of programming concepts are covered including data types, selection, iteration, arrays, methods, classes and objects, serialisation, file handling and string handling. This is more than enough to allow the development of applications that emulate commercial application code.

All examples in the modules are fully commented to ensure you can understand the code and to enhance your knowledge of the Java programming language. Reading the comments in the code examples will enhance your understanding of Java and will help explain why the code does something or what the code is doing.

After you have completed the core modules, you will look at common programming routines and use Java to code them. The routines include linear search, binary search, bubble sort and insertion sort.

The book then completes with Labs (exercises) for the majority of the programming modules you have covered. Each Lab exercise is supported with a working solution just, in case you have difficulty completing any of the labs.

The book is ideal for beginners, those refreshing their Java skills or those moving from another programming language. It is ideally suited for those **students** studying programming at high school or at university and for **teachers** who deliver programming lessons. The book offers detailed explanations and the code has excellent comments to support learning. By using clean code with proper naming the code is intuitive to read and understand.

Reading the book is one thing but actually coding the examples using the Eclipse Integrated Development Environment is the most important thing, if you wish to get the best understanding of the Java language. Hands on experience whilst reading this book is the key to success.

Remember

"Life begins at the edge of our comfort zone"

Think about now and believe.

Often the thought of getting started can make us 'frightened' and 'uncomfortable'.

Programming can be rewarding and by going through the modules in this book you will learn that programming is within your grasp and that it is realistic to program in the Java language.

Think about learning as a dot. When you start learning Java the dot is small but as you progress with the modules, the dot will increase in size. It is not how big the dot becomes that is important but simply that the dot is increasing. No matter how 'expert' someone is at Java there will always be an opportunity to learn more and as such the dot continually gets larger.

Note

Another version of this book is also available with step-by-step instructions and screenshots for the IntelliJ IDEA Integrated Development Environment. The code and examples in both books are the same.

The completed code for each module of the book is available at the GitHub repository:

https://github.com/gerardbyrne/Program_Practically_With_Java-EclipseIDEVersion.git

Program Practically

Java

Module 01

Introduction – what is a program?

Programming languages
A recipe
Input, output and process
Packages and classes
Variables
Console, form and web

Gerry Byrne

Program Practically – Introduction

Computer Program

We will be using Java to write computer programs, just like many programmers in companies around the world who use Java to write programs in the commercial environment. So, a very good starting point before we write programs (code) is to fully understand what a computer program is. We can think of a computer program as:

- a sequence of data instructions created by a programmer
- instructions that tell the computer what operations it should execute
- instructions that tell the computer how it should execute an operation
- instructions written in a special programming language e.g. Java, C#, C++, COBOL

Besides Java there are a large number of programming languages available to developers when creating their application. Each programming language will have particular advantages and disadvantages when compared to other programming languages, but they will all be useful for writing computer applications. It is important to understand that some programming languages are:

- more powerful than others e.g. Java
- better for developing applications requiring fast processing e.g. C
- better for developing web based software applications e.g. JavaScript
- better for developing computer games e.g. C++
- better for data analytics e.g. Python
- better for scripting e.g. Perl

The points above should help us understand that there are many programming languages available for software developers, but they all have concepts that can be applied across the majority of the languages. So, by the time we finish reading this book, entering and running all the example code and doing all the exercises, we will be in a strong position to recognise and apply constructs in the C# programming language or the C++ language and indeed other programming languages, as well as our main focus, the Java language.

Programming Languages

The language we will be using is Java but there are a large number of programming languages available for developers to use and create their application. It is certainly great to have a choice of programming languages but at times this makes it difficult to choose the correct one when writing a software application. In the list below, we can see some facts about programming languages:

- there are many different programming languages to choose from
- each language has its own set of very strict language rules
- Java is one such programming language
- other languages include C#, C++, Visual Basic, Python, JavaScript, Cobol, Swift Objective C, Ruby, Go
- programming languages such as Java, C#, C++ and Visual Basic are **high-level languages** since they have a high correlation with a spoken and written language
- assembly language is called a **low-level language** as it has a low correlation to a spoken and written language and is more like the language the computer can understand
- every computer program will need to be 'translated' into 'machine code' that the computer can understand e.g. byte code, object code and binary code
- the process of 'translation' is carried out by **compilers**, **interpreters** or **assemblers**.

A computer program – can we compare it to a recipe used for baking or cooking?

Let us think about a recipe that we might use in our kitchen to create the end product of **fifteens**. The information we need might be written in a book or on a website like this:

Ingredients

- 15 digestive biscuits
- 15 marshmallows
- 15 glacé cherries, cut into halves or smaller
- About 150ml of condensed milk
- 100g desiccated coconut

Instructions

- add 15 digestive biscuits to a bag and 'smash' the biscuits with a rolling pin until they are fine crumbs
- place the crumbs in a mixing bowl
- slice the 15 marshmallows into pieces, we decide how big the marshmallows should be
- slice the 15 cherries in half or smaller, we decide how big the cherries should be
- add the cherries and marshmallows to the digestive biscuit crumbs in the mixing bowl
- stir the mixture until the cherries and marshmallows are spread evenly around the biscuit crumbs
- pour the 150ml of condensed milk on top of the biscuit, glacé cherries and marshmallows mix
- mix the contents in the bowl and add more condensed milk if required, so that the mixture is not dry
- cut a large piece of tinfoil
- spread half of the coconut onto the tinfoil
- scoop the wet biscuit, glacé cherry and marshmallow mix onto the tinfoil
- add the other half of the coconut to the mixture
- roll the tinfoil over the mixture to create a sausage shape
- move the rolled mixture to the fridge
- leave in the fridge for 3 or 4 hours
- remove the roll from the fridge and cut it into 15 slices

As we can see, the recipe contains:

- a list of instructions (directions) written in a language (in this case it is English):
    - likewise a computer program contains a list of statements (directions) written in a programming language such as Java
- a list of ingredients. The ingredients are of various types e.g. biscuits, marshmallows, glacé cherries, condensed milk, desiccated coconut:
    - likewise a computer program contains a list of variables (ingredients). The variables will be of various types e.g. numbers, text

The following two code examples show the structure of code for Java and Python. Even at this early stage, by looking at the code examples, we should see some similarities between the two different programming languages, Java and Python. By the end of this course we will become more familiar with programming and other programming languages will be less 'daunting' to look at and to program with.

Example code

This example shows Java code which will ask the user to input two values and then totals the values. The program is like our recipe, it is a set of instructions.

```java
int counter = 0;
int totalofallclaims = 0;                        variables (list of ingredients)
int inputnumber = 0;


while (counter < 2)
{
   System.out.println("What is the value of the claim: -- ");
   inputnumber = myScanner.nextInt();

   // Add the number to the total
   totalofallclaims = totalofallclaims + inputnumber;     statements (list of statements)
   counter = counter + 1;

   // Print out the total of the claims that have been entered
   System.out.println("The total of the claims that have been input is " + totalofallclaims);
}
```

Example code

This example shows Python code which will ask the user to input two values and then totals the values. The program is like our recipe, it is a set of instructions.

```
counter = 0
totalofallclaims = 0
```
variables (list of ingredients)

```
while counter < 2:

    #Input a number
    inputnumber = int(input("What is the value of the claim: -- "))

    #Add the number to the total
    totalofallclaims = totalofallclaims + inputnumber

    #Add one to the value of count
    counter = counter + 1
```
statements (list of statements)

```
# Print out the total of the claims that have been entered
print("The total of the claims that have been input is ", totalofallclaims)
```

The basic operations of a computer

Under the direction of a program, written in a programming language and converted to machine readable code, the computer can perform the following:

Input The computer can accept user input from the keyboard

Process The computer can perform arithmetic calculations and other types of processing

Output The computer can display a message or result on the screen or other device

Combination The computer can combine these operations in **three** ways:

> **Sequentially**
> A sequence of operations is performed one after the other
>
> **Repeatedly**
> A sequence of operations is performed a number of times
>
> **Selectively**
> One, two or more sequences of operations are performed depending upon a condition e.g. is counter <2

Subprograms A program can contain a number of smaller programs, usually called methods or functions which are the core of modern application development and writing clean code

Java program application formats

Every programming language will have a structure which we need to understand if we wish to write code using that language. In the Java programming language, there are basic elements that all Java programs must have, and these basic elements depend on which type of application is being developed. In this book we will be concentrating on writing code for **console applications** and, as we go through the book applications, we will gain more understanding of console applications. Using Java, we can write applications for a number of different formats:

Format 1 - Console application

In a console application we use the command prompt, better known as the console, to accept **input** from the user and to display **output** data for the user. In the distant past we only had console applications, there were no windows applications. The diagram below shows what the console looks like.

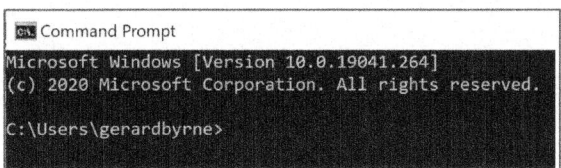

We can think of the console as a black and white screen (although the colours can be changed) where input from the user is accepted and output from the computer program is displayed. Nowadays, whilst many applications have a fancy front end, Java console applications are still used to perform many tasks which are not dependent on 'pretty' user interfaces (UI).

We will be using an Integrated Development Environment (IDE) called Eclipse. When we write our Java code in the editor of Eclipse, we will need to run it to make sure it works properly, so our Java console application will run in a console window which may have a black background and grey text or a white background and black text or some other combination of colours.

In learning to program it is very important that we understand the programming concepts and forget about user interface design, which can be built into the applications that we create after learning all the core programming concepts. In reality we need to concentrate on ensuring that our code is well designed and works as required. There would be no point in having code that did not work properly and there would definitely be no point in having a well-designed ('pretty') user interface that was not functioning as expected because the code behind it was not working correctly.

The diagram below shows the console window for a very basic Java console application. It also shows the code that has been written to produce the console application. The code will be explained later in this module.

```java
package com.gerrybyrne.module02;

public class Program
{
    public static void main(String[] args)
    {
        System.out.println();
    } // End of main() method
} // End of class
```

Console
<terminated> Program [Java Application] C:\Users\gerardbyrne\.p2\p

Format 2 - Window application (Swing)

In a Form application we use a window called a Form onto which we add objects.
The diagram below shows the code that has been written to produce a very basic Java Swing Form application (window application).

```java
package com.gerry;

import javax.swing.*;
import java.awt.*;

public class JavaSwingFormExample
{
    static private JFrame frame;
    static private JTextField textField;

    public static void main(String[] args)
    {
        EventQueue.invokeLater(new Runnable()
        {
            @Override
            public void run()
            {
                try
                {
                    //Create and set up the window
                    JFrame frame = new JFrame();
                    frame.setDefaultCloseOperation(JFrame.EXIT_ON_CLOSE);
                    frame.setTitle("COURSE");
                    JLabel label = new JLabel("Program Practically With Java");
                    frame.add(label);

                    //Display the window
                    frame.setMinimumSize(new Dimension(200, 200));
                    frame.pack();
                    frame.setVisible(true);
                } // End of try section
                catch (Exception e)
                {
                    e.printStackTrace();
                } // End of catch section
            } // End of run() method
        });
    } // End of main() method
} // End of JavaSwingFormExample class
```

We use a Graphical User Interface (GUI) to design the form using objects such as:

- text boxes
- labels
- radio buttons
- checkboxes
- buttons

The screenshot below shows a Swing Window Form application.

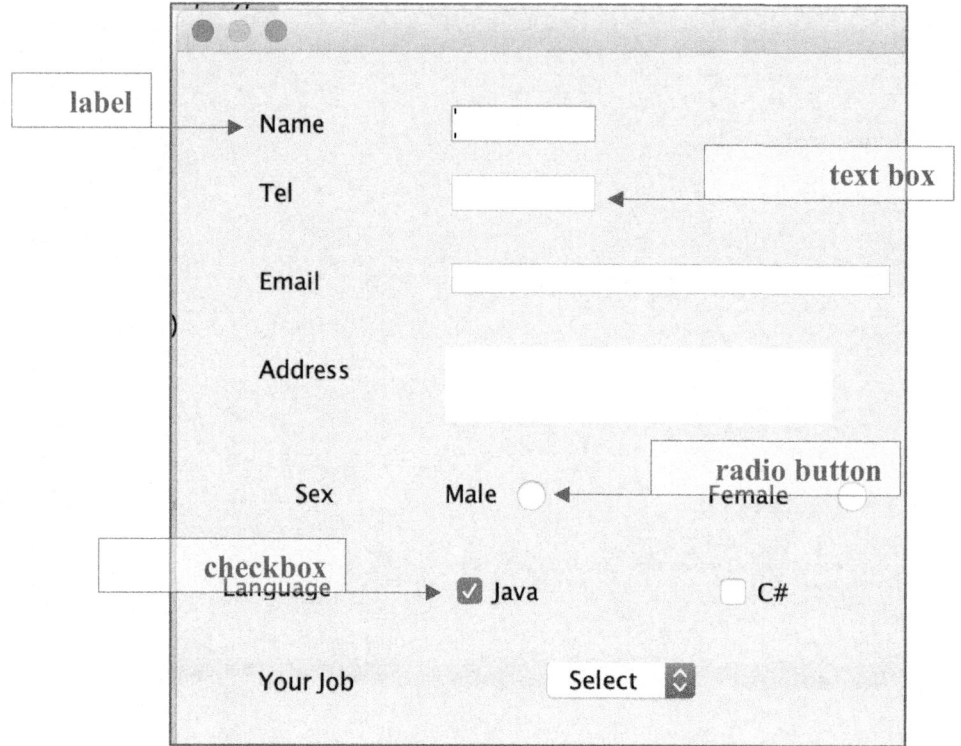

The GUI therefore makes the application different from a console application, which is less concerned with a 'pretty' user interface. A Window Form application can also be known as a desktop application.

Format 3 - Web application

Another very common application is a web application which is developed for use in a browser.

No matter which of the three formats we decide to develop for, the code we write will be Java. So, we need a solid knowledge of the Java language and then we can learn to develop applications which have a better Graphical User Interface than a console application.

The structure of a Java program

In this book concentrating on console applications will allow us to focus on the Java programming language concepts, rather than worrying about the design of a user interface.

We saw in an earlier diagram of the console application, the general form of a **Java c**onsole application. The program code is shown:

```
package com.gerry;

public class Program
{
        public static void main(String[] args)
        {
        System.out.println();
        } // End of main() method
} // End of class
```

The following points will help us fully understand the basic form of the Java console application code:

Package
- all code in a Java application is enclosed within a **package** or **packages**. In this example the single package is called **com.gerry.** The application code starts with the line:

    package com.gerry;

    Essentially a package is like a folder, an area to store classes (code). Packages provide us as developers with a way to keep one set of names separate from another. The class names declared in one package do not conflict with the same class names declared in another.

    Think about a Word document that we create and save as JavaNotes.docx and:

- understand that the document will be saved in a folder on the storage device
- understand that we cannot create a new Word document and save it with the same name in the same folder as the JavaNotes.docx document, as this would cause the operating system to ask us if we wanted to replace (overwrite) the existing file
- on the other hand, if we save the file with the same name but in a different folder this will be fine

The reason for this is that the folders allow us to keep files separate from one another and the actual name of the file will include the folder name.

Example:
C:\Gerry\Documents\MyNotes\JavaNotes.docx
C:\Gerry\Documents\MyClassNotes\JavaNotes.docx

In the same way that we have different folders to separate our Word (or other) documents, we have packages in Java to separate our classes (code files).
Just like every Word document will be in a folder, every class must be inside a package, even if it is the default package. The package com.gerry is essentially two folders, one called **com** and inside this is a folder called **gerry**.

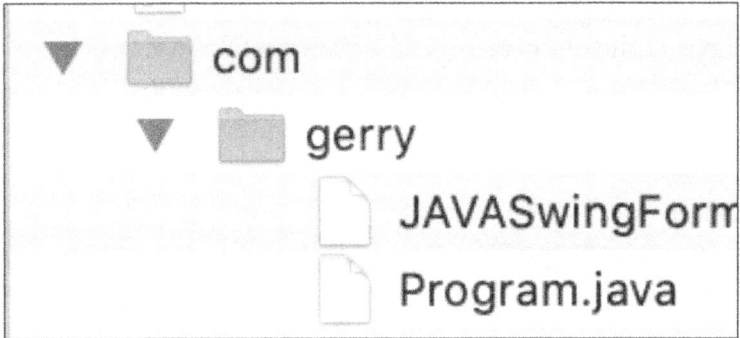

Packages are therefore used in Java to avoid name conflicts and to control the access to classes etc. With packages, it makes it easier to locate related classes that hold our code and they provide a structure for projects which, in a commercial application could contain hundreds of classes and other files.

Java has many built in packages which we will make extensive use of in our coding. Some examples of the packages in Java are shown in the diagram below:

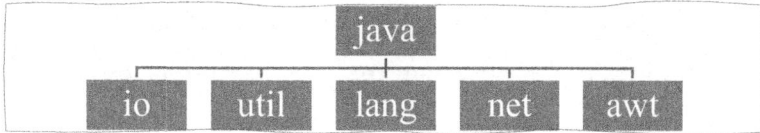

Class

- within the package we will have a **class.** The class is the container into which our Java code will go, it is where our Java code will be wrapped. In this example our class is called **Program**. So, the class looks like this:

public class Program
{
} // End of class

- after the class 'signature' is the **opening curly brace** which is matched by the **closing curly brace**, which is the last thing in our class. Therefore, our code is wrapped within the class braces.

Opening and closing braces are widely used to contain blocks of code and segregate the blocks of code from each other. We will see this when we get to the methods module and in the modules on iteration and selection.

Method

- the main entry point of our console application will be the **method** called **main**. A method is simply a number of lines of code, a block of code. Later, in another module, we will look at methods in detail.

- our lines of code for the main method are enclosed between the **opening curly brace** which is matched by the **closing curly brace**.

public static void main(String[] args)
{
} // End of main() method

- the main method has two keywords before it:
  - **static** - later in another module when we look at classes and methods in detail we will become familiar with the use of the keyword static. Static means the item does not move, it belongs to this class but, for now, just forget about static and simply accept its use in the code as shown.
  - **void** - means that when all the lines of code in the method are executed no value will be returned from the method, it is a void, empty of a return. We will see more about this when we look at methods in details in a later.

- the main method has some text within the brackets:
  - **String[]** – we will see more about this when we look at arrays in detail in a later module. Essentially it means that the main method can accept (be given) one or more inputs which are of type **String**. The **[]** brackets indicate that it is an **array** of strings (one or more string values). So, the main method can accept an array of Strings (a number of values of type String).

  - **args** - args is the name of the String array. If we change the name from args to something else it will not affect the running of the program. In the example shown below args has been amended to the name **gerry** and the program has been run. The result is the same as that shown earlier, the only difference being the name of the array.

```
1  package com.gerry;
2
3  public class Program
4  {
5      public static void main(String[] gerry)
6      {
7          System.out.println();
8      }
9  }
```

Problems @ Javadoc Declaration **Console** Terminal Covera
<terminated> Program [Java Application] /Library/Java/JavaVirtualMachines/jdk1.8.0_14

It should be noted that not all our code will be written inside the main method, but it will definitely be written within a class which is always contained within a package.

Import

As we have read earlier, a console application is contained within a **package.** A package may be thought of as a storage area for some **classes** which themselves contain **methods**. The Java language has thousands of base classes stored in packages. When we write our Java code examples, we will create many more classes and we must follow the same practices as Oracle and store our classes within our own packages. Storing our classes in packages makes code more manageable and easier to maintain.

So, a package can be likened to the folders that we keep our files in. We create different folders to hold different files in a structure that best suits our system. Likewise, we can create packages to hold our Java classes and we can use the packages created by Oracle in our code to get access to the Java base classes.

The lines of code at the start of the program code usually have a format that starts with the keyword **import**. The keyword **import** refers to the fact that we wish to use classes that are contained in the package that follows the word **using**. Remember, packages contain classes that themselves contain methods and it will be these methods, blocks of code, that we will use.

Import statement	Description
import java.lang.Math.*;	// imports everything inside the java.lang.Math package
import java.io.*;	// imports everything inside java.io package
import java.lang.System.*;	// imports everything inside the java.lang.System package
import java.util.Scanner;	// imports a class that allows us to accept input data
import java.util.Calendar;	// imports only the Calendar class
import java.util.Date;	// imports only the Date class
import java.util.ArrayList;	// imports only the ArrayList class

Classes

As stated earlier a console application is contained within a package and within the package there will be a **class** or **classes.** A class is used to allow us as developers to create our own 'types' using Java code. A class is like an outline that will let us define the 'type' we want using other types, methods and variables.

In the example code we saw earlier we have a class called Program. As we become more proficient in our Java coding, we will begin to develop our own more complex classes.

Here we will look at some examples that could be created in real applications:
- a class for the type **pizza** to define that all pizzas have
  - a pizza base
  - a pizza sauce and
  - toppings

Once we define the blueprint class for the pizza we will be able to use the class to create specific types of pizza. For example, we can create a Hawaiian pizza or a Vegetarian pizza. The two classes, Hawaiian pizza and Vegetarian pizza, are called instances of the class and each instance will contain a pizza base, a pizza sauce and a topping(s)

- a class for the type **InsuranceQuote** to define that all insurance quotes must have
  - an applicant's forename
  - an applicant's surname
  - an applicant's date of birth
  - a method to calculate the insurance premium

Once we define the blueprint class for the InsuranceQuote we will be able to use the class to create specific types of InsuranceQuote. We can create a CarInsuranceQuote or a HomeInsuranceQuote which are called instances of the class (instance classes) and each instance will contain an applicant's forename, an applicant's surname, an applicant's date of birth and a method to calculate the insurance premium.

What we should be clear about is that by the time we start our module on classes and objects, which is a complex topic, we will be well prepared and should find the complex topic more manageable.

The starting point, before we code, is to be clear about the following concepts:
- a **class exists inside a package**
- a **class can contain variables** e.g. forename, surname, dateofbirth
- a **class can contain methods** e.g. calculateinsurancepremium()

The term **instance** has been used to describe our **copy** of the class. It is also acceptable to say that our copy is an **occurrence** of the class. More importantly, it is possible to say our copy is an **object**. We will study **classes** and **objects** in more detail in a future module.

As we go through the course modules, we will be reminded of the fact that **a class contains variables and methods**. This is a key concept and will be relevant when writing all code. We will also see later that instead of saying variable we will say **property** when we talk about them in classes, but in our learning, just think variables.

To expand this key concept of variables and methods within a class, take a closer look at the way they have been written:

    variable **forename**
    variable **surname**
    variable **surname**
    method **calculateinsurancepremium()**

- notice that a variable has a name that we give to it. It is one word
- notice that a method has a name that we give to it followed by the open bracket followed by the close bracket i.e. ()
  So **()** means a method. Remember the main method
     static void main(String[] args)
  it has the () brackets.

The main method is interesting because it accepts an input. As developers we can code any method to accept input, alternatively, we can code a method so it does not accept a value or values.

Naming A Class (class identifiers)

In Java we use the following rules when naming a class:
- the class name (identifier) should start with a Unicode characters, an underscore, a $ or a digit 0 to 9
- following the first character the class name should be a sequence of Unicode characters, an underscore, a $ or a digit 0 to 9
- upper and lower case letters are distinct, so the class name is case sensitive, although as a rule we should use a capital letter for class names
- the name can be any length, unlimited! Well that's what the Java specification might say, but we need to also consider the operating system we use. In practical terms we should think of a maximum of 255 characters. This will mean that including the .java extension there will be 5 more characters i.e., 260 characters. So, make the class name a maximum of 255 characters including the 5 character .java.

Valid class identifier examples

Class Name	Class Name
Program	Bank_Account
Customer	Customer_Order
Employee	Mailing-List-For-Customers
Student	_Student_Results_For_Test
Author	Car_Insurance_Quote
$double	Currency_Converter_Euro_To_Dollars

Invalid class identifier examples

Class Name	Class Name
Program Version 1	Bank Account

1Customer	\Customer Order
decimal	Mailing List For Customers
%Student	Student Results For Test
*Author	-Car-Insurance-Quote

In terms of **clean code** some things should be considered as good practise:

- when naming a class we should use a noun phrase
- the class name should describe what the class does, make the name descriptive
- use the singular rather than the plural e.g., use Agent rather than Agents
- start the class name with a capital letter
- keep the class name and the filename the same, this is not always required but it would be seen as the norm and makes for consistent naming across all classes
- use camel case in the class name, this is better than using underscores

Module summary

In this module we have learnt about programming languages and some features that apply to Java. We have learnt that:

- a computer program is a set of instructions created by a programmer
- a computer program is like a cooking or baking recipe
- the computer can perform input, process and output with the help of a program
- Java programs can be written for **console**, **Window** or **Web** applications
- there is a structure to all Java programs which include the use of packages, classes and methods, including the main method
- the keyword import is used to 'import' the classes (methods and variables) contained within the named package
- classes contain variables (properties) and methods
- methods always have the () after them e.g. main()

This is only module 1 and yet we have made great progress in learning to code. **The fundamentals are so important** and are the foundation from which we build real applications. Now we have some fundamental concepts we can progress to other aspects of programming.

What a great achievement for us.

We have learnt so much about the terms and concepts used in Java programming. We will need all this information when we start writing and reading Java code. Everything we have learnt in this module will be reinforced throughout all the other modules. We have just picked up some of the building blocks necessary to allow us to be a Java programmer.

Program Practically

Java

Module 02

Introduction – Input and Output

Console input
Console output
System.out
Scanner class
Imports

Gerry Byrne

Program Practically - Writing to and reading from the console

We learnt in module 1 that:

Under the direction of a program, written in a programming language and converted to machine readable code, the computer can perform the following:

Input   The computer can accept user input from the keyboard.

Process   The computer can perform arithmetic calculations and other types of processing.

Output   The computer can display a message or result on the screen or other device.

This module will concentrate on how to **output to the console**. We will also use a basic Java command to **read from the console**, which is an example of **input**. It is very important to understand that what we learn by completing the simple examples in this module will:

- help us build more complex code examples in future modules
- show us commands that are used in real world applications
- get us started with two important aspect of any programming language – **input** and **output**

Looking back at something that was shown in module 1:

> We can think of the console as a black and white screen (although the colours can be changed) where input from the user is accepted and output from the computer program is displayed.

So, our console will display data and in the Java programming language we can achieve this with the line of code:

>   System.*out*.println();

Analysing this line of code.

- **Fact 1**

    Here we can see the keyword **System.** System is a final class within the java.lang package and included in the class are facilities to handle standard input, standard output and error output streams. So, we can see that this means System allows us to interact with the console, yes, the 'screen' we mentioned earlier where input from the user is accepted and output from the computer program is displayed.

- **Fact 2**

    The second part is the full stop (or period as it is also known). In programming languages like Java, the full stop means that we want to use a part or element of the **object** that appears to the left of the full stop, in this case the **out**. The object will generally be a class, and we talked about classes in the previous module. Now, if we consider that System is a class and we once again go back to what we learnt in the previous module:

    > "As we go through the course modules, we will be reminded of the fact that **a class contains variables and methods**. This is a key concept and will be relevant when writing all code".

So, if System is a class, it can contain variables and methods, therefore when we add the full stop after the class name, we are saying we want to use either a variable or a method that is inside the class. It was also said in the previous module:

> "Likewise, we can create packages to hold our classes and we can use the packages created by Oracle in our code to get access to the **Oracle base classes**".

Oracle base classes will be like the classes we write, they contain variables and methods which we as developers can use, without having to write them. System is one such base class and it therefore contains variables and methods that we can use.

out is a variable (member) of the System class. It is very special as it is of the data type **PrintStream,** but let's not concern ourselves with this now, we will just use the statement to perform input and output.

- **Fact 3**

The third part is println()

Looking back to what we learnt in the previous module:

"So () means a method"

We should now be able to recognise that println() is indeed a method and, as it has nothing between the brackets (), we should also be aware that this means the method takes in no value.

- **Fact 4**

println() belongs to a class System which is contained in the java.lang package (we saw the java.lang connection in the diagram we saw earlier).

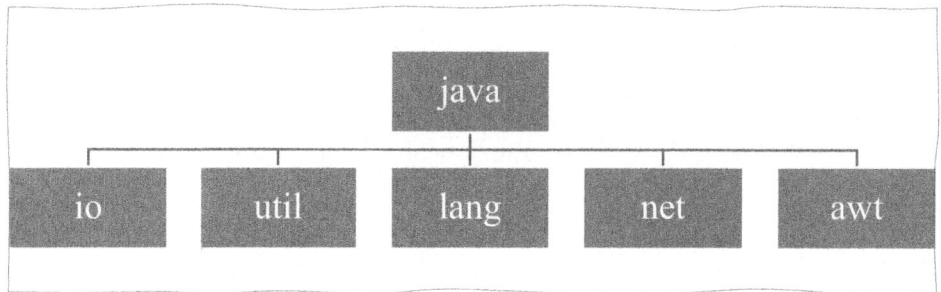

It is not obvious from the line of code that println() belongs to the System class, but it will become obvious as we start to write the code in our Integrated Development Environment (IDE). To explain this, we can think back to what we learnt in the previous module:

"The lines of code at the start of the program code usually have a format that starts with the keyword **import**. The word **import** refers to the fact that we wish to use classes (and ultimately the methods and variables in the classes) that are contained in the package that follows the word import".

import static java.lang.System.*;

So, we can see a package called **java.lang** being used in our Java code and this illustrates another important concept to get used to when programming:

"we will use classes that already exist to help us build our own applications using Java code".

Always remember the key fact that **a class contains variables and methods**, so when we tell our code to use an existing class, which exists in a package, we are doing this to get access to variables and methods that already exist and will help us in building our application with Java code.

When we use an Integrated Development Environment like Eclipse or IntelliJ we will receive assistance when we type a class name (or package name) followed by the dot. We call this **dot notation**, and it presents us with a list of variables and methods that exist in the class, very handy for us as developers. The diagram below shows an example of the packages appearing as part of the Integrated Development Environment assistance and also the variables (properties) and methods that exist in the System class appearing, when we use the Eclipse Integrated Development Environment.

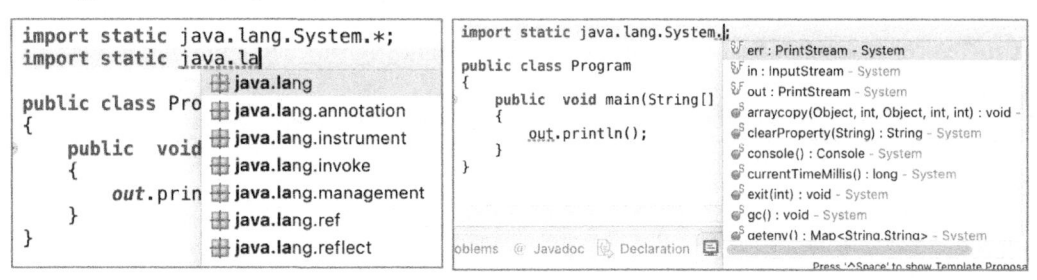

If we study the icons this will help when we are coding our applications. There are different icons representing aspects of the class. For now, simply get familiar with two of the icons that represent the variables (properties) and the methods:

△	default field (package visible)	C	constructor
□	private field	A	abstract member
◇	protected field	F	final member
○	public field	S	static member
		⊙	synchronized member
▲	default method (package visible)	N	native method
■	private method	T	transient field
◆	protected method	V	volatile field
●	public method	▷	type with public static void main(String[] args)

The two terms and concepts, field and method, are highly important when we write programs in any programming language. It is essential that we become familiar with both terms as we will use the terms throughout the modules, and we will use them in every program we write during the modules. We will give a preliminary explanation of the two terms below:

The field

A **field** is represented in a few different ways depending on the type of field. A **field** is also called a property, variable or member of the class. Look back to what we learnt in previous module:

> "We will also see later that we use a different word from variable (property) when we talk about classes, but in our learning, they will be referred to as variables"

So, another name for a **variable** that we will use is **field** or **property.** We will also see the word **member.**

The Method

A **method** is represented in a few different ways depending on the type of method. A method is a block of code.

Let's code some Java

Now it is time for us to do some Java coding. The Java console application we will code will use the **System.out.println()** method to output data to the console window and then use some of the methods of the Scanner class to read keyboard input from the class.

The diagram below shows some of the methods that exist in the Scanner class:

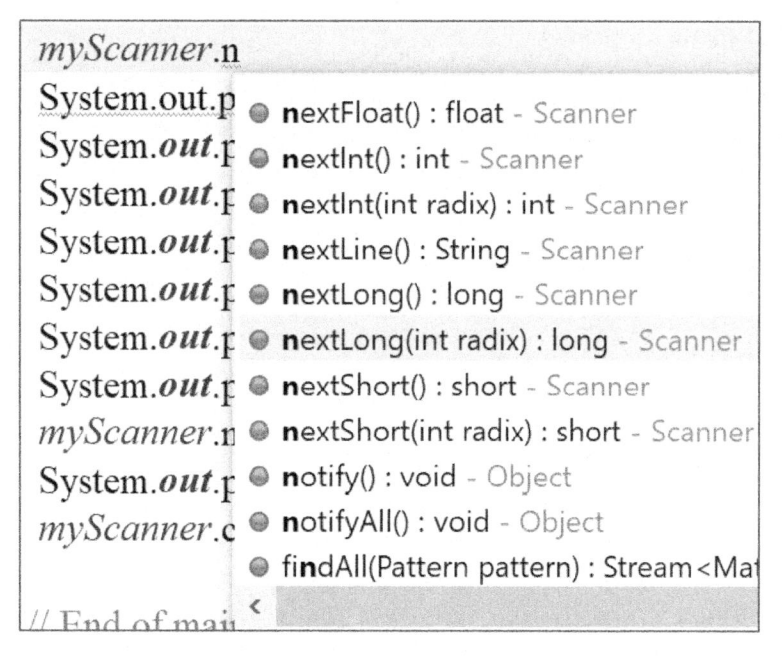

```
myScanner.n
System.out.p    ● nextFloat() : float - Scanner
System.out.p    ● nextInt() : int - Scanner
System.out.p    ● nextInt(int radix) : int - Scanner
System.out.p    ● nextLine() : String - Scanner
System.out.p    ● nextLong() : long - Scanner
System.out.p    ● nextLong(int radix) : long - Scanner
System.out.p    ● nextShort() : short - Scanner
myScanner.n     ● nextShort(int radix) : short - Scanner
System.out.p    ● notify() : void - Object
myScanner.c     ● notifyAll() : void - Object
                ● findAll(Pattern pattern) : Stream<Mat
// End of mai
```

Create a workspace (a folder to hold one or more projects)

All our code will be saved in one location called a workspace. The workspace is a folder on our computer. Once we create the workspace, we will create projects within it and these projects are folders within the workspace. So, now we need to create a workspace at a location of our choice on our computer.

1. Open the Eclipse Integrated Development Environment.
2. At the opening screen use the Browse button to locate the directory or drive where we wish to create our code using the browse button.
3. Now we will add the name **PracticallyJava** to the end of the path location, as shown.

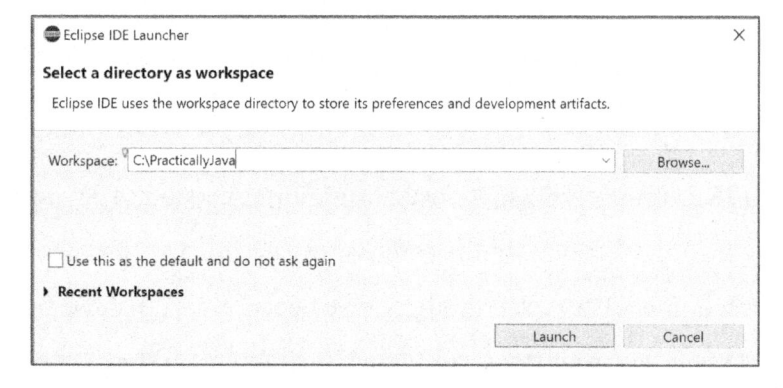

```
● Eclipse IDE Launcher                                              ×
Select a directory as workspace
Eclipse IDE uses the workspace directory to store its preferences and development artifacts.

Workspace:  C:\PracticallyJava                        ∨    Browse...


☐ Use this as the default and do not ask again
▸ Recent Workspaces

                                              Launch      Cancel
```

4. Click on the **Launch** button.
5. Click on the **File** menu.
6. Choose **New**.
7. Choose **Project**.
8. Expand the Java folder.
9. **Choose Java Project** as the project type.

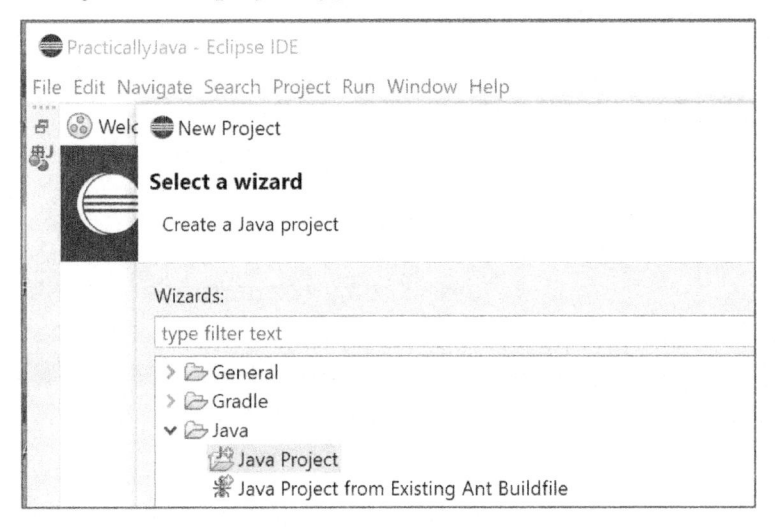

10. Click on the **Next** button.
11. In the name area type the name of the project – **PracticallyJava.**

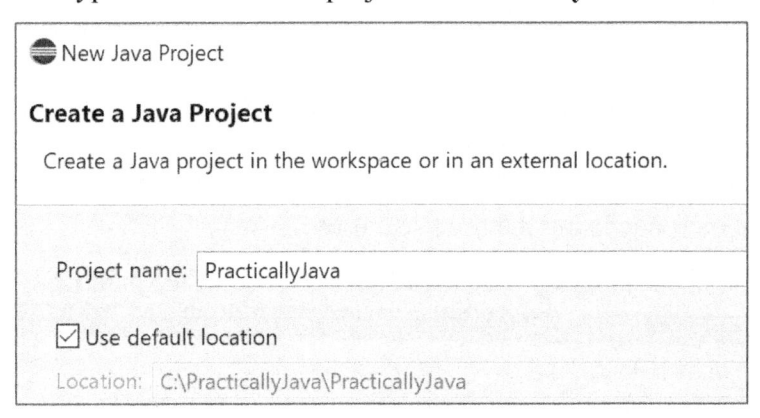

12. In the Select a JRE drop down list choose our required version of Java (usually this will be the highest version we have). In the screenshot **version 1.8** has been selected. Version 1.8 is widely used in industry even though newer versions with some additional features are available. **When learning the fundamentals of Java version 1.8 is very suitable**.

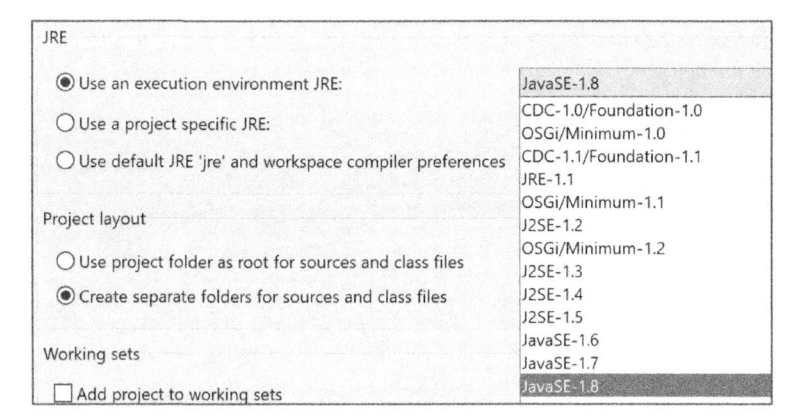

13. Leave the rest of this form as it is and then click the **Next** button.
14. Click on the **Libraries** tab.

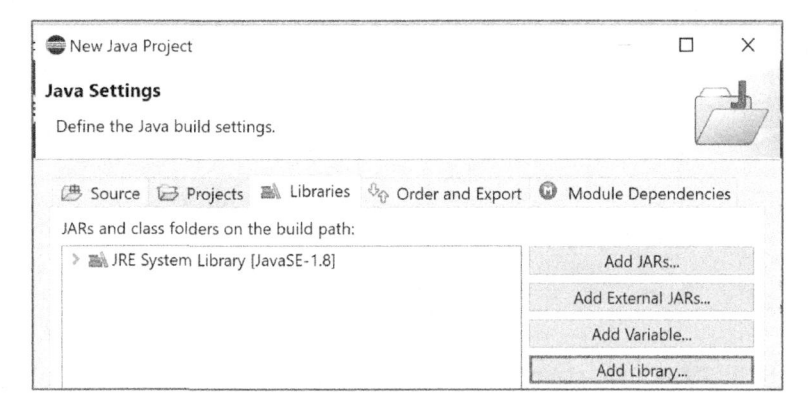

We should see that Java 1.8, or whatever version we choose, will be shown as the JRE System Library.

15. Click the **Finish** button.

You may get a pop-up window appear and say that a Java project is associated with a Java perspective. This is telling us that the Eclipse IDE will show our Java project with tools and windows associated with a Java project. This makes it easier for us to find the required tools to create our Java code.

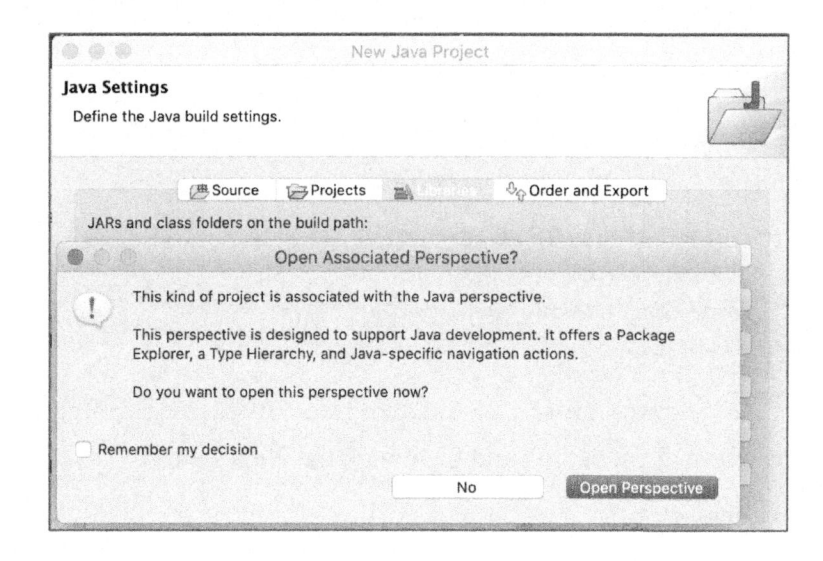

If this window appears click the **Open Perspective** button.

16. Close the welcome screen, if it appears, by clicking on the X on the Welcome screen tab at the top.

Look at the top right of the Eclipse screen. We should see something like the following:

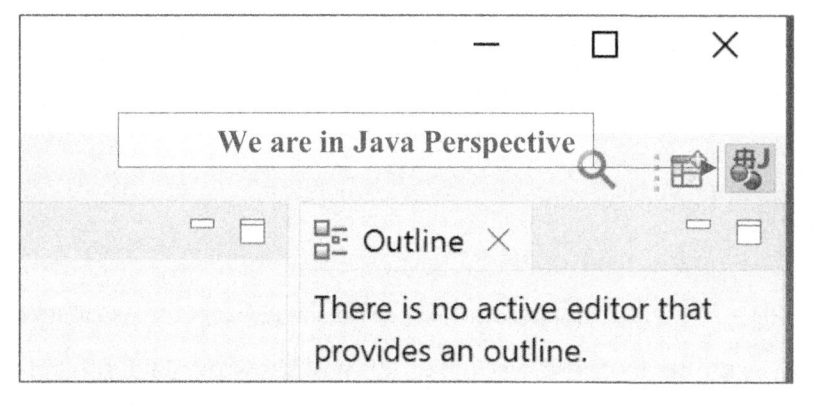

Notice the **J** in the top right corner – this indicates that we are in the Java perspective.

Now look in the **Package Explorer** panel on the left. We should see the name of our project, **JavaExamples**, beside the folder icon. Remember the project goes in a folder inside the namespace:

- our workspace is **LearnToCodeJava**
- our project is **JavaExamples**

- the workspace and project are folders:
    - the top level folder is the **workspace** called **LearnToCodeJava**
    - the inner folder is the **project folder** called **JavaExamples**

The folder structure can also be seen in 'File Explorer' of our operating system:

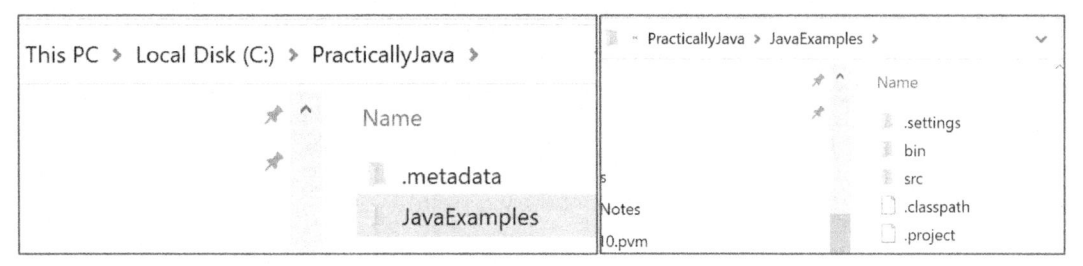

17. Within Eclipse expand the JavaExamples project folder by clicking on the arrow to the left of the folder icon.
18. Expand the JRE System Library by clicking on the arrow to the left of the books icon.

We will see a series of **jar** files. These are **Java Archive (jar) files** and they hold packages which hold classes which hold variables and methods.

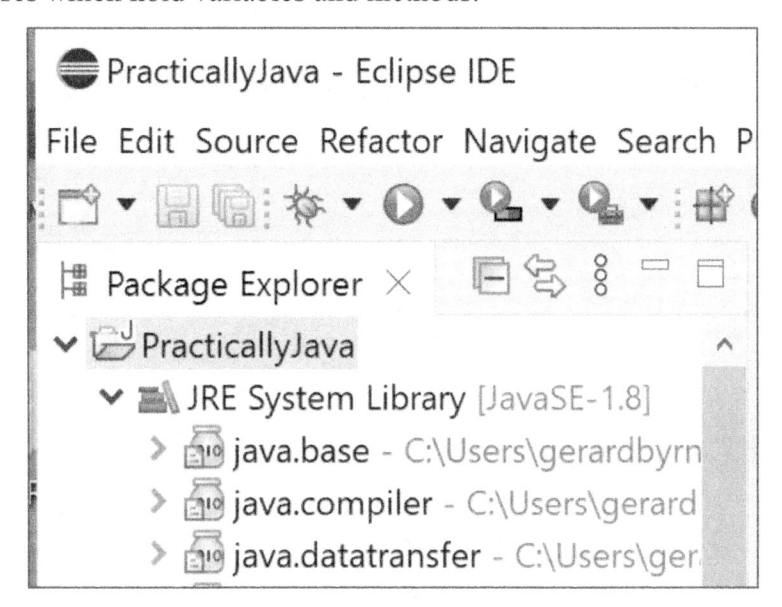

Now we will create a package that will hold our class(es), which will hold our variables and methods. Remember, classes in Java will be held within a package. In other words, these jar files come as part of Java 1.8 and they have code which we as developers can access and which helps make our development simpler.

Packages - important points about packages

- packages are (and should) be used in all Java applications and we will definitely use them in each project we create during our course modules
- package names in Java are by custom and practice lower case
- each part of the package name is separated by a period (.)
- each part represents a new folder within the project we have created
- we choose the package name, but in industry we might use a structure such as:
- company web address reversed, followed by the department name, followed by the project name e.g. **com.gerrybyrne.claims.repairshopapplication**
- a package will hold our class(es), which will hold our variables and methods
- all classes in Java will be held within a package

Create a package (a folder or folders to hold our Java code)

19. Right click on the **src** folder.
20. Choose **New**.
21. Choose **Package**.

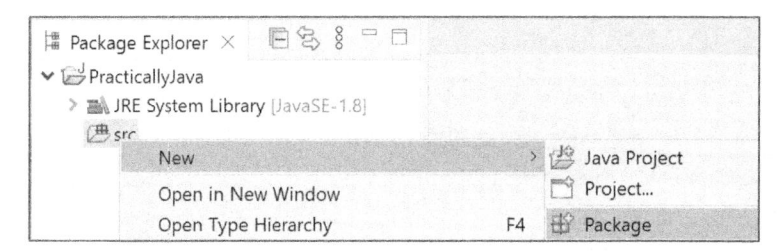

22. Name the package **com.gerrybyrne**.

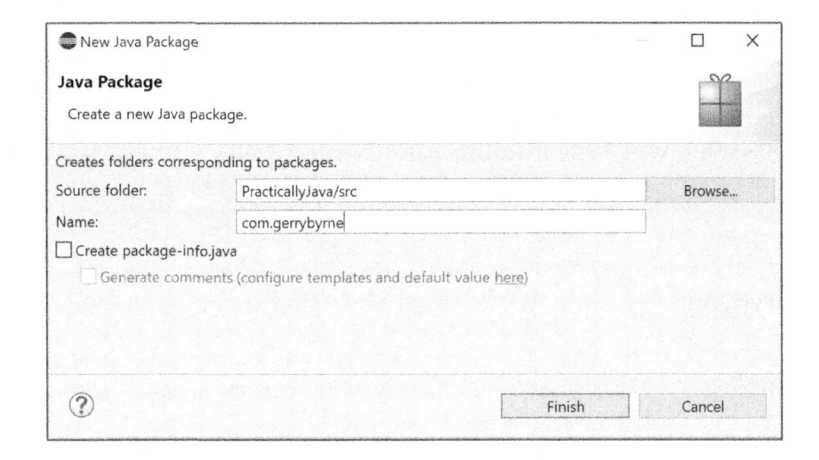

23. Click the **Finish** button.
24. Right click on the package icon.
25. Choose **New**.
26. Choose **Class**.

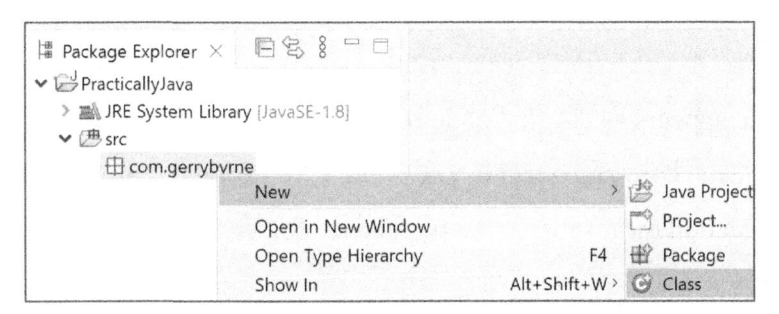

27. Name the class **Example1**.
28. Put a **tick in the checkbox** beside the public static void main(String[] args) box.

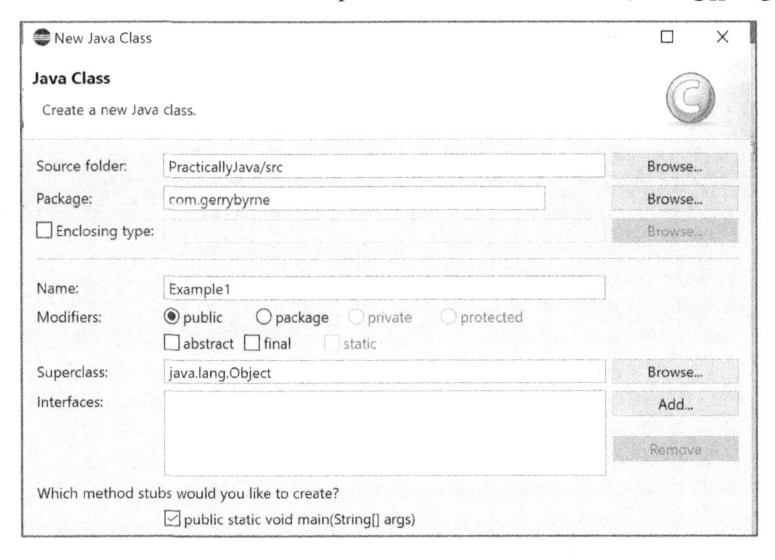

29. Click on the **Finish** button.

The Example1 class code will appear in the editor window and will be similar to the following:

package com.gerrybyrne;

public class Example1
{
    public static void main(String[] args)
    {
        // TODO Auto-generated method stub

    } // End of main method()
} // End of Example1 class

Note

The package name appears as the first code line and is the name we gave it and therefore represents two folders, **com** and **gerrybyrne,** which are inside the project folder, JavaExamples, which in turn is inside the workspace folder LearnToCode as shown below:

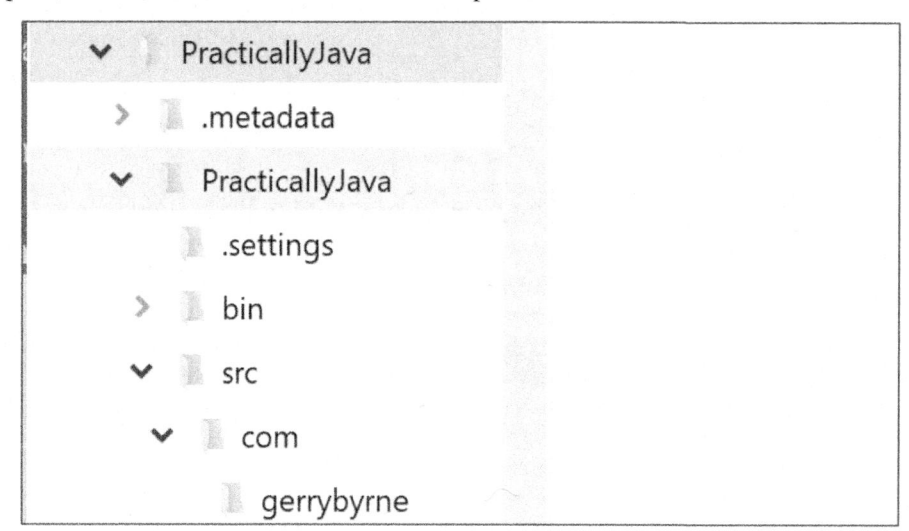

```
v  PracticallyJava
   >  .metadata
   v  PracticallyJava
         .settings
      >  bin
      v  src
         v  com
               gerrybyrne
```

30. Amend the code to add some println() statements, these allow us to display content to the console:

```java
package com.gerrybyrne;

public class Example1
{
    public static void main(String[] args)
    {
        System.out.println();
        System.out.println("------- Build your Java muscle -------");
        System.out.println("--------- Learn To Code --------");
        System.out.println();
        System.out.println();
    } // End of main method()
} // End of Example1 class
```

If we study the code carefully, we will see that there are no import statements in the code. This is fine, but we could add, after the package statement on line one, the import line for the System as shown below:

```
import static java.lang.System.*;
```

This would mean we do not need the keyword System in the lines of code within the main method. If we were to amend the code using this import our code would look like this:

```java
package com.gerrybyrne;
import static java.lang.System.*;

public class Example1 {

    public static void main(String[] args)
    {
        out.println();
        out.println("------- Build your Java muscle -------");
        out.println("--------- Learn To Code --------");
        out.println();
        out.println();
    } // End of main method()
} // End of Example1 class
```

As developers it is our choice. The reality is that some industry developers may use the shortened version and others will not. We will therefore see in nearly every commercial Java application code a lot of using statements at the top of the code, including **import System.**

31. Click on the **green Run button** at the top of the screen or click on the Run menu and choose the Run option:

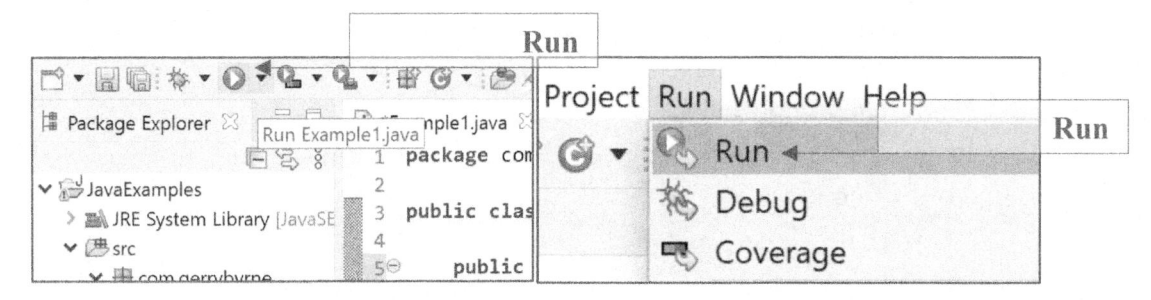

32. Save the files if we are requested to do so.

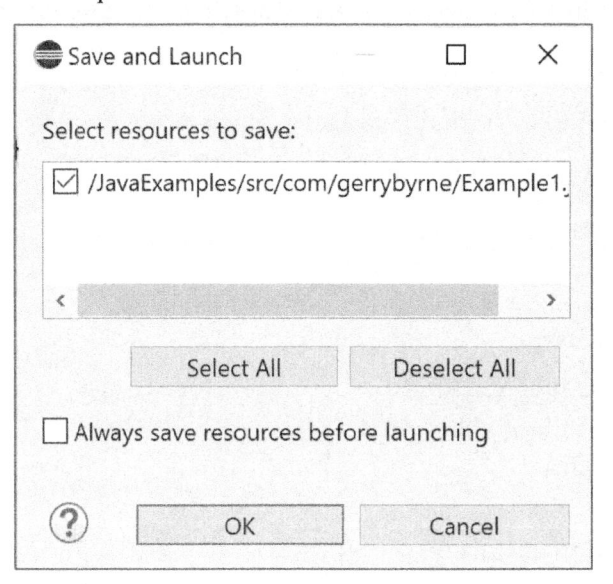

33. Look in the Console window at the bottom of the screen and we should see the output from the println() statements.

The console window will appear with the 5 lines written, a blank line to start, two lines of text and another two blank lines. The cursor may be flashing on the sixth line, or click in the console window to see the flashing cursor.

```
 Problems  @ Javadoc  Declaration  Console  X
Example1 [Java Application] C:\Users\gerardbyrne\.p2\pool\plug

------- Build your Java muscle -------
--------- Learn To Code --------   ◄      Console output
```

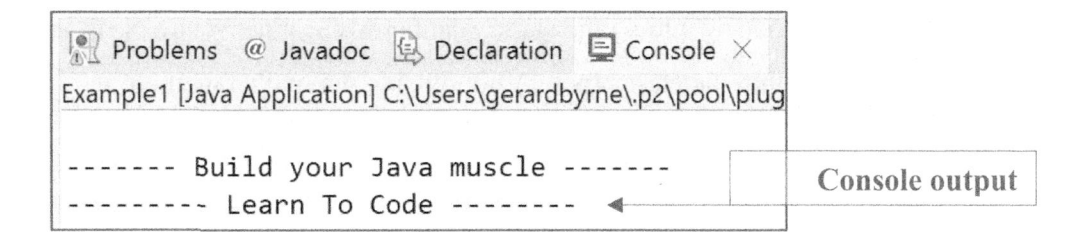

Input from the console

Up to know we have coded for **output** but now we will code to accept **input** from the console. This is a little tricky and involves a number of concepts which will become clearer when we have studied the module on classes and objects. For now, just accept that we will always add these two lines to our code if it involves reading user input through the console:

import java.util.Scanner;   and

Scanner myScanner = **new** Scanner(System.in);

- the statement **import java.util.Scanner;** will appear at the top of the code

- the statement **Scanner myScanner = new Scanner(System.in);** will appear within the class code. For the present moment, as we learn the fundamentals of Java, we will locate this line inside the main() method. Later, we may choose to locate the line outside the main() method but inside the class.

So, let's keep it simple for now and as we develop our skills we will see how and why we would put the line at the **class level** rather than at the **method level**.

34. Amend the code by adding the System import statement which goes in a line under the package statement, usually just after the last import statement.

   Our new code will be
   package com.gerrybyrne;

   import static java.lang.System.*;

   import java.util.Scanner;

35. Amend the code by adding the static Scanner myScanner = new Scanner(System.in); statement within the class brace {} but outside the main() method.

```java
public class Example1
{
/*
   Creating an instance of the Scanner class so we can use it. The name
   we will use is myScanner as this will help us to remember that it is
   something created by us
*/
static Scanner myScanner = new Scanner(System.in);

   public static void main(String[] args)
   {
      System.out.println();
      System.println("------- Build your Java muscle -------");
      System.println("--------- Learn To Code --------");
      System.out.println();
      System.out.println();
   } // End of main method()
} // End of Example1 class
```

Code analysis

- **import java.util.Scanner;**

    this is the import statement we use to allow us to use the Scanner class. The import statement is coded at the top of the code outside the class declaration braces{}.

- **Scanner myScanner = new Scanner(System.*in*);**

    this is creating a copy (instance) of the Scanner class so we can use it. We are not allowed use the Scanner class directly, we must use a copy (instance).

    This statement can be placed:
    - inside the class but outside the main method and if this is where we place the statement, then the word **static** will have to appear in front on the word Scanner as shown:

        static Scanner myScanner = new Scanner(System.*in*);

> **public static void** main(String[] args)

or

- o inside the main method and if this is where we place the statement, then the word static does **not** get used in front on the word Scanner as shown:

  public static void main(String[] args)
  {
     Scanner myScanner = **new** Scanner(System.*in*);

36. Amend the code to add a statement that requests the user to press a key on the keyboard:

    Our new code will be

    public static void main(String[] args)
    {
       System.*out*.println();
       System.*out*.println("------- Practically Java -------");
       System. println("------- Build your Java muscle -------");
       System. println("--------- Learn To Code --------");
       System.*out*.println();
       System.*out*.println();
       System.*out*.println("Press any letter on the keyboard to continue");
     } // End of main method()
    } // End of Example1 class

37. Now add a line of code to read the user input from the console window using the **next()** method from the Scanner class. Remember, we created an instance of the Scanner class and called it myScanner. Also, add a line of code that will display a message, Goodbye, after the console input has been read.

    Our new code will be

    public static void main(String[] args)
    {
       System.*out*.println();
       System. println("------- Build your Java muscle -------");
       System. println("--------- Learn To Code --------");
       System.*out*.println();
       System.*out*.println();

System.*out*.println("Press any letter on the keyboard to continue");

myScanner.next();
System.*out*.println("Goodbye");
} // End of main method()
} // End of Example1 class

38. Finally, we will add a line of code to close our instance of the Scanner class (this is a very important action as we never want to open and forget to close).

System.*out*.println("Press any letter on the keyboard to continue");
myScanner.next();
System.*out*.println("Goodbye");

myScanner.close();
} // End of main method()
} // End of Example1 class

39. Click on the **File** menu.
40. Choose **Save** to save the amended code.
41. Click on the green **Run** button at the top of the screen.
42. Click in the Console window at the bottom of the screen.

The console window will appear and ask us to press any letter on the keyboard.

43. Type any letter key to continue e.g. a
44. Press the **Enter** key.

The message saying Goodbye will be displayed in the console window and our instance of the Scanner class will be closed.

```
Problems   @ Javadoc   Declaration   Console  ×
<terminated> Example1 [Java Application] C:\Users\gerardbyrne\.p2\po

------- Build your Java muscle -------
--------- Learn To Code --------


Press any letter on the keyboard to continue
a
Goodbye
```

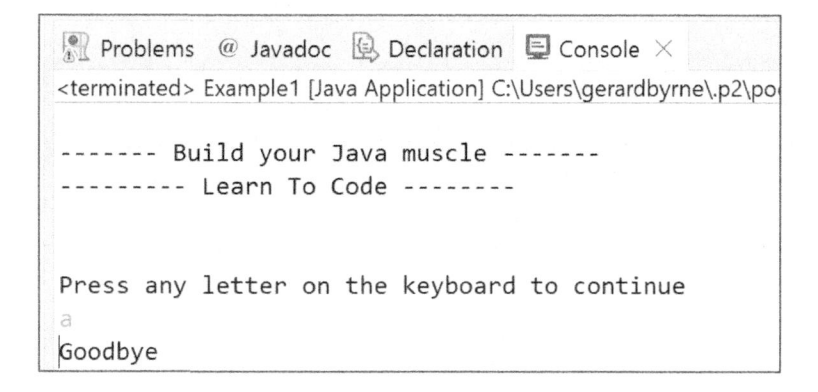

Code Analysis

System.out.println()

this means write a line to the console and since there is no information between the brackets () the line will be blank. With the println() command, the cursor will move to the next line as its final act.

System. println("------- Build your Java muscle -------");

this means write a line to the console and, since there is information between the brackets (), the line displays the text exactly as shown between the double quotes "".

The double quotes indicate that the text is always going to be whatever has been typed between the double quotes, it is a **String**. The text is a String, it is a **constant** and the String data is enclosed in double quotes. We could say it is **not a variable so it is a constant**. A constant will not change throughout the lifetime of the application and it is said to be **immutable**.

With the println() command the cursor will move to the next line as its final act.

myScanner.**next();**

this means read a String from the console, so we are using **Input.**

Let us analyse this myScanner.next() line of code

- **Fact 1**

    Here we have used **myScanner**, which is our instance of the Scanner class, to interact with the console where **input** from the user will be accepted. This is different to the **output** from the computer program when we used the System.out.println() method.

- **Fact 2**

    The second part is the **dot**, the **full stop** (or **period** as it is also known). As we learnt earlier:
    - in Java code the full stop means that we want to use a part or element of the **object** that appears to the left of the full stop.
    - the part or element will be a **variable** or a **method**.

- **Fact 3**

    The third part is **next()**

    We should now be able to recognise that **next()** is indeed a method, it has the brackets **()** at the end. As this method has nothing between the brackets () we should be aware that this means the method takes in no value. he brackets are just empty, there are no parameters.

Now we have the concept of the input and output and can see that we have started using lines of Java programming code that industry developers use, we can progress to using other programming concepts in our code.

Code Review and summary

Our completed code is:

```java
package com.gerrybyrne;

import static java.lang.System.*;

import java.util.Scanner;

public class Example1
{
    /*
        Creating an instance of the Scanner class so we can use it. The name
        we will use is myScanner as this will help us to remember that it is
        something created by us
    */
    static Scanner myScanner = new Scanner(System.in);

    public static void main(String[] args)
    {
        System.out.println();
        System.out.println("------- Build your Java muscle -------");
        System.out.println("--------- Learn To Code --------");
        System.out.println();
        System.out.println();
        System.out.println("Press any letter on the keyboard to continue");
        myScanner.next();
        System.out.println("Goodbye");

        myScanner.close();
    } // End of main method()
} // End of Example1 class
```

and the program code produces the following console output:

```
Problems  @ Javadoc  Declaration  Console
<terminated> Example1 [Java Application] C:\Users\gerardbyrne\.p2\pool\plu

------- Practically Java -------
--------- Learn To Code --------


Press any letter on the keyboard to continue
a
Goodbye
```

The following points are important in understanding this Java program and will be applicable to many of the programs we write in the future modules:

- the **import statements** at the top of the code represent classes that we need to help our program work

- import refers to the fact that we wish to use classes and ultimately the methods and variables in the classes that are contained in the package that follows the import keyword

- classes are program code that hold **variables** (properties) and **methods** that are made available to the programmer

- we are developing a Java project and the project has a class called **Example1**

- it is in this **Example1** class that we have written our code. In future projects we can rename the Example1 class or add a new class and give it a name of our choice

- this class has what is called an **access modifier** in front to word class. The access modifier is **public** so we are telling the class that it is accessible by other code in our project (this is a simplified definition but sufficient for us at the moment).

    public class Example1
    {
        public static void main(String[] args)
        {

- the curly left brace on the line following class name, Example1, matches the closing brace in the last line of the example. This is because **the whole class definition is between the open and close braces**.

- the curly left brace following the class name can be on the same line as the class name or it can be moved to the line after the class name, it's personal choice. In our code example the opening (left) curly brace has been put on the line following the class name.

- Inside the opening curly brace for the class we have the statement static Scanner myScanner = **new** Scanner(System.*in*); which gives us access to the Scanner class whose methods can be used to read the keyboard input

- the code in this class is in the form of a method, in this case a method called **main**

- this method also has what is called an **access modifier** in front of the words static void. The access modifier is **public** and therefore we are telling the main method that it is accessible by other code in our project.

    public class Example1
    {
        public static void main(String[] args)
        {

- the first line of the method is called the **method signature** (header)

- the words **static** and **void** are important and are used regularly. As we can see we have used them both with the main method. These two words are examples of **Java keywords**, words that have a special meaning in a Java program and that cannot be used for any other purpose.

- the other keywords in this example are **public** and **class**

- the method signature defines the name of the method e.g. **main**, and is followed by the method body, which is enclosed in braces

- the **System.out.println()** statement displays the text contained between the brackets () and inside the quotes, in a console window

- the **myScanner.next()** statement waits to read the input from the console until a space is encountered. The input is determined when the Enter key has been pressed

- each of the lines of code within the main method constitute Java statements i.e. commands to be carried out

- each Java statement is terminated by a semicolon

We have seen and applied the concept of **input** and **output** and we have started using lines of Java programming code that industry developers use.

As we progress, we will be using other programming concepts in our code, but we have made great progress in learning the basics of writing a Java application using an Integrated Development Environment.

Our Java code has Java statements and if we refer back to the recipe from module 1 we will see that they are like the ingredients of the recipe.

Another great achievement for us in our learning.

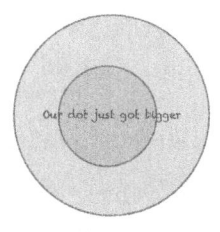

Our dot just got bigger

Program Practically

Java

Module 03

Introduction – Commenting code

Why comment?
Single line comments
Inline comments
Multiple line comments (block comments)
Comments versus proper names
Clean code

Gerry Byrne

Program Practically - Commenting code for readability

We learnt in module 2 that:

Our application code can involve input and output and that the input and output is completed in the console window. We can say this is the visible part of our application for the user, and it is important they have a good experience when seeing the output from our application. The user experience is often referred to as the UX and can involve the use of colours, emphasis, layout etc by the developer to make the application readable and pleasing to look at.

This module will concentrate on how to create a good user experience **for the developer** when they are creating, reading and amending code. It is particularly important to understand that we as developers should be having a good user experience when we look at any application code, whether it is our code our someone else's.

As a starting point we will say that one of the current themes in the world of programming in the commercial environment is to write code that is **self-documenting**. This is a great idea and one that we can achieve by writing Java code statements that will be easily understood by other developers who will read or use the code. In fact, it can even make the original writer of the code, us, understand it better when returning to it to make amendments.

Before we start to code, we should keep the strategy of **self-documenting code** foremost in our thoughts. Writing self-document code is easy to do and can involve:

- adding **astutely placed comments** (explanations) in our code
- not overusing comments, not everything will need a comment if the code is written well, but comments can be a big help to the reader
- our **variable names** being such that they explain the purpose of the variable
- our **method names** being such that they explain the purpose of the method
- our **class names** being such that they explain the purpose of the class

Another strategy is to use colours in the coding statements, we should have already seen that the Eclipse Integrated Development Environment has coloured parts of our code. Examples of the code colouring are:

Red - for Java keywords

```
Example1.java
1  package com.gerrybyrne;
2
3  import static java.lang.System.*;
4  import java.util.Scanner;
5
6  public class Example1
7  {
```

Green - for Java comments

```
public class Example1
{
    /*
     Creating an instance of the Scanner class so we can use it. The name
     we will use is myScanner as this will help us to remember that it is
     something created by us
     */
```

This code colouring is one way in which we can help ourselves and other developers who might have to read our code.

Note

In the code examples we will use throughout the modules in this course, there will be lots of comments used to help us understand the code, but if these were commercial applications we would not have as many comments.

Make sure to read the code comments in the course code examples as they have invaluable information that adds to and supplements the text of this book.

Comments can be used to give information such as:
- a description indicating the purpose of the application
- information about the developer or developers
- the date on which the program was first create

- the date when maintenance occurred e.g. when lines of code were amended, added or deleted
- the purpose of a method
- what a line or lines of code are doing

In the programming industry there is currently a strong emphasis on writing **clean code** and self-documenting code forms a part of this concept. If we write self-documenting code, then there should be little need for lots of comments.

Java single line comments

Single line comments in Java, and many other programming languages, are preceded by two forward slash symbols, //. The // indicates a single line comment which is generally used for brief comments. Some developers will write the comments above the code whilst others will use the comment on the same line as the code. Both types are shown below.

Example 1

This example shows three single line comments which could be used at the start of a program to give the user information about the program, developer and creation date:

```
// Program Description:   A simple Java program to output text and read input
// Author:                Gerry Byrne
// Date of creation:      01/10/2021
```

Example 2

This example shows a single line comment which gives the user information about the class called Program that follows the comment. The comment appears above the code statement.

```
// This is our only class and it will contain the main method
class Program
```

Example 3

This example shows a single line comment which gives the user information about the line of code. In this case the single line comment appears on the same line as the code statement.

myScanner.next();// This code line waits for the user to input a String

Before we start writing the code for this module, let us think about the package we created for the first module. When we created it, we gave the package the name com.gerrybyrne, which was perfectly fine. Now when we code the example in this module, where will we put our code?

Well, we can do this in:

- the existing package, where we can amend the existing class or create a new class to hold the new code
- a new package which we can create

For this exercise we will create a new package, but what should we call it? If we think about what we have just talked about, self-documenting code, we should question the name of the package we created in the last module, com.gerrybyrne. Maybe it should have been named it better e.g.

- com.gerrybyrne.moduleone
- moduleone.code

If we decide that a name change would be appropriate, we can **rename** the package, but will the code in the class need to be changed as it has the package name as the first line of code? Great question, and it is important for us the think like this when we go to make changes which could filter throughout the class or all classes we create.

The answer is extremely helpful for us because the Integrated Development Environment will automatically amend all occurrences of the package name if it is renamed. That is the power of a good Integrated Development Environment like Eclipse or IntelliJ, it saves us as developers lots of time and helps us be more efficient.

Rename the package

1. Make sure the workspace and project are open in Eclipse.
2. Expand the **src** folder by clicking on the > symbol to the left of it.
3. Expand the package, **com.gerrybyrne**, by clicking on the > symbol to the left of it. We will see the Example1 class we created in the last module.
4. Right click on the **package** name.
5. Choose **Refactor** from menu that appears.
6. Choose **Rename** from next menu that appears.

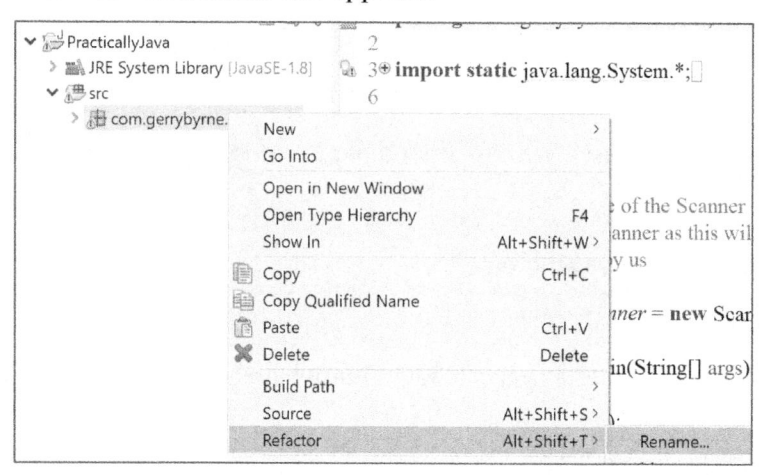

7. Enter the new name for the package, we will call it **com.gerrybyrne.module02**.

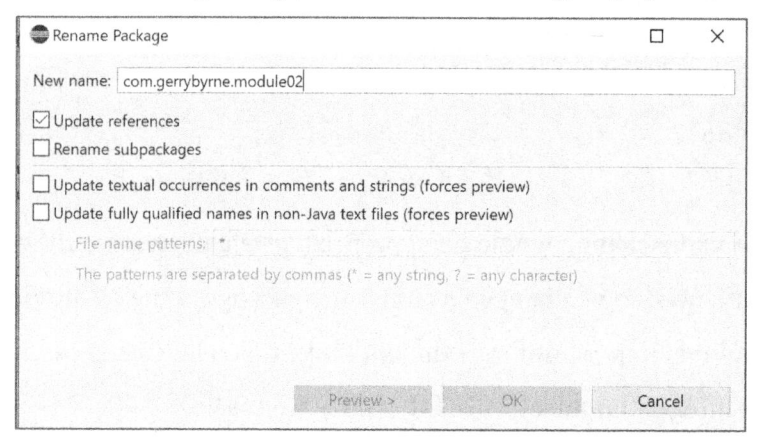

8. Click the **OK** button

If you get a warning message, click the Continue button.

The package has been renamed in the Package Explorer window and equally important in the code within the class.

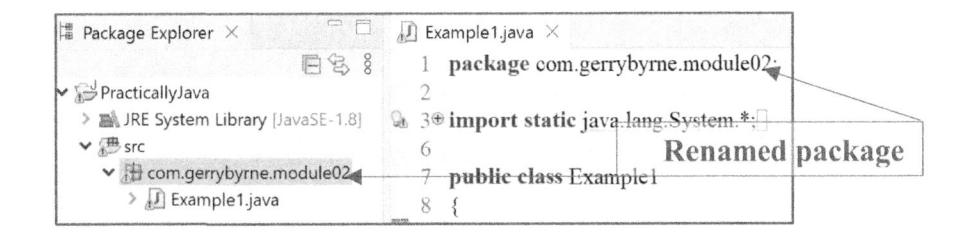

This is a better name for the package as it infers that it relates to module02.

Create a new package

9. Right click on the **src** folder.
10. Choose **New**.
11. Choose **Package**.

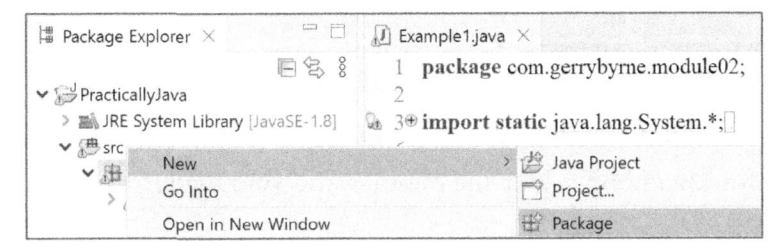

12. Enter the new name for the package, we will call it **com.gerrybyrne.module03**.

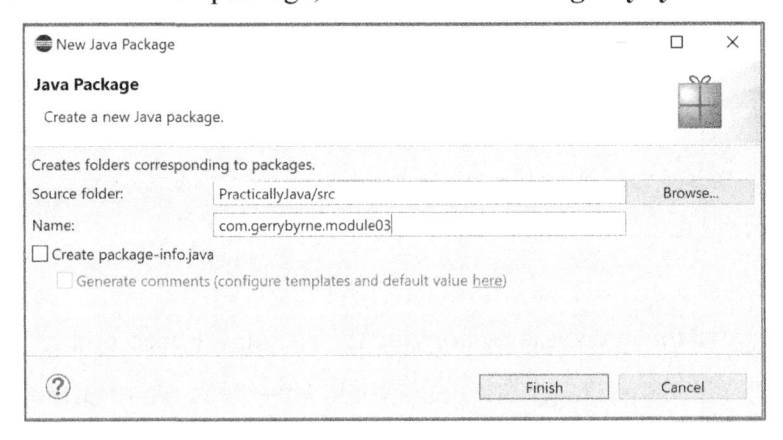

13. Click the **Finish** button.
14. Right click on the **com.gerrybyrne.module03** package.
15. Choose **New**.
16. Choose **Class**.

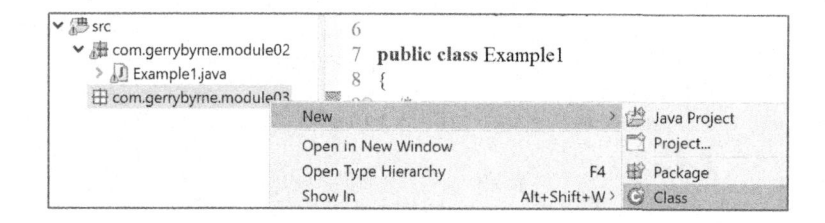

17. Name the class **Example2**.

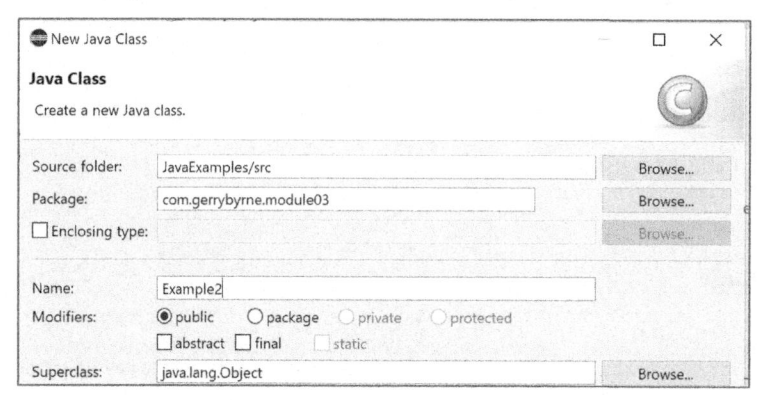

18. Put a **tick in the checkbox** beside the public static void main(String[] args) box.

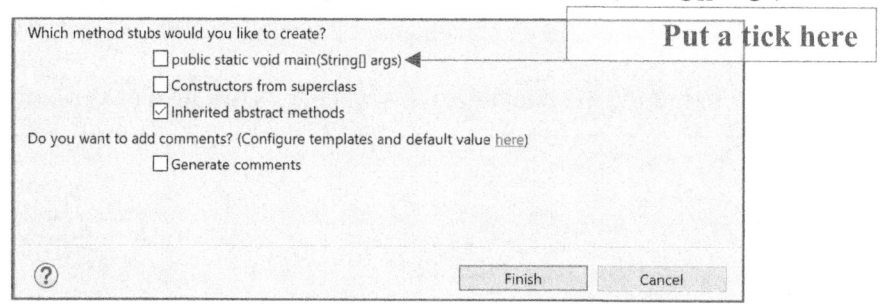

19. Click the **Finish** button.

We could have created the new class by copying the Example1 class and pasting it into the com.gerrybyrne.module03 package. The code would have been renamed automatically so that the first line of code showed the correct package name. We will use this copy and paste feature later.

20. Open the Example1 class in the module02 package and copy the code which is inside the class, between the open and close braces.
21. Open the Example2 class we have just created.
22. Paste the copied code inside the class over writing the main method.

23. Move back to the Example1 class and copy the static Scanner *myScanner* = new Scanner(System.*in*); line of code.
24. Move back to the Example1 class and paste the static Scanner *myScanner* = new Scanner(System.*in*); line of code into the code within the class but outside the main method.

Our new code will be

    package com.gerrybyrne.module03;

    import static java.lang.System.*;

    import java.util.Scanner;

    public class Example2
    {
      /*
        Creating an instance of the Scanner class so we can use it. The name
        we will use is myScanner as this will help us to remember that it is
        something created by us
      */
      static Scanner *myScanner* = **new** Scanner(System.*in*);

      public static void main(String[] args)
      {
        System.*out*.println();
        System.*out*.println("------- Build your Java muscle -------");
        System.*out*.println("--------- Learn To Code --------");
        System.*out*.println();
        System.*out*.println();
        System.*out*.println("Press any letter on the keyboard to continue");
        myScanner.next();
        System.*out*.println("Goodbye");

        myScanner.close();
      } // End of main method()
    } // End of Example2 class

We may notice that the import statement may not be automatically added to our code by the Integrated Development Environment and the import static java.lang.System.*; may not added because we have specifically used the System keyword in the println() code lines.

25. Hover over the red underlined Scanner.
26. Choose the Import 'Scanner' (java.util) option from the pop up window.

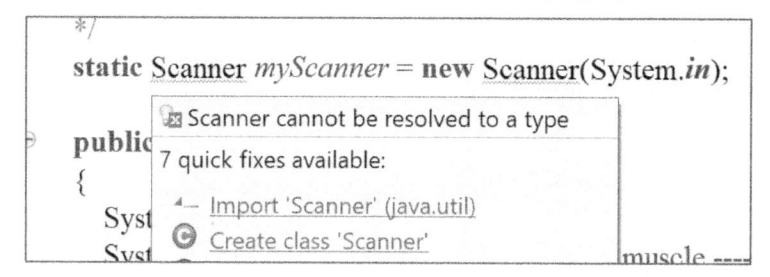

The import statement is now added to the code.

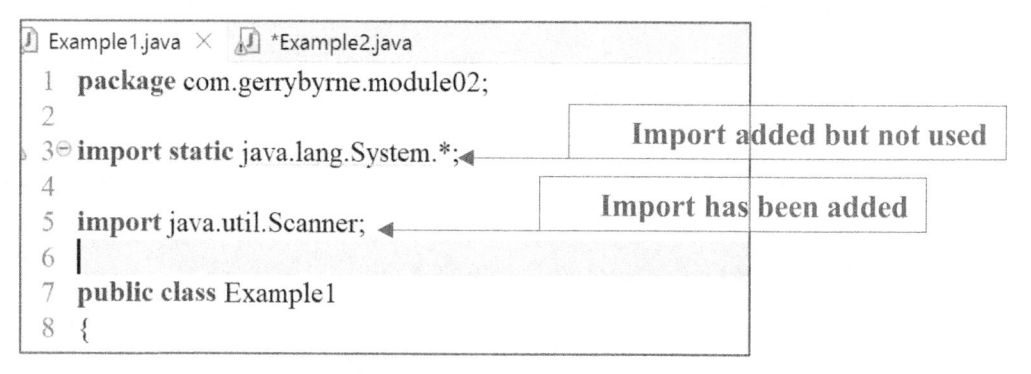

The Integrated Development Environment is great at helping us write clean code and having the unnecessary System import statement would not fit well with the clean code concept. There is a concept in programming known as **YAGNI** which stands for, **You Ain't Going To Need It** and having unused imports or code fits into this.

Amend the code to include comments

27. Add the following comments to our program code to show the use of single line comments before a line of code and at the end of the code line.

Our new code will be

```java
// Program Description:    A simple Java program to output text and read input
// Author:                 Gerry Byrne
// Date of creation:       01/10/2021
```
Single line comments before program code

```java
package com.gerrybyrne.module03;

import java.util.Scanner;
```
Single line comments before program code

```java
//This is our only class and it will contain the Main method
public class Example2
{
    /*
      Creating an instance of the Scanner class so we can use it. The name
      we will use is myScanner as this will help us to remember that it is
      something created by us
    */
    static Scanner myScanner = new Scanner(System.in);

    public static void main(String[] args)
    {
        System.out.println();
        System.out.println("------- Build your Java muscle -------");
        System.out.println("--------- Learn To Code --------");
        System.out.println();
        System.out.println();
        System.out.println("Press any letter on the keyboard to continue");
        myScanner.next();   //This code line waits for the user to input something
        System.out.println("Goodbye");
        myScanner.close();
    } // End of main method()
} // End of Example2 class
```
Inline comment

28. Click on the **File** menu.
29. Choose **Save All.**
30. Click on the green **Run** button at the top of the screen.
31. Click in the Console window at the bottom of the screen.

The console window will appear and ask us to press any letter on the keyboard e.g. a.

32. Press any letter key to continue e.g. **a**.
33. Press the **Enter** key.

The message saying Goodbye will be displayed in the console window and our instance of the Scanner class will be closed.

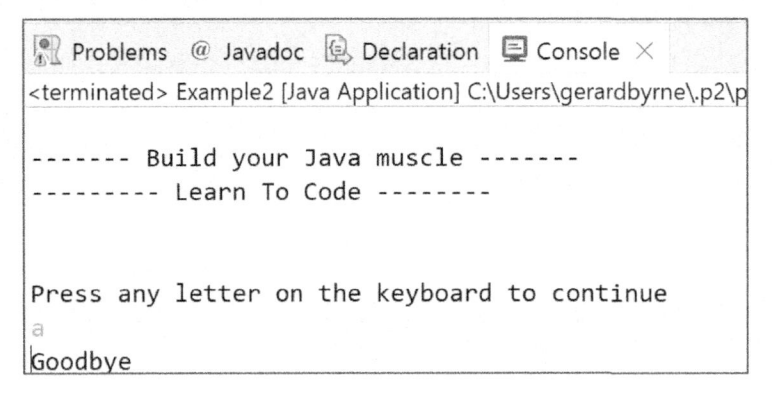

```
Problems  @ Javadoc  Declaration  Console  X
<terminated> Example2 [Java Application] C:\Users\gerardbyrne\.p2\p

------- Build your Java muscle -------
--------- Learn To Code --------


Press any letter on the keyboard to continue
a
Goodbye
```

The code has produced an application which performs exactly as it did before we added the comment lines. So, **comments are for a reader of the code** and do not change what the application does. The **comments are ignored in the process of building (compiling)** the program from the source code we have written.

Java Multiple line comments

Multiple line comments, also called **comment blocks,** are enclosed between the symbols /* and */. These are used for longer comments. The /* is the start and the */ is the end symbol.

```
/*      Longer comments in a Java program can easily
        extend over a number of lines as long as they start with the
        proper characters. This is an example of multiple line comments
*/
```

34. Add the following multiple line comments to our program code:

    Our new code will be

    ```
    // Program Description:   A simple Java program to output text and read input
    // Author:                Gerry Byrne
    // Date of creation:      01/10/2021
    /*
    ```

The package is simply an area that holds our class.
This package has used the dot . to separate sections of the package name.
The parts essentially represent folders within our workspace.
Package names are by tradition all small letters
*/
package com.gerrybyrne.module03;
import java.util.Scanner;
//This is our only class and it will contain the Main method
public class Example2
{
/*
Creating an instance of the Scanner class so we can use it. The name
we will use is myScanner as this will help us to remember that it is
something created by us
*/
static Scanner *myScanner* = **new** Scanner(System.*in*);

/*
We now have our main method which will contain all our code.
As we become a better developer, we will not have all our code
contained within the main method.
This would be seen as poor code and not fitting in with the design
principle of modular code.
*/

public static void main(String[] args)
{

35. Click on the **File** menu.
36. Choose **Save All**.
37. Click on the green **Run** button at the top of the screen.
38. Click in the Console window at the bottom of the screen.

The console window will appear and ask us to press any letter on the keyboard e.g. a.

39. Press any letter key to continue e.g. **a**.
40. Press the **Enter** key.

The message saying Goodbye will be displayed in the console window and our instance of the Scanner class will be closed. The addition of comments has not altered the running of the code and the application output.

```
Problems   @ Javadoc   Declaration   Console  X
<terminated> Example2 [Java Application] C:\Users\gerardbyrne\.p

------- Build your Java muscle -------
--------- Learn To Code --------


Press any letter on the keyboard to continue
a
Goodbye
```

Module summary

We have added comments to our code to help us understand what we are doing and to reinforce certain aspects of Java programming e.g. some information about packages and the main() method. Remember the golden rule, only use comments when we need to.

The code including the names of
- the workspace
- the project
- the class
- the variables
- the constants

should be self-documenting and no comments should be necessary for them.

Some people would say:

"If we cannot write legible code, then it is unlikely we will be able to write legible comments".

Harsh! Maybe, but it reinforces the point that comments should not be a replacement for self-documenting code.

Another great achievement for us in our learning.

Our dot just got bigger

Program Practically

Java

Module 04

Data types

Java primitive data types
Value types
char versus String
Data type conversion – implicit and explicit
Widening and narrowing conversions
Escape sequences \t and \n
Using the Scanner class to read console input as a specific data type

Gerry Byrne

Program Practically - Data types, variables and conversion

We learnt in module 3 that:

Whilst we can use single and multiple line comments, they should not be a replacement for self-documenting code. Comments are there to help the reader of the code but when the code is written expressively with proper class names, variable names etc. there is a limited need for comments and in reality, we should try for a zero need for comments approach.

In this module we will use code which is well documented for the purposes of helping us understand the code, it is not how we would do it in a real application.

We will learn from this module about the very important concepts of, **data types and variables**. We will use data types and variables in all the Java programs in this book, that is how crucial they are to Java programming. We should also be aware that data types and variables exist in all programming languages and are a fundamental building block for the code we will write.

Data Types

There are different data types in Java, but we will use the category called **Value Types**. **In Java there are 8 primitive (built in) data types**. Value types will contain data and we will hold data for value types such as:

        boolean   **char**

arithmetic integral types

        byte   **short**   **int**   **long**

arithmetic floating-point types

        float   **double**

Notice that **char (one character)** is a data type but there is **no String** (more than one character). Java still supports strings, but strings are a reference to an **instance of the class String.** Do not worry about this statement too much, we will use strings and characters in our programming. However, note the capital **S** in the String and the lower-case letters in the other data types.

In Java, and indeed in other languages, the value types are referred to as **primitive types** and primitive types are predefined by Java, with their names being **reserved keywords**. When we declare a data type, we are reserving memory to store a value. Each data type will have a particular size of memory that needs to be set aside.

The primitive data types in Java are shown below along with their size and default values:

Java data type	default	Size	Description
boolean	false	1 byte	Contains either true or false
char	\u0000	2 bytes	Contains a single character

Integral types

byte	0	1	May contain integers from -128 to 127
short	0	2	Ranges from 32,768 to 32,767
int	0	4	Ranges from -2,147,483,648 to 2,147,483,647
long	0	8	Ranges from -9,223,372,036,854,775,808 to 9,223,372,036,854,775,807

Floating point types

float	0.0	4	unlimited
Double	0.0	8	unlimited

Points to note

- data types are represented in the Java language using **keywords**, so each of the above data type names, **float**, **double** etc. is a keyword in Java
- keywords are the words defined by the language and cannot be used as identifiers
- it is worth noting that **String** is also an acceptable data type in Java, so String is a keyword in Java

Conversion from one data type to another

Sometimes when we code, we will receive a message to the effect that data cannot be converted from one data type to another data type. This will become clearer as we go through the course modules, but what we will learn is that, when we want to convert from one data type to another data type this can happen in one of two ways:

- **implicit** conversion   this means that we do not need to do anything as the conversion is automatically handled by our code.
  The Java Virtual Machine (JVM) handles the conversion.

- **explicit** conversion   this means that we will need to code the data type conversion. It is not an automatic thing.
  The Java Virtual Machine (JVM) will complain, through an error message, that it cannot handle the conversion.

Converting

We will be able to perform data type conversions using methods from the classes supplied to us by Java. The class methods allow us to perform:

- **widening conversions**

  Widening occurs when a small primitive data type value is automatically accommodated in a bigger (wider) primitive data type.

  If we convert from an **int** to a **double** this is an example of a widening conversion.

If we convert from a **char** to a **String** this is an example of a widening conversion.

Widening conversions that are acceptable are:

- byte   -   is convertible to short, int, long, float, or double
- short   -   is convertible to int, long, float, or double
- char   -   is convertible to int, long, float, or double
- int   -   is convertible to long, float, or double
- long   -   is convertible to float or double
- float   -   is convertible to double

Automatic conversion will take place if the two data types are compatible, as above, and the destination data type is larger than the data type being converted. **Automatic conversion is therefore essentially a widening conversion.**

- **narrowing conversions**

Narrowing occurs when a larger primitive data type value is accommodated in a smaller (narrower) primitive data type.

If we convert from a value that includes a fraction (decimal, float etc) to an integer data type the fractional part will be lost, a narrowing has occurred.

Narrowing conversions that are acceptable:

- short   -   is convertible to byte or char
- char   -   is convertible to byte or short
- int   -   is convertible to byte, short, or char
- long   -   is convertible to byte, short, or char
- float   -   is convertible to byte, short, char, int, or long
- double -   is convertible to byte, short, char, int, long, or float

We will learn more about these types of conversions as we code the examples.

When we use narrowing conversions in our code, we will see that we must explicitly do the conversion by placing the new data type in parenthesis (), like a method. The data type to convert to, sits in front of the object to be converted. We will see this as we carry out the examples in this book, but here is an example of what the code lines might look like.

The code below shows an example of the conversion we have just talked about, int to byte, using **(byte)**. The narrowing conversion is performed using **casting**.

```java
package com.consoleexamples;
class Test {
    public static void main(String args[])
    {
        byte commissionfactor;
        byte commissionpremium;
        int commissionvalue = 257;
        double monthlyinsurancepremium = 296.99;
        System.out.println("Narrowing conversion from int to byte.");

        //(byte) means we wish to convert to byte the commissionvalue
        commissionfactor = (byte) commissionvalue;

        System.out.println("\nThe car emmision value is: "+ commissionvalue +
        but when converted to a byte the car emmission factor is: " + commissionfactor);
        System.out.println("\nConversion of double to byte.");
        /* (byte) means we wish to convert to byte the monthlyinsurancepremium
        So, we will now have 296.99 minus 256 which is 40 (forgetting the
        decimal places) */
        commissionpremium = (byte) monthlyinsurancepremium;
        System.out.println("\nThe monthly insurance premium is: " +
monthlyinsurancepremium + "\nand the car emmission premiumwhen is: "+
commissionpremium);
    }
}
```

More of this later.

Now we will look at adding code that will help in building an application to simulate a car insurance quotation application. Firstly, we will create a String variable called vehicleManufacturer that will hold the value typed in by the user at the console. Remember to read the comments carefully as they fully explain what we are doing.

Create a new package

1. Right click on the **src** folder.
2. Choose **New**.
3. Choose **Package**.
4. Enter the new name for the package, we will call it **com.gerrybyrne.module04**.
5. Click the **Finish** button.

Copy and paste a Java file from one package to another package

6. In the Package Explorer window right click on the **Example2** file in the com.gerrybyrne.module03 package.
7. Choose **Copy**.

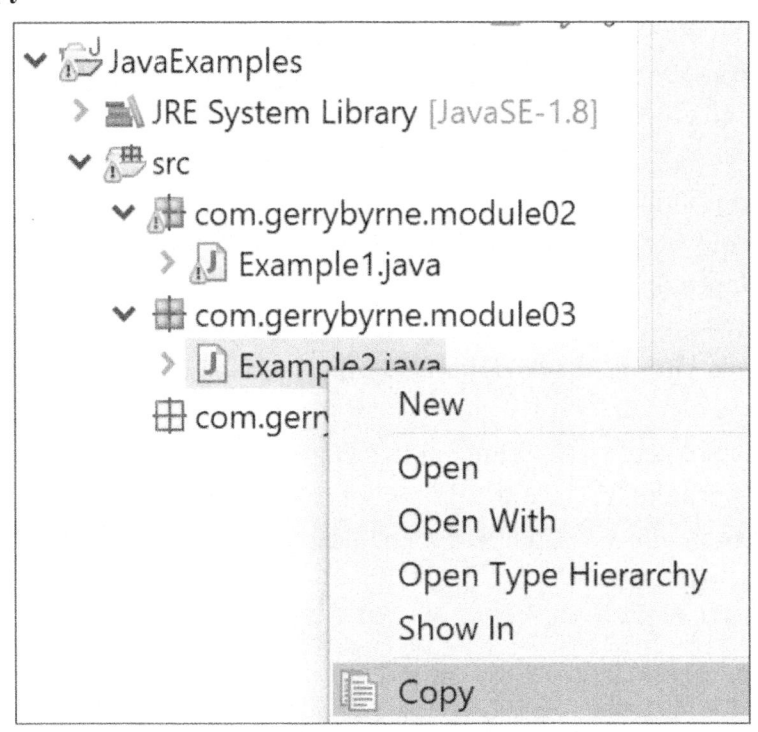

8. In the Package Explorer window right click on the com.gerrybyrne.module04 package.
9. Choose **Paste**.

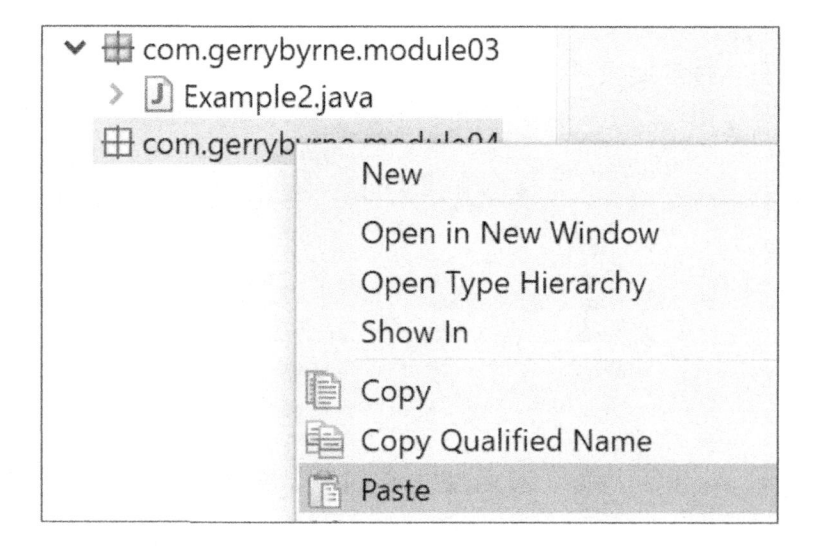

```
  v  ⊞ com.gerrybyrne.module03
     >  [J] Example2.java
     ⊞ com.gerryb────────────────
                  │ New                  │
                  │ Open in New Window   │
                  │ Open Type Hierarchy  │
                  │ Show In              │
                  │ 📋 Copy              │
                  │ 📋 Copy Qualified Name│
                  │ 📋 Paste             │
                  └──────────────────────┘
```

10. Expand the com.gerrybyrne.module04 package by clicking on the > symbol beside the name.

The Java file will be located in this package and it is obviously called Example2, but we will rename it to call it Example3. In module 2 we renamed the package by using the refactor option followed by the rename option, now we will do the same for the class. Once again, the package name statement which is the first line of code in the class, should automatically be amended.

Rename the Java file

11. Right click on the **Example2** file in the com.gerrybyrne.module04 package.
12. Choose **Refactor**.
13. Choose **Rename**.

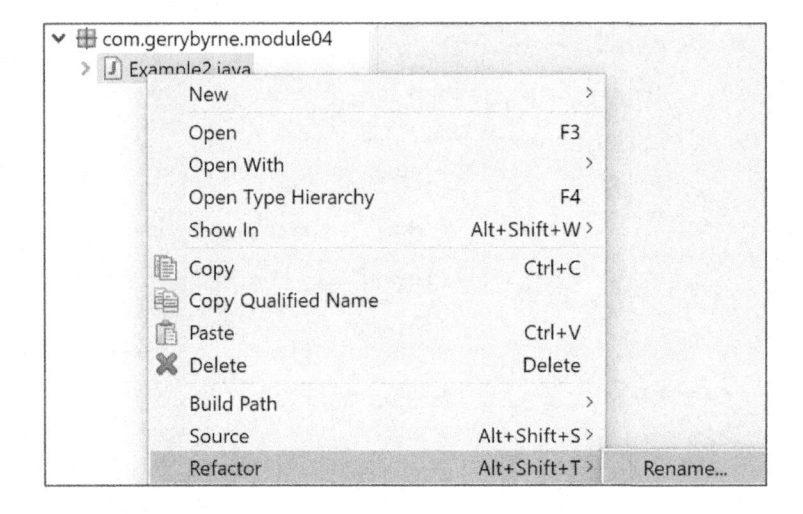

14. Enter the name for the Java class, in our case this will be **Example3**.
15. Click the **Finish** button.
16. Click the **Finish** button.

The new filename appears in the Package Explorer window and within the class code, we can also see that the class has the correct package at the top of the code.

Amend the Java code

17. Amend the existing code by adding the String variable called **vehicleManufacturer**:

    Our new code will now be

    public static void main(String[] args)
    {
    /*
    In this section we will add the variables we will use throughout the program code. These are variables that are going to be of a specific data type. Once we declare a variable and have said what its data type is, we cannot change the variables data type.
    The data type is immutable, it cannot be changed over time. First we will add

a variable called vehicleManufacturer of data type string.
*/
String vehicleManufacturer;

18. Amend the existing code to display a different heading and message:

Our new code will now be

String vehicleManufacturer;

System.out.println();
System.out.println("------- Car Quotation Application -------");
System.out.println();
System.out.println("Type the vehicle manufacturer and press the enter key");
System.out.println();

19. Amend the code to make an instance of the Scanner class at the class level.

Our new code will now be

public class Example3
{
static Scanner *myScanner* = new Scanner(System.*in*);

public static void main(String[] args)
{

20. Amend the existing code to read the user input and assign it to the vehicleManufacturer variable:

Our new code will now be

System.out.println("------- Car Quotation Application -------");
System.out.println();
System.out.println("Type the vehicle manufacturer and press the enter key");
System.out.println();
/*
The next line of code tells the program to wait for the user to input something. When the user presses the Enter key this will indicate that the input has been completed. We have also said that we want the data entered at the console to

be assigned to the variable vehicleManufacturer which we set up earlier with a data type of string. What we can now see is that the data entered through the console is going to be held in the program as data type String.
*/

vehicleManufacturer = myScanner.next();

21. Amend the existing code to display a blank line and then close the Scanner:

    System.out.println();
    myScanner.close();
    } // End of main method()
    } // End of class

22. Click on the **File** menu.
23. Choose **Save All**.
24. Click on the green Run button at the top of the screen.
25. Click in the Console window at the bottom of the screen.
26. Type **Ford** as the manufacturer name.
27. Press the **Enter** key on the keyboard.

In our code we read the String that the user inputs (Ford), using the **next()** method of the Scanner class, and assigned this string of data to the variable, vehicleManufacturer, which we set up. This is great, but surely we want to use the value once we have it! We will now use the value we have stored (containing the String Ford) and print it to the console using the println() method.

28. Amend the code to display the vehicleManufacturer value which has been read from the console:

    Our new code will now be

    vehicleManufacturer = myScanner.next();

    /*
    The next line of code tells the program to display the text between the double quotes "" and to add on to this text (indicated by the +) the

value of the variable called vehicleManufacturer which has been assigned the value typed in by the user at the console (Ford). The + means to concatenate the text and the variable, in other words join them
*/

System.out.println("Your car manufacturer is recorded as " + vehicleManufacturer);

System.out.println();
myScanner.close();
} //End of main() method
} // End of class

29. Click on the **File** menu.
30. Choose **Save All**.
31. Click on the green Run button at the top of the screen.
32. Click in the Console window at the bottom of the screen.
33. Type **Ford** as the manufacturer name.
34. Press the **Enter** key on the keyboard.

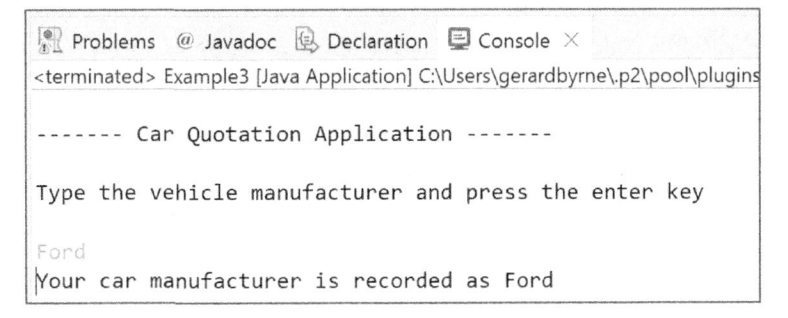

```
Problems  @ Javadoc  Declaration  Console  ×
<terminated> Example3 [Java Application] C:\Users\gerardbyrne\.p2\pool\plugins

------- Car Quotation Application -------

Type the vehicle manufacturer and press the enter key

Ford
Your car manufacturer is recorded as Ford
```

Using the \t escape sequence to tab items

Now we will display an additional line for a 'header'. The Java code for this line will use the **escape sequence \t** to **tab** the text on the lines. The \t is an escape sequence that we might use to tab the output at this place. In other words, leave a fixed amount of space (usually 4 spaces, but this can be configured by the developer) at this position in the text.

35. Amend the code to add the additional 'header' line:

Our new code will now be

System.out.println();

```
System.out.println("------- Car Quotation Application -------");
System.out.println("\tCar\tInsurance\tApplication\n");
System.out.println();
System.out.println("Type the vehicle manufacturer and press the enter key");
System.out.println();
```

36. Click on the **File** menu.
37. Choose **Save All**.
38. Click on the green Run button at the top of the screen.
39. Click in the Console window at the bottom of the screen.
40. Type **Ford** as the manufacturer name.
41. Press the **Enter** key on the keyboard.

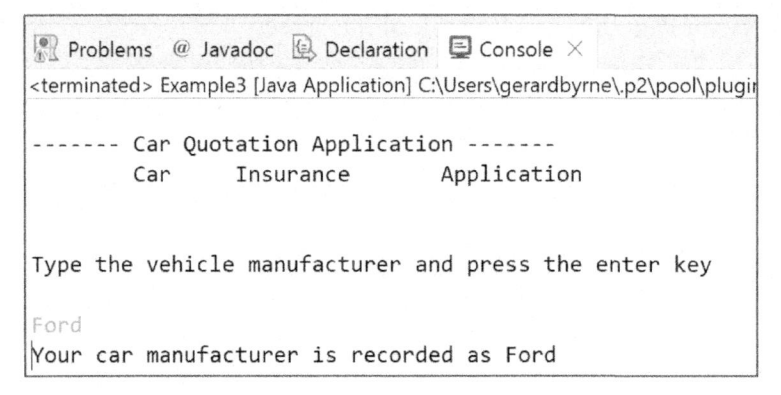

```
------- Car Quotation Application -------
        Car     Insurance       Application


Type the vehicle manufacturer and press the enter key

Ford
Your car manufacturer is recorded as Ford
```

Note how the space between the words Car and Insurance is not 1 but whatever number of spaces has been set in the Eclipse Integrated Development Environment, which is usually 4.

Code analysis

As we can see, the code includes extensive comments which are aimed at explaining the code being used. For the code that we have just added the following points are important:

- we have added a section within the main method where we declare the variables to be used in the program
- in this section we have declared a variable called **vehicleManufacturer** which will hold data of type **String**

Read this line String vehicleManufacturer; as - "**a variable called vehicleManufacturer of data type String**"

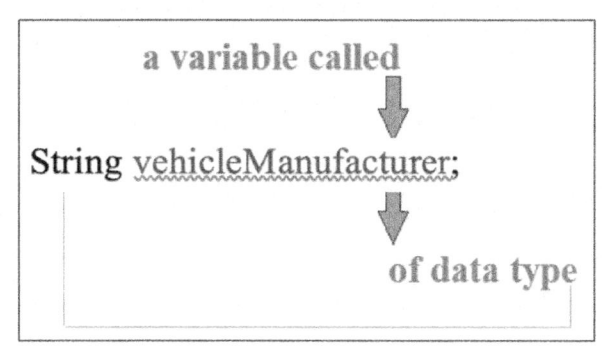

```
                a variable called
                       ↓
       String vehicleManufacturer;
                       ↓
                              of data type
```

All variables and objects should be read in a similar way, as we will see in later modules.

- the variable, vehicleManufacturer, has been declared in the main method and will only be visible to code which is inside the open and close curly braces of the main method. This means that **the scope of the variable is the main method,** between the curly braces

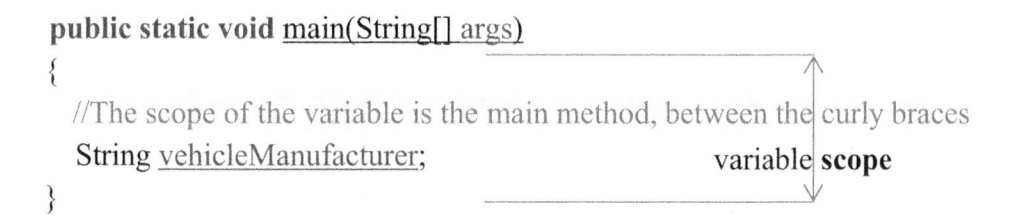

    ```
    public static void main(String[] args)
    {
       //The scope of the variable is the main method, between the curly braces
        String vehicleManufacturer;                              variable scope
    }
    ```

- on executing the System.out.println("Type the vehicle manufacturer and press the enter key"); statement which displays what is between the double quotes "", the cursor will move to a new line after displaying the text.

    Taking a new line can also be achieved by using a 'strange' ending, **\n**.

    This is what is called an **escape sequence** and this \n escape sequence means add a **new line**. So \n is just like println(). We could use the print() method and add the escape sequence \n at the end of the line instead of the println() method e.g.

System.*out*.print("Type the vehicle manufacturer and press the enter key\n");

The other escape sequence we used is **\t** which means **tab** the output at this place. In other words, leave a fixed amount of space at this position in the text. The example of code using \t was:

String vehicleManufacturer;
System.out.println();
System.out.println("------- Car Quotation Application -------");
System.out.println("\tCar\tInsurance\tApplication\n");
System.out.println();
System.out.println("Type the vehicle manufacturer and press the enter key");
System.out.println();

and the console output would be

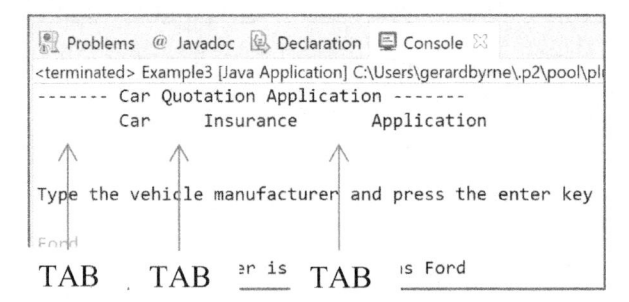

```
Problems  @ Javadoc  Declaration  Console
<terminated> Example3 [Java Application] C:\Users\gerardbyrne\.p2\pool\pl
------- Car Quotation Application -------
       Car      Insurance       Application

Type the vehicle manufacturer and press the enter key
Ford
```
TAB   TAB   er is   TAB   is Ford

- in the code we have entered the statement myScanner.next(). However, this is included as part of a line which says that we want the variable vehicleManufacturer to be made equal to myScanner.next(). This is known as **an assignment,** where we assign a value to a variable. The variable is vehicleManufacturer and the value is whatever the user inputs at the console.

  vehicleManufacturer = myScanner.next();

  Read the line like this:
  The variable called vehicleManufacturer is assigned
  the value of myScanner.next()

- System.out.println("Your car manufacturer is recorded as " + vehicleManufacturer);

This is an interesting line of code that is effectively **three parts** within the brackets ()

- the first part is what we have used before, it is simply text, **a String between double quotes** "", and as we know this tells the program to display this exact text in the Console
- the second part is **a plus sign** (+) and we might be thinking this means add. Well, we are indeed correct, as the plus sign is being used here to say we want to add whatever comes after the plus sign to the text we have just written. This is called **concatenation** and we mentioned it earlier.
- the third part is the **name of the variable** and so the value that is entered at the console by the user e.g. Ford is added to the end of the text - 'Your car manufacturer is recorded as '

So, this line means that the console will have the following displayed:

Your car manufacturer is recorded as Ford

```
Problems  @ Javadoc  Declaration  Console  X
<terminated> Example3 [Java Application] C:\Users\gerardbyrne\.p2\pool\plugir

------- Car Quotation Application -------
        Car       Insurance        Application


Type the vehicle manufacturer and press the enter key

Ford
Your car manufacturer is recorded as Ford  ←  Concatenated String
```

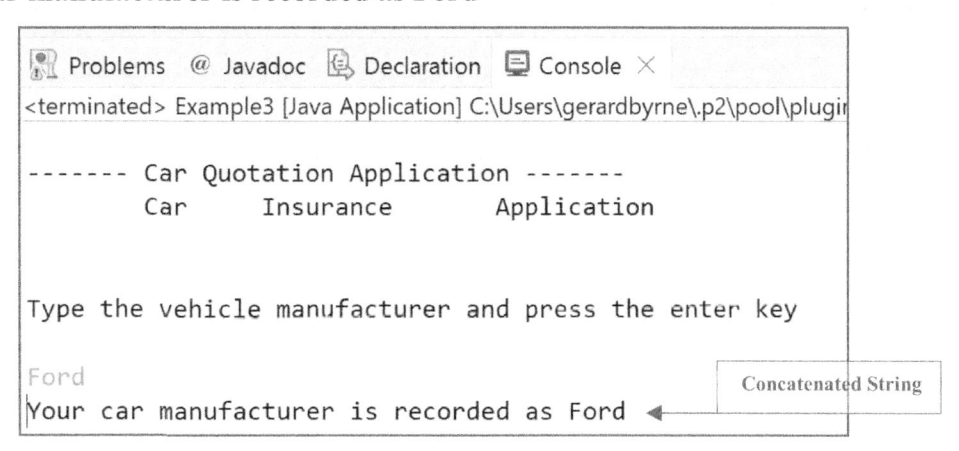

The **plus sign (+) or plus symbol is used to add string parts together**. We can also use the more widely used term **concatenate** to refer to what the plus sign (+) in this context does.

As we go through the course modules, we will also see the plus sign (+) used as the mathematical plus where it will add two numerical values.

Amazing, we are now able to:

- write to the console
- read from the console
- set up a variable
- assign a value that has been read in from the console to a variable
- display text to the console which is a concatenation of text and variables

We will now amend the code to ask the user to input other details about the vehicle being insured. In this case it will be the model of the vehicle. This is the same process as we have already completed and coding this should help reinforce our learning.

The steps are:
- set up a variable that will hold the data requested from the user. The variable will be of a particular **data type**, in this case **String**
- display a message that we want the user to input some data
- use the **next()** method from the Scanner instance, myScanner, to get the data entered

1. Amend the existing code by adding the String variable called vehicleModel:

    public static void main(String[] args)
    {
    /*
    In this section we will add the variables we will use throughout the program code. These are variables that are going to be of a specific data type. Once we declare a variable and have said what its data type is, we cannot change the variables data type. The data type is immutable, it cannot be changed over time.
    First, we will add a variable called vehicleManufacturer of data type String then another String variable called vehicleModel. */
    String vehicleManufacturer;

    String vehicleModel;
2. Amend the existing code to ask for user input, read the user input and assign it to the vehicleModel variable :

    System.out.println("Your car manufacturer is recorded as " + vehicleManufacturer);
    /*

```
      In the next three lines we display a question for the user, read
      whatever data the user inputs at the console, assign this data to the
      variable called vehicleModel and write out the concatenated text
   */
   System.out.println("What is the model of the vehicle?\n");

   vehicleModel = myScanner.next();
```

3. Amend the code to display the vehicleModel which has been read from the console:

```
   /*
      In the next three lines we display a question for the user, read
      whatever data the user inputs at the console, assign this data to the
      variable called vehicleModel and write out the concatenated text
   */
   System.out.println("What is the model of the vehicle?\n");
   vehicleModel = myScanner.next();

   System.out.println("You have told us that the vehicle model is " + vehicleModel);

   System.out.println();
   myScanner.close();
      } //End of main() method
   } // End of class
```

4. Click on the **File** menu.
5. Choose **Save All**.
6. Click on the green Run button at the top of the screen.
7. Click in the Console window at the bottom of the screen.
8. Type **Ford** as the manufacturer name.
9. Press the **Enter** key on the keyboard.
10. Type **Fiesta** as the model name.
11. Press the **Enter** key on the keyboard.

We will see that the console window now displays the concatenated text for the model.

```
 Problems   @ Javadoc   Declaration   Console  ×
<terminated> Example3 [Java Application] C:\Users\gerardbyrne\.p2\pool\plugins\org.eclipse.

------- Car Quotation Application -------
        Car       Insurance        Application


Type the vehicle manufacturer and press the enter key
Ford
Your car manufacturer is recorded as Ford
What is the model of the vehicle?
Fiesta
You have told us that the vehicle model is Fiesta   ◄────── Concatenated String
```

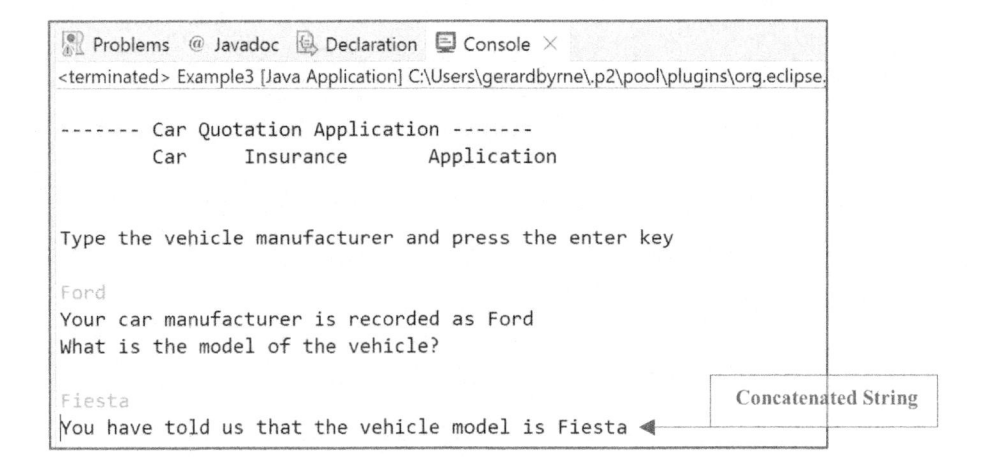

Amend the Java code to accept user input for the vehicle colour

We will now amend the code to ask the user to input other details about the vehicle being insured. In this case it will be the colour of the vehicle. Once again this is exactly the same process as we have already completed and coding this should help reinforce our learning.

The steps are:
- set up a variable that will hold the data requested from the user. The variable will be of a particular **data type** (in this case **String**)
- display a message that we want the user to input some data
- use the **myScanner.next()** method to get the data entered

12. Amend the existing code by adding the String variable called vehicleColour:

    Our new code will now be

    public static void main(String[] args)
    {
        Scanner myScanner = **new** Scanner(System.in);
        /*
        In this section we will add the variables we will use throughout the program code.
        These are variables that are going to be of a specific data type. Once we declare a
        variable and have said what its data type is, we cannot change the variables data type.
        The data type is immutable, it cannot be changed over time.
        First, we will add a variable called vehicleManufacturer of data type String then
        another String variable called vehicleModel and then another String variable called
        vehicleColour. */

String vehicleManufacturer;
String vehicleModel;

String vehicleColour;

13. Amend the existing code to ask for user input, read the user input and assign it to the vehicleColour variable:

    ```
    /* In the next three lines we display a question for the user, read
       whatever data the user inputs at the console, assign this data to the
       variable called vehicleModel and write out the concatenated text */
    System.out.println("What is the model of the vehicle?\n");
    vehicleModel = myScanner.next();
    System.out.println("You have told us that the vehicle model is " + vehicleModel);

    System.out.println("What is the colour of the vehicle?\n");
    vehicleColour = myScanner.next();
    ```

14. Amend the code to display the vehicleColour value which has been read from the console:

    ```
    System.out.println("What is the model of the vehicle?\n");
    vehicleModel = myScanner.next();
    System.out.println("We have told us that the vehicle model is " + vehicleModel);
    System.out.println("What is the colour of the vehicle?\n");
    vehicleColour = myScanner.next();

    System.out.println("We have told us that the vehicle colour is " + vehicleColour);

    System.out.println();

    myScanner.close();
    } //End of main() method
    } // End of class
    ```

15. Click on the **File** menu.
16. Choose **Save All**.
17. Click on the green Run button at the top of the screen.
18. Click in the Console window at the bottom of the screen.

19. Type **Ford** as the manufacturer name.
20. Press the **Enter** key on the keyboard.
21. Type **Fiesta** as the model name.
22. Press the **Enter** key on the keyboard.
23. Type **Blue** as the vehicle colour.
24. Press the **Enter** key on the keyboard.

We will see that the console window now displays the concatenated text for the colour.

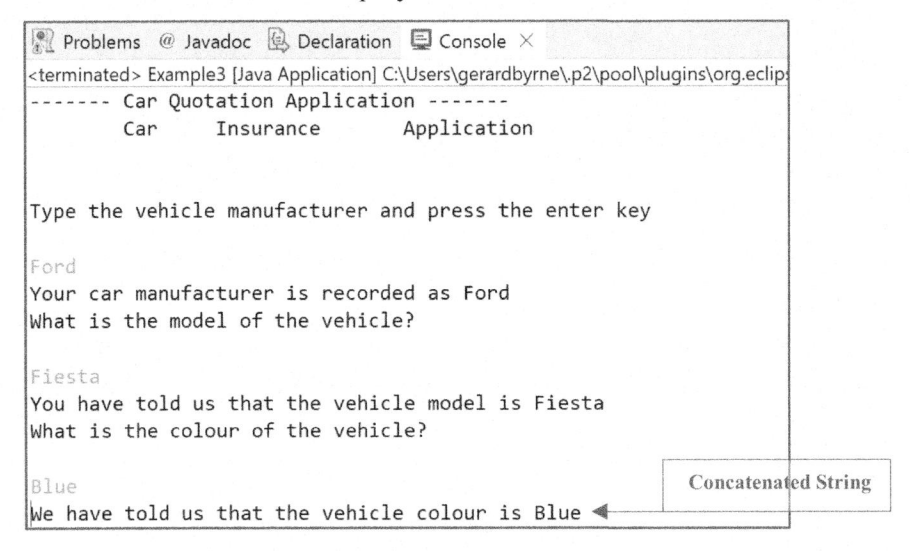

```
------- Car Quotation Application -------
        Car      Insurance      Application


Type the vehicle manufacturer and press the enter key

Ford
Your car manufacturer is recorded as Ford
What is the model of the vehicle?

Fiesta
You have told us that the vehicle model is Fiesta
What is the colour of the vehicle?

Blue
We have told us that the vehicle colour is Blue
```

Concatenated String

Something a little different with our variables

We will now amend the code to ask the user to input other details about the vehicle being insured. In this case we will amend the code to ask the user to input details about the age, in years, of the vehicle. We might use the age of the vehicle in a mathematical formula that will calculate the insurance premium to be charged. Once again this is the same process as we have already completed, **with one difference**, the variable is not of data type String, it will be of **data type int.**

So, the steps are:

- set up a variable that will hold the data requested from the user. The variable will be of a particular data type in this case it will be an **int**
- display a message that we want the user to input some data

- use the **myScanner.next()** method to get the data entered

This will be interesting as we will be accepting input from the console and we have seen from the previous examples that console input is accepted as a String. So, how can we now assign the String that the user enters for the age of the vehicle, to the variable of data type int, that we create to hold the data? We will see how to handle this shortly.

1. Amend the code to add the variables we require:

    String vehicleModel;
    String vehicleColour;

    int vehicleAgeInYears;

2. Amend the existing code to ask for user input, read the user input and assign it to the vehicleAgeInYears variable:

    vehicleColour = myScanner.next();
    System.*out*.println("You have told us that the vehicle colour is " + vehicleColour);

    System.*out*.println("What is the age, in full years, of the vehicle? \n");
    vehicleAgeInYears = myScanner.nextInt();

3. Click on the **File** menu.
4. Choose **Save All**.

All is well in our code as we can see, there are no red lines in the code editor window.

As we program, we will make mistakes and the **Java Virtual Machine** will help us as much as it can to correct them. These errors are called **compile time errors** as they are occurring at compile time rather than when we run the code and we may get a **runtime error**. We will get used to the error messages and become familiar with their meaning and how to resolve the issues in our code.

In this example the **conversion is handled by the Scanner class method, nextInt()**. When we read the earlier text, we were asked the question:

"So how can we now assign the String that the user enters for the age of the vehicle, to the variable of data type int that we will create to hold the data?"

We now know that this is handled by the Scanner class methods, in this case the method handling the conversion is the nextInt() method.

At other times in our code we will need to handle the conversions ourselves, as the Java Virtual Machine will tell us that it cannot do this conversion for us, **it is not implicit**, we have to tell the Java Virtual Machine how to do it, **we must be explicit**.

Remember we read this text earlier:

When we want to convert from one data type to another data type this can happen either by:

- **implicit** conversion — this means that we do not need to do anything as the conversion is automatically handled by our code.
  The Java Virtual Machine handles the conversion.

- **explicit** conversion — this means that we will need to code the data type conversion. It is not an automatic occurrence.
  The Java Virtual Machine will complain, through an error message, it cannot handle the conversion.

The conversion of input from the console is a simple process in Java if we use the Scanner class and its associated methods.

Code Analysis
- we have just used another method, as we can see from the () in the code
- the method is called nextInt and as it is a method it is written as **nextInt()**

- the nextInt () method has the keyword **Scanner** (or really the instance of the Scanner that we called myScanner) in front of it followed by a dot, a full stop. As we have already learnt, the full stop is dot notation in Java code and means that we want to use a part or element (variable or method) of the **object** that appears to the left of the full stop, in our case the Scanner object. We also know that Scanner must be a class which has variables and methods that we have access to.
- the Scanner class methods will do conversions from one data type to another data type for us. We do not need to write our own code to do the conversions. This is a great example of **reusable code** where code is written once and can be reused as often as required. Some of the methods that are accessible to us from the Scanner class are shown in the diagram below:

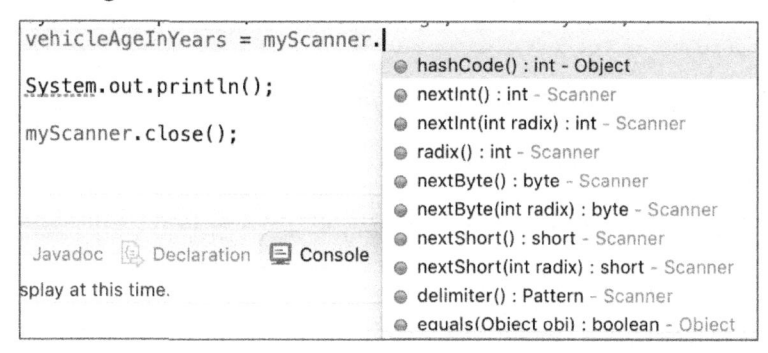

- the nextInt() method is used to convert from one data type to another data type so it needs know what is to be converted. This is clearly shown when we click on nextInt() in the pop-up window after typing the full stop:

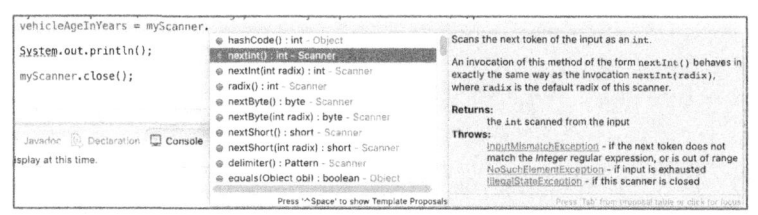

- when the nextInt() method scans the next token of the input and attempts to convert it to an int, it is possible an error will occur. The method will therefore:
  - return the int scanned from the input or
  - throw an exception, which can be one of three types:
    - **InputMismatchException**

> this is returned if the next token read in does not match the Integer regular expression or is out of range

- **NoSuchElementException**

  this is returned if the input is exhausted

- **IllegalStateException**

  this is returned if this scanner is closed

Great, we can see that the method nextInt() does the conversion for us. **How?** We do not need to know, simply accept that this method, which is part of the Scanner class, has been written, thoroughly tested and used by all developers when they wish to do a similar conversion.

This is the power of using existing code, and as developers we have access to many pieces of existing code. Using code methods from the Java language, from other developers in our organisation or other developers elsewhere, forms an integral part of modern programming.

Now we need to display a message to tell the user what has been read in.

This will be interesting as we are reading a **String** from the console and then converting it to an **int** data type. So, will we be able to use an int in our println() method or will it need to be converted back to a string?

5. Amend the code to display the message about the age of the vehicle:

```
vehicleAgeInYears = myScanner.nextInt();
System.out.println("You have told us that the vehicle age is " + vehicleAgeInYears);
  System.out.println();
myScanner.close();
   } //End of main() method
} // End of class
```

Do we see any error message? No, we should not see an error.

6. Click on the **File** menu.
7. Choose **Save All**.
8. Click on the green **Run** button at the top of the screen.
9. Click in the Console window at the bottom of the screen.
10. Type **Ford** as the manufacturer name.
11. Press the **Enter** key on the keyboard.
12. Type **Fiesta** as the model name.
13. Press the **Enter** key on the keyboard.
14. Type **Blue** as the vehicle colour.
15. Press the **Enter** key on the keyboard.
16. Type **5** as the vehicle age.
17. Press the **Enter** key on the keyboard.

We will see that the console window now displays the concatenated text for the age of the vehicle.

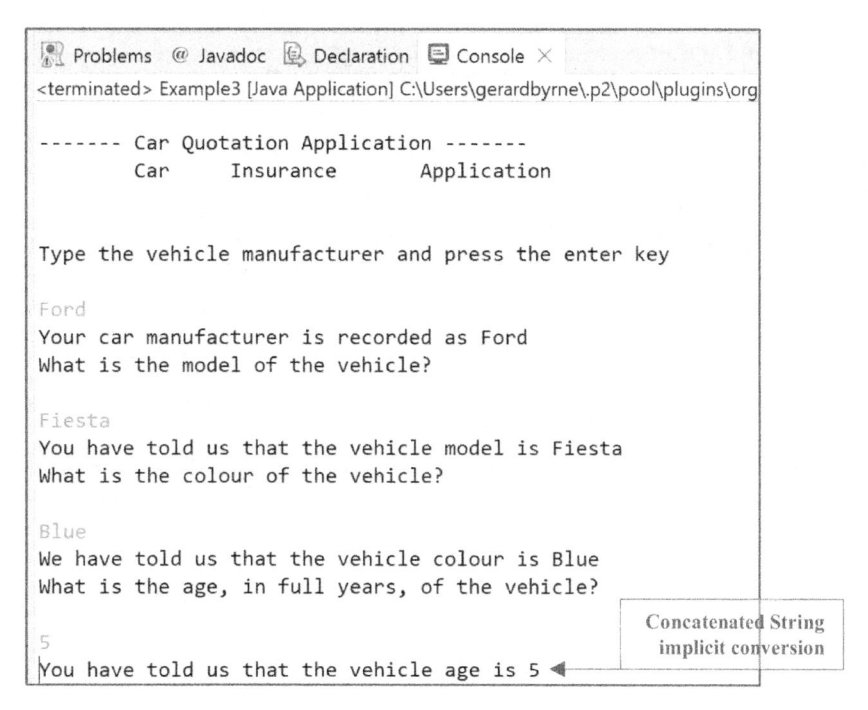

```
Problems  @ Javadoc  Declaration  Console  X
<terminated> Example3 [Java Application] C:\Users\gerardbyrne\.p2\pool\plugins\org

------- Car Quotation Application -------
         Car      Insurance      Application


Type the vehicle manufacturer and press the enter key

Ford
Your car manufacturer is recorded as Ford
What is the model of the vehicle?

Fiesta
You have told us that the vehicle model is Fiesta
What is the colour of the vehicle?

Blue
We have told us that the vehicle colour is Blue
What is the age, in full years, of the vehicle?

5
You have told us that the vehicle age is 5
```
Concatenated String implicit conversion

Code Analysis

- we have concatenated a string data type and an int data type using the + concatenator

- this works fine simply because the compiler actually does the conversion of the int data type to a string data type for us. It is an example of an **implicit conversion**

Remember what we read earlier:

- **implicit** conversion   this means that **we do not need to do anything** as the **conversion is automatically** handled by our code.
The Java Virtual Machine handles the conversion.

Amazing, we are now able to convert from one data type to another data type using the Scanner class. We are able to use the nextInt() method to convert a string to an int and we should now be able to use the same concept for converting a String to another data type. We are also more familiar with the meaning of explicit and explicit conversions.

Amend the Java code to accept user input for the vehicle value as a floating-point type.

We will now amend the code to ask the user to input details about the value of the vehicle. This is exactly the same process as we have already completed so we will follow the same steps as before. Our main decision in this process will be what data type to use for the value of the vehicle input. Three options could be considered:

float
 the float data type is a single-precision 32-bit floating point. As a rule, use a float (instead of double) to save memory. **A float should not be used for precise values, such as currency.** It would probably be more applicable to use the java.math.BigDecimal class.

double
 the double data type is a double-precision 64-bit floating point. For decimal values, the double data type is usually the default choice. **A double should not be used for precise values, such as currency.** It would probably be more applicable to use the java.math.BigDecimal class.

BigDecimal

The BigDecimal class provides operations on double numbers for arithmetic, scale handling, rounding etc. BigDecimal can handle very large and very small floating-point numbers with great precision.

This can be summarised to say that, when choosing a data type for the value of the vehicle, it is our choice, and depends on the accuracy we need for the value. Float is the least accurate, double is the next most accurate and BigDecimal is the most accurate. Here we are able to use any of the three but for this example we will use double, which would generally tend to be the default for most scenarios.

1. Amend the existing code by adding the variable called vehicleEstimatedCurrentPrice which is of data type double:

   String vehicleColour;
   int vehicleAgeInYears;

   double vehicleEstimatedCurrentPrice;

2. Amend the existing code to ask for user input, read the user input and assign it to the vehicleEstimatedCurrentPrice variable:

   System.*out*.println("You have told us that the vehicle age is " + vehicleAgeInYears);

   System.*out*.println("What is the estimated value of the vehicle?\n");
   vehicleEstimatedCurrentPrice = myScanner.nextDouble();
   System.*out*.println();
   myScanner.close();
   } // End of main() method
   } // End of class

3. Amend the code to display the vehicleEstimatedCurrentPrice value which has been read from the console:

   System.*out*.println("You have told us that the vehicle age is " + vehicleAgeInYears);
   System.*out*.println("What is the estimated value of the vehicle?\n");
   vehicleEstimatedCurrentPrice = myScanner.nextDouble();

```
        System.out.println("You have told us that the estimated vehicle price is £ " +
vehicleEstimatedCurrentPrice);
        System.out.println();
        myScanner.close();
 } // End of main() method
 } // End of class
```

4. Click on the **File** menu.
5. Choose **Save All**.
6. Click on the green **Run** button at the top of the screen.
7. Click in the Console window at the bottom of the screen.
8. Type **Ford** as the manufacturer name.
9. Press the **Enter** key on the keyboard.
10. Type **Fiesta** as the model name.
11. Press the **Enter** key on the keyboard.
12. Type **Blue** as the vehicle colour.
13. Press the **Enter** key on the keyboard.
14. Type **5** as the vehicle age.
15. Press the **Enter** key on the keyboard.
16. Type **6999.99** as the estimated vehicle value.
17. Press the **Enter** key on the keyboard.

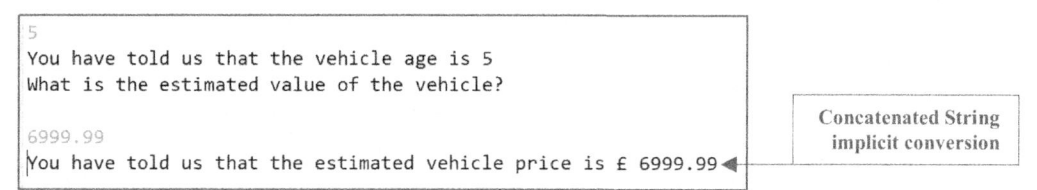

```
5
You have told us that the vehicle age is 5
What is the estimated value of the vehicle?

6999.99
You have told us that the estimated vehicle price is £ 6999.99
```

Concatenated String implicit conversion

Amend the Java code to accept user input for the vehicle mileage as an int

We will now amend the code to ask the user to input details about the number of kilometres recorded on the odometer of the vehicle.

1. Amend the existing code by adding the int variable called vehicleCurrentMileage:

    int vehicleAgeInYears;

```
double vehicleEstimatedCurrentPrice;

int vehicleCurrentMileage;
```

2. Amend the code to display the vehicleCurrentMileage value which has been read in:

```
System.out.println("You have told us that the estimated vehicle price is £ " +
vehicleEstimatedCurrentPrice);

System.out.println("What is the current mileage (in km) of the vehicle?\n");
vehicleCurrentMileage = myScanner.nextInt();
System.out.println("You have told us that the vehicle mileage is " +
vehicleCurrentMileage + " km");
    System.out.println();
    myScanner.close();
  } // End of main() method
} // End of class
```

Amend the Java code to accept user input for the driver date of birth as a String

We will now amend the code to ask the user to input the date of birth of the main driver of the vehicle. **Dates are tricky to handle**, so, initially we will read the input into a String and then we will convert it to a date.

3. Amend the existing code by adding the String variable called dateOfBirthOfMainDriver:

```
double vehicleEstimatedCurrentPrice;
int vehicleCurrentMileage;
String dateOfBirthOfMainDriver;
```

4. Amend the existing code to ask for user input, read the user input and assign it to the dateOfBirthOfMainDriver variable:

```
System.out.println("You have told us that the vehicle mileage is " +
vehicleCurrentMileage + " km");
```

myScanner.nextLine();

```
System.out.println("What is the date of birth (dd-mm-yyyy) of the main driver of the vehicle?\n");

dateOfBirthOfMainDriver = myScanner.nextLine();

System.out.println();
myScanner.close();
    } // End of main() method
} // End of class
```

Now we will need to create a date format and then use it to convert the **dateOfBirthOfMainDriver** string to this new date format.

5. Amend the code to create the Date format, don't worry too much about this statement for now, it will make more sense once we have completed the module on classes and objects:

```
System.out.println("What is the date of birth (dd-mm-yyyy) of the main driver of the vehicle?\n");

dateOfBirthOfMainDriver = myScanner.nextLine();

SimpleDateFormat myDateFormat = new SimpleDateFormat("dd-mm-yyyy");
```

6. Amend the code to import the required library for the **SimpleDateFormat** class:

```
package com.consoleexamples;

import java.util.Scanner;

import java.text.SimpleDateFormat;

//This is our only class and it will contain the Main method
public class Example3
{
```

7. Amend the code to convert **(parse)** the dateOfBirthOfMainDriver string to the new date format, do not worry about the error yet:

   dateOfBirthOfMainDriver = myScanner.nextLine();
   SimpleDateFormat myDateFormat=**new** SimpleDateFormat("dd-mm-yyyy");

   Date dateOfBirthOfMainDriverInDateFormat =
               myDateFormat.parse(dateOfBirthOfMainDriver);

8. Amend the code to import the Date class:

   package com.consoleexamples;
   import java.util.Date;

   import java.util.Scanner;
   import java.text.SimpleDateFormat;

   //This is our only class and it will contain the Main method
   public class Example3

We will need to use a **try catch** block around this code as we will see from the error message. It is important to realise that whilst a conversion will be attempted there is no guarantee that it will be successful. For this reason, we are being forced to handle any possible error using the try catch block of code. As we code more, we will see that it is important to handle errors so that our application does not just suddenly 'crash'.

9. Hover over the red underline.

   Date dateOfBirthOfMainDriverInDateFormat = myDateFormat.parse(dateOfBirthOfMainDr

   Unhandled exception type ParseException
   2 quick fixes available:
   System.*out*.println();   Add throws declaration
   myScanner.close();   Surround with try/catch

   } // End of main method()

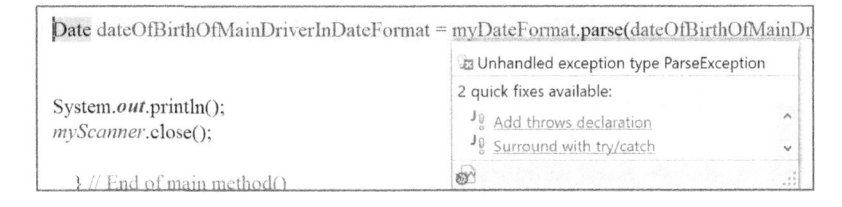

10. Choose the **Surround with try/catch** option by clicking on the option.

    The code will appear as shown below:

```
   dateOfBirthOfMainDriver = myScanner.nextLine();
   SimpleDateFormat myDateFormat=new SimpleDateFormat("dd-mm-yyyy ");

   try
   {
      Date dateOfBirthOfMainDriverInDateFormat =
      myDateFormat.parse(dateOfBirthOfMainDriver);
   }
   catch (ParseException e)
   {
      // TODO Auto-generated catch block
      e.printStackTrace();
   }
```

11. Amend the code to display the message

```
   try
   {
      Date dateOfBirthOfMainDriverInDateFormat =
      myDateFormat.parse(dateOfBirthOfMainDriver);

      System.out.println("You have told us that the main driver was born on " +
      dateOfBirthOfMainDriverInDateFormat);
   }
```

12. Click on the **File** menu.
13. Choose **Save All**.
14. Click on the green **Run** button at the top of the screen.
15. Click in the Console window at the bottom of the screen.
16. Type **Ford** as the manufacturer name.
17. Press the **Enter** key on the keyboard.
18. Type **Fiesta** as the model name.
19. Press the **Enter** key on the keyboard.
20. Type **Blue** as the vehicle colour.
21. Press the **Enter** key on the keyboard.
22. Type **5** as the vehicle age.
23. Press the **Enter** key on the keyboard.

24. Type **6999.99** as the estimated vehicle value.
25. Press the **Enter** key on the keyboard.
26. Press the **Enter** key on the keyboard.
27. Type **50000** as the number of kilometres on the odometer of the vehicle.
28. Press the **Enter** key on the keyboard.
29. Type **01-01-1998** as the date of birth for the main driver of the vehicle.
30. Press the **Enter** key on the keyboard.

The date, entered as a String, is converted to a Date and is displayed in a date format depending on the setup preferences on your computer. We can change the format in our code, but that's just too much for us at the moment.

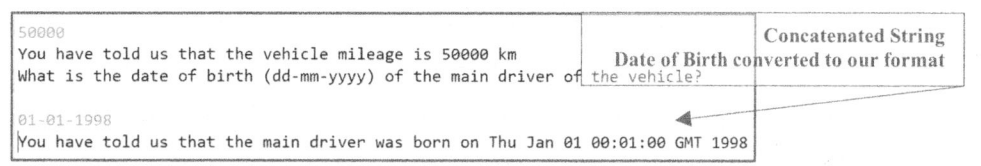

```
50000
You have told us that the vehicle mileage is 50000 km
What is the date of birth (dd-mm-yyyy) of the main driver of the vehicle?
01-01-1998
You have told us that the main driver was born on Thu Jan 01 00:01:00 GMT 1998
```

Concatenated String
Date of Birth converted to our format

Code Analysis

- we have used data types int, double, string and we have just used a data type of **Date**
- when we read the console input, we have used our own **SimpleDateFormat** to convert the string input by the user.
- this is similar to an **explicit conversion**

Module Summary

In this module we have learnt about the very important programming concepts of **data types**, **variables** and **conversions**. We have learnt that:

- there are value types in Java that include **boolean and char**
- there are arithmetic value types such as **byte, short, int, double**
- there are arithmetic floating-point value types such as **float and double**
- the value types in Java are referred to as **primitive types** and they are part of the language, they are built into the language, we do not need to create them
- sometimes variables need to be converted from one data type to another data type and this is either done **explicitly** or **implicitl**
- there are conversions called widening conversions where the converted data changes from a smaller data type to a larger data type
- there are conversions called narrowing conversions where the converted data changes from a larger data type to a smaller data type and data can be lost
- there are **variables** in code, and they have a **scope**
- use of comments is important, at times
- escape sequences such as \n and \t are useful for presentation of data in the console
- data can be read from the console using the Scanner class
- data can be written to the console using the System.out.println() or System.out.print()
- there is a **BigDecimal** class that can be used in operations on double numbers

This is great progress in such a short period of study. We should also be aware that Java has other data types and we will use them as required by our code.

Another great achievement for us in our learning

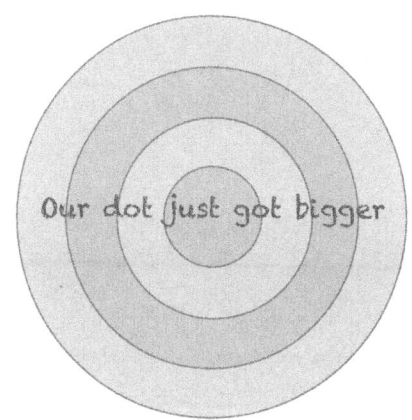

Our dot just got bigger

Program Practically

Java

Module 05

Conversion – Casting and Parsing

Casting from one numeric data type to another
Parsing a String to a numeric data type
Wrapper classes

Gerry Byrne

Program Practically - Data types, variables, casting and parsing

We learnt in module 4 that:

We can declare variables which are of a particular data type and then assign values to them in our code. We can accept user input and assign the value input by the user to the variable. We also saw that there are times when we will need to convert a variable from one data type to another. We learnt about narrowing and widening conversions and in particular we used a conversion from an int to a byte which involved casting, (byte).

Conversions using casting and parsing

In this module we will continue the theme of conversion and look at both casting and parsing as forms of conversion from one data type to another. First let us look at the difference between casting and parsing.

Casting

In Java, casting is a method used to **convert one numeric data type to another**. Casting is used as an explicit conversion telling the compiler what to do, and to be aware that there may be a loss of data. So, we use casting to achieve a **numeric conversion** where the destination data type we are assigning the value to is of a lesser precision. **Casting is a conversion from one numeric data type to another numeric data type**.

Think back to what we have read about the numeric data types. We start with a less precise data type, byte and move to the most precise long data type. Data types in Java are shown below along with their size and default values:

Java data type	default	Size	Description
boolean	false	1 byte	Contains either true or false
char	\u0000	2 bytes	Contains a single character

Integral types

Java data type	default	Size	Description
byte	0	1 byte	May contain integers from 128 to 127
short	0	2 bytes	Ranges from 32,768 to 32,767
int	0	4 bytes	Ranges from -2,147,483,648 to 2,147,483,647
long	0	8 bytes	Ranges from -9,223,372,036,854,775,808 to 9,223,372,036,854,775,807

Floating point types

Java data type	default	Size	Description
float	0.0	4 bytes	unlimited
double	0.0	8 bytes	unlimited

So, if we were to take a data type in the table and try to assign it to a variable which has a data type above it in the table, we are moving to a less precise format and therefore we must use a cast (casting). Shortly we will code an example of **int to short**.

Parsing

In Java, parsing is a method used to convert a **String to a primitive data type**. With parsing we use methods of type parseDATATYPE(), where the DATATYPE will be replaced by the data type it is being converted to e.g. parse**Int**(), parse**Double**(), parse**Byte**(), parse**Float**() etc. The operation is named **parsing**. The parsing methods are available through Wrapper classes, but let's not worry about this now, just concentrate on the fact that we can do some conversions using parsing.

Let's code some Java

Now we will look at using casting in different ways. Remember to read the comments carefully as they fully explain what we are doing.

Create a new package

In the last module we saw how to create a new package, then copy and paste a Java class file from another package to the new package. Now we will do something different, this time by copying the package com.gerrybyrne.module04 and renaming it com.gerrybyrne.module05. By copying the package we will also get the Java files that are within it. This is just what we want as it will mean we do not have to copy and paste the files.

1. Right click on the package **com.gerrybyrne.module04**.

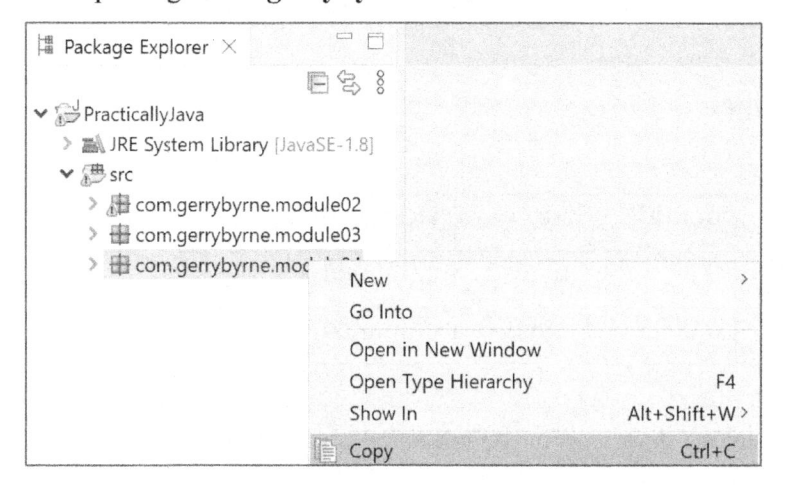

2. Choose **Copy**.
3. Right click on the **src** folder.
4. Choose **Paste**.
5. Rename the package as **com.gerrybyrne.module05.**

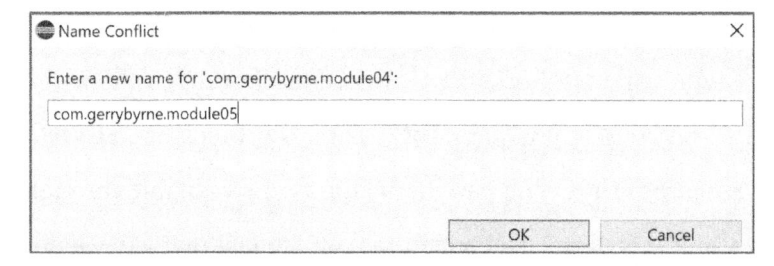

6. Choose the **OK** button.
7. Expand the com.gerrybyrne.module05 package by clicking on the > symbol beside the name.
8. Right click on the **Example3** file.
9. Choose **Refactor**.
10. Choose **Rename**.
11. Enter the new name for the file, we will call it **Example4**.
12. Click the **Finish** button.
13. Click the **Finish** button.

Amend the Java code to use a casting from int to short

14. Amend the existing code by adding two new variables, one of data type int and called maximumAmountForRepairCosts and the other of data type short and called minmumAmountForRepairCosts

    int vehicleCurrentMileage;
    String dateOfBirthOfMainDriver;

    // max value of short is 2,147,483,647
    int maximumAmountForRepairCosts = 32767;

    // max value of short is 32,767
    short maximumAmountForCarHire = 0;

15. Click on the **File** menu.
16. Choose **Save All**.
17. Amend the code to assign the value of the variable maximumAmountForRepairCosts to the variable called maximumAmountForCarHire:

    catch (ParseException e)
    {
        e.printStackTrace();
    }
    /*

Now we are trying to put the <u>int</u> variable maximumAmountForRepairCosts into the short variable maximumAmountForCarHire. This is not possible without something being changed. This is where the error message will appear and a cast comes into play
*/
maximumAmountForCarHire = <u>maximumAmountForRepairCosts</u>;

System.*out*.println();
myScanner.close();

} // End of main method()
} // End of Example4 class

As we see the variable called maximumAmountForRepairCosts is underlined with red. So, we need to fix the issue, once we understand what is causing the error.

18. Hover over the red underline and read the pop-up message.

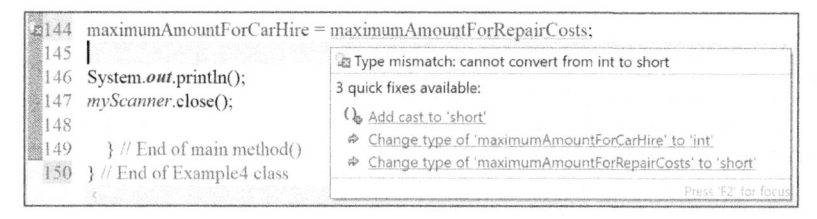

```
144  maximumAmountForCarHire = maximumAmountForRepairCosts;
145
146  System.out.println();         Type mismatch: cannot convert from int to short
147  myScanner.close();            3 quick fixes available:
148                                  Add cast to 'short'
149     } // End of main method()   Change type of 'maximumAmountForCarHire' to 'int'
150  } // End of Example4 class     Change type of 'maximumAmountForRepairCosts' to 'short'
                                                                Press 'F2' for focus
```

As we see from the message, we are being told that maximumAmountForRepairCosts **cannot be implicitly converted from an int data type to a short** data type.

Even though the error message does not specifically say it, the cause of the error is that we are trying to perform a narrowing conversion, and this cannot be done implicitly, we must perform the conversion with an explicit conversion, a **cast** in this case.

The error message gives us options to fix the issue - to perform a cast or changing the data type of one of the variables.

This means that we can perform the conversion using a cast. We will be casting the variable maximumAmountForRepairCosts, which is of data type int, so it fits into a data type short.

19. Click on the **Add cast to 'short'** option or amend the code as shown below to perform the casting manually:

/* Now we are trying to put the int variable maximumAmountForRepairCosts into the short variable maximumAmountForCarHire. This is not possible without something being changed. This is where the error message will appear and a cast comes into play */
maximumAmountForCarHire = (short) maximumAmountForRepairCosts;

As we will see, the red underline error has disappeared. We have fixed the conversion issue. The solution was to add a cast where the cast is () brackets with the type of conversion to be accomplished **(short).**

Solution is called casting

maximumAmountForCarHire = (short)maximumAmountForRepairCosts;

20. Amend the code to display the maximumAmountForCarHire and maximumAmountForRepairCosts values:

Our new code will now be

maximumAmountForCarHire = **(short)** maximumAmountForRepairCosts;

System.out.println("The int variable maximumAmountForRepairCosts has a value of " + maximumAmountForRepairCosts);

System.out.println("\nThe short variable maximumAmountForCarHire has a value of " + maximumAmountForCarHire);

System.out.println();
myScanner.close();

Now, running this application with the int variable being set to have its maximum value of 32767, will be fine, this means the **casting will take place without loss of accuracy, on this occasion**.

21. Click on the **File** menu.
22. Choose **Save All**.
23. Click on the green **Run** button at the top of the screen.
24. Click in the Console window at the bottom of the screen.
25. Type **Ford** as the manufacturer name.
26. Press the **Enter** key on the keyboard.
27. Type **Fiesta** as the model name.
28. Press the **Enter** key on the keyboard.
29. Type **Blue** as the vehicle colour.
30. Press the **Enter** key on the keyboard.
31. Type **5** as the vehicle age.
32. Press the **Enter** key on the keyboard.
33. Type **6999.99** as the estimated vehicle value.
34. Press the **Enter** key on the keyboard.
35. Press the **Enter** key on the keyboard.
36. Type **50000** as the number of kilometres on the odometer of the vehicle.
37. Press the **Enter** key on the keyboard.
38. Type **01-01-1998** as the date of birth for the main driver of the vehicle.
39. Press the **Enter** key on the keyboard.

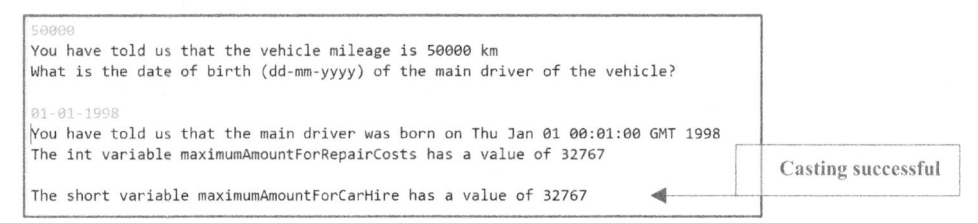

```
50000
You have told us that the vehicle mileage is 50000 km
What is the date of birth (dd-mm-yyyy) of the main driver of the vehicle?

01-01-1998
You have told us that the main driver was born on Thu Jan 01 00:01:00 GMT 1998
The int variable maximumAmountForRepairCosts has a value of 32767

The short variable maximumAmountForCarHire has a value of 32767
```

Casting successful

If we amended the code so that the int variable is set to have a value of 32768, which is one more than the maximum value of the short data type (32767) there will be an issue, this means the **casting will take place with loss of accuracy**.

40. Amend the code to change the value of the int variable so that it is one more than the maximum value of a short data type. This will mean that when we cast the int variable it will be too large for the variable maximumAmountForCarHire (data type short) to hold:

```java
// max value of short is 2,147,483,647
int maximumAmountForRepairCosts = 32768;

// max value of short is 32,767
short maximumAmountForCarHire = 0;
```

41. Click on the **File** menu.
42. Choose **Save All**.
43. Click on the green **Run** button at the top of the screen.
44. Click in the Console window at the bottom of the screen.
45. Type **Ford** as the manufacturer name.
46. Press the **Enter** key on the keyboard.
47. Type **Fiesta** as the model name.
48. Press the **Enter** key on the keyboard.
49. Type **Blue** as the vehicle colour.
50. Press the **Enter** key on the keyboard.
51. Type **5** as the vehicle age.
52. Press the **Enter** key on the keyboard.
53. Type **6999.99** as the estimated vehicle value.
54. Press the **Enter** key on the keyboard.
55. Press the **Enter** key on the keyboard.
56. Type **50000** as the number of kilometres on the odometer of the vehicle.
57. Press the **Enter** key on the keyboard.
58. Type **0-/01-1998** as the date of birth for the main driver of the vehicle.
59. Press the **Enter** key on the keyboard.

This will give us an output and no compile error but, the result is not correct.

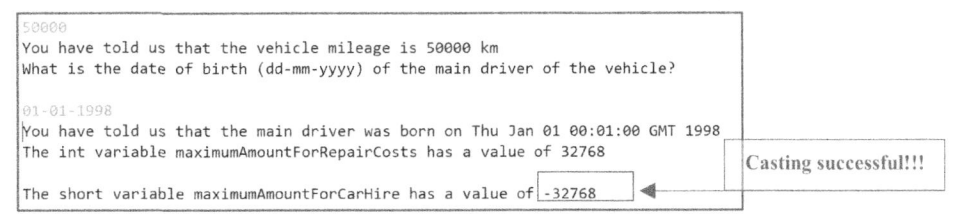

```
50000
You have told us that the vehicle mileage is 50000 km
What is the date of birth (dd-mm-yyyy) of the main driver of the vehicle?
01-01-1998
You have told us that the main driver was born on Thu Jan 01 00:01:00 GMT 1998
The int variable maximumAmountForRepairCosts has a value of 32768

The short variable maximumAmountForCarHire has a value of -32768
```

Casting successful!!!

Certainly not what we expected and therefore, not very good coding. As developers, we need to be careful when we use casting and indeed any type of conversion.

60. Change the value back to 32767.

Amend the Java code to use a Boolean data type and use parsing for the conversion

We will now amend the code to ask the user to input **True** or **False** at the console. Remember that console input is a String. We will then assign the console input to a variable of data type **boolean**.

1. Amend the code to add two new variables, one of data type string and the other of data type bool (Boolean):

   ```
   // max value of short is 32,767
   short maximumAmountForCarHire = 0;

   String fullyComprehensiveUserInput = "True";
   boolean fullyComprehensiveRequirement = true;
   ```

2. Amend the code to ask the user for input:

   ```
   catch (ParseException e)
   {
       // TODO Auto-generated catch block
       e.printStackTrace();
   }
   System.out.println("Do we require fully comprehensive insurance (enter the word true or false)?\n");
   ```

3. Amend the code to assign the value of the variable fullyComprehensiveRequirement to the value entered by the user at the console:

   ```
   catch (ParseException e)
   {
   ```

```
            // TODO Auto-generated catch block
            e.printStackTrace();
    }
        System.out.println("Do we require fully comprehensive insurance (enter the word true or false)?\n");
        fullyComprehensiveRequirement = Boolean.parseBoolean(myScanner.next());
```

In the example we have used the Boolean class and chose the parseBoolean() method. The Boolean class is a Wrapper class as we mentioned previously. We know we are using a method because of the (). The method is given (passed) the value to be parsed (converted). In this case the value is being read from the keyboard as a String using the next() method from the myScanner instance (copy) of the Scanner class.

4. Amend the code to display the value of the variable fullyComprehensiveRequirement which is of data type bool

   ```
   System.out.println("Do you require fully comprehensive insurance (enter the word true or false)?\n");
   fullyComprehensiveRequirement = Boolean.parseBoolean(myScanner.next());

   System.out.println("It is " + fullyComprehensiveRequirement + " that we require fully comprehensive insurance");
   ```

5. Click on the **File** menu.
6. Choose **Save All**.
7. Click on the green **Run** button at the top of the screen.
8. Click in the Console window at the bottom of the screen.
9. Type **Ford** as the manufacturer name.
10. Press the **Enter** key on the keyboard.
11. Type **Fiesta** as the model name.
12. Press the **Enter** key on the keyboard.
13. Type **Blue** as the vehicle colour.
14. Press the **Enter** key on the keyboard.
15. Type **5** as the vehicle age.
16. Press the **Enter** key on the keyboard.

17. Type **6999.99** as the estimated vehicle value.
18. Press the **Enter** key on the keyboard.
19. Press the **Enter** key on the keyboard.
20. Type **50000** as the number of kilometres on the odometer of the vehicle.
21. Press the **Enter** key on the keyboard.
22. Type **01-01-1998** as the date of birth for the main driver of the vehicle.
23. Press the **Enter** key on the keyboard.
24. Type **true** for the answer to the question It is true that we require fully comprehensive insurance.

The output will be as shown below:

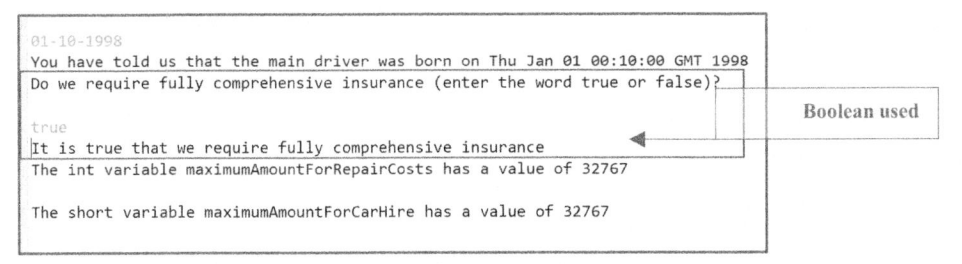

```
01-10-1998
You have told us that the main driver was born on Thu Jan 01 00:10:00 GMT 1998
Do we require fully comprehensive insurance (enter the word true or false)?
true
It is true that we require fully comprehensive insurance
The int variable maximumAmountForRepairCosts has a value of 32767

The short variable maximumAmountForCarHire has a value of 32767
```

Boolean used

Amend the Java code to use parsing for the conversion of the age read in as a String

We will now amend the code to ask the user to input the age of the vehicle again, but this time we will read the user input as a String using the next() method. We will use the parsing method parseInt() from the Integer class. We know parseInt() is a method because of the (). We will then assign the parsed console input to the variable vehicleAgeInYears which is of data type int.

1. Amend the code to comment the two lines of code showing the maximum values of the variables maximumAmountForRepairCosts and maximumAmountForCarHire:

```
/* Now we are trying to put the int variable maximumAmountForRepairCosts
   into the short variable maximumAmountForCarHire. This is not possible
   without something being changed. This is where the error message will
   appear and a cast comes into play
*/
```

maximumAmountForCarHire = (**short**) maximumAmountForRepairCosts;

```
/*
    System.out.println("The int variable maximumAmountForRepairCosts has a
    value of " + maximumAmountForRepairCosts);

    System.out.println("\nThe short variable maximumAmountForCarHire has a
    value of " + maximumAmountForCarHire);
*/
System.out.println();
myScanner.close();
```

2. Amend the code to repeat the 3 lines of code related to the vehicle age:

```
/*
    System.out.println("The int variable maximumAmountForRepairCosts has a
    value of " + maximumAmountForRepairCosts);

    System.out.println("\nThe short variable maximumAmountForCarHire has a
    value of " + maximumAmountForCarHire);
*/

System.out.println("What is the age, in full years, of the vehicle? \n");

vehicleAgeInYears = Integer.parseInt(myScanner.next());

System.out.println("You have told us that the vehicle age is " + vehicleAgeInYears);

System.out.println();
myScanner.close();
```

Here we have asked the user to input the vehicle age and we have used the next() method of the Scanner class to read it, so it is a String. However, we have enclosed this inside an Integer.parseInt(). This means use the parseInt(0 method of the Integer class to covert the String to an int.

3. Click on the **File** menu.
4. Choose **Save All**.

5. Click on the green **Run** button at the top of the screen.
6. Click in the Console window at the bottom of the screen.
7. Type **Ford** as the manufacturer name.
8. Press the **Enter** key on the keyboard.
9. Type **Fiesta** as the model name.
10. Press the **Enter** key on the keyboard.
11. Type **Blue** as the vehicle colour.
12. Press the **Enter** key on the keyboard.
13. Type **5** as the vehicle age.
14. Press the **Enter** key on the keyboard.
15. Type **6999** as the estimated vehicle value.
16. Press the **Enter** key on the keyboard.
17. Press the **Enter** key on the keyboard.
18. Type **50000** as the number of kilometres on the odometer of the vehicle.
19. Press the **Enter** key on the keyboard.
20. Type **01-01-1998** as the date of birth for the main driver of the vehicle.
21. Press the **Enter** key on the keyboard.
22. Type **true** for the answer to the question It is true that we require fully comprehensive insurance.
23. Type **5** as the vehicle age.

The output will be as shown below and we can see that the String value for the age of the vehicle that was entered by the user has been parsed and becomes an integer.

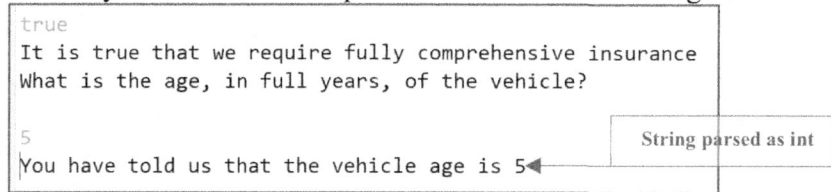

```
true
It is true that we require fully comprehensive insurance
What is the age, in full years, of the vehicle?

5
You have told us that the vehicle age is 5    ← String parsed as int
```

Parsing

In Java, parsing simply means converting something from text (data type String) to another data type, e.g. a numeric such as int. Many Java data types already have methods written that will perform the parsing for us. We have used two parsing methods (remember methods belong to classes):

- Boolean.parseBoolean()
- Integer.parseInt()

Others include:

- Byte.parseByte();
- Float.parseFloat();
- Double.parseDouble();

One important thing to note is the capital letter of the 'data type'. When we see the capital letter, we are not using a data type the way we did when we were defining a variable, we are using **an object**, **a class**, a **Wrapper class** is the fancy name for it.

Wrapper Class	method name	Conversion type
Boolean	parseBoolean()	String to boolean
Integer	parseInt()	String to integer
Byte	parseByte()	String to byte
Float	parseFloat()	String to float
Double	parseDouble()	String to double

Instead of using this casting method:

byte commissionfactor;
int commissionvalue = 257;

//(byte) means we wish to convert to byte the commissionvalue
commissionfactor = (byte) commissionvalue;

we could use this parsing method:

byte commissionfactor;
String commissionvalue="9";

/* Take the commissionvalue variable which is of data type int and use
   the parseByte() method from the class (object) called Byte to parse
   the variable which is apssed into the method. */
commissionfactor = Byte.parseByte(commissionvalue);

But please remember the difference between parsing and casting.

- casting involves changing the data type of a variable and is for number to number conversion
- parsing means taking the string and working out its logical value. This is a complex process as a String is represented by a series of ASCII codes and the parsing algorithm has to go through each of the ASCII character codes and convert them to their numeric value
- using the example above we had:
    - String commissionvalue="9";
    - this would be reprersented in ASCII code as 57
    - so the conversion algorithm has to take the value 57 and convert it to the integer 9
- using another example which has a decimal point:
    - String commissionvalue="9.99";
    - this could be reprersented as 57465757
    - so the conversion algorithm has to take the value 57 and convert it to the integer 9.99
- in reality parsing converts the data but casting does not

Module summary

In this module we have learnt about the particularly important programming concepts of parsing and casting and have seen the 'subtle' difference between them. We have seen that in parsing we use the Wrapper class which represents the data type e.g. Integer, and we noted that this class, like all classes, starts with a capital letter. Each wrapper class has methods that will perform the parsing e.g. parseInt and the method will be passed the name of the variable to be parsed (converted).

Yet another great achievement for us in our learning.

Our dot just got bigger

Program Practically

Java

Module 06

Arithmetic

Arithmetic using standard operators, + - * /

Arithmetic using non-standard operators, % += -= *= /=

Square root as a special method from the Math class

Formatting output to 2 decimal places

Gerry Byrne

Program Practically - Arithmetic Operations

We learnt in module 5 that:

Variables can be 'converted' from one data type to another which is referred to as **casting** or converting a String value to a numeric value which is called **parsing**. Parsing uses methods from a wrapper class to convert the String data to a numeric data type value. These are important concepts and widely used in all programming languages by professional developers. As we develop our Java skills throughout the modules, we will use these concepts, so it is worthwhile constantly reminding ourselves of the differences between casting and parsing and how they are used within Java code.

Arithmetic in our business logic

The code, or business logic as it is often called, of many applications will have some degree of computation or calculation. In Java it is possible to perform operations, on integers and other numerical data types, that we can perform in normal mathematics.

We will probably be aware from our mathematics lessons at school, that mathematical operations are performed in a specific order, and therefore we need to ensure that formulae are written in such a way that the mathematical operators work in the correct order. Based on this knowledge we should recognise that calculations involving combinations of the mathematical operators such as add (+), subtract (-), multiply (*) and divide (/) can return a different value (answer) when the order is changed. The normal algebraic rules of **precedence (priority)** apply in every programming language, including Java, and need to be thoroughly understood and applied. The precedence can be understood using the acronym BODMAS which means:

- **B**rackets
- p**O**wers
- **D**ivision   These two operations have the same priority

- **Multiplication**
- **Addition**   These two operations have the same priority
- **Subtraction**

Division and Multiplication operations have the same priority.

Addition and Subtraction operations have the same priority.

As stated earlier it is vitally important that we get the correct answer when we execute calculations in our code, therefore, we need to ensure that mathematical formulae are written correctly in our code. Big problems can be caused by, and for developers, when they code their formulae incorrectly. Often the coding errors in mathematical formulae are caused because developers misuse, or do not use, brackets ( ) to group expressions within their formulae.

Example 1

6 * 5 - 3	we could take this to mean
6 * 5	this part is equal to 30
30 – 3	this part is equal to 27

If this was the intention it should be written as

(6 * 5) - 3   now the brackets make it clear that 6 is multiplied by 5 and the answer will have 3 subtracted from it to give an answer of 27.

Alternatively we could take it to mean

6 * 5 - 3
5 - 3   this part is equal to 2
6 * 2   this part is equal to 12

If this was the intention it should be written as

6 * (5 - 3)   now the brackets make it clear that 3 is subtracted from 5 and the answer is multiplied by 6 to give an answer of 12.

Example 2

2 + 4 × 3 − 1

2 + 12 − 1

14 − 1

13

If we use brackets it can make the visualisation of the actual order much easier

2 + 4 × 3 − 1   can be written as   2 + (4 x 3) -1

Without brackets it can be harder to see what needs to be done in the formula. By using brackets ( ) to group expressions within the formula we can make it much easier to understand.

Common arithmetical operators

Within Java we have access to a number of arithmetical operators, including those shown below, which we will use in this module and in many programs that we write:

Add   +
Subtract   -
Multiply   *
Divide   /
Modulus   %   the remainder

Integer Division

Integer division in any programming language, just as in mathematics, is an interesting operation in that we get an answer with a remainder, even if the remainder is 0. In programming when two integer values are divided using the / operator, the result will be the *whole* part of the division, the *remainder* is not taken into account.

Example

19/5   will give an answer of   3

As we can see this is the whole number part and there is no indication of the remainder. Where has the remainder of 4 gone?

It has effectively been lost as we have not used the division operator in its full format. We need to use the division operator alongside the ***modulus*** operator (%). The modulus operator **%** gives the ***remainder*** after the division has been performed.

Example:

19%5 will give an answer of   4

Therefore, to do a division properly we need to combine the division and the modulus parts.

Now it is time for us to do some Java coding. The Java console application we will code will use the mathematical operators to perform arithmetic. We will read data input from the console, using the Scanner class method and will write to the console using the System.out.println() method. As we are dealing with mathematical operators our data will need to be numerical, so, our code will apply some conversion. We will also apply some casting, in particular when undertaking division which involve int data types.

We should use the same workspace that we created for the earlier modules, as this will mean we will still be able to see the code we have written for the previous modules. The approach of keeping all our separate projects in one workspace is a good idea while studying this book and coding the examples.

The code for this module uses arithmetic within an insurance quote example and builds on our learning from the previous modules.

Amend the Java project to add a new package and within it the class

1. Right click on the **src** folder.
2. Choose **New**.

3. Choose **Package**.
4. Name the package **com.gerrybyrne.module06**.
5. Click the **Finish** button.
6. Right click on the package icon.
7. Choose **New**.
8. Choose **Class**.
9. Name the class **Arithmetic**.
10. Put a tick in the checkbox beside the public static void main(String[] args) box.
11. Click on the Finish button.

The **Arithmetic** class code will appear in the editor window and will be similar to the following:

package com.gerrybyrne.module06;

public class Arithmetic
{

    public static void main(String[] args)
    {
      // **TODO** Auto-generated method stub

    } // End of main method()
} // End of Arithmetic class

Look at the structure of the Solution in the Package Explorer window:
- the com.gerrybyrne.module06 package is now included in the workspace alongside the other packages we have created for the other modules
- the com.gerrybyrne.module06 package has the Arithmetic Java class with some template code and it should be open in the editor window. If it is not opened, double click on the Arithmetic file in the project window

We should now be getting a better understanding of the structure for projects and packages and, as we learn more, we will see how to add different classes to our projects and packages, with only one class containing the main() method. Obviously, we will need to have different names for each class in a project, so, once we have named classes it is still possible to rename them. We can start by doing this in our project and will rename the file, Arithmetic, and call it **QuoteArithmetic**.

12. Right click on the file **Arithmetic** file in the Package Explorer window.
13. Choose **Refactor** from the menu that appears.
14. Choose **Rename** from the next menu that appears.
15. Type **QuoteArithmetic** as the new file name.
16. Click the **Finish** button.
17. Click the second **Finish** button.

The file name is amended, as can be seen in the Package Explorer window.

Now we will add the variables that will be used in our code. In the code below there are detailed comments to help us get a full understanding of the code.

Amend the Java project to add the variables we require

18. Amend the template code as shown below by adding the variables we will use in our insurance quotation application code:

```
// Program Description:    A Java program to perform arithmetical operations
// Author:                 Gerry Byrne
// Date of creation:       01/10/2021

package com.gerrybyrne.module06;
public class QuoteArithmetic {
public static void main(String[] args)
{
  /*
   We will setup our variables that will be used in the mathematical
   calculation used to produce an insurance quotation for a vehicle.
   First we will setup the variables that will hold the user input and
   that will be used in calculating the quote
  */
```

```
int vehicleAgeInYears;
int vehicleCurrentMileage;

/*
    For the quotation we will use 10000 kilometres as a base line for
    calculating a mileage factor. If the average kilomteres travelled
    per year is above the     base mileage of 10000 the mileage factor will
    be above 1, if the average kilomteres travelled per year is the lower
    than the base mileage of 10000 the mileage factor will be below 1
*/
double quoteAverageExpectedKilometres = 10000;

/*
    For the quotation we will use £100 as a base figure (this is just
    an example) and this figure will be multiplied by the mileage and age factors
*/
double quoteBaseRate = 100.00;

/*
    For the quotation we will use 10 as a base figure for the age of
    the vehicle (this is just an example). If the vehicle is older than
    10 years, the age factor will be above 1. If the vehicle is younger
    than 10 years the age factor will be below 1
*/
int quoteBaseAge = 10;

/* This variable will be used to hold the value of the age factor */
double quoteAgeFactor;

/*
    This variable holds the quote amount based on the age factor and
    the base rate
*/
double quoteAgeFactorPremium;

/*
    This variable holds the quote mileage factor based on the number of
    kilometres travelled each year and how the kilometres per year is a
    ratio of the average expected 10000 kilometres as decided by the
    insurance company
*/
```

double quoteMileageFactor;

/*
This variable will hold the amount for the quote based only on the mileage factor. The quote also has to take into account the age of the vehicle
*/
double quoteMileageFactorPremium;

/*
This variable will hold the discount amount. A discount will be applied to the quote based on the age of the vehicle. The age of the vehicle is divided into 1 to get the discount.

The decimal value is a representation of the discount and will then be multiplied by the quote value to get the actual discount in terms of £s
*/
double quoteDiscount;

/*
This variable holds the total of the age factor premium and the mileage factor premium and will be used by the discount calculation to get the discount amount
*/
double quoteAmountForPremium;

/* This variable holds the final quotation value, the premium */
double quoteFinalAmountForPremium;

} // End of main() method
} // End of QuoteArithmetic class

Amend the Java code to output some information

Now we will write some information to the console and ask the user to input some data.

19. Amend the code, by adding these print lines to the end of the code, as shown:

/* This variable holds the final quotation value, the premium */

```
        double quoteFinalAmountForPremium;

    System.out.println();
    System.out.println("------- Car Quotation Application -------");
    System.out.println("\tCar\tInsurance\tApplication\n");
    System.out.println();
    System.out.println("What is the age, in full years, of the vehicle?\n");

    } // End of main() method
} // End of QuoteArithmetic class
```

Amend the Java code to read user input and perform some calculations

Now we will:

- read the user input data for the vehicle age from the console and convert it to an int.
- use the vehicle age to calculate an age factor by dividing it into the base age we set up in the variables.
- calculate the premium based on the age factor and quote base rate (£100).

20. Amend the code to create an instance of the Scanner class so we can read from the console, as shown:

    ```
    public static void main(String[] args)
    {
        Scanner myScanner = new Scanner(System.in);
    ```

21. Add the Scanner class import as shown:

    ```
    package com.gerrybyrne.module06;

    import java.util.Scanner;

    public class QuoteArithmetic
    {
    ```

22. Amend the code, by adding these lines to the end of the code that:

- reads the input and convert, using casting, to an int
- performs a calculation using division and which involves converting, using casting, two variables that are being used in the division
- performs a calculation using multiplication

```
System.out.println("What is the age, in full years, of the vehicle?\n");
/*
    Perform the conversion from string to int as we will use the age of
    the vehicle in our calculation and it needs to be numeric
*/
vehicleAgeInYears = (int)(myScanner.nextInt());

/*
    Perform the conversion from string to double as we will use the age of
    the vehicle in our calculation and it needs to be numeric
    Example: For a 5 year old car the factor is 10/5 = 2
*/
quoteAgeFactor = (double)(quoteBaseAge) / (double)(vehicleAgeInYears);

/* The quote amount based on the age is £100 multiplied by the age factor
    Example £100 * 2 = £200
*/
quoteAgeFactorPremium = quoteBaseRate * quoteAgeFactor;

} // End of main() method

} // End of QuoteArithmetic class
```

Now we will:
- read the user input data for the vehicle mileage from the console and convert it to an int
- use the vehicle mileage and divide it by the age of the vehicle to get the average yearly mileage
- divide this value by the 10000, which is the expected yearly mileage, to calculate a mileage factor
- calculate the premium based on the mileage factor and the quote base rate (£100)

23. Amend the code, by adding these lines to the end of the code, as shown:

quoteAgeFactor = (**double**)(quoteBaseAge) / (**double**)(vehicleAgeInYears);

/* The quote amount based on the age is £100 multiplied by the age factor
   Example £100 * 2 = £200 */
quoteAgeFactorPremium = quoteBaseRate * quoteAgeFactor;

/* Ask the user for the number of kilometres on the odometer */
System.*out*.println("What is the current mileage (in km) of the vehicle?\n");
vehicleCurrentMileage = (**int**)(myScanner.nextInt());

/* Calculate the mileage factor. This is based on the number of kilometres
   travelled each year and how the kilometres per year is a ratio of the average
   expected 10000 kilometres as decided by the insurance company
   Example: For a 5 year old car with 60000km the factor is
           (60000/5)/10000 = 12000/10000 = 1.2
*/
quoteMileageFactor = (vehicleCurrentMileage / vehicleAgeInYears) /
   quoteAverageExpectedKilometres;

/* The quote amount based on the mileage is £100 multiplied by the mileage factor
   Example £100 * 1.2 = £120
*/
quoteMileageFactorPremium = quoteBaseRate * quoteMileageFactor;

  } // End of main() method
} // End of QuoteArithmetic class

Now we will add the two values we have just calculated to give us the premium.

24. Amend the code, by adding these lines to the end of the code, as shown (there are plenty of comment lines to help you understand):

/* The quote amount based on the mileage is £100 multiplied by the mileage factor
   Example £100 * 1.2 = £120
*/
quoteMileageFactorPremium = quoteBaseRate * quoteMileageFactor;

/* Calculate the quotation based on a base rate of £100. This base rate is
   multiplied by the vehicle age factor and by the vehicle mileage factor.

So, the older the vehicle the cheaper the quote or the neour the vehicle the
more expensive the quote.
The more kilometres travelled on average per year the more expensive the quote or
the less kilometres travelled on average per year the cheaper the quote
Example: For a 5 year old car, 60000km, age factor is 2 and mileage factor is 1.2
 The quote is (£100 * 2) + (£100 * 1.2) = £200 + £120 = £320
*/

/* The quote amount based on the age premium plus the mileage premium
  Example £2000 + £120 = £320
*/
quoteAmountForPremium = quoteAgeFactorPremium + quoteMileageFactorPremium;

 } // End of main() method
} // End of QuoteArithmetic class

Now we will calculate the discount based on the calculated premium and the vehicle age.

25. Amend the code, by adding these lines to the end of the code, as shown:

    quoteAmountForPremium = quoteAgeFactorPremium + quoteMileageFactorPremium;

    /* The discount amount is based on the age of the vehicle
       Example 5 year old vehicle gives discount of 1/5 = 20 percent
    */
    quoteDiscount = (1 /**(double)** vehicleAgeInYears) * quoteAmountForPremium;

     } // End of main() method
    } // End of QuoteArithmetic class

Now we will calculate the discount based on the calculated premium and the vehicle age.

26. Amend the code, by adding these lines to the end of the code, as shown:

    quoteDiscount = (1 /**(double)** vehicleAgeInYears) * quoteAmountForPremium;

    /* The final quote with the discount applied
       Example 5 year old vehicle gives discount of 100/5 = 20 percent
       20% of £320 is £64. So, the actual amount is £320 - £64 = £256

```
    */
    quoteFinalAmountForPremium = quoteAmountForPremium - quoteDiscount;

    } // End of main() method
} // End of QuoteArithmetic class
```

Now we will write the quote details to the console.

27. Amend the code, by adding these print lines to the end of the code:

```
/*
    The final quote based with the discount applied
    Example 5 year old vehicle gives discount of 100/5 = 20 percent
    20% of £320 is £64. So the actual amount is £320 - £64 = £256
*/
quoteFinalAmountForPremium = quoteAmountForPremium - quoteDiscount;

System.out.println("*********************************************\n");
System.out.println("Quotation price is for 1 year starting today    \n");
System.out.println("*********************************************\n");

System.out.println("The age of the vehicle is: \t\t" + vehicleAgeInYears);

System.out.println("The age factor for this vehicle is : " + quoteAgeFactor);

System.out.println();
System.out.println("The average kilometres per year is: \t" + (vehicleCurrentMileage / vehicleAgeInYears));

System.out.println("The mileage factor is :\t\t\t" + quoteMileageFactor);
System.out.println();

System.out.println("The quotation is :\t\t\t£" + quoteAmountForPremium);
System.out.println();

System.out.println("The discount is :\t\t\t£" + quoteDiscount);
System.out.println();

System.out.println("The final discounted amount is :\t£" + quoteFinalAmountForPremium);
```

```
System.out.println("*************************************************\n");
} // End of main() method

} // End of QuoteArithmetic class
```

28. Amend the code to display a blank line and then close the Scanner:

```
System.out.println("The final discounted amount is :\t£" +
quoteFinalAmountForPremium);
System.out.println("*************************************************\n");

myScanner.next();
myScanner.close();
} // End of main() method

} // End of QuoteArithmetic class
```

29. Click on the **File** menu.
30. Choose **Save All**.
31. Click on the green **Run** button at the top of the screen.
32. Click in the Console window at the bottom of the screen.
33. Type **5** as the age of the vehicle.
34. **Press the Enter key** on the keyboard.
35. Type **60000** as the number of kilometres on the odometer.
36. **Press the Enter key** on the keyboard.

The console window will appear with the quotation details.

```
What is the age, in full years, of the vehicle?

5
What is the current mileage (in km) of the vehicle?

60000
***************************************************

Quotation price is for 1 year starting today

***************************************************

The age of the vehicle is:             5
The age factor is for this vehicle is: 2.0

The average kilometres per year is:    12000
The mileage factor is :                1.2

The quotation is :                     £320.0

The discount is :                      £64.0      ◄── Not formatted

The final discounted amount is :       £256.0
***************************************************
```

Now let us pose the question, is the quotation amount correct?

- well, we should have known what to expect before we started typing the code
- we need to know the formulae before we code, but we should also have tested data in our head that will tell us what to expect for the quote answer
- if we followed a Test-Driven Development methodology, we would write a test first

The mathematics:

quoteAgeFactor	=	10/5	=	2.0		
quoteAgeFactorPremium	=	£100 * 2.0	=	£200		
quoteMileageFactor	=	(60000/5)/ 10000	=	12000/10000	=	1.2
quoteMileageFactorPremium	=	£100 * 1.2	=	£120		
quoteAmountForPremium	=	£200 + £120	=	£320;		
quoteDiscount	=	(1/5) * £320	=	£64		
quoteFinalAmountForPremium	=	£320 - £64	=	£256		

The format method

What we also see is that our output does not have 2 figures after the decimal point. The println() method simply prints out a line of code but cannot format it. If we wish to have formatted text, we can use the format method.

The format method formats multiple arguments based on a **format string**. The format string consists of static text embedded with **format specifiers**.

Format strings support many features. In this tutorial, we'll just cover some basics. For a complete description, see **format string syntax** in the API specification.

Example:

int number= 2;
double squareRootOfNumber= Math.sqrt(myNumber);

System.out.format("The square root of %d is %f.%n", number, squareRootOfNumber);

The output would be:

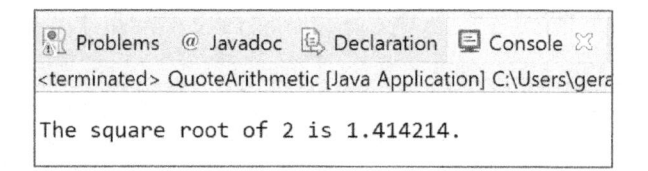

```
Problems  @ Javadoc  Declaration  Console
<terminated> QuoteArithmetic [Java Application] C:\Users\gera
The square root of 2 is 1.414214.
```

So, we should see that the %d matches the first variable in the list after the ending double quote and the %f matches the second variable in the list. We have already seen the %n and this mean a new line should be taken.

The three format specifiers are:

- %d   d means format an integer value as a decimal value
- %f   f means format a floating-point value as a decimal value
- %n   n outputs a platform-specific line terminator

Other format specifiers include:

d	A decimal integer
f	A float
n	A new line character appropriate to the platform running the application. We should always use %n, rather than \n
tB	A date & time conversion—locale-specific full name of month
td, te	A date & time conversion—2-digit day of month. td has leading zeroes as needed, te does not
ty, tY	A date & time conversion—ty = 2-digit year, tY = 4-digit year
tl	A date & time conversion—hour in 12-hour clock
tM	A date & time conversion—minutes in 2 digits, with leading zeroes as necessary
tp	A date & time conversion—locale-specific am/pm (loour case)
tm	A date & time conversion—months in 2 digits, with leading zeroes as necessary
tD	A date & time conversion—date as %tm%td%ty

Example code from the Oracle documentation shows some use of the specifiers and the resulting output.

```java
import java.util.Calendar;
import java.util.Locale;

public class TestFormat
{
    public static void main(String[] args)
    {
        long n = 461012;
        System.out.format("%d%n", n);        // --> "461012"
        System.out.format("%08d%n", n);      // --> "00461012"
        System.out.format("%+8d%n", n);      // --> " +461012"
        System.out.format("%,8d%n", n);      // --> " 461,012"
        System.out.format("%+,8d%n%n", n);   // --> "+461,012"

        double pi = Math.PI;

        System.out.format("%f%n", pi);       // --> "3.141593"
        System.out.format("%.3f%n", pi);     // --> "3.142"
        System.out.format("%10.3f%n", pi);   // --> "     3.142"
```

```
System.out.format("%-10.3f%n", pi);     // --> "3.142"
System.out.format(Locale.FRANCE, "%-10.4f%n%n", pi);   // --> "3,1416"

Calendar c = Calendar.getInstance();
System.out.format("%tB %te, %tY%n", c, c, c);    // --> "May 29, 2006"

System.out.format("%tl:%tM %tp%n", c, c, c);     // --> "2:34 am"

System.out.format("%tD%n", c);     // --> "05/29/06"
  } // End of main method()
}// End of TestFormat class
```

37. Amend the code by adding the import statements for Locale and Calendar to the start of the code:

    package com.gerrybyrne.module06;

    import java.util.Calendar;
    import java.util.Locale;
    import java.util.Scanner;

    public class QuoteArithmetic
    {

38. Amend the code by replacing some println() methods with format() methods where required, as shown

    ```
    System.out.println("**********************************************\n");
    System.out.println("Quotation price is for 1 year starting today   \n");
    System.out.println("**********************************************\n");

    System.out.println("The age of the vehicle is: \t\t" + vehicleAgeInYears);

    //System.out.println("The age factor for this vehicle is : " + quoteAgeFactor);
    System.out.format("The age factor for this vehicle is : %.2f" , quoteAgeFactor);

    System.out.println();
    System.out.println("The average kilometres per year is: \t" + (vehicleCurrentMileage / vehicleAgeInYears));
    ```

```java
// System.out.println("The mileage factor is :\t\t\t" + quoteMileageFactor);
System.out.format("The mileage factor is :\t\t\t%.2f" , quoteMileageFactor);
System.out.println();

//System.out.println("The quotation is :\t\t\t£" + quoteAmountForPremium);
System.out.format("The quotation is :\t\t\t£%.2f" , quoteAmountForPremium);
System.out.println();

//System.out.println("The discount is :\t\t\t£" + quoteDiscount);
System.out.format("The discount is :\t\t\t£%.2f" , quoteDiscount);
System.out.println();

//System.out.println("The final discounted amount is :\t£" + quoteFinalAmountForPremium);
System.out.format("The final discounted amount is :\t£%.2f%n" , quoteFinalAmountForPremium);

System.out.println("*************************************************\n");
myScanner.next();
myScanner.close();
    } // End of main method()
} // End of QuoteArithmetic class
```

39. Click on the **File** menu.
40. Choose **Save All**.
41. Click on the green **Run** button at the top of the screen.
42. Click in the Console window at the bottom of the screen.
43. Type **5** as the age of the vehicle.
44. Press the **Enter** key on the keyboard.
45. Type **60000** as the number of kilometres on the odometer.
46. Press the **Enter** key on the keyboard.

The console window will appear with the quotation details.

Decimal format – 2 decimal places

```
What is the age, in full years, of the vehicle?

5
What is the current mileage (in km) of the vehicle?

60000
*************************************************

Quotation price is for 1 year starting today

*************************************************

The age of the vehicle is:              5
The age factor for this vehicle is:     2.00
The average kilometres per year is:     12000
The mileage factor is :                 1.20
The quotation is :                      £320.00
The discount is :                       £64.00
The final discounted amount is :        £256.00
*************************************************
```

Formatted to 2 decimal places (applied to the monetary values)

Other operators

There are two other arithmetic operators which are included with Java:

++   Means add one to the value.

    Example

        double quoteMileageFactor= 1.2;

        quoteMileageFactor ++;

        quoteMileageFactor will now be 2.2

We will see this ++ operator when we come to code with loops (iteration)

--   Means subtract one from the value.

    Example

        double quoteMileageFactor= 1.2;

        quoteMileageFactor --;

        quoteMileageFactor will now be 0.2

We can use this operator when we code with loops (iteration).

Apart from the mathematical operators, +, -, *, / and % there are other operators included in Java. We will now look at what are called **assignment operators** which store a value in the object on the left-hand side. In the code examples below we will use a **compound assignment**, where an arithmetic operation is performed before the value is stored in the object on the left-hand side.

Up to now in our code we have used one operator the = symbol e.g.
        quoteAgeFactorPremium = quoteBaseRate * quoteAgeFactor;
The = operator is a **simple operator**.
Now we will use the compound assignment operators as shown below:

+=   Means take the value on the right of the = and add it to the value of the object on the left of the = and then store the new value in the object on the left.
       Example
            double quoteMileageFactor= 1.2;
            quoteMileageFactor += 1;
       quoteMileageFactor will now be 2.2

-=   Means take the value on the right of the = and subtract it from the value on the left of the = and then store the new value in the object on the left.
       Example
            double quoteMileageFactor= 1.2;
            quoteMileageFactor -= 1;
       quoteMileageFactor will now be 0.2

*=   Means take the value on the left of the = and multiply it by the value on the right of the = and then store the new value in the object on the left.
       Example
            double quoteMileageFactor= 1.2;
            quoteMileageFactor *= 2;
       quoteMileageFactor will now be 2.4

/=   Means take the value on the left of the = and divide it by the value on the right of the = and then store the new value in the object on the left.

Example

> **double** quoteMileageFactor= 1.2;
>
> quoteMileageFactor /= 1;
>
> **quoteMileageFactor will now be 0.6**

We will now amend the code to use some of the operators we have just read about.

Plus Equals (+=)

1. Amend the code, by adding one line of the code:

   /* Calculate the mileage factor. This is based on the number of kilometres travelled each year and how this is a ratio of the average expected 10000 kilometres as decided by the insurance company.
   Example:
   For a 5 year old car, 60000km the factor is (60000/5)/10000 = 12000/10000 = 1.2 */
   quoteMileageFactor = (vehicleCurrentMileage / vehicleAgeInYears) / quoteAverageExpectedKilometres;

   quoteMileageFactor +=1;

2. Click on the **File** menu.
3. Choose **Save All**.
4. Click on the green **Run** button at the top of the screen.
5. Click in the Console window at the bottom of the screen.
6. Type **5** as the age of the vehicle.
7. **Press the Enter key** on the keyboard.
8. Type **60000** as the number of kilometres on the odometer.
9. **Press the Enter key** on the keyboard.

The console window will appear with the quotation details as shown below. The images show the new calculations compared with the calculations prior to the increment of the variable **quoteMileageFactor**. We can see that the mileage factor has increased by 1 to the value 2.2.

```
What is the age, in full years, of the vehicle?     What is the age, in full years, of the vehicle?
5                                                    5
What is the current mileage (in km) of the vehicle? What is the current mileage (in km) of the vehicle?
60000                                                60000
***************************************************  ***************************************************
Quotation price is for 1 year starting today         Quotation price is for 1 year starting today
***************************************************  ***************************************************
The age of the vehicle is:              5            The age of the vehicle is:              5
The age factor for this vehicle is:     2.00         The age factor for this vehicle is:     2.00
The average kilometres per year is:     12000        The average kilometres per year is:     12000
The mileage factor is :                 1.20         The mileage factor is :                 2.20
The quotation is :                      £320.00      The quotation is :                      £420.00
The discount is :                       £64.00       The discount is :                       £84.00
The final discounted amount is :        £256.00      The final discounted amount is :        £336.00
```

We will continue amending the code to use some of the operators we have just read about.

Minus Equals (-=)

1. Amend the code, by adding one line of the code, as shown:

   quoteMileageFactor = (vehicleCurrentMileage / vehicleAgeInYears) / quoteAverageExpectedKilometres;

   quoteMileageFactor -=1;

2. Click on the **File** menu.
3. Choose **Save All**.
4. Click on the green **Run** button at the top of the screen.
5. Click in the Console window at the bottom of the screen.
6. Type **5** as the age of the vehicle.
7. **Press the Enter key** on the keyboard.
8. Type **60000** as the number of kilometres on the odometer.
9. **Press the Enter key** on the keyboard.

The console window will appear with the quotation details as shown below. The images show the new calculations compared with the calculations prior to the decrement of the variable **quoteMileageFactor**. We can see that the mileage factor has decreased by 1 to the value 0.2.

```
What is the age, in full years, of the vehicle?    What is the age, in full years, of the vehicle?

5                                                  5
What is the current mileage (in km) of the vehicle? What is the current mileage (in km) of the vehicle?

60000                                              60000
***************************************            ****************************************

Quotation price is for 1 year starting today       Quotation price is for 1 year starting today

***************************************            ****************************************

The age of the vehicle is:            5            The age of the vehicle is:            5
The age factor for this vehicle is:   2.00         The age factor for this vehicle is:   2.00
The average kilometres per year is:   12000        The average kilometres per year is:   12000
The mileage factor is :               1.20         The mileage factor is :               0.20
The quotation is :                    £320.00      The quotation is :                    £220.00
The discount is :                     £64.00       The discount is :                     £44.00
The final discounted amount is :      £256.00      The final discounted amount is :      £176.00
```

Multiply Equals (*=)

1. Amend the code, by adding one line of the code, as shown:

   quoteMileageFactor = (vehicleCurrentMileage / vehicleAgeInYears) / quoteAverageExpectedKilometres;

   quoteMileageFactor *=2;

2. Click on the **File** menu.
3. Choose **Save All**.
4. Click on the green **Run** button at the top of the screen.
5. Click in the Console window at the bottom of the screen.
6. Type **5** as the age of the vehicle.
7. **Press the Enter key** on the keyboard.
8. Type **60000** as the number of kilometres on the odometer.
9. **Press the Enter key** on the keyboard.

The console window will appear with the quotation details as shown below. The images show the new calculations compared with the calculations prior to the multiplication of the variable **quoteMileageFactor**. We can see that the mileage factor has multiplied by 2, doubled, to the value 2.4.

```
What is the age, in full years, of the vehicle?     What is the age, in full years, of the vehicle?

5                                                    5
What is the current mileage (in km) of the vehicle? What is the current mileage (in km) of the vehicle?

60000                                                60000
**************************************************  **************************************************

Quotation price is for 1 year starting today         Quotation price is for 1 year starting today

**************************************************  **************************************************

The age of the vehicle is:              5            The age of the vehicle is:              5
The age factor for this vehicle is:     2.00         The age factor for this vehicle is:     2.00
The average kilometres per year is:     12000        The average kilometres per year is:     12000
The mileage factor is :                 1.20         The mileage factor is :                 2.40
The quotation is :                      £320.00      The quotation is :                      £440.00
The discount is :                       £64.00       The discount is :                       £88.00
The final discounted amount is :        £256.00      The final discounted amount is :        £352.00
**************************************************  **************************************************
```

Divide Equals (/=)

1. Amend the code, by adding one line of the code, as shown:

   quoteMileageFactor = (vehicleCurrentMileage / vehicleAgeInYears) / quoteAverageExpectedKilometres;

   quoteMileageFactor /=2;

2. Click on the **File** menu.
3. Choose **Save All**.
4. Click on the green **Run** button at the top of the screen.
5. Click in the Console window at the bottom of the screen.
6. Type **5** as the age of the vehicle.
7. **Press the Enter key** on the keyboard.
8. Type **60000** as the number of kilometres on the odometer.
9. **Press the Enter key** on the keyboard.

The console window will appear with the quotation details as shown below. The images show the new calculations compared with the calculations prior to the division of the variable **quoteMileageFactor**. We can see that the mileage factor has been divided by 2, halved, to the value 0.6

```
What is the age, in full years, of the vehicle?          What is the age, in full years, of the vehicle?

5                                                         5
What is the current mileage (in km) of the vehicle?      What is the current mileage (in km) of the vehicle?

60000                                                     60000
****************************************************     ****************************************************

Quotation price is for 1 year starting today             Quotation price is for 1 year starting today

****************************************************     ****************************************************
The age of the vehicle is:              5                The age of the vehicle is:              5
The age factor for this vehicle is:     2.00             The age factor for this vehicle is:     2.00
The average kilometres per year is:     12000            The average kilometres per year is:     12000
The mileage factor is :                 1.20             The mileage factor is :                 0.60
The quotation is :                      £320.00          The quotation is :                      £260.00
The discount is :                       £64.00           The discount is :                       £52.00
The final discounted amount is :        £256.00          The final discounted amount is :        £208.00
```

Square root

Here we will use the Math class and the sqrt() method. The sqrt() method accepts the numeric value which is to be operated on.

1. Amend the code, by replacing the quoteMileageFactor assignment as shown:

    quoteMileageFactor = (vehicleCurrentMileage / vehicleAgeInYears) / quoteAverageExpectedKilometres;
    quoteMileageFactor = Math.sqrt(quoteMileageFactor);

2. Click on the **File** menu.
3. Choose **Save All**.
4. Click on the green **Run** button at the top of the screen.
5. Click in the Console window at the bottom of the screen.
6. Type **5** as the age of the vehicle.
7. **Press the Enter key** on the keyboard.
8. Type **60000** as the number of kilometres on the odometer.
9. **Press the Enter key** on the keyboard.

The console window will appear with the quotation details as shown below. The images show the new calculations compared with the calculations prior to the square root of the variable

quoteMileageFactor. We can see that the mileage factor has been calculated as the square root of 1.2, which is 1.1.

This means 1.1 times 1.1 equals 1.2. But this is not true, it should be 1.095445115010332. The issue is the number of decimal places we have asked for using the format() method. We have asked for 2.

```
What is the age, in full years, of the vehicle?
5
What is the current mileage (in km) of the vehicle?
60000
*******************************************

Quotation price is for 1 year starting today

*******************************************

The age of the vehicle is:              5
The age factor for this vehicle is:     2.00
The average kilometres per year is:     12000
The mileage factor is :                 1.20
The quotation is :                      £320.00
The discount is :                       £64.00
The final discounted amount is :        £256.00
```

```
What is the age, in full years, of the vehicle?
5
What is the current mileage (in km) of the vehicle?
60000
*******************************************

Quotation price is for 1 year starting today

*******************************************

The age of the vehicle is:              5
The age factor for this vehicle is:     2.00
The average kilometres per year is:     12000
The mileage factor is :                 1.10
The quotation is :                      £309.54
The discount is :                       £61.91
The final discounted amount is :        £247.64
*******************************************
```

We can now change the format() for the mileage factor, quoteMileageFactor, so we have 15 figures after the decimal point.

10. Amend the code, by changing the .2 to .16 in the line of code, as shown:

System.*out*.format("The mileage factor is :\t\t\t%.16f" , quoteMileageFactor);
System.*out*.println();

11. Click on the **File** menu.
12. Choose **Save All**.
13. Click on the green **Run** button at the top of the screen.
14. Click in the Console window at the bottom of the screen.
15. Type **5** as the age of the vehicle.
16. Press the **Enter** key on the keyboard.
17. Type **60000** as the number of kilometres on the odometer.
18. Press the **Enter** key on the keyboard.

The console window will appear with the quotation details as shown below. The images show the new 16 decimal place numeric output compared with the 2 decimal place numeric output.

```
What is the age, in full years, of the vehicle?
5
What is the current mileage (in km) of the vehicle?
60000
***************************************************
Quotation price is for 1 year starting today
***************************************************
The age of the vehicle is:              5
The age factor for this vehicle is:     2.00
The average kilometres per year is:     12000
The mileage factor is :                 1.20
The quotation is :                      £320.00
The discount is :                       £64.00
The final discounted amount is :        £256.00
***************************************************
```

```
What is the age, in full years, of the vehicle?
5
What is the current mileage (in km) of the vehicle?
60000
***************************************************
Quotation price is for 1 year starting today
***************************************************
The age of the vehicle is:              5
The age factor for this vehicle is:     2.00
The average kilometres per year is:     12000
The mileage factor is :                 1.0954451150103321
The quotation is :                      £309.54
The discount is :                       £61.91
The final discounted amount is :        £247.64
***************************************************
```

Note

The other calculations which depend on the quoteMileageFactor still have the same value. This should indicate to us that even though 2 decimal places were displayed the underlying figure was more accurate than the 2 decimal places.

Module summary

In this module we have learnt about the very important concept of arithmetic operations which will be widely used in real world applications. We also saw that arithmetic performed on variables or values can result in inaccuracies because the display does not show the required number of decimal places. We therefore saw the use of the printf() method where we could specify the number of decimal places required in the output. Besides the popular arithmetic operators +, -, * and / we also saw some 'strange' operators, +=, -=, *=, /=.

Yet another great achievement for us in our learning. Be proud of the learning to date.

Program Practically

Java

Module 07

Selection

Selection using if construct
Selection using if else construct
Selection using if else if construct
Selection using switch construct
Switch on numeric and String values
Logical operators AND, OR and NOT
ToUppercase() and ToLowercase()

Gerry Byrne

Program Practically - Selection

We learnt in module 6 that:

We could apply arithmetic operations on some variables or values and we could use the printf() method to specify the number of decimal places required in the output. We also investigated the use of less familiar arithmetic operators such as +=, -=, *=, /=.

Selection

In this module we will learn about the very important of concept selection and its use within an application. However, the concept of selection should be familiar to us through our everyday life. Many of the things we do in everyday life require us to make decisions. When making decisions in everyday life we will be directed down one path or another, as shown in the diagram below.

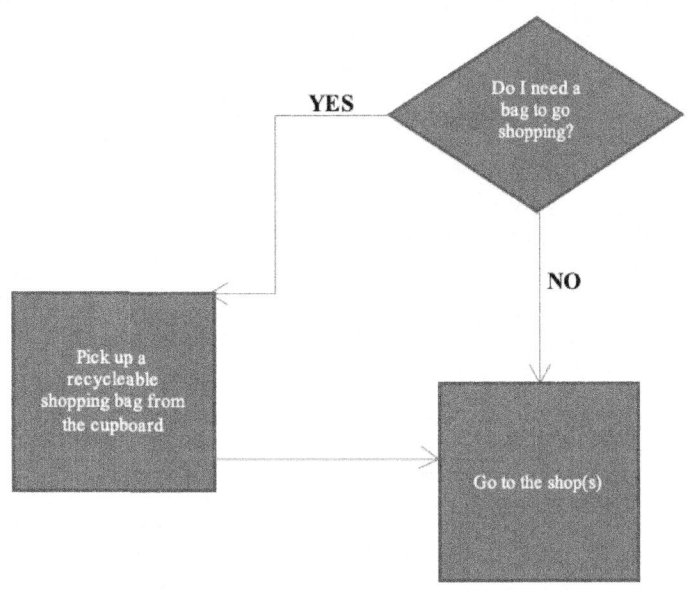

In a similar manner the programs we, and every developer, write normally will require us to make decisions. Decisions in our code will change the flow of execution depending on the decision made. This can be clearly seen in the diagram above where:

- a **yes** decision changes execution down the yes path and
- a **no** decision changes execution down the no path

In this example the execution eventually returns to a common path (Go to the shop(s)).

In programming making decisions can be achieved in a number of ways and we will now look at the use of the **SELECTION** statements within Java.

Comparison Operators

To build our program code to make decisions we need to make use of comparison operators to construct a condition. The operators we can use are familiar mathematical expressions e.g. less than, greater than and equal to. In Java the symbols used for the operators are:

Symbol	Meaning
<	Less than
<=	Less than or equal to
>	Greater than
>=	Greater than or equal to
==	Equal to
!=	Not equal to
&&	logical AND
||	logical OR
!	logical NOT

It is important we fully understand that when testing if one piece of data is equal to another, we use the **double equals (==)**, because, as mentioned previously, a single equal symbol (=) is an assignment operation.

The primary selection constructs (statements) that we will use in our Java code will be:
- if
- if-else
- if else if construct
- switch

and we will also look at the logical operators AND (&&), || (OR) and ! (NOT)

if statement

The **if** construct is used whenever a choice has to be made between two alternative actions. The construct will enable a block of code to be executed depending upon whether or not a condition is true. If the condition is not true (false) the code does not execute the block of code associated with the if statement and simply moves to the next code statement.

The general format of the **if construct** is:

```
if( condition )
{
    // perform these statements when condition is true
}
```

In simple terms all we are doing with the if construct is saying "is something true", is it true or is it false. So, the statement:

        if(condition)   means   if(true)

(remember true is a boolean data type).

In most programs selection will be a key element but for an insurance program, selection statements may include:

- checking the maximum **years of no claims** a driver has and informing the user that:
    - the value is within the **years of no claims** limit and will be used (this is the true part)

  or
    - just moving to the next code statement

- checking the **maximum cost** that can be charged to a credit card and informing the user that:
    - the insurance cost is under or equal to the credit card limit and can be processed (this is the true part)

  or
    - just moving to the next code statement

if-else statement

The general format of the **if-else construct** is:

    if(condition)
    {
      // perform these statements when condition is true
    }
    else
    {
      // perform these statements when condition is false
    }

In simple terms all we are doing with the if-else construct is saying. "is something true", is it true or is it false. So, the statement:

| if(condition) | means | if(true) |
| else | means | it is not true it is **false** |

(remember true is a boolean data type)

The else part of the if-else construct may be omitted depending on requirements. If it is omitted it is essentially an if statement, which is what we have just looked at.

Using the same insurance program criteria as we used in the if statement above, we can see how the if-else construct could be applied. The program selection statements may include:

- checking the maximum **years of no claims** a driver has and informing the user that:

    o the value is within the **years of no claims** limit and will be used (this is the true part)

or

    o the value is over the **years of no claims** limit and will be reduced to 10 years (this is the false part, the else part

- checking the maximum cost that can be charged to a credit card and informing the user that:
    - the insurance cost is under or equal to the credit card limit and can be processed

or

    - the insurance cost is over the credit card limit and the user will need to call the company to give additional information

The **if else** statement is used to make a selection within a program and the following points are important in understanding the format of the if else statement:

- the if statement will test if a particular *condition* statement is true e.g.

    if (yearsofnoclaims > 10)

- if the condition is true then the program will execute a block of code e.g.

    ```
    if (yearsofnoclaims > 10)
    {
    // This block of code will be executed if the yearsofnoclaims is greater than 10
    }
    ```

- if the condition is false then the program will execute a different block of code, the else part that handles a false condition (executed when the statement is not true) e.g.

    ```
    if (yearsofnoclaims > 10)
    {
    // This block of code will be executed if the yearsofnoclaims is greater than 10
    }
    else
    {
    // This block of code will be executed if the yearsofnoclaims is
    // less than or equal to 10
    }
    ```

- it is essential that the two different blocks of code are clearly indicated and to ensure this, we use the curly braces.

  { **opening (left) curly brace**

  } **closing (right) curly brace**

- The two different blocks of code are separated using the **else** keyword.

```
if (yearsofnoclaims > 10)
{
BLOCK ONE
// This block of code will be executed if the yearsofnoclaims is greater than 10
}
else
{
BLOCK TWO
// This block of code will be executed if the yearsofnoclaims is less
// than or equal to 10
}
```

Switch statement

A switch statement can have a number of advantages over the equivalent if-else statements including being easier to:

- read
- debug and
- maintain

In using a switch construct we will have multiple cases and the matching case will be the one that will have its code executed.

Switch also has some disadvantages depending on the version of Java we use. From Java 7 onwards, the match expression can be of primitive data type byte, short, char and int as well as a String object.

The general format of the **switch construct** is:

```
switch (expression)
{
```

```
        case 1:
        {
            statements;
            break;
        }
        case 2:
        {
            statements;
            break;
        }
        default:
        {
            statements;
            break;
        }
        break;
} // End of switch statement
```

Using the same insurance program criteria as we used in the if and if-else constructs above, we can see how the switch construct could be applied. The program selection statements may include:

- checking the maximum **years of no claims** a driver has and informing the user that if:

    o the value is 0 years the **discount is 0%**

    o the value is 5 years the **discount is 5%**

    o the value is 10 years the **discount is 10%**

As a switch statement this would be:

```
switch (years_of_no_claims)
{
  case 0:
  {
    discount = 0.00;
    break;
  }
```

```
        case 5:
        {
            discount = 5.00;
                break;
        }
        case 10:
        {
            discount = 10.00;
                break;
        }
        default:
        {
            discount = 0.00;
                break;
        }
    } // End of switch statement
```

Let's code some Java

The if construct

We will now use the **if construct** which has one block of code, between the curly braces, that is executed if the condition inside the brackets evaluates as boolean true. If the condition evaluates to boolean false then, with the if construct, there is no other block of code associated with it so, the next line in the program after the close curly brace, is executed. The evaluation to boolean true would be equivalent to the area highlighted by the green rectangle in the diagram below (the pathway to the left).

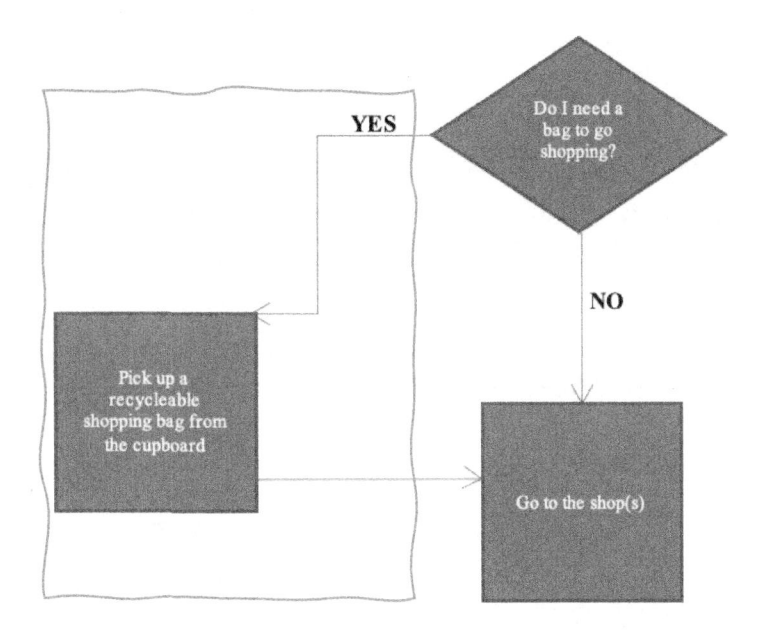

We should use the same workspace that we created for the earlier modules, as this will mean we will still be able to see the code we have written for the previous modules. The approach of keeping all our separate projects in one workspace is a good idea while studying this book and coding the examples.

This module will concentrate on selection, use an insurance quote example and build on our learning from the previous modules.

1. Right click on the **src** folder.
2. Choose **New**.
3. Choose **Package**.
4. Name the package **com.gerrybyrne.module07**.
5. Click the **Finish** button.
6. Right click on the package icon.
7. Choose **New**.
8. Choose **Class**.
9. Name the class **Selection**.
10. Put a tick in the checkbox beside the public static void main(String[] args) box.
11. Click on the **Finish** button.

The **Selection** class code will appear in the editor window and will be similar to the following:

```java
package com.gerrybyrne.module07;

public class Selection
{
    public static void main(String[] args)
    {
        // TODO Auto-generated method stub

    } // End of main method()

} // End of Selection class
```

Now we will add the variables that will be used in our code. In the code below there are detailed comments to help us get a full understanding of the code.

12. Amend the code to add the variables:

```java
// Program Description:    A simple Java program to perform selection
// Author:                 Gerry Byrne
// Date of creation:       01/10/2021

package com.gerrybyrne.module07;
public class Selection
{
  public static void main(String[] args)
  {
    /*
    We will setup our variables that will be used in the
    quote application
    */
    int yearsOfNoClaims;

  } // End of main() method
} // End of Selection class
```

We will now request the user to input some data. To allow input we need to create an instance of the Scanner class and this will require an import statement.

13. Amend the code to create an instance of the Scanner class, calling the instance **myScanner** and importing the Scanner class.

    package com.gerrybyrne.module07;

    import java.util.Scanner;

    public class Selection
    {
        public static void main(String[] args)
        {
            Scanner myScanner = **new** Scanner(System.*in*);

            /*
            We will setup our variables that will be used in the
            quote application
            */
            int yearsOfNoClaims;

14. Amend the code to request user input and then convert it to an int:

    /*
    We will setup our variables that will be used in the quote application
    */
    int yearsOfNoClaims;

    /*
    Read the user input and convert it to an int
    */
    System.*out*.println("How many full years of no claims does the driver have?\n");

    yearsOfNoClaims = myScanner.nextInt();

        } // End of main method()
    } // End of Selection class

15. Amend the code to:
    - check if the number of years of no claims is greater than 10 and
      - if this is true, to execute some code

    otherwise
      - move to the next set of code lines

```java
// Read the user input and convert it to an int //
System.out.println("How many full years of no claims does the driver have?\n");
yearsOfNoClaims = myScanner.nextInt();

/*
Now we will check if the years of no claims is greater than 10 if
it is true then we execute some lines of code which exist between
the curly braces, else the program just moves to the next code line
after the closing curly brace, which is to read a key
*/
if (yearsOfNoClaims > 10)
{
  /*
  This block of code will be executed if the yearsofnoclaims
  is more than 10
  */
  System.out.println("Years of no claims is more than 10");
}
```

16. Amend the code to close the instance of the Scanner that was created:

```java
if (yearsOfNoClaims > 10)
{
  /*
  This block of code will be executed if the yearsofnoclaims
  is more than 10
  */
  System.out.println("Years of no claims is more than 10");
}

// Close the myScanner instance we opened
```

      myScanner.close();
  } // End of main() method
} // End of class

17. Click on the **File** menu.
18. Choose **Save All**.
19. Click on the green **Run** button at the top of the screen.
20. Click in the Console window at the bottom of the screen.
21. Type **10** as the number of years of no claims.
22. Press the **Enter** key on the keyboard.

The console window will show no additional data as the code has evaluated that 10 is not greater than (>) 10, so it skips the if block of code and moves to the next line of code after the closing curly brace. This statement simply closes the Scanner.

23. Click on the green **Run** button at the top of the screen.
24. Click in the Console window at the bottom of the screen.
25. Type **20** as the number of years of no claims.
26. Press the **Enter** key on the keyboard.

The code has evaluated that 20 is greater than (>) 10 so it executes the if block of code and then it moves to the next line of code which is to close the Scanner.

The console window will appear as shown:

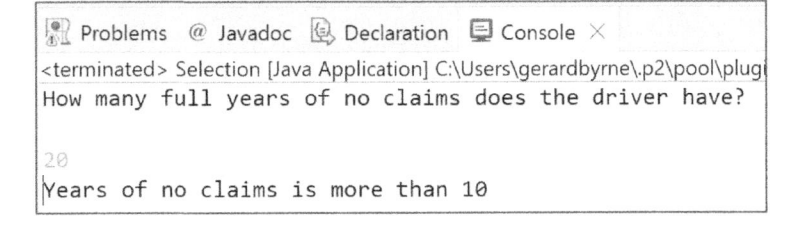

```
Problems  @ Javadoc  Declaration  Console  X
<terminated> Selection [Java Application] C:\Users\gerardbyrne\.p2\pool\plug
How many full years of no claims does the driver have?

20
Years of no claims is more than 10
```

The if-else construct

We will now use the **if-else construct** which is an extension of the if construct we have just used. In the if construct we had one block of code, between the curly braces, that was executed when the condition inside the brackets evaluated to true. When the condition evaluated to false this block of code was passed over and the next line in the program was executed. Now, in the if-else construct there will be a second block of code, with its own set of curly braces. This second block of code will be executed when the condition evaluates as false. This would be the equivalent to the area highlighted in red in the diagram below, the right-hand pathway.

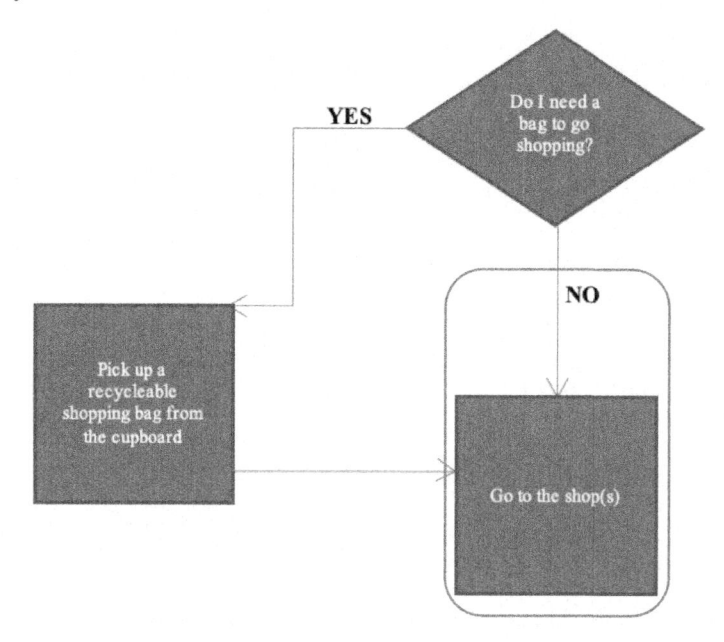

1. Amend the code to add the else part of the construct:

   ```
   if (yearsOfNoClaims > 10)
   {
       /*
       This block of code will be executed if the yearsofnoclaims
       is more than 10
       */
       System.out.println("Years of no claims is more than 10");
   }
   else
   {
       /*
   ```

This block of code will be executed if the yearsofnoclaims is not more than 10
We need to be careful when we are dealing with boundaries and in this example we should realise that the >10 means 11, 12, 13 etc. The not greater than 10 then means 10, 9, 8 etc. In other words, 10 is included in the else part. We could also use >= 10 if we wanted 10 to be included in the true section
*/
System.*out*.println("Years of no claims is less than or equal to 10");
}

// Close the myScanner instance we opened
myScanner.close();

} // End of main method()
} // End of Selection class

2. Click on the **File** menu.
3. Choose **Save All**.
4. Click on the green **Run** button at the top of the screen.
5. Click in the Console window at the bottom of the screen.
6. Type **20** as the number of years of no claims.
7. **Press the Enter key** on the keyboard.

The console window will appear as shown and we can see that **the true block of code has been executed**:

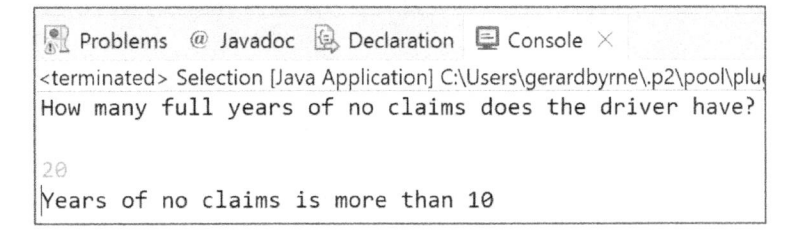

```
Problems  @ Javadoc  Declaration  Console
<terminated> Selection [Java Application] C:\Users\gerardbyrne\.p2\pool\plu
How many full years of no claims does the driver have?
20
Years of no claims is more than 10
```

8. Click on the green **Run** button at the top of the screen.
9. Click in the Console window at the bottom of the screen.
10. Type **10** as the number of years of no claims.
11. **Press the Enter key** on the keyboard.

The console window will appear as shown and we can see that **the false (else) block of code has been executed**:

```
Problems  @ Javadoc  Declaration  Console
<terminated> Selection [Java Application] C:\Users\gerardbyrne\.p2\pool\plu
How many full years of no claims does the driver have?

10
Years of no claims is less than or equal to 10
```

The if else if construct

The if-else construct we have just used has two blocks of code, one for the boolean true and the other for the boolean false. However, what would happen if we had other choices when the first condition was not true? Well, the Java language provides us with a solution which is an extension of the if-else construct. The if part of the construct can be followed by an **else if** statement. The general format will be:

```
if (first expression is true)
{
 /*
   This block of code will be executed if the first
   expression is true
 */
}
else if (second expression is true))
{
 /*
   This block of code will be executed if the second
   expression is true
 */
}
else if (third expression is true))
{
 /*
   This block of code will be executed if the third
   expression is true
 */
}
else
{
 /*
```

       This block of code will be executed if the first
       expression, second expression and third expression
       are all false
       */
   }

1. Amend the code to add the **else if** parts of the construct, **replacing the existing else code block**:

   if (yearsOfNoClaims > 10)
   {
       //This block of code will be executed if the yearsofnoclaims is more than 10
       System.*out*.println("Years of no claims is more than 10");
   }
   else if (yearsOfNoClaims > 8)
   {
       /* This block of code will be executed if the yearsofnoclaims is more than 8
       which means 9, 10, 11, 12 etc. However, if yearsofnoclaims is 11, 12 etc it
       will have been detected in the yearsofnoclaims > 10 block so really it will
       only be the 9 and 10 that will be detected in this block */
       System.*out*.println("Years of no claims is either 9 or 10");
   }
   else if (yearsOfNoClaims > 6)
   {
       /* This block of code will be executed if the yearsofnoclaims is more than 6
       which means 7, 8, 9, 10 etc. However, if yearsofnoclaims is 9, 10 etc it will
       have been detected in the yearsofnoclaims > 8 block so really it will only
       be the 7 and 8 that will be detected in this block */
       System.*out*.println("Years of no claims is either 7 or 8");
   }
   else if (yearsOfNoClaims > 4)
   {
       /* This block of code will be executed if the yearsofnoclaims is more than 4
       which means 5, 6, 7, 8 etc. However, if yearsofnoclaims is 7, 8 etc it will
       have been detected in the yearsofnoclaims > 6 block so really it will only
       be the 5 and 6 that will be detected in this block */
       System.*out*.println("Years of no claims is either 5 or 6");
   }
   else if (yearsOfNoClaims > 2)
   {

/* This block of code will be executed if the yearsofnoclaims is more than 2
which means 3, 4, 5, 6 etc. However, if yearsofnoclaims is 5, 6 etc it will
have been detected in the yearsofnoclaims > 4 block so really it will only
be the 3 and 4 that will be detected in this block */
System.*out*.println("Years of no claims is either 3 or 4");
}
else
{
/* This block of code will be executed if the yearsofnoclaims is not more than 2.
For this block of code to be executed none of the conditions above must have
been true (and none of the blocks of code were executed)*/
System.*out*.println("Years of no claims is 2, 1, 0 \n or indeed a negative number of
years \n because of a penalty being enforced on our policy");
}
/* After the true or false block is executed this is the next line to be executed */
// Close the myScanner instance we opened
myScanner.close();

2. Click on the **File** menu.
3. Choose **Save All**.
4. Click on the green **Run** button at the top of the screen.
5. Click in the Console window at the bottom of the screen.

The console window will appear and ask the question. Now we can try the values 10, 8, 6, 4, and 2 which will test the 5 else blocks. We will start with 10.

6. Type **10** as the number of years of no claims.
7. **Press the Enter key** on the keyboard.

The console window will appear as shown and we can see that the first else if block of code has been executed:

```
Problems   @ Javadoc   Declaration   Console  X
<terminated> Selection [Java Application] C:\Users\gerardbyrne\.p2\pool\plug
How many full years of no claims does the driver have?

10
Years of no claims is either 9 or 10
```

8. Click on the green **Run** button at the top of the screen.
9. Click in the Console window at the bottom of the screen.
10. Type **8** as the number of years of no claims.
11. **Press the Enter key** on the keyboard.

The console window will appear as shown and we can see that the second else if block of code has been executed:

```
Problems   @ Javadoc   Declaration   Console  X
<terminated> Selection [Java Application] C:\Users\gerardbyrne\.p2\pool\plug
How many full years of no claims does the driver have?
8
Years of no claims is either 7 or 8
```

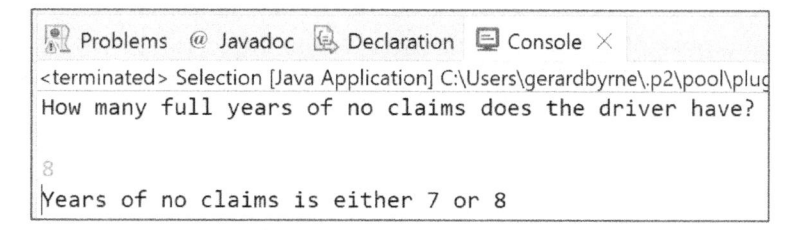

12. Click on the green **Run** button at the top of the screen.
13. Click in the Console window at the bottom of the screen.
14. Type **6** as the number of years of no claims.
15. **Press the Enter key** on the keyboard.

The console window will appear as shown and we can see that the third else if block of code has been executed:

```
Problems   @ Javadoc   Declaration   Console  X
<terminated> Selection [Java Application] C:\Users\gerardbyrne\.p2\pool\plug
How many full years of no claims does the driver have?
6
Years of no claims is either 5 or 6
```

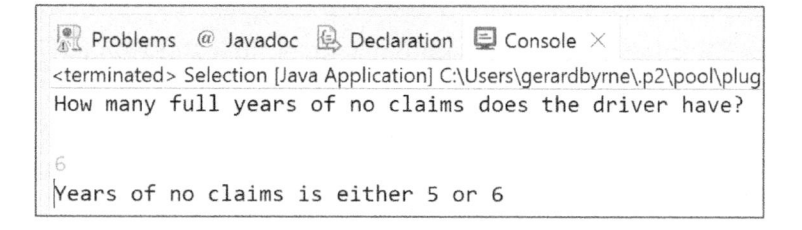

16. Click on the green **Run** button at the top of the screen.
17. Click in the Console window at the bottom of the screen.
18. Type **4** as the number of years of no claims.
19. **Press the Enter key** on the keyboard.

The console window will appear as shown and we can see that the fourth else if block of code has been executed:

```
Problems  @ Javadoc  Declaration  Console ×
<terminated> Selection [Java Application] C:\Users\gerardbyrne\.p2\pool\plug
How many full years of no claims does the driver have?

4
Years of no claims is either 3 or 4
```

20. Click on the green **Run** button at the top of the screen.
21. Click in the Console window at the bottom of the screen.
22. Type **2** as the number of years of no claims.
23. **Press the Enter key** on the keyboard.

The console window will appear as shown and we can see that the fifth else if block of code has been executed:

```
Problems  @ Javadoc  Declaration  Console ×
<terminated> Selection [Java Application] C:\Users\gerardbyrne\.p2\pool\plug
How many full years of no claims does the driver have?

2
Years of no claims is 2, 1, 0
 or indeed a negative number of years
 because of a penalty being enforced on our policy
```

As we can see, the code works fine and our test values have shown the correct blocks of code were executed. If we formatted the code within our Integrated Development Environment as shown below, we could see why the if else if construct is often called the **if else ladder** (the code moves into the right for each section):

```
if (yearsOfNoClaims > 10)
{
  /*
   This block of code will be executed if the yearsofnoclaims is
   more than 10
  */
  Console.WriteLine("Years of no claims is more than 10");
}
else
  if (yearsOfNoClaims > 8)
  {
```

```java
      /*
        This block of code will be executed if the yearsofnoclaims is more
        than 8 which means 9, 10, 11, 12 etc. However, if yearsofnoclaims
        is 11, 12 etc it will have been detected in the yearsofnoclaims > 10
        block so really it will only be the 9 and 10 that will be detected
        in this block
      */
      System.out.println("Years of no claims is either 9 or 10");
    }
    else
      if (yearsOfNoClaims > 6)
      {
        /*
          This block of code will be executed if the yearsofnoclaims is
          more than 6 which means 7, 8, 9, 10 etc. However, if
          yearsofnoclaims is 9, 10 etc it will have been detected in the
          yearsofnoclaims > 8 block so really it will only be the 7 and 8
          that will be detected in this block
        */
        System.out.println("Years of no claims is either 7 or 8");
      }
      else
        if (yearsOfNoClaims > 4)
        {
          /*
            This block of code will be executed if the yearsofnoclaims is
            more than 4 which means 5, 6, 7, 8 etc. However, if
            yearsofnoclaims is 7, 8 etc it will have been detected in the
            yearsofnoclaims > 6 block so really it will only be the 5 and
            6 that will be detected in this block
          */
          System.out.println("Years of no claims is either 5 or 6");
        }
        else
          if (yearsOfNoClaims > 2)
          {
            /*
              This block of code will be executed if the yearsofnoclaims
              is more than 2 which means 3, 4, 5, 6 etc. However, if
              yearsofnoclaims is 5, 6 etc it will have been detected in
              the yearsofnoclaims > 4 block so really it will only be the
```

```
            3 and 4 that will be detected in this block
        */
            System.out.println("Years of no claims is either 3 or 4");
        }
    else
    {
        /*
            This block of code will be executed if the yearsofnoclaims
            is not more than 2. For this block of code to be executed
            none of the conditions must have been true (and none of the
            blocks of code were executed
        */
```

So, do we think the code is OK because it executes properly?

We might say yes, but that would mean we are only concerned about the code execution. Let's think differently and consider the code readability, maintainability and efficiency. These aspects of code also play an important role in the code development process. It is not all about our view, there may be others involved in the process. We must take a wider view of code development and not just think about our own small world view. We must think in terms of the wider view (think about the word Weltanschauung which means world view). By thinking wider, we will think about others who are required to read our code, those who will have to maintain our code and those who will use the code and want it to operate at the highest efficiency level.

The code can indeed be made better in terms of readability, maintainability and efficiency by using another selection construct, the **switch construct**. It is important for us to understand that, in terms of efficiency, switch is not always faster than the if else-if construct.

The Switch construct

The **switch construct** is an alternative to the if-else construct we have just used. It is commonly used in programming if a single expression is tested against three or more conditions. As we read earlier, the general format of the **switch construct** is:

```
switch (expression)
{
  case value1:
  {
    statements;
    break;
  }
  case value2:
  {
    statements;
    break;
  }
  case value3:
  {
    statements;
    break;
  }
  default:
  {
    statements;
    break;
  }
} // End of switch construct
```

We will now apply this format to the if else-if construct we have just written. To do this we will create a new class, rather than trying to manipulate the existing code.

1. Right click on the **com.gerrybyrne.module07** package.
2. Choose **New**.
3. Choose **Class**.
4. Name the class **Switch**.
5. Put a tick in the checkbox beside the public static void main(String[] args) box.
6. Click on the **Finish** button.

The **Switch** class code will appear in the editor window and will be similar to the following:

package com.gerrybyrne.module07;

```java
public class Switch
{
    public static void main(String[] args)
    {
        // TODO Auto-generated method stub

    } // End of main method()
} // End of Switch class
```

Now we will add the variables that will be used in our code. In the code below there are detailed comments to help us get a full understanding of the code. As the application will require the user to input data, we will need to import the Scanner class and create an instance of it for use in the code.

7. Amend the code to create an instance of the Scanner class, calling the instance **myScanner** and importing the Scanner class.

```java
package com.gerrybyrne.module07;

import java.util.Scanner;

public class Switch {

    public static void main(String[] args)
    {
        Scanner myScanner = new Scanner(System.in);
```

8. Amend the code to setup a variable for the years of no claims and then add the code that will ask the user for input, read the console input and convert it to data type int.

```java
public static void main(String[] args)
{
    Scanner myScanner = new Scanner(System.in);

    /*
    We will setup our variables that will be used in the quote application
```

```
*/
int yearsOfNoClaims;

/* Read the user input and convert it to an int */
System.out.println("How many full years of no claims does the driver have?\n");

yearsOfNoClaims = myScanner.nextInt();
```

9. Amend the code to add the **switch construct** and ensure we close the Scanner:

```
/* Read the user input and convert it to an int */
System.out.println("How many full years of no claims does the driver have?\n");

yearsOfNoClaims = myScanner.nextInt();

/*
Now we will check if the years of no claims is greater than 10
if it is true then we execute some lines of code which exist
between the curly braces, else the program just moves to the
next code line which is to read a key
*/
switch (yearsOfNoClaims)
{
case 11:
case 12:
case 13:
case 14:
case 15:
/*
This block of code will be executed if the yearsofnoclaims is more than 10
*/
System.out.println("Years of no claims is more than 10 but less than 16");
break;
case 9:
case 10:
/*
This block of code will be executed if the yearsofnoclaims is either 9 or 10
*/
System.out.println("Years of no claims is either 9 or 10");
break;
```

```java
case 7:
case 8:
/*
This block of code will be executed if the yearsofnoclaims is either 7 or 8
*/
System.out.println("Years of no claims is either 7 or 8");
break;
case 5:
case 6:
/*
This block of code will be executed if the yearsofnoclaims is either 5 or 6
*/
System.out.println("Years of no claims is either 5 or 6");
break;
case 3:
case 4:
/*
This block of code will be executed if the yearsofnoclaims is either 3 or 4
*/
System.out.println("Years of no claims is either 3 or 4");
break;
default:
/*
This block of code will be executed if the yearsofnoclaims is
 not one of the values in the case statements 4 to 15. That
means if the value is more than 15 or less than 4 this block
will be executed.
We need to think, is this what we really want. Certainly it
does not give us the same result as the if else-if
*/
System.out.println("Years of no claims is either less than 3 or greater than 15");
break;
    } //End of switch construct

    myScanner.close();

  } // End of main method()
} // End of Switch class
```

10. Click on the **File** menu.

11. Choose **Save All**.
12. Click on the green **Run** button at the top of the screen.
13. Click in the Console window at the bottom of the screen.

The console window will appear and ask the question. Now we can try the values 15, 10, 8, 6, 4, and 2 which will test the 5 case blocks. We will start with 15.

14. Type **15** and press the Enter key.

The console window will appear as shown and we can see that the first case block of code has been executed:

```
Problems  @ Javadoc  Declaration  Console  ×
<terminated> Switch [Java Application] C:\Users\gerardbyrne\.p2\pool\plugins
How many full years of no claims does the driver have?

15
Years of no claims is more than 10 but less than 16
```

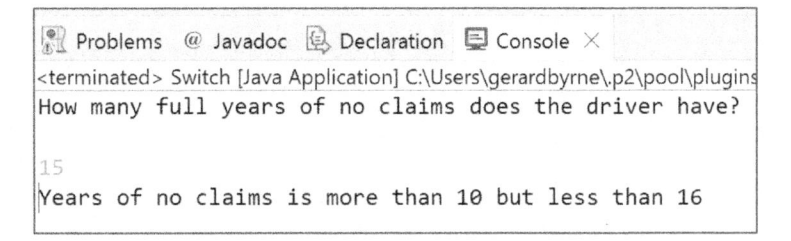

15. Click on the green **Run** button at the top of the screen.
16. Click in the Console window at the bottom of the screen.
17. Type **10** as the number of years of no claims.
18. **Press the Enter key** on the keyboard.

The console window will appear as shown and we can see that the second case block of code has been executed:

```
Problems  @ Javadoc  Declaration  Console  ×
<terminated> Switch [Java Application] C:\Users\gerardbyrne\.p2\pool\plugin
How many full years of no claims does the driver have?

10
Years of no claims is either 9 or 10
```

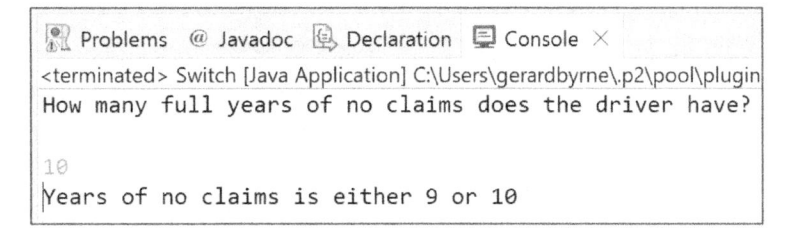

19. Click on the green Run button at the top of the screen.
20. Click in the Console window at the bottom of the screen.
21. Type **8** as the number of years of no claims.
22. **Press the Enter key** on the keyboard.

The console window will appear as shown and we can see that the third case block of code has been executed:

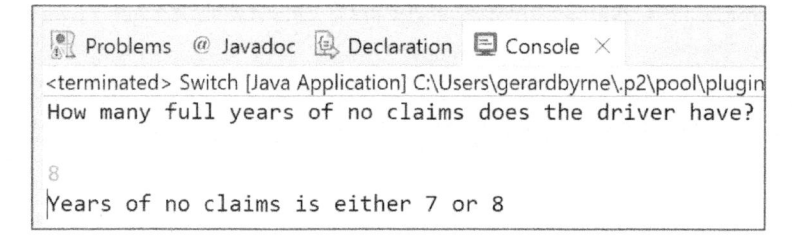

```
Problems  @ Javadoc  Declaration  Console ×
<terminated> Switch [Java Application] C:\Users\gerardbyrne\.p2\pool\plugin
How many full years of no claims does the driver have?
8
Years of no claims is either 7 or 8
```

23. Click on the green **Run** button at the top of the screen.
24. Click in the Console window at the bottom of the screen.
25. Type **6** as the number of years of no claims.
26. **Press the Enter key** on the keyboard.

The console window will appear as shown and we can see that the fourth case block of code has been executed:

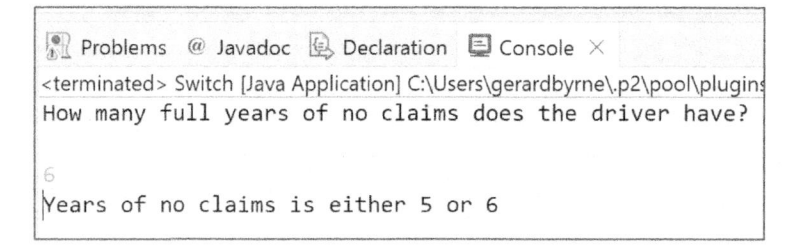

```
Problems  @ Javadoc  Declaration  Console ×
<terminated> Switch [Java Application] C:\Users\gerardbyrne\.p2\pool\plugins
How many full years of no claims does the driver have?
6
Years of no claims is either 5 or 6
```

27. Click on the green **Run** button at the top of the screen.
28. Click in the Console window at the bottom of the screen.
29. Type **4** as the number of years of no claims.
30. **Press the Enter key** on the keyboard.

The console window will appear as shown and we can see that the fifth case block of code has been executed:

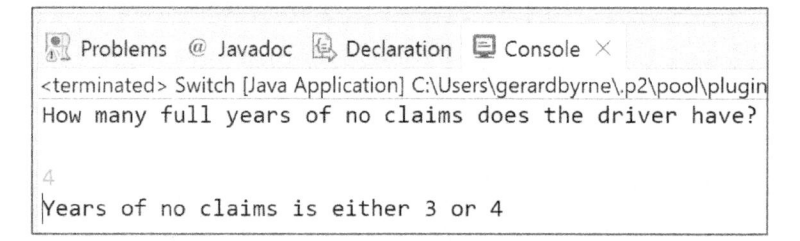

```
Problems  @ Javadoc  Declaration  Console ×
<terminated> Switch [Java Application] C:\Users\gerardbyrne\.p2\pool\plugin
How many full years of no claims does the driver have?
4
Years of no claims is either 3 or 4
```

31. Click on the green **Run** button at the top of the screen.

32. Click in the Console window at the bottom of the screen.
33. Type **2** as the number of years of no claims.
34. **Press the Enter key** on the keyboard.

The console window will appear as shown and we can see that the sixth case block of code has been executed, this is actually the default case:

```
Problems  @ Javadoc  Declaration  Console ×
<terminated> Switch [Java Application] C:\Users\gerardbyrne\.p2\pool\plugins\org.ec
How many full years of no claims does the driver have?

2
Years of no claims is either less than 3 or greater than 15
```

The switch construct is a replacement for the if else-if construct.

As we can see, the only issue in our case construct code arises for the equivalent of yearsOfNoClaims >10.

- in the if else-if, the yearsOfNoClaims >10 handled values 11, 12, 13, 14, 15, 16, 17 etc.
- in the switch statement we had to individually state case 11, case 12, case 13, case 14, case 15 but to do this for all values above 10 would be a long and wasteful process
- so, we may need to think of a better way to do this, or just use the if else-if construct
- the case construct in Java does not always allow for the use of a range of numbers or even > 10 as the case. The switch statement should not be used for condition checking

Switch with strings

The Java switch programs we have been writing have used an integer. We have therefore executed one block of code, or another, based on the integer value in the case statement. Java also allows us to use the switch construct with a **String**. When we use a String, the construct is the same as we have already coded, but the string must be enclosed in double quotes "".

We will now use a String in the switch construct and to do this we will amend a copy of the last program, **Switch**, so the data read from the console is not converted to an int, we will just keep it as a String. To achieve this, we will also need to change the data type of the variable, yearsOfNoClaims, from int to String.

Rather than changing the existing Switch.java, class we will create a copy of the class, rename it and then change the code in the copied class. This is a great technique, as we can reuse existing code and save lots of time having to start a program from 'scratch'.

1. Right click on the **Switch.java** class in the **com.gerrybyrne.module07** package.
2. Choose **Copy**.
3. Right click on the **com.gerrybyrne.module07** package.
4. Choose **Paste**.

The Name Conflict dialog box will appear, and we can keep the SwitchV2 name or give the copy of the class a new name.

5. Type **SwitchString** for the new name for this class.

If we look in the Package Explorer panel, we will see the new class.

6. Double click on the SwitchString class in the Package Explorer panel to open the code in the editor window.
7. Ensure that the name of the class is **SwitchString**, if not, amend the code as shown below to change the class name.

```
package com.gerrybyrne.module07;
import java.util.Scanner;

public class SwitchString {

    public static void main(String[] args)
    {
        Scanner myScanner = new Scanner(System.in);
```

8. Amend the code to change the data type of the variable to **String** instead of an int.

```java
public static void main(String[] args)
{
Scanner myScanner = new Scanner(System.in);
/* We will setup our variables that will be used in the quote application */
String yearsOfNoClaims;
```

9. Amend the code to remove the nextInt() automatic conversion of the data input by the user, as we want to use next() to obtain a String.

```java
Scanner myScanner = new Scanner(System.in);
/* We will setup our variables that will be used in the quote application */
String yearsOfNoClaims;

/* Read the user input as a String */
System.out.println("How many full years of no claims does the driver have?\n");

yearsOfNoClaims = myScanner.next();
```

10. Amend the code to add the new format for the first case block. This will mean enclosing the numbers in double quotes as they are being entered as strings.

```java
switch (yearsOfNoClaims)
{
  case "11":
  case "12":
  case "13":
  case "14":
  case "15":
  /*
    This block of code will be executed if the yearsofnoclaims is
    more than 10
  */
  System.out.println("Years of no claims is more than 10 but less than 16");
  break;
```

11. Amend the code to add the new format for the second and remaining case blocks.

```
/*
  This block of code will be executed if the yearsofnoclaims
```

                is more than 10
            */
            System.out.println("Years of no claims is more than 10 but less than 16");
            break;
        case "9":
        case "10":
            /*
                This block of code will be executed if the yearsofnoclaims
                is either 9 or 10
            */
            System.out.println("Years of no claims is either 9 or 10");
            break;
        case "7":
        case "8":
            /*
                This block of code will be executed if the yearsofnoclaims
                is either 7 or 8
            */
            System.out.println("Years of no claims is either 7 or 8");
            break;
        case "5":
        case "6":
            /*
                This block of code will be executed if the yearsofnoclaims
                is either 5 or 6
            */
            System.out.println("Years of no claims is either 5 or 6");
            break;
        case "3":
        case "4":
            /*
                This block of code will be executed if the yearsofnoclaims
                is either 3 or 4
            */
```

12. Click on the **File** menu.
13. Choose **Save All.**
14. Click on the green **Run** button at the top of the screen.
15. Click in the Console window at the bottom of the screen.
```

The console window will appear and ask the question. Now we can try the values 15, 10, 8, 6, 4, and 2 which will test the 5 case blocks. We will start with 15.

16. Type **15** and press the Enter key.

The console window will appear as shown and we can see that the first case block of code has been executed:

```
Problems  @ Javadoc  Declaration  Console  ×
<terminated> SwitchString [Java Application] C:\Users\gerardbyrne\.p2\pool\
How many full years of no claims does the driver have?

15
Years of no claims is more than 10 but less than 16
```

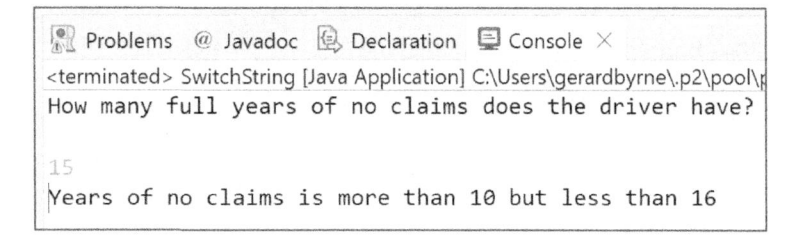

17. Click on the green **Run** button at the top of the screen.
18. Click in the Console window at the bottom of the screen.
19. Type **10** as the number of years of no claims.
20. **Press the Enter key** on the keyboard.

The console window will appear as shown and we can see that the second case block of code has been executed:

```
Problems  @ Javadoc  Declaration  Console  ×
<terminated> SwitchString [Java Application] C:\Users\gerardbyrne\.p2\pool\
How many full years of no claims does the driver have?

10
Years of no claims is either 9 or 10
```

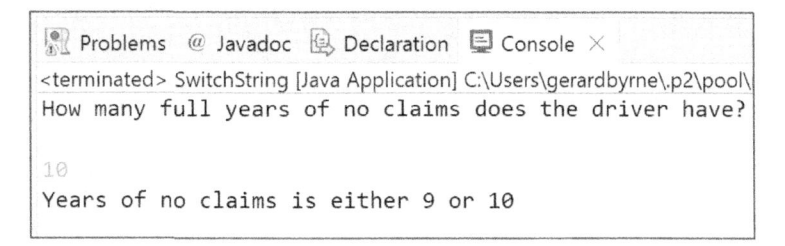

21. Click on the green **Run** button at the top of the screen.
22. Click in the Console window at the bottom of the screen.
23. Type **8** as the number of years of no claims.
24. **Press the Enter key** on the keyboard.

The console window will appear as shown and we can see that the third case block of code has been executed:

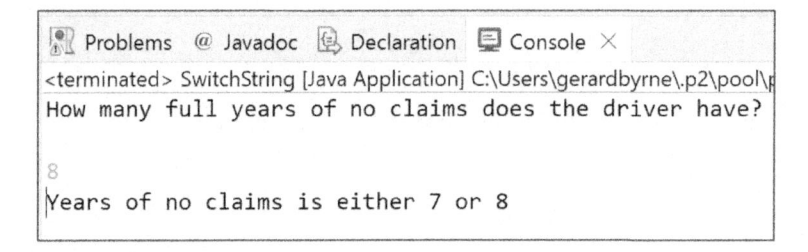

```
Problems  @ Javadoc  Declaration  Console  ×
<terminated> SwitchString [Java Application] C:\Users\gerardbyrne\.p2\pool\
How many full years of no claims does the driver have?

8
Years of no claims is either 7 or 8
```

25. Click on the green **Run** button at the top of the screen.
26. Click in the Console window at the bottom of the screen.
27. Type **6** as the number of years of no claims.
28. **Press the Enter key** on the keyboard.

The console window will appear as shown and we can see that the fourth case block of code has been executed:

```
Problems  @ Javadoc  Declaration  Console  ×
<terminated> SwitchString [Java Application] C:\Users\gerardbyrne\.p2\pool\
How many full years of no claims does the driver have?

6
Years of no claims is either 5 or 6
```

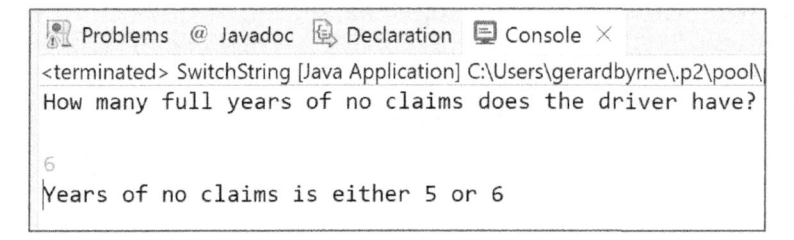

29. Click on the green **Run** button at the top of the screen.
30. Click in the Console window at the bottom of the screen.
31. Type **4** as the number of years of no claims.
32. **Press the Enter key** on the keyboard.

The console window will appear as shown and we can see that the fifth case block of code has been executed:

```
Problems  @ Javadoc  Declaration  Console  ×
<terminated> SwitchString [Java Application] C:\Users\gerardbyrne\.p2\pool\
How many full years of no claims does the driver have?

4
Years of no claims is either 3 or 4
```

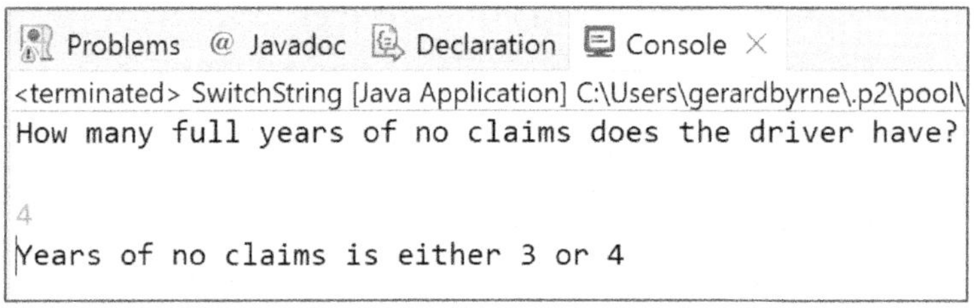

33. Click on the green **Run** button at the top of the screen.
34. Click in the Console window at the bottom of the screen.

35. Type **2** as the number of years of no claims.
36. **Press the Enter key** on the keyboard.

The console window will appear as shown and we can see that the sixth case block of code has been executed, this is actually the default case:

```
Problems  @ Javadoc  Declaration  Console ×
<terminated> SwitchString [Java Application] C:\Users\gerardbyrne\.p2\pool\plugins\c
How many full years of no claims does the driver have?
2
Years of no claims is either less than 3 or greater than 15
```

Switch with strings

Here we will code an additional example where we will again use the printformat method for writing a concatenated string.

As we saw earlier in our coding, by using the System.out.format() method we could format the output. With this method for displaying data, there is no concatenation and instead we are writing data to the console in a different way using a % 'placeholder':

- the placeholder has the format **%type**
- there can be more than one placeholder in the print line

With concatenation the example would be:

System.out.println("\nThe " + vehicleModel + " manufacturer is " + vehicleManufacturer);

With the new format() method the format of the code will be:

System.out.format("\nThe %s manufacturer is %s", vehicleModel, vehicleManufacturer);

Effectively the two code lines above mean the same thing.

The format method is very neat and has the advantage that we do not have to keep opening and closing the double quotes to insert the concatenation + symbol. We simply have all the variables at the end of the format() method.

We will now create a new class and use the format() method in the new code.

1. Right click on the **com.gerrybyrne.module07** package.
2. Choose **New**.
3. Choose **Class**.
4. Name the class **SwitchStringVehicleModel.**
5. Put a **tick in the checkbox** beside the public static void main(String[] args) box.
6. Click the **Finish** button.
7. Amend the code to import the Scanner class and instantiate the Scanner class withing the main() method:

    package com.gerrybyrne.module07;
    import java.util.Scanner;

    public class SwitchStringVehicleModel
    {
      public static void main(String[] args)
      {
        Scanner myScanner = **new** Scanner(System.*in*);

8. Amend the code to add the variables we will use:

        public static void main(String[] args)
        {
          Scanner myScanner = **new** Scanner(System.*in*);
          /*
            In this section we declare the two variables of data type
            String that we will use throughout the program code.
          */
          String vehicleModel;
          String vehicleManufacturer;
        } // End of main method()
      } // End of SwitchStringVehicleModel class

9. Amend the code to ask the user for input regarding the vehicle model and assign the input value to the vehicleModel variable:

> String vehicleModel;
> String vehicleManufacturer;
>
> System.*out*.println();
> System.*out*.println("What is the model of the vehicle?\n");
> /*
>   In this section we read the user input from the console.
>   The console input is by default a String data type which
>   means we can directly assign the value to the String
>   variable called vehicleModel.
> */
> vehicleModel = myScanner.next();
>
>   } // End of main method()
> } // End of SwitchStringVehicleModel class

10. Amend the code to add the Switch statement that will accept String values:

> vehicleModel = myScanner.next();
> /*
>   In this section we use the String variable called vehicleModel
>   in the case statement to decide which block of code will be
>   executed. The blocks of code therefore will be based on the
>   model of the vehicle and the code will set the value of the
>   variable called vehicleManufacturer.
> */
> **switch** (vehicleModel)
> {
>   **case** "Edge":
>   **case** "Fiesta":
>   **case** "Focus":
>   **case** "Kuga":
>   **case** "Mondeo":
>   **case** "Mustang":
>   vehicleManufacturer = "Ford";
>   **break**;
>   **case** "Astra":

```java
            case "Corsa":
            case "Insignia":
            case "Viva":
                vehicleManufacturer = "Vauxhall";
                break;
            case "Altima":
            case "Juke":
            case "Sentra":
                vehicleManufacturer = "Nissan";
                break;
            case "C-Class":
            case "E-Class":
            case "S-Class":
            case "GLA":
            case "GLC":
            case "GLE":
                vehicleManufacturer = "Mercedes Benz";
                break;
            default:
                vehicleManufacturer = "unknown";
                break;
        }// End of Switch statement
    } // End of main method()
} // End of SwitchStringVehicleModel class
```

11. Amend the code to print a message using the println() method:

```java
        } // End of Switch statement
        /*
            Here we will write the same message to the console in two different
            ways so we can use a new technique.

            In this statement we are writing data to the console in our normal
            way with a concatenated (joined) String and this works fine
        */
        System.out.println("\nThe " + vehicleModel + " manufacturer is " +
                vehicleManufacturer);

    } // End of main method()
} // End of SwitchStringVehicleModel class
```

12. Amend the code to print a message using the format() method which uses placeholders to match the variables to be displayed:

    System.*out*.println("\nThe " + vehicleModel + " manufacturer is " + vehicleManufacturer);

    /*
    In this statement we are writing data to the console in a different
    way using a String which has the %s 'placeholder'. Each place holder
    has a position and this position represents the position of the
    variable name in the comma separated list at the end of the statement.

    The example below effectively means:
    System.out.println("\nThe vehicleModel manufacturer is
    vehicleManufacturer ");

    This new format is very neat and means we do not have to keep opening
    and closing the double quotes and having the concatenation + symbol.
    */
    System.*out*.format("\nThe %s manufacturer is %s
    ",vehicleModel,vehicleManufacturer);

    } // End of main method()
    } // End of SwitchStringVehicleModel class

13. Amend the code to close the Scanner which was opened at the start of the program:

    System.*out*.format("\nThe %s manufacturer is %s
         ",vehicleModel,vehicleManufacturer);
    myScanner.close();

    } // End of main method()
    } // End of SwitchStringVehicleModel class

14. Click on the **File** menu.
15. Choose **Save All**.
16. Click on the green **Run** button at the top of the screen.
17. Click in the Console window at the bottom of the screen.

The console window will appear and ask the question. Now we can try the string values **Mustang**, **Corsa**, **Juke**, **S-Class** and **Pacifica** which will test the 5 case blocks. We will start with Mustang.

18. Type **Mustang** and press the Enter key.

The console window will appear as shown and we can see that the first case block of code has been executed:

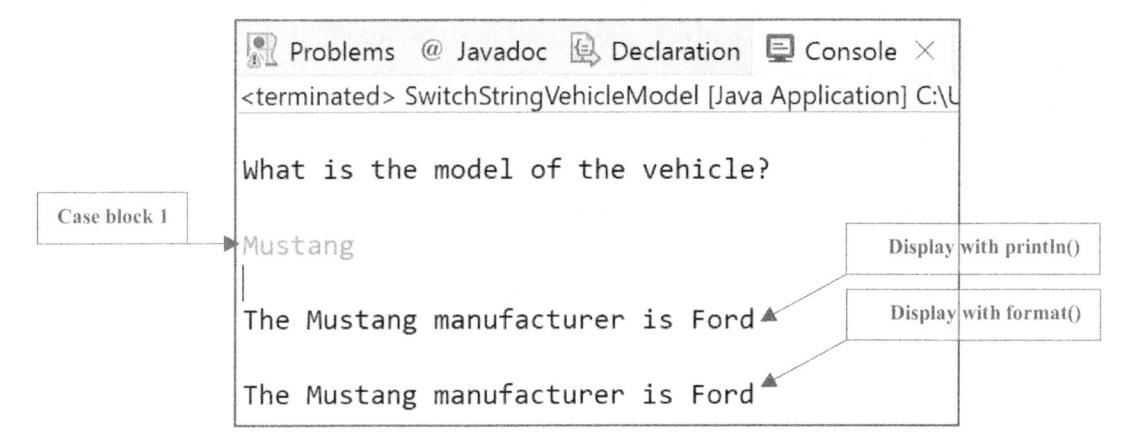

```
Problems  @ Javadoc  Declaration  Console  ×
<terminated> SwitchStringVehicleModel [Java Application] C:\U

What is the model of the vehicle?
Mustang

The Mustang manufacturer is Ford

The Mustang manufacturer is Ford
```

Case block 1 → Mustang
Display with println()
Display with format()

19. Click on the green **Run** button at the top of the screen.
20. Click in the Console window at the bottom of the screen.
21. Type **Corsa** and press the Enter key.

The console window will appear as shown and we can see that the second case block of code has been executed:

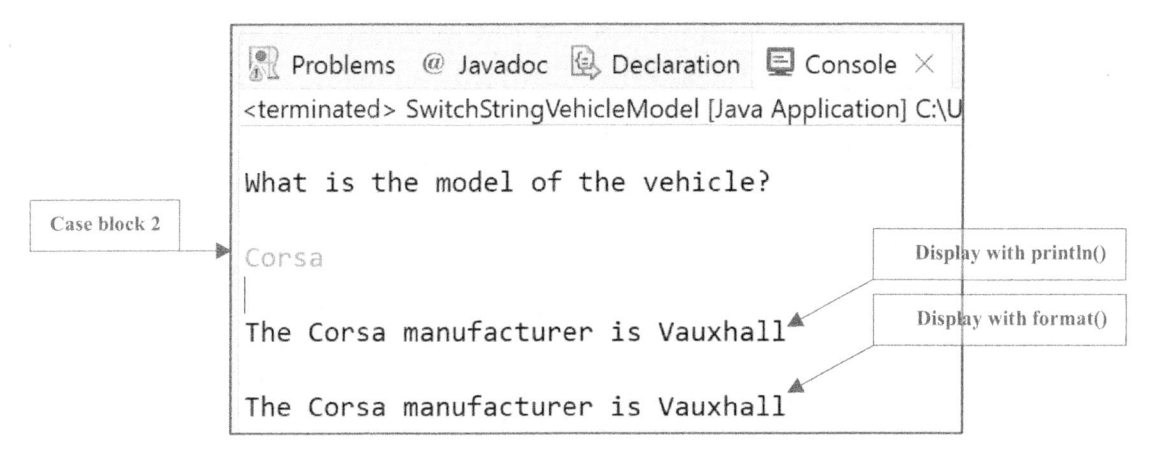

```
Problems  @ Javadoc  Declaration  Console  ×
<terminated> SwitchStringVehicleModel [Java Application] C:\U

What is the model of the vehicle?
Corsa

The Corsa manufacturer is Vauxhall

The Corsa manufacturer is Vauxhall
```

Case block 2 → Corsa
Display with println()
Display with format()

22. Click on the green **Run** button at the top of the screen.
23. Click in the Console window at the bottom of the screen.

24. Type **Juke** and press the Enter key.

The console window will appear as shown and we can see that the third case block of code has been executed:

```
Problems  @ Javadoc  Declaration  Console  X
<terminated> SwitchStringVehicleModel [Java Application] C:\

What is the model of the vehicle?
Juke

The Juke manufacturer is Nissan
The Juke manufacturer is Nissan
```

Case block 3 → Juke
Display with println()
Display with format()

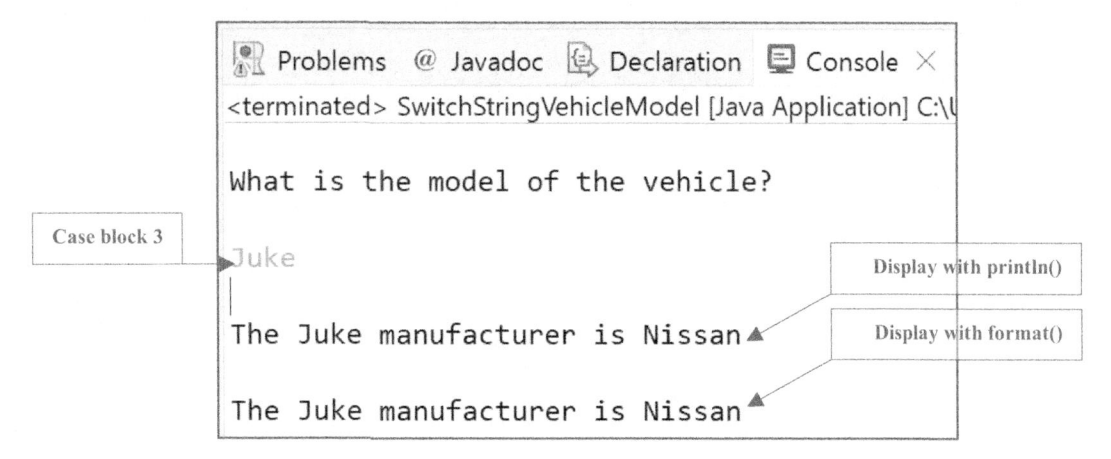

25. Click on the green **Run** button at the top of the screen.
26. Click in the Console window at the bottom of the screen.
27. Type **S-Class** and press the Enter key.

The console window will appear as shown and we can see that the fourth case block of code has been executed:

```
Problems  @ Javadoc  Declaration  Console  X
<terminated> SwitchStringVehicleModel [Java Application] C:\

What is the model of the vehicle?
S-Class

The S-Class manufacturer is Mercedes Benz
The S-Class manufacturer is Mercedes Benz
```

Case block 4 → S-Class
Display with println()
Display with format()

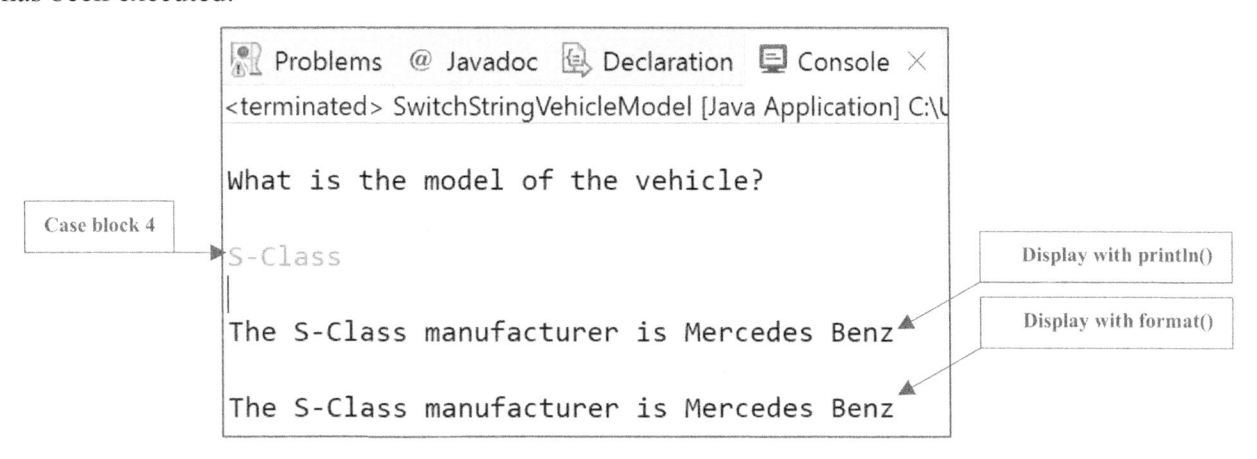

28. Click on the green **Run** button at the top of the screen.
29. Click in the Console window at the bottom of the screen.
30. Type **Pacifica** and press the Enter key.

The console window will appear as shown and we can see that the fifth case block (called **default**) of code has been executed:

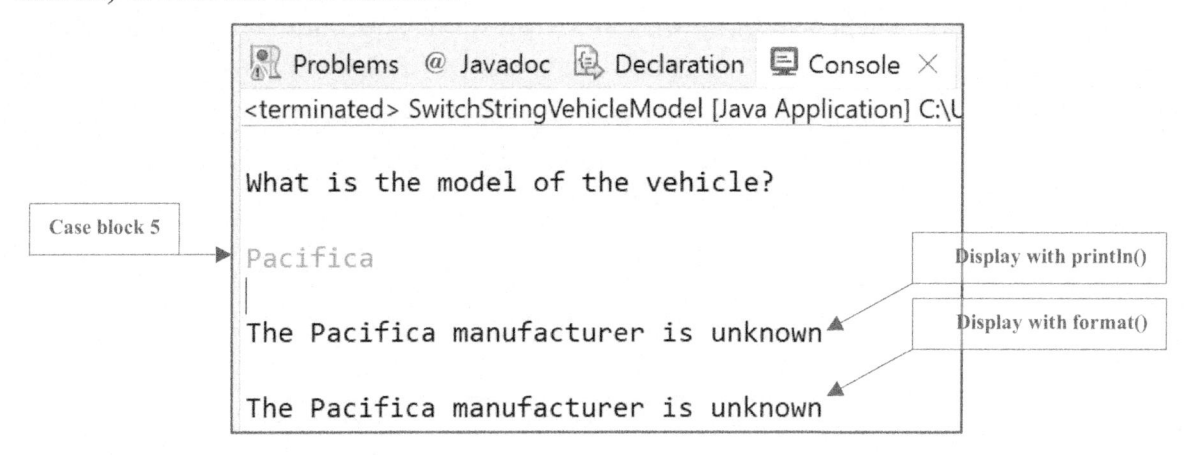

```
Problems  @ Javadoc  Declaration  Console  X
<terminated> SwitchStringVehicleModel [Java Application] C:\U
What is the model of the vehicle?
Pacifica

The Pacifica manufacturer is unknown

The Pacifica manufacturer is unknown
```

Case block 5 → Pacifica

Display with println()
Display with format()

An issue to be considered when using strings with the case statement is that checking is case sensitive. This should be no surprise to us really, as we will be familiar with writing and will know that these are all different (strings):

- Mustang
- MUSTANG
- mustang
- mUSTANG

So, if these are all different in our writing, then we can imagine that the Java compiler will also treat them as being different. This will mean that the user needs to input the data in precisely the same way as we as the developer have checked the string in the switch statement. This is certainly an issue and not a very satisfactory experience for the end user. To avoid such issues different techniques can be used by us as developers, such as using a method to convert the user input to **uppercase and then having the case statements have uppercase text**. As a 'taster' for the future modules this might be coded as:

```
switch (vehicleModel.toUpperCase())
{
case "EDGE":
case "FIESTA":
case "FOCUS":
case "KUGA":
case "MONDEO":
case "MUSTANG":
    vehicleManufacturer = "Ford";
    break;
```

and if the user inputs any string it will be converted to uppercase when the switch statement is executed. So, if the user enters:

    mUsTaNg   the code will convert it to uppercase   **MUSTANG**

and the case statement will find the correct manufacturer.

We could also use the **ToUpperCase()** method on the output as shown below:

System.out.format("\nThe %s manufacturer is %s", vehicleModel.ToUpperCase(), vehicleManufacturer);

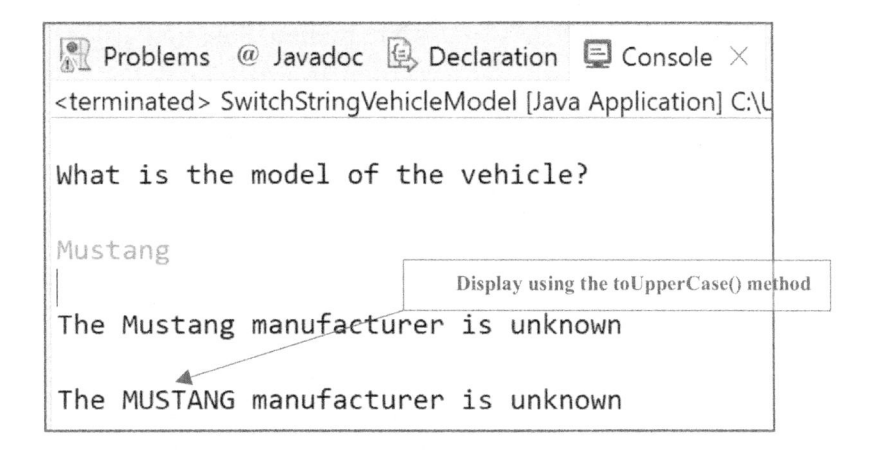

```
What is the model of the vehicle?

Mustang

The Mustang manufacturer is unknown

The MUSTANG manufacturer is unknown
```

Display using the toUpperCase() method

For now, do not worry about this.

Logical operators

We said earlier "**we will also look at the logical operators AND (&&), || (OR) and ! (NOT)**". Well, now is the time to use them by building on the if construct we have learnt.

AND

Looking at the AND operator we will see that both parts must be TRUE for the whole statement to be TRUE. An example of using AND in the if construct is:

```
if (yearsOfNoClaims > 10 AND policyHolderAge > 50)
{
    // Some business logic
}
```

Looking at all the possibilities for an AND the table would look like this:

First part		Second part		Result
TRUE	AND	TRUE	=	TRUE
TRUE	AND	FALSE	=	FALSE
FALSE	AND	TRUE	=	FALSE
FALSE	AND	FALSE	=	FALSE

OR

Looking at the OR operator we will see that only one part must be TRUE for the whole statement to be TRUE. An example of using AND in the if construct is:

```
if (yearsOfNoClaims > 10 OR policyHolderAge > 50)
{
    // Some business logic
}
```

Looking at all the possibilities for an OR the table would look like this:

First part		Second part		Result
TRUE	OR	TRUE	=	TRUE
TRUE	OR	FALSE	=	TRUE
FALSE	OR	TRUE	=	TRUE
FALSE	OR	FALSE	=	FALSE

NOT

Looking at the NOT operator we will see that the current value becomes the opposite of what it is, TRUE becomes FALSE and FALSE becomes TRUE. An example of using NOT in the if construct is:

```
if (!yearsOfNoClaims > 10)
{
    // Some business logic
}
```

Looking at all the possibilities for a NOT the table would look like this:

!TRUE	=	FALSE
!FALSE	=	TRUE

In Java the logical operators will only evaluate the second part of the expression if it is necessary. Why, we might ask. Well, we will see that it makes sense to use this **short circuit** evaluation to save needless evaluation.

Examples

AND

In our truth table we saw that the only combination that evaluates to TRUE is when both parts of the expression are TRUE. So, we can short circuit any combinations that start with a FALSE.

if(6>7 AND 9<10)   equates to   if(FALSE AND TRUE)   equates to FALSE

as the first part evaluates to FALSE there is no point in evaluating the second part.

OR

In our truth table we saw that a TRUE or a FALSE as the first part could lead to an overall evaluation of TRUE. So, we cannot short circuit when using the OR construct.

Let's code some Java using AND operator

1. Right click on the com.gerrybyrne.module07 package icon.
2. Choose **New**.
3. Choose **Class**.
4. Name the class **SelectionAnd**.
5. Put a tick in the checkbox beside the public static void main(String[] args) box.
6. Click on the **Finish** button.

The **SelectionAnd** class code will appear in the editor window and will be similar to the following:

package com.gerrybyrne.module07;

public class SelectionAnd
{
　　public static void main(String[] args)
　　{
　　　　// TODO Auto-generated method stub
　　} // End of main method()
} // End of SelectionAnd class

Now we will add the variables that will be used in our code. In the code below there are detailed comments to help us get a full understanding of the code.

7. Amend the code to add the variables and an instance of the Scanner class to allow us to accept user input:

　　package com.gerrybyrne.module07;

　　import java.util.Scanner;

　　public class SelectionAnd
　　{
　　　public static void main(String[] args)
　　　{
　　　　　Scanner myScanner = **new** Scanner(System.*in*);

```
/* We will setup our variables that will be used in the quote application */
int yearsOfNoClaims;
int ageOfDriver = 0;

    } // End of main method()
} // End of SelectionAnd class
```

8. Amend the code to request user input for the years of no claims and convert it to an int:

   int yearsOfNoClaims;
   int ageOfDriver = 0;

   /* Read the user input and convert it to an int */
   System.*out*.println("How many full years of no claims does the driver have?\n");

   yearsOfNoClaims = myScanner.nextInt();

9. Amend the code to request user input for the driver age and convert it to an int:

   int yearsOfNoClaims;
   int ageOfDriver = 0;

   /* Read the user input and convert it to an int */
   System.*out*.println("How many full years of no claims does the driver have?\n");
   yearsOfNoClaims = myScanner.nextInt();

   System.*out*.println("What is the current age of the driver?\n");

   ageOfDriver = myScanner.nextInt();

10. Amend the code to check if the number of years of no claims is greater than 10 and if the age of the driver is greater than 40 then:
    - if these are both true we execute code in the if block otherwise
    - move to the else block and execute the code in this block

      System.*out*.println("What is the current age of the driver?\n");
      ageOfDriver = myScanner.nextInt();
      /*

Now we will check if the years of no claims is greater than 10 AND if the age of the driver is greater than 40. If both are TRUE we have the Boolean expression TRUE AND TRUE which equates to TRUE and we then we execute some lines of code which exist between the curly braces of the code block, otherwise the program moves to the else code block and execute some lines of code in this code block
*/
```
    if (yearsOfNoClaims > 10 && ageOfDriver > 40)
{
  /*
    This block of code will be executed if the both
    parts of the condition are TRUE
  */
    System.out.println("This quote is eligible for a 10% discount");
} // End of True part
else
{
  /*
    This block of code will be executed if the one
    part of the condition is FALSE
  */
    System.out.println("This quote is ineligible for a discount");
} // End of False part

  } // End of main method()
} // End of SelectionAnd class
```

11. Amend the code to close the instance of the Scanner that was created:

```
    System.out.println("This quote is ineligible for a discount");
} // End of False part

    myScanner.close();

  } // End of main method()
} // End of SelectionAnd class
```

Testing TRUE AND TRUE

12. Click on the **File** menu.
13. Choose **Save All**.
14. Click on the green **Run** button at the top of the screen.
15. Click in the Console window at the bottom of the screen.
16. Type **20** as the number of years of no claims.
17. Press the **Enter** key on the keyboard.
18. Type **50** as the current age of the driver.
19. Press the **Enter** key on the keyboard.

The console window will show the message that a discount is applicable as 20 is greater than 10 AND 50 is greater than 40.

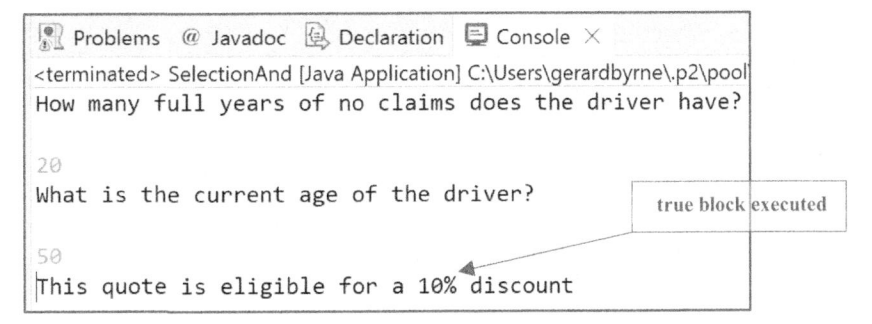

```
Problems  @ Javadoc  Declaration  Console  X
<terminated> SelectionAnd [Java Application] C:\Users\gerardbyrne\.p2\pool
How many full years of no claims does the driver have?

20
What is the current age of the driver?          true block executed

50
This quote is eligible for a 10% discount
```

Testing FALSE AND TRUE

20. Click on the green **Run** button at the top of the screen.
21. Click in the Console window at the bottom of the screen.
22. Type **10** as the number of years of no claims.
23. Press the **Enter** key on the keyboard.
24. Type **50** as the current age of the driver.
25. Press the **Enter** key on the keyboard.

The console window will show the message that no discount is applicable as 50 is greater than 40 BUT 10 is not greater than 10.

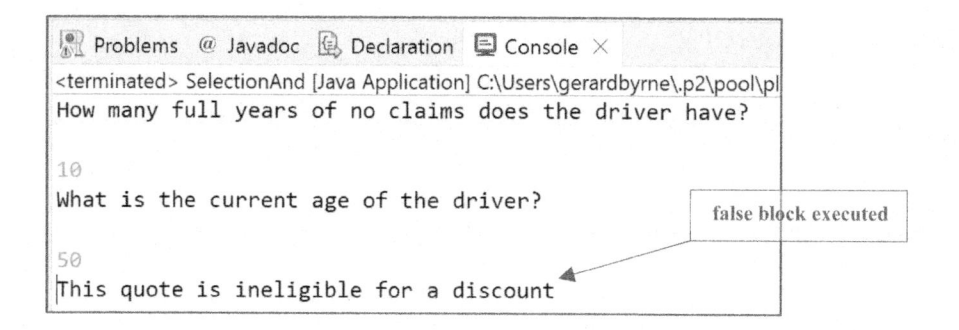

```
Problems  @ Javadoc  Declaration  Console ×
<terminated> SelectionAnd [Java Application] C:\Users\gerardbyrne\.p2\pool\pl
How many full years of no claims does the driver have?

10
What is the current age of the driver?

50
This quote is ineligible for a discount
```
false block executed

Testing TRUE AND FALSE

26. Click on the green **Run** button at the top of the screen.
27. Click in the Console window at the bottom of the screen.
28. Type **20** as the number of years of no claims.
29. Press the **Enter** key on the keyboard.
30. Type **30** as the current age of the driver.
31. Press the **Enter** key on the keyboard.

The console window will show the message that no discount is applicable as 20 is greater than 10 BUT 30 is not greater than 40.

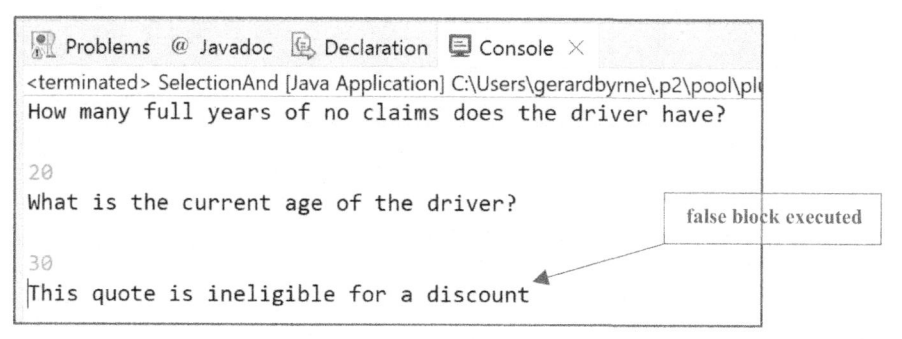

```
Problems  @ Javadoc  Declaration  Console ×
<terminated> SelectionAnd [Java Application] C:\Users\gerardbyrne\.p2\pool\pl
How many full years of no claims does the driver have?

20
What is the current age of the driver?

30
This quote is ineligible for a discount
```
false block executed

Let's code some Java using OR operator

1. Right click file **SelectionAnd**, in the Package explorer panel.
2. Choose **Copy**.
3. Right click on the **com.gerrybyrne.module07** package.
4. Choose **Paste**.
5. Rename the file as **SelectionOR**.
6. Click on the **OK** button.

We will amend the code to use the logical operator OR rather than the logical operator AND.

7. Amend the code to change the && (AND) to || (OR) and the comments. This means:
   - check if the number of years of no claims is greater than 10 OR if the age of the driver is greater than 40
     - if these are both true we execute code in the if block
     - if one of these is true we execute code in the if block otherwise
     - move to the else block and execute the code in this block

```
ageOfDriver = myScanner.nextInt();

/*
Now we will check if the years of no claims is greater than 10 OR
if the age of the driver is greater than 40.
If both are TRUE we have the Boolean expression TRUE AND TRUE which equates
to TRUE or
if one of them is TRUE we have the Boolean expression TRUE OR FALSE or
FALSE OR TRUE which equates to TRUE
and we then we execute some lines of code which exist between the
curly braces of the code block, otherwise the program moves to the
else code block and executes some lines of code in this code block
*/

if (yearsOfNoClaims > 10 || ageOfDriver > 40)
{
    /*
    This block of code will be executed if one
    part of the condition is TRUE
    */
    System.out.println("This quote is eligible for a 10% discount");
} // End of True part
else
{
    /* This block of code will be executed if both parts of the condition are FALSE */
    System.out.println("This quote is ineligible for a discount");
} // End of False part
```

Testing TRUE OR TRUE

8. Click on the **File** menu.
9. Choose **Save All**.
10. Click on the green **Run** button at the top of the screen.
11. Click in the Console window at the bottom of the screen.
12. Type **20** as the number of years of no claims.
13. Press the **Enter** key on the keyboard.
14. Type **50** as the current age of the driver.
15. Press the **Enter** key on the keyboard.

The console window will show the message that a discount is applicable as 20 is greater than 10 OR 50 is greater than 40. In this case both are TRUE which equates to TRUE.

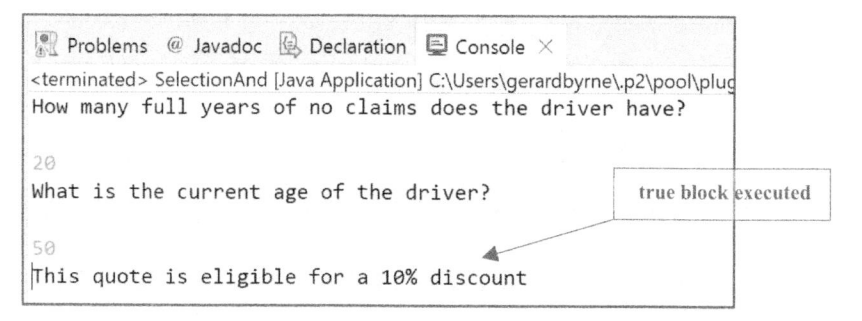

```
Problems  @ Javadoc  Declaration  Console ×
<terminated> SelectionAnd [Java Application] C:\Users\gerardbyrne\.p2\pool\plug
How many full years of no claims does the driver have?

20
What is the current age of the driver?            true block executed

50
This quote is eligible for a 10% discount
```

Testing FALSE OR TRUE

16. Click on the green **Run** button at the top of the screen.
17. Click in the Console window at the bottom of the screen.
18. Type **10** as the number of years of no claims.
19. Press the **Enter** key on the keyboard.
20. Type **50** as the current age of the driver.
21. Press the **Enter** key on the keyboard.

The console window will show the message that a discount is applicable as 10 is not greater than 10 (FALSE) OR 50 is greater than 40 (TRUE). In this case we have FALSE OR TRUE which equates to TRUE.

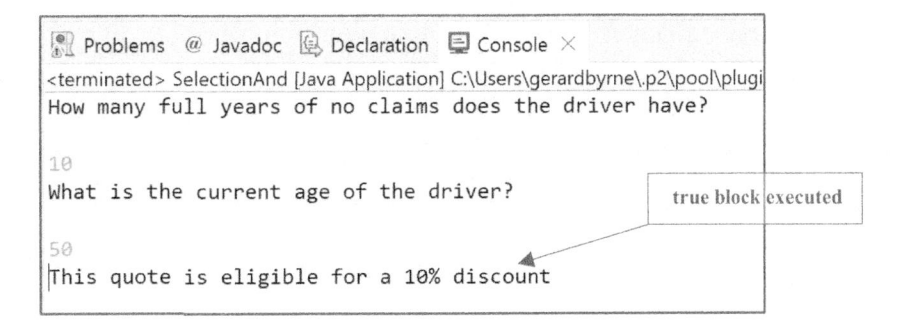

```
Problems  @ Javadoc  Declaration  Console ×
<terminated> SelectionAnd [Java Application] C:\Users\gerardbyrne\.p2\pool\plugi
How many full years of no claims does the driver have?

10
What is the current age of the driver?            true block executed

50
This quote is eligible for a 10% discount
```

Testing TRUE OR FALSE

22. Click on the green **Run** button at the top of the screen.
23. Click in the Console window at the bottom of the screen.
24. Type **20** as the number of years of no claims.
25. Press the **Enter** key on the keyboard.
26. Type **30** as the current age of the driver.
27. Press the Enter key on the keyboard.

The console window will show the message that a discount is applicable as 20 is greater than 10 (TRUE) OR 30 is greater than 40 (FALSE). In this case we have TRUE OR FALSE which equates to TRUE.

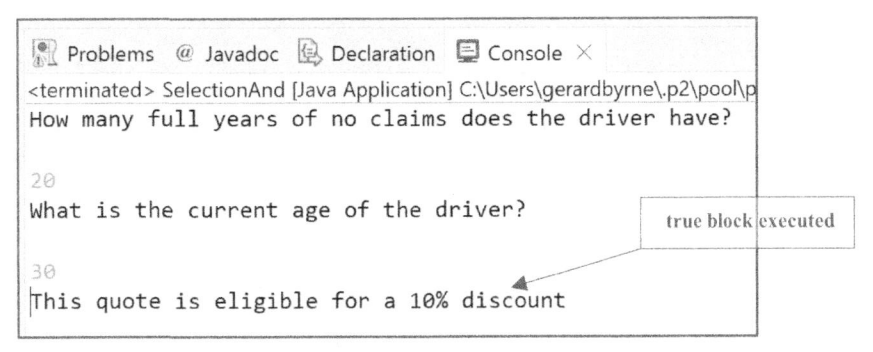

```
Problems  @ Javadoc  Declaration  Console ×
<terminated> SelectionAnd [Java Application] C:\Users\gerardbyrne\.p2\pool\p
How many full years of no claims does the driver have?

20
What is the current age of the driver?            true block executed

30
This quote is eligible for a 10% discount
```

Testing FALSE OR FALSE

28. Click on the green **Run** button at the top of the screen.
29. Click in the Console window at the bottom of the screen.
30. Type **10** as the number of years of no claims.
31. Press the **Enter** key on the keyboard.
32. Type **30** as the current age of the driver.
33. Press the **Enter** key on the keyboard.

The console window will show the message that a discount is applicable as 10 is greater than 10 (FALSE) OR 30 is greater than 40 (FALSE). In this case we have FALSE OR FALSE which equates to FALSE.

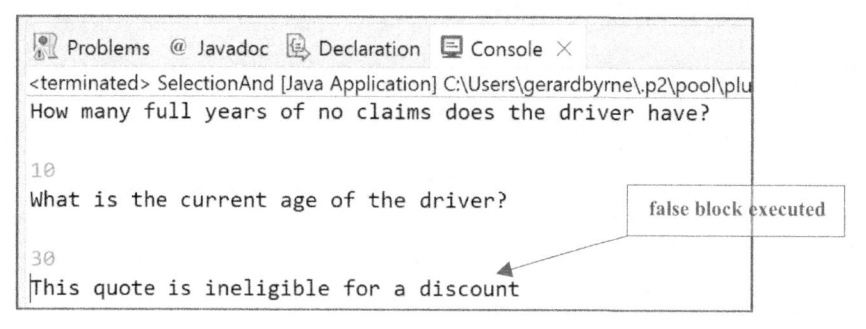

```
Problems  @ Javadoc  Declaration  Console  X
<terminated> SelectionAnd [Java Application] C:\Users\gerardbyrne\.p2\pool\plu
How many full years of no claims does the driver have?

10
What is the current age of the driver?                    false block executed

30
This quote is ineligible for a discount
```

Let's code some Java using NOT operator

1. Right click on the file **SelectionAnd** in the Package explorer panel.
2. Choose **Copy**.
3. Right click on the **com.gerrybyrne.module07** package.
4. Choose **Paste**.
5. Rename the file as **SelectionNOT**.
6. Click on the **OK** button.

Now we will amend the code to use the logical operator NOT.

7. Amend the code to change the AND expression by adding an extra set of brackets () around it and putting a !, NOT, before the new brackets. We will leave the comments as they are. This means we are now doing the following:

    - checking if the number of years of no claims is greater than 10 AND if the age of the driver is greater than 40
        - if these are both true the expression in the brackets equates to true but we negate it (!) to false and we do not execute the code in the if block
        - if one of these is false the expression in the brackets equates to false but we negate it (!) to true and we execute the code in the if block

- if these are both false the expression in the brackets equates to false but we negate it (!) to true and we execute the code in the if block

```
if (!(yearsOfNoClaims > 10 && ageOfDriver > 40))
{
    /*
     This block of code will be executed if the both
     parts of the condition are TRUE
    */
    System.out.println("This quote is eligible for a 10% discount");
} // End of True part
```

Testing TRUE AND TRUE

8. Click on the **File** menu.
9. Choose **Save All**.
10. Click on the green **Run** button at the top of the screen.
11. Click in the Console window at the bottom of the screen.
12. Type **20** as the number of years of no claims.
13. Press the **Enter** key on the keyboard.
14. Type **50** a as the current age of the driver.
15. Press the **Enter** key on the keyboard.

The console window will show the message that a discount is not applicable as we have an overall TRUE negated to a FALSE (20 is greater than 10 AND 50 is greater than 40 means TRUE then negated to FALSE so no discount is applicable).

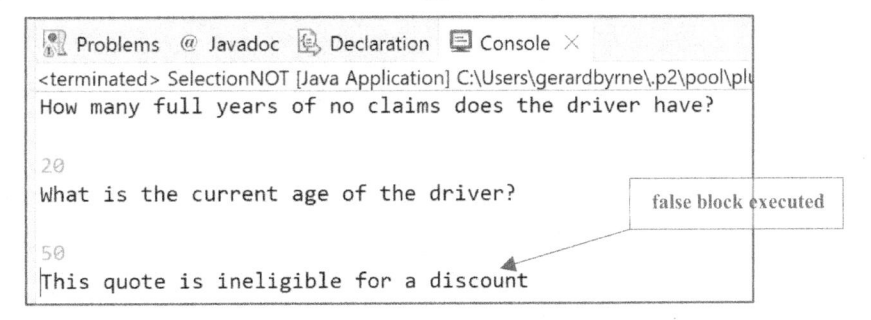

```
Problems  @ Javadoc  Declaration  Console ×
<terminated> SelectionNOT [Java Application] C:\Users\gerardbyrne\.p2\pool\pl
How many full years of no claims does the driver have?

20
What is the current age of the driver?                    false block executed

50
This quote is ineligible for a discount
```

Testing FALSE AND TRUE

16. Click on the green **Run** button at the top of the screen.
17. Click in the Console window at the bottom of the screen.
18. Type **10** as the number of years of no claims.
19. Press the **Enter** key on the keyboard.
20. Type **50** as the current age of the driver.
21. Press the **Enter** key on the keyboard.

The console window will show the message that a discount is applicable as we have an overall FALSE negated to a TRUE (10 is not greater than 10 AND 50 is greater than 40 means FALSE then negated to TRUE so a discount is applicable).

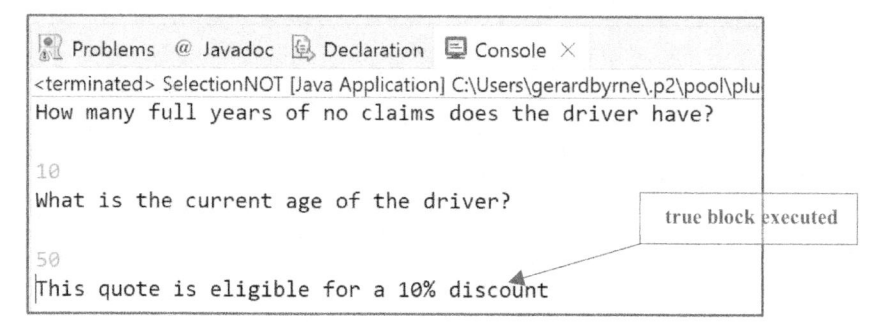

```
Problems  @ Javadoc  Declaration  Console  X
<terminated> SelectionNOT [Java Application] C:\Users\gerardbyrne\.p2\pool\plu
How many full years of no claims does the driver have?

10
What is the current age of the driver?

50
This quote is eligible for a 10% discount
```
true block executed

Testing TRUE AND FALSE

22. Click on the green **Run** button at the top of the screen.
23. Click in the Console window at the bottom of the screen.
24. Type **20** as the number of years of no claims.
25. Press the **Enter** key on the keyboard.
26. Type **30** as the current age of the driver.
27. Press the **Enter** key on the keyboard.

The console window will show the message that a discount is applicable as we have an overall FALSE negated to a TRUE (20 is greater than 10 AND 30 is not greater than 40 means FALSE then negated to TRUE so a discount is applicable).

```
Problems  @ Javadoc  Declaration  Console  ×
<terminated> SelectionNOT [Java Application] C:\Users\gerardbyrne\.p2\pool\pl
How many full years of no claims does the driver have?

20
What is the current age of the driver?

30
This quote is eligible for a 10% discount
```

← true block executed

Module Summary

In this module we have learnt about a very important programming concept called **selection**.

We have learnt that:

- selection in Java can have different formats, including
    - the **if** construct
    - the **if else** construct
    - the **if else-if** construct
    - the **switch** construct (and the case label)
- the case construct can use numeric or string data types
- the case label is case sensitive
- there is a different way to display data to the console with the use of the format() method and 'placeholders' (%)
- Java has a string handling class with useful methods, one of which is the ToUpperCase() method
- we can have more than one class in a package

Yet another great achievement for us in our learning. Be proud of the learning to date.

Our dot just got bigger

Program Practically

Java

Module 08

Iteration

Iteration using for construct

Iteration using while construct

Iteration using do while construct

Iteration using for each construct

Using the break and continue statements

Gerry Byrne

Program Practically - Iteration (Looping)

We learnt in module 7 that:

Selection is a particularly important programming concept in all programming languages. To use selection in our Java code we have several options and the best option to choose will depend on the particular task the code has to perform. The different formats for the selection construct are the if construct, the if else construct, the if else-if construct and the switch construct with its case label. The switch construct can use numeric or string data types and when we use strings it is case sensitive. To help in using strings with the switch construct we can make use of the ToUpperCase() or ToLowerCase() methods. We also learnt that displaying data to the console could be achieved using the format() method and 'placeholders' (%).

In terms of the project structure, we learnt that not only can we have multiple packages but within a package we can have multiple classes, each having to have unique name.

Introduction to Iteration

Many of the things we do in everyday life require iteration. Think about making a number of slices of toast in a toaster. The instructions could be:

- take a slice of bread from the recycleable packaging
- put the slice of bread in the toaster
- pull the toaster lever down to start the heating process
- when the toast pops up remove the slice of toast from the toaster
- put the slice of toast on a plate
- **repeat** the process the required number of times

Think about brushing our teeth – move the toothbrush left and right the required number of times.

The concept of iteration is important in programming and the Java language offers us a number of different structures to perform iteration. In this module we will look at the Java iteration (loops) constructs and concepts including:

- the **for** loop
- the **while** loop
- the **do** loop
- the **foreach** loop
- the **break** statement
- the **continue** statement

The principle of iteration is to repeat a sequence of Java instructions (a block of code) a number of times. The number of times is determined by the type of loop structure, as we will see when we code each type of loop structure.

For Loop

The first structure we will look at is the **For Loop** which will allow us to repeat a sequence of instructions a set number of times. The for statement will repeat the block of code, a number of lines of code, while a Boolean expression evaluates to true.

The format of the for loop is shown below:

```
for(<Start value>; <Condition>; <increment value>)
{
   <statements>
}
```

There are 3 parts to the for construct, the:

- **start value** – **which will be of data type int**
- **condition** – **which will equate to true or false**
- **increment** – **which will change the start value by a specified amount**

Example:

```
for (int counter = 0; counter < 2; counter++)
{
        block of code statements
}
```

In the example code:

- a local variable called **counter** is set up inside the brackets ()
- the **variable** will be used as the loop counter and help to decide how many times the block of code is executed
- the variable is created as an integer and set to have an **initial value of 0** (it does not have to be 0 as the starting point). **This is the first part of the for loop, the start value**
- the loop counter is **compared** with the value 2, and if it less than 2, the execution of the block of code continues. **This is the second part of the for loop, the condition**
- the loop counter is **incremented** (increased) by 1. **This is the third part of the for loop, the increment, we could also decrement**
- each section is separated by a semi-colon ;
- all of this is enclosed in the brackets ()
- the block of code to be executed the required number of times is enclosed between curly braces {}

The for statement can be exited early, if this is required, by using the **break** statement. It is also possible to have the code move to the next iteration in the loop by using the keyword **continue**.

This module will concentrate on iteration using an insurance quote example and will build on our learning from the previous modules.

1. Right click on the **src** folder.
2. Choose **New**.
3. Choose **Package**.
4. Name the package **com.gerrybyrne.module08.**
5. Click the **Finish** button.
6. Right click on the package icon.
7. Choose **New**.
8. Choose **Class**.
9. Name the class **Iteration**.

10. Put a tick in the checkbox beside the public static void main(String[] args) box.
11. Click on the **Finish** button.

The **Iteration** class code will appear in the editor window and will be similar to the following code:

```java
package com.gerrybyrne.module08;

public class Iteration
{
    public static void main(String[] args)
    {
        // TODO Auto-generated method stub

    } // End of main method()
} // End of Iteration class
```

When a vehicle is involved in an accident and requires repair, it could go to a repair centre which has been nominated by the insurance company. When the repairs are completed the repair centre will recoup their costs from the insurance company. We will now develop a program that will ask the user from the repair shop to enter the details required by the insurance company. The details will be:

- the repair shop unique id   (String)
- the vehicle insurance policy number   (String)
- the claim amount and   (double)
- the date of the claim   (date)

Now we will add the variables that will be used in our code. In the code below there are detailed comments to help us get a full understanding of the code.

Let's code some Java

12. Amend the code to create an instance of the Scanner class, calling the instance myScanner and importing the Scanner class

```java
package com.gerrybyrne.module08;

import java.util.Scanner;

public class Iteration {

    public static void main(String[] args)
    {
        Scanner myScanner = new Scanner(System.in);
```

13. Amend the code to add the variables we will require:

```java
    public static void main(String[] args)
    {
        Scanner myScanner = new Scanner(System.in);
        /*
        We will set up the variables to be used in the quote application
        The details will be:
            - the repair shop unique id              (String)
            - the vehicle insurance policy number    (String)
            - the claim amount and                   (double)
            - the date of the claim                  (date)
        */
        String repairShopID;
        String vehiclePolicyNumber;
        String claimDate;
        double claimAmount;
    } // End of main method()
} // End of Iteration class
```

14. Amend the code to include a for construct which will iterate twice:

```java
        double claimAmount;

        for (int claimsCounter= 0; claimsCounter < 2; claimsCounter ++)
        {
        } // End of for loop
    } // End of main method()
} // End of Iteration class
```

15. Amend the code to ask the user to input the repair shop id, accept the input, keep it as a String and assign the value to the variable called repairShopID:

    ```
    for (int claimsCounter= 0; claimsCounter < 2; claimsCounter ++)
    {
      /* Read the user input for the repair shop id and keep it as a string */
      System.out.println("What is our repair shop id?\n");
      repairShopID = myScanner.next();
    } // End of for loop

      } // End of main method()
    } // End of Iteration class
    ```

16. Amend the code to ask the user to input the vehicle policy number, accept the input, keep it as a String and assign the value to the variable called vehiclePolicyNumber:

    ```
    for (int claimsCounter= 0; claimsCounter < 2; claimsCounter ++)
    {
      /* Read the user input for the repair shop id and keep it as a string */
      System.out.println("What is our repair shop id?\n");
      repairShopID = myScanner.next();

      /* Read the user input for the vehicle policy number and keep it as a string */
      System.out.println("What is the vehicle policy number?\n");
      vehiclePolicyNumber = myScanner.next();
    } // End of for loop
      } // End of main method()
    } // End of Iteration class
    ```

17. Amend the code to ask the user to input the repair amount, accept the input, convert it to a double and assign the value to the variable called claimAmount:

    ```
    for (int claimsCounter= 0; claimsCounter < 2; claimsCounter ++)
    {
      /* Read the user input for the repair shop id and keep it as a string */
      System.out.println("What is our repair shop id?\n");
      repairShopID = myScanner.next();

      /* Read the user input for the vehicle policy number and keep it as a string */
    ```

```
        System.out.println("What is the vehicle policy number?\n");
        vehiclePolicyNumber = myScanner.next();

        /*Read the user input for the repair amount and convert it to a double*/
        System.out.println("What is the amount being claimed for the repair?\n");
        claimAmount = myScanner.nextDouble();
     } // End of for loop

  } // End of main method()
} // End of Iteration class
```

18. Amend the code to ask the user to input the repair date, accept the input, keep it as a String and assign the value to the variable called claimDate:

```
        /*Read the user input for the repair amount and convert it to a double*/
        System.out.println("What is the amount being claimed for the repair?\n");
        claimAmount = myScanner.nextDouble();

        /*Read the user input for the repair date leaving it as a String */
        System.out.println("What was the date of the repair?\n");
        claimDate = myScanner.next();
     } // End of for loop

  } // End of main method()
} // End of Iteration class
```

19. Amend the code to display the details that have been entered by the user. The displaying of the details will occur at the end of each iteration and there will therefore be two displays:

```
        /* Read the user input for the repair date leaving it as a String */
        System.out.println("What was the date of the repair?\n");
        claimDate = myScanner.next();

        System.out.println("The details entered for repair " +
        (claimsCounter + 1) + " are");
        System.out.println("Repair shop id:\t" + repairShopID);
        System.out.println("Policy number:\t" + vehiclePolicyNumber);
```

```
            System.out.println("Claim amount:\t" + claimAmount);
            System.out.println("Claim date:\t" + claimDate);
        } // End of for loop

    } // End of main method()
} // End of Iteration class
```

When the code is executed the user will be asked to input 2 sets of details as:

- the counter will start at 0 and the block of code is executed
- then the counter is incremented to 1 and the block of code is executed
- when it is incremented to 2 it will be checked against the comparator (claimsCounter < 2) and as it is not less than 2 the loop will be exited

20. Click on the **File** menu.
21. Choose **Save All**.
22. Click on the green **Run** button at the top of the screen.
23. Click in the Console window at the bottom of the screen.

The console window will appear and ask the user to input the repair shop id.

24. Type **RS000001** and press the Enter key.

The console will now ask the user to input the vehicle policy number.

25. Type **VP000001** and press the Enter key.

The console will now ask the user to input the claim amount.

26. Type **1999.99** and press the Enter key.

The console will now ask the user to input the date of the repair

27. Type **01/10/2021** and press the Enter key.

The display of the details entered for claim 1 will appear in the console window.

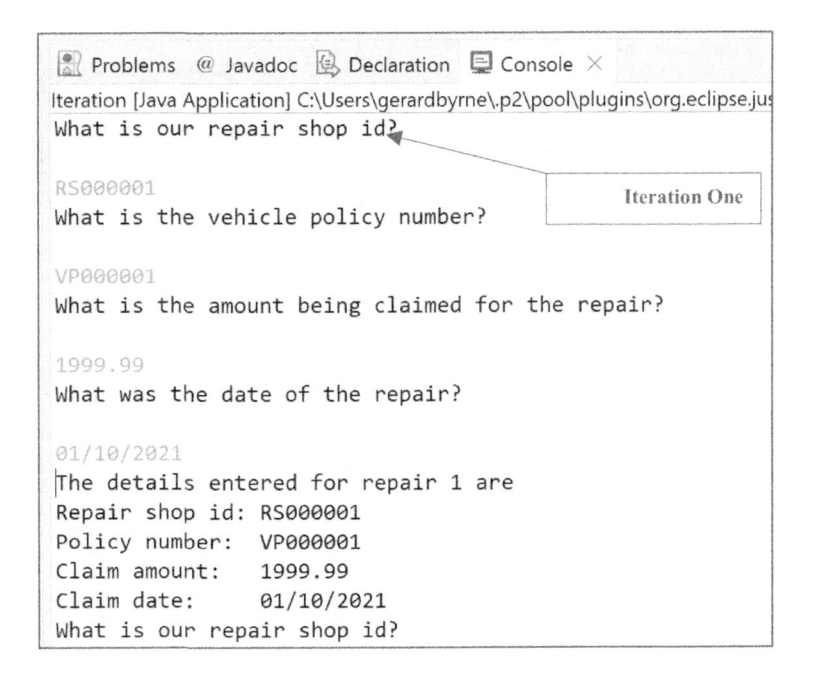

```
 Problems  @ Javadoc   Declaration   Console  ×
Iteration [Java Application] C:\Users\gerardbyrne\.p2\pool\plugins\org.eclipse.ju
What is our repair shop id?

RS000001
What is the vehicle policy number?          Iteration One

VP000001
What is the amount being claimed for the repair?

1999.99
What was the date of the repair?

01/10/2021
The details entered for repair 1 are
Repair shop id: RS000001
Policy number:  VP000001
Claim amount:   1999.99
Claim date:     01/10/2021
What is our repair shop id?
```

Iteration one is now completed, the block of code has been executed. The claims counter will now be incremented by 1 and becomes a 1. The comparison is made to see if the claims counter value is less than 2, and as it is the iterations continue.

The console window will now ask the user to input the repair shop id.

28. Type **RS000001** and press the Enter key.

The console will now ask the user to input the vehicle policy number.

29. Type **VP001234** and press the Enter key.

The console will now ask the user to input the claim amount.
30. Type **2500.99** and press the Enter key.

The console will now ask the user to input the date of the repair

31. Type **16/08/2021** and press the Enter key.

The display of the details entered for claim 2 will appear in the console window.

```
What is our repair shop id?

RS000001
What is the vehicle policy number?

VP001234
What is the amount being claimed for the repair?

2500.99
What was the date of the repair?

16/08/2021
The details entered for repair 2 are
Repair shop id: RS000001
Policy number:  VP001234
Claim amount:   2500.99
Claim date:     16/08/2021
```
Iteration Two

Iteration two is now completed, the block of code has been executed for the second time. The claims counter will now be incremented by 1 and becomes a 2. The comparison is made to see if the claims counter value is less than 2, and as it is not the iterations will end.

The code moves to the next line, which in this case does not exist, so the application stops. **We should see that all the details we entered are lost. In the next module we will look at storing the details in an array, in this module we are concentrating on loops (iterations).**

The iteration (loop) works fine but we could improve the situation by adhering to the principle of writing maintainable code:

- in the loop we have used a **hard-coded value** in the comparator i.e. the 2
- in this case 2 is known as a '**magic number**', as it just appears
- this has worked fine but when we wish to loop more times, our code would need to be changed
- ideally, we need to set up a **variable** that will store the value for the number of times that the loop is to be executed
- we will now amend the code in two stages just to show clearly the process of developing code that is more maintainable

The first stage will be to:

- set up a variable called **numberOfClaimsBeingMade** of data type int
- assign the value 2 to the variable
- remove the hard coded 2 from the loop and replace it with the variable numberOfClaimsBeingMade

32. Amend the code to implement these changes, starting by adding the variable and assigning the initial value:

```
String repairShopID;
String vehiclePolicyNumber;
String claimDate;
double claimAmount;
/*
  Set up a variable called numberOfClaimsBeingMade of data type int
  and assign the variable the value 2
*/
int numberOfClaimsBeingMade = 2;
```

33. Amend the code to remove the hard coded number (magic number) and replace it with the variable name:

```
/*
  Remove the hard coded 2 from the loop and replace it with the variable
  numberOfClaimsBeingMade
*/
for (int claimsCounter= 0; claimsCounter < numberOfClaimsBeingMade; claimsCounter ++)
{
    /* Read the user input for the repair shop id and keep it as a string */
    System.out.println("What is our repair shop id?\n");
    repairShopID = myScanner.next();
```

34. Click on the **File** menu.
35. Choose **Save All**.

If we ran the program, we would see nothing has changed but our code is a little better as we have used a variable in the loop. However, the code will still have to be amended if the user is required to enter a different number of claims than 2. Our code can be improved by removing the assigned value of 2 and replacing it with a value entered by the user. This will mean the code is written once and does not need to be changed, as the control lies with the value typed in by the user. Writing highly maintainable code is very important.

The second stage will therefore be to:
- ask the user to input the number of claims they wish to make
- read the value from the console
- assign the converted value to the variable numberOfClaimsBeingMade

36. Amend the code to implement these changes, start by removing the initial value:

    double claimAmount;

    /* Set up a variable called numberOfClaimsBeingMade of data type int */
    int numberOfClaimsBeingMade; // removed the = 2

37. Amend the code to ask the user to input the number of claims:

    /*
    Set up a variable called numberOfClaimsBeingMade of data type int
    and assign the variable the value 2
    */
    int numberOfClaimsBeingMade; // removed the 2 int numberOfClaimsBeingMade = 2;

    /*
    Read the user input for the number of claims being made and convert
    the string value to an integer data type using the nextInt() method
    */
    System.*out*.println("How many claims are we wishing to make?\n");

    numberOfClaimsBeingMade = myScanner.nextInt();

38. Click on the **File** menu.

39. Choose **Save All.**
40. Click on the green **Run** button at the top of the screen.
41. Click in the Console window at the bottom of the screen.

The console window will appear and ask the user how many claims they wish to make.

42. Type **2** and press the Enter key.

The console window will appear and ask the user to input the repair shop id.

43. Type **RS000001** and press the Enter key.

The console will now ask the user to input the vehicle policy number.

44. Type **VP000001** and press the Enter key.

The console will now ask the user to input the claim amount.

45. Type **1999.99** and press the Enter key.

The console will now ask the user to input the date of the repair

46. Type **01/10/2021** and press the Enter key.

The display of the details entered for claim 1 will appear in the console window.

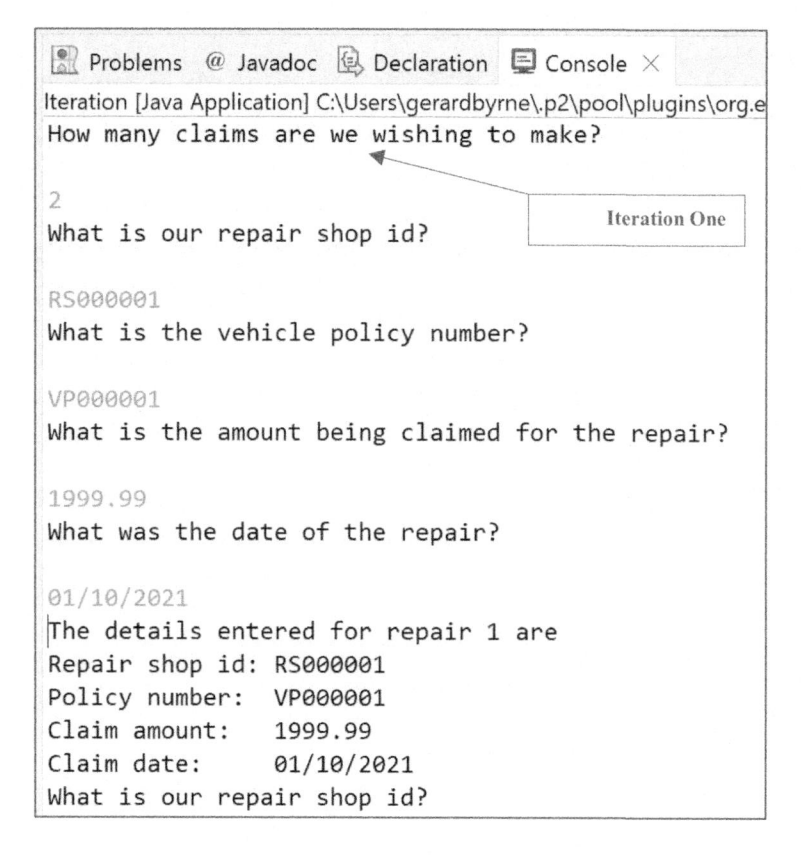

```
Problems  @ Javadoc   Declaration   Console  ×
Iteration [Java Application] C:\Users\gerardbyrne\.p2\pool\plugins\org.e
How many claims are we wishing to make?

2
What is our repair shop id?                    Iteration One

RS000001
What is the vehicle policy number?

VP000001
What is the amount being claimed for the repair?

1999.99
What was the date of the repair?

01/10/2021
The details entered for repair 1 are
Repair shop id: RS000001
Policy number:  VP000001
Claim amount:   1999.99
Claim date:     01/10/2021
What is our repair shop id?
```

Iteration one is now completed, the block of code has been executed. The claims counter will now be incremented by 1 and becomes a 1. The comparison is made to see if the claims counter value is less than 2, and as it is, the iterations continue.

The console window will now ask the user to input the repair shop id.

47. Type **RS000001** and press the Enter key.

The console will now ask the user to input the vehicle policy number.

48. Type **VP001234** and press the Enter key.

The console will now ask the user to input the claim amount.

49. Type **2500.99** and press the Enter key.

The console will now ask the user to input the date of the repair

50. Type **16/08/2021** and press the Enter key.

The display of the details entered for claim 2 will appear in the console window.

```
What is our repair shop id?

RS000001
What is the vehicle policy number?          Iteration Two

VP001234
What is the amount being claimed for the repair?

2500.99
What was the date of the repair?

16/08/2021
The details entered for repair 2 are
Repair shop id: RS000001
Policy number:  VP001234
Claim amount:   2500.99
Claim date:     16/08/2021
```

Iteration two is now completed, the block of code has been executed for the second time. The claims counter will now be incremented by 1 and becomes a 2. The comparison is made to see if the claims counter value is less than 2, and as it is not the iterations will end.

Wow! Very good, we have a nice application that can handle multiple claims from a user.

Break Statement

Control of the for loop is determined by the three sections as shown:

```
        section 1       section 2      section 3
    for(<Start value>; <Condition>; <increment value>)
    {
       <statements>
    }
```

- the first section determines the start value of the counter
- the second section determines when the loop has completed enough iterations
- the third section increments the counter

However, the control may be modified by using the **break** statement. The **break** statement forces a loop to exit immediately.

We will create a variable called maximumNumberOfClaims and set its value to 0. This means that for this example the user will not be able to enter any claims (it's just an example). Now we will check inside the loop if the counter has reached the value set for the maximumNumberOfClaims i.e. 0. If the value of the counter has reached 0 the loop will be exited.

51. Amend the code to implement this break statement by adding the new variable called maximumNumberOfClaims:

    int numberOfClaimsBeingMade; // removed the = 2
    int maximumNumberOfClaims = 0;

52. Amend the code to implement this break statement within an if selection block:

    /* Read the user input for the number of claims being made and convert
       the string value to an integer data type using the nextInt() method */
    System.out.println("How many claims are we wishing to make?\n");
    numberOfClaimsBeingMade = myScanner.nextInt();

    /* As we are using a variable in the loop our code is flexible and can be
       used for any number of claims. An ideal situation and good code.
    */

    for (int claimsCounter= 0; claimsCounter < numberOfClaimsBeingMade; claimsCounter++)
    {
       /*
         We will use the if statement to perform a boolean test and if the test
         produces a true value we will break out of the loop. There is no else
         part to the if statement so if the boolean test produces a false value
         the loop simply continues executing the block of code
       */
       if (claimsCounter == maximumNumberOfClaims)
       {
          /*
            We have reached the maximum number of claims allowed in one session
            so we will break out of the loop early
          */

```
            System.out.println("Breaking out of the loop?\n");
            break;
        }

        /*
          Read the user input for the repair shop id and keep it as a string
        */
        System.out.println("What is our repair shop id?\n");
        repairShopID = myScanner.next();
```

53. Amend the code to display a message that the application has finished:

```
        System.out.println("Policy number:\t" + vehiclePolicyNumber);
        System.out.println("Claim amount:\t" + claimAmount);
        System.out.println("Claim date:\t" + claimDate);
    } // End of for loop

    System.out.println("End of program?\n");
    } // End of main() method
} // End of class
```

54. Click on the **File** menu.
55. Choose **Save All**.
56. Click on the green **Run** button at the top of the screen.
57. Click in the Console window at the bottom of the screen.

The console window will appear and ask the user how many claims they wish to make.

58. When the console window appears **type 3** for the number of claims we wish to make (remember that we have set a variable that will stop the iteration when the counter is 0, so the number entered here will be irrelevant!)
59. Press the **Enter** key.
60. Press the **Enter** key again to continue and close the console window.

The **break** statement has been executed and we are not asked any of the questions as the loop was exited.

```
Problems  @ Javadoc  Declaration  Console  ×
<terminated> Iteration [Java Application] C:\Users\gerardbyrne\
How many claims are we wishing to make?

3
Breaking out of the loop?

End of program?
```

Continue Statement

Control of the loop may also be modified by using the **Continue** statement. The **continue** statement forces the code to move to the next iteration in the loop. So, the loop continues (skipping the rest of the code in the current iteration) unlike the break statement where the loop is exited with no more iterations taking place.

Let's look at a sample scenario where the number of claims to be entered is keyed in as 3.

- we will enter 3 for the number of claims to be made
- when the counter starts the value will be set to 0
- when the check is made it performs a division by 2
- when the division is applied, the remainder is evaluated to see if it is a 0
- if the remainder is a 0, the counter number is an even number and so the code will stop this iteration and continue to the next iteration if there is one
- so, for the first iteration the number is even, and no questions will be asked

- the counter is incremented by 1 and will now have a value of 1
- when the check is made it performs a division by 2
- the remainder is evaluated to see if it is 0, in this case it will not be 0 (it will be 1)
- so, the questions will be asked

- the counter is incremented by 1 and will now have a value of 2
- when the check is made it performs a division by 2
- the remainder is evaluated to see if it is 0, in this case it will be 0

- so, the questions will not be asked

- the counter is incremented by 1 and will now have a value of 3

- the loop will be ended as the loop has been executed three times, but only once was the counter an odd number so the questions were only asked once. We skipped out of the existing loop twice through the use of the continue statement

61. Amend the code by changing the value of the variable maximumNumberOfClaims to 5:

    int numberOfClaimsBeingMade;
    int maximumNumberOfClaims = 5;

62. Amend the code to add a line at the start of the for loop that informs us of the counters current value:

    ```
    /*
      As we are using a variable in the loop our code is flexible and can be
      used for any number of claims. An ideal situation and good code.
    */
    for (int claimsCounter= 0; claimsCounter < numberOfClaimsBeingMade; claimsCounter ++)
    {
    System.out.println("The current value of the counter is :" + claimsCounter + "\n");
    ```

63. Amend the code to implement this continue statement:

    ```
    /*
      We have reached the maximum number of claims allowed in one session
      so we will break out of the loop early
    */
    System.out.println("Breaking out of the loop?\n");
    break;
    }
    ```

    /*
      We will use the if statement to perform a boolean test and if the test
      produces a true value we will continue with the loop but will skip
      out of this current iteration. In this example we will check if the

```
   value of the counter is even (when we divide by 2 the remainder is 0.
   If it is an even number we will skip the rest of this iteration by
   using the continue statement. There is no else part to the if
   statement so if the boolean test produces a false value the loop
   carries on executing the block of code
*/
if (claimsCounter % 2 == 0)
{
   /*
     We have reached the maximum number of claims allowed in one session
     so we will break out of the loop early
   */
   continue;
}

/*
  Read the user input for the repair shop id and keep it as a string
*/
System.out.println("What is our repair shop id?\n");
repairShopID = myScanner.next();
```

64. Click on the **File** menu.
65. Choose **Save All**.
66. Click on the green **Run** button at the top of the screen.
67. Click in the Console window at the bottom of the screen.

The console window will appear and ask the user how many claims they wish to make.

68. Type **3** and press the Enter key.

The console window will show that the current value of the claims counter is 0. The console window will immediately show that the current value of the claims counter is 1. This means no block of code was executed the first time as the 0 value of the claims counter was an even number and as such the continue statement was executed, putting the code to the next iteration, skipping the code in the current iteration.

```
Problems  @ Javadoc  Declaration  Console  X
Iteration [Java Application] C:\Users\gerardbyrne\.p2\pool\plugins\org.
How many claims are we wishing to make?

3
The current value of the counter is :0

The current value of the counter is :1

What is our repair shop id?
```

As the value of the claims counter is now 1 and this is not an even number the block of code in the current iteration is executed. So, the questions are asked.

69. Type **RS000001** for the repair shop id and press the Enter key.

The console will now ask the user to input the vehicle policy number.

70. Type **VP000001** and press the Enter key.

The console will now ask the user to input the claim amount.

71. Type **1999.99** and press the Enter key.

The console will now ask the user to input the date of the repair

72. Type **01/10/2021** and press the Enter key.

Iteration one is now completed, the block of code has been executed. The claims counter will now be incremented by 1 and becomes a 2.

```
Problems   @ Javadoc   Declaration   Console  X
<terminated> Iteration [Java Application] C:\Users\gerardbyrne\.p2\pool\
How many claims are we wishing to make?

3
The current value of the counter is :0

The current value of the counter is :1

What is our repair shop id?

RS000001
What is the vehicle policy number?

VP000001
What is the amount being claimed for the repair?

1999.99
What was the date of the repair?

01/10/2021
The details entered for repair 2 are
Repair shop id: RS000001
Policy number:  VP000001
Claim amount:   1999.99
Claim date:     01/10/2021
The current value of the counter is :2

End of program?
```

The claims counter value of 2 is an even number and as such the continue statement was executed, putting the code to the next iteration, skipping the code in the current iteration. The claims counter will now be incremented by 1 and becomes a 3 and as this is not less than the numberOfClaimsBeingMade the loop has completed and will be exited.

While Loop

When we use a **while loop** it will check a condition and then continue to execute a block of code if the condition evaluates to true. As the condition is evaluated at the start, before each execution, it is possible that the while loop will not execute the block of code at all. The while loop is said to 'execute zero or more times'. So, yes, it is possible that the loop does not execute the block of code.

Like the for loop, the while loop can be exited early, if this is required, by using the **break** statement. It is also possible to have the code move to the next iteration in the loop using the keyword **continue**.

The format of the **while loop** is shown below:

```
while (<Condition>)
{
   <statements>
}
```

Example:

```
int counter = 0;
    while (counter < 2)
    {
        Block of code
        counter++
    }
```

Code Analysis

In the example:
- a variable called counter is set up outside the while loop, it cannot be created inside the brackets () as it can be in the for loop
- the variable is initialised before entering the while loop

- the loop counter is compared with the value 2 and if it less than 2 the execution of the block of code continues

- the loop counter is increased (incremented) by 1

- the Boolean test is enclosed inside the brackets ()

- the block of code to be executed the required number of times is enclosed between curly braces {}

- when the condition is TRUE, the statements in the braces will execute

- once the statements have executed control returns to the beginning of the while loop to check the condition again

- when the condition is FALSE, the while statements in the braces are skipped and execution begins after the closing brace of that block of code

We will use the same example for this exercise as we did in the for loop exercise. To avoid having to enter the code again we can copy and paste from the last program as we use a while loop.

1. Right click on the **com.gerrybyrne.module08** package in the Package Explorer panel.
2. Choose **New**.
3. Choose **Class**.
4. Name the class **WhileIteration**.
5. Put a tick in the checkbox beside the public static void main(String[] args) box.
6. Click on the **Finish** button.
7. Amend the code to set up and initialise the variables etc, copy the code from the last program:

   package com.gerrybyrne.module08;

   import java.util.Scanner;

   public class WhileIteration

```java
{
    public static void main(String[] args)
    {
        Scanner myScanner = new Scanner(System.in);

        /*
        We will set up the variables to be used in the quote application
        The details will be:
        - the repair shop unique id  (String)
            - the vehicle insurance policy number   (String)
            - the claim amount and  (double)
        - the date of the claim  (date)
        */
        String repairShopID;
        String vehiclePolicyNumber;
        String claimDate;
        double claimAmount;

        /*
        Set up variable called numberOfClaimsBeingMade,
        maximumNumberOfClaims,numberOfClaimsEntered of data type int
        */
        int numberOfClaimsBeingMade;
        int maximumNumberOfClaims = 0;
        int numberOfClaimsEntered = 0;
```

8. Amend the code to ask the user how many claims are being made:

```java
        int numberOfClaimsBeingMade;
        int maximumNumberOfClaims = 0;
        int numberOfClaimsEntered = 0;

        /*
        Read the user input for the number of claims being made and convert
        the string value to an integer data type using the nextInt() method
        */
        System.out.println("How many claims are we wishing to make?\n");

        numberOfClaimsBeingMade = myScanner.nextInt();
```

9. Amend the code to include the start of a while loop:

numberOfClaimsBeingMade = myScanner.nextInt();

/*
Here we use the while iteration which uses a Boolean test to see if
the number of claims entered by the user so far is less than the
number of claims being made. If the comparison equates to true then
the while loop block of code is executed. If the comparison equates
to false then the while loop block of code is not executed.
As we are using a variable in the loop our code is flexible and can be
used for any number of claims. An ideal situation and good code.
*/
while (numberOfClaimsEntered < numberOfClaimsBeingMade)
{

10. Amend the code to read the user input from within the while loop, copy the code from the last program:

    while (numberOfClaimsEntered < numberOfClaimsBeingMade)
    {
    /* Read the user input for the repair shop id and keep it as a string */
    System.*out*.println("What is our repair shop id?\n");
    repairShopID = myScanner.next();

    /* Read the user input for the vehicle policy number and keep it as a string */
    System.*out*.println("What is the vehicle policy number?\n");
    vehiclePolicyNumber = myScanner.next();

    /*Read the user input for the repair amount and convert it to a double*/
    System.*out*.println("What is the amount being claimed for the repair?\n");
    claimAmount = myScanner.nextDouble();

    /*Read the user input for the repair date leaving it as a String */
    System.*out*.println("What was the date of the repair?\n");
    claimDate = myScanner.next();

11. Amend the code to display the details that have been entered, copy the code from the last program and make the small amendment to the first line which shows the 'counter':

    /*Read the user input for the repair date leaving it as a String */

```
            System.out.println("What was the date of the repair?\n");
            claimDate = myScanner.next();

            System.out.println("The details entered for repair " + (numberOfClaimsEntered
+ 1) + " are");
            System.out.println("Repair shop id:\t" + repairShopID);
            System.out.println("Policy number:\t" + vehiclePolicyNumber);
            System.out.println("Claim amount:\t" + claimAmount);
            System.out.println("Claim date:\t" + claimDate);

            /* Increment the loop counter by 1 */
            numberOfClaimsEntered++;

        } // End of While loop
```

12. Amend the code to close the Scanner (as is good practise) and add the end of main and class braces:

```
            /* Increment the loop counter by 1 */
            numberOfClaimsEntered++;
        } // End of While loop

        myScanner.close();
        System.out.println("End of program\n");
    } // End of main() method
} // End of WhileIteration class
```

When the code is executed, the user will be asked to input the number of claims to be entered. We will enter 2. When the code is executed, the user will therefore be asked to input 2 sets of details as:

- the counter in the while loop will be the variable called numberOfClaimsEntered which will start at 0
- at the start of the while loop the numberOfClaimsEntered is compared to the variable numberOfClaimsBeingMade(which is 2)
- the comparison produces a true value and the block of code is executed
- next the numberOfClaimsEntered variable is incremented by 1 (it is now 1)

- the numberOfClaimsEntered is now 1 and is compared to the variable numberOfClaimsBeingMade (which is 2)
- the comparison produces a true value and the block of code is executed
- in this example the block of code is execute
- next the numberOfClaimsEntered variable is incremented by 1 (it is now 2)
- the numberOfClaimsEntered is now 2 and is compared to the variable numberOfClaimsBeingMade (2)
- the comparison produces a false value and the block of code is not executed

13. Click on the **File** menu.
14. Choose **Save All**.
15. Click on the green **Run** button at the top of the screen.
16. Click in the Console window at the bottom of the screen.

The console window will appear and ask the user how many claims they wish to make.

17. Type **2** and press the Enter key.

The console window will appear and ask the user to input the repair shop id.

18. Type **RS000001** and press the Enter key.

The console will now ask the user to input the vehicle policy number.

19. Type **VP000001** and press the Enter key.

The console will now ask the user to input the claim amount.

20. Type **1999.99** and press the Enter key.

The console will now ask the user to input the date of the repair

21. Type **01/10/2021** and press the Enter key.

```
Problems  @ Javadoc  Declaration  Console  ×
WhileIteration [Java Application] C:\Users\gerardbyrne\.p2\pool\plugins
How many claims are we wishing to make?

2
What is our repair shop id?

RS000001
What is the vehicle policy number?

VP000001
What is the amount being claimed for the repair?

1999.99
What was the date of the repair?

01/10/2021
The details entered for repair 1 are
Repair shop id: RS000001
Policy number:  VP000001
Claim amount:   1999.99
Claim date:     01/10/2021
What is our repair shop id?
```

Iteration one is now completed, the block of code has been executed. The claims counter, which is the variable numberOfClaimsEntered, will now be incremented by 1 and therefore becomes a 1. The comparison is made to see if this value is less than 2, and as it is (condition is true) the iterations continue.

The console window will now ask the user to input the repair shop id.

22. Type **RS000001** and press the Enter key.

The console will now ask the user to input the vehicle policy number.

23. Type **VP001234** and press the Enter key.

The console will now ask the user to input the claim amount.

24. Type **2500.99** and press the Enter key.

The console will now ask the user to input the date of the repair

25. Type **01/10/2021** and press the Enter key.

Iteration two is now completed, the block of code has been executed for the second time. The claims counter, numberOfClaimsEntered, will now be incremented by 1 and becomes a 2. The comparison is made to see if this value is less than 2 (the number of claims being made), and as it is not (condition is false) the iterations will end.

```
What is our repair shop id?

RS000001
What is the vehicle policy number?

VP001234
What is the amount being claimed for the repair?

2500.99
What was the date of the repair?

01/10/2021
The details entered for repair 2 are
Repair shop id: RS000001
Policy number:  VP001234
Claim amount:   2500.99
Claim date:     01/10/2021
End of program
```

Break Statement

Control of the While loop is determined by the Boolean section (condition) as shown:

       Boolean section
    while (<Condition>)
    {
       <statements>
    }

the boolean section determines if the counter has reached its target.
However, the control may be modified by using the **Break** statement.

The **break** statement forces a loop to exit immediately.

We will now add a break statement as we did with the for loop. We have a variable called **maximumNumberOfClaims** which is set to the value 0. This means that for this example the user will not be able to enter any claims (it's just an example). Now we will check inside the while condition if the counter has reached the maximumNumberOfClaims, i.e. 0. If the value of the counter has reached 0 the loop will be exited.

26. Amend the code to implement this break statement using an if construct inside the while loop:

    ```
    while (numberOfClaimsEntered < numberOfClaimsBeingMade)
    {
      /*
        We will use the if statement to perform a boolean test and if the
        test produces a true value we will break out of the loop.
        If the boolean test produces a false value the loop simply continues
        executing the block of code
      */
      if (numberOfClaimsEntered == maximumNumberOfClaims)
      {
        /*
          We have reached the maximum number of claims allowed in one
          session so we will break out of the loop early
        */
        break;
      }

      /* Read the user input for the repair shop id and keep it as a string */
      System.out.println("What is our repair shop id?\n");
    ```

27. Click on the **File** menu.
28. Choose **Save All**.
29. Click on the green **Run** button at the top of the screen.
30. When the console window appears type **3** for the number of claims we wish to make (remember that we have set a variable that will stop the iteration when the counter is 0, so the number entered here will be irrelevant!).
31. Press the **Enter** key.

The **break** statement has been executed and we are not asked any of the questions as the loop was exited.

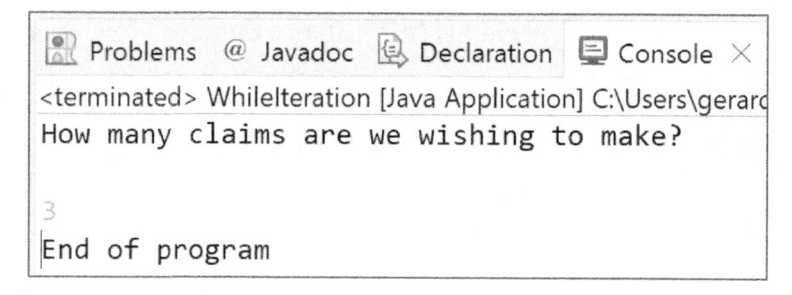

```
Problems  @ Javadoc  Declaration  Console  X
<terminated> WhileIteration [Java Application] C:\Users\gerard
How many claims are we wishing to make?

3
End of program
```

Continue Statement

Control of the while loop may also be modified by using the **Continue** statement. The **continue** statement forces the code to move to the next iteration in the loop. So, the loop continues (skipping the rest of the code in the current iteration) unlike the break statement where the loop is exited with no more iterations taking place. This is exactly the same as we saw in the for loop. We will now add a continue statement in the same way as we did with the for loop.

We will use the same sample scenario as used in the for loop, where the number of claims to be entered is keyed in as 3.

32. Amend the code by changing the value of the variable maximumNumberOfClaims to 5

    int numberOfClaimsBeingMade;
    int maximumNumberOfClaims = 5; // was int maximumNumberOfClaims = 0;
    int numberOfClaimsEntered = 0;

33. Amend the code to add a line at the start of the for loop that informs us of the counters current value:

    while (numberOfClaimsEntered < numberOfClaimsBeingMade)
    {
    System.*out*.println("The current value of the counter is :" + numberOfClaimsEntered + "\n");

34. Amend the code to implement this continue statement, after the end of the if statement:

```java
if (numberOfClaimsEntered == maximumNumberOfClaims)
{
    /*
        We have reached the maximum number of claims allowed in one
        session so we will break out of the loop early
    */
    break;
}
/*
    We will use the if statement to perform a boolean test and if the test
    produces a true value we will continue with the loop but will skip out
    of this current iteration. In this example we will check if the value
    of the counter is even (when we divide by 2 the remainder is 0). If
    it is an even number we will skip the rest of this iteration by using
    the continue statement. There is no else part to the if statement so
    if the boolean test produces a false value the loop carries on
    executing the block of code
*/
if (numberOfClaimsEntered% 2 == 0)
{
    /*
        We have reached the maximum number of claims allowed in one
        session so we will break out of the loop early.
        Increment the loop counter by 1
    */
    numberOfClaimsEntered++;
    continue;
}

/*
    Read the user input for the repair shop id and keep it as a string
*/
System.out.println("What is our repair shop id?\n");
repairShopID = myScanner.next();
```

35. Click on the **File** menu.
36. Choose **Save All**.
37. Click on the green **Run** button at the top of the screen.

The console window will appear and ask the user to input the number of claims to be made.

38. Type **3** and press the Enter key.

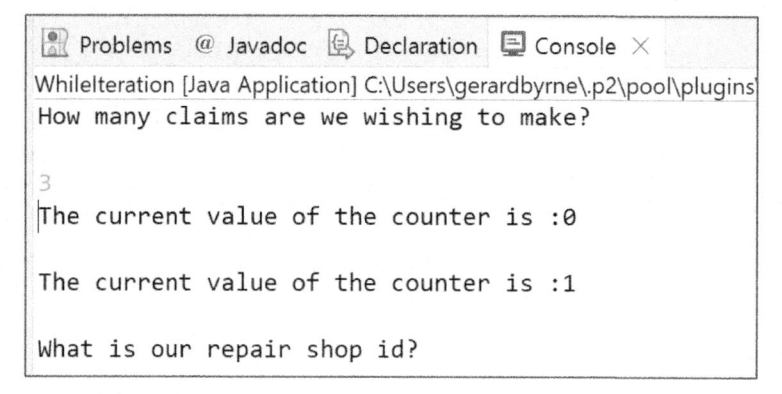

```
Problems  @ Javadoc  Declaration  Console ×
WhileIteration [Java Application] C:\Users\gerardbyrne\.p2\pool\plugins
How many claims are we wishing to make?

3
The current value of the counter is :0

The current value of the counter is :1

What is our repair shop id?
```

The console window will show that the current value of the claims counter is 0. The console window will immediately show that the current value of the claims counter is 1. This means no block of code was executed the first time as the 0 value of the (numberOfClaimsEntered) counter was an even number and as such the continue statement was executed, putting the code to the next iteration, skipping the code in the current iteration.

As the value of the counter is now 1 and this is not an even number the block of code in the current iteration is executed. So, the questions are asked.

39. Type **RS000001** for the repair shop id and press the Enter key.

The console will now ask the user to input the vehicle policy number.

40. Type **VP000001** and press the Enter key.

The console will now ask the user to input the claim amount.

41. Type **1999.99** and press the Enter key.

The console will now ask the user to input the date of the repair

42. Type **01/10/2021** and press the Enter key.

Iteration one is now completed, the block of code has been executed. The counter will now be incremented by 1 and becomes a 2.

```
What is our repair shop id?

RS000001
What is the vehicle policy number?

VP000001
What is the amount being claimed for the repair?

1999.99
What was the date of the repair?

01/10/2021
The details entered for repair 2 are
Repair shop id: RS000001
Policy number:  VP000001
Claim amount:   1999.99
Claim date:     01/10/2021
The current value of the counter is :2

End of program
```

The counter value of 2 is an even number and as such the continue statement was executed, putting the code to the next iteration, skipping the code in the current iteration. The counter will now be incremented by 1 and becomes a 3 and as this is not less than the variable numberOfClaimsBeingMade the loop has completed and will be exited.

Do (While) loop

The **do loop** is like the while loop, except that it has the Boolean check at the end rather than the start**.** This means that the do loop is guaranteed to execute at least once unlike the while loop which may never be executed, remember the 'execute zero or more times' phrase associated with the while loop. The do while loop will check a condition at the end of the first iteration and then continue to execute the loop if the Boolean condition evaluates as true.

The do while loop is said to 'execute at least once'. Like the for and while loops, the do while loop can be exited early, if this is required, by using the **break** statement. It is also possible to have the code move to the next iteration in the loop by using the keyword **continue**.

The format of the **do while loop** is shown below:
```
do
{
   <statements>
}
while (<Condition>)
```

Example:
```
int counter = 0;
do
{
  Block of code
  counter++
} while (counter < 2);
```

Code Analysis

In the example:

- a variable called counter is set up outside the do while loop, it cannot be created inside the brackets () as it can be in the for loop

- the variable is initialised before entering the do while loop

- the block of code between the {} braces is executed

- inside the block of code the counter is incremented

- the loop counter is compared with the value 2 and if it less than 2 the execution of the block of code continues

- the loop counter is increased (incremented) by 1

- the Boolean test is enclosed inside the brackets ()

- when the condition is true, the statements in the braces will execute

- once the statements have executed, control returns to the beginning of the do while loop

- when the condition is false, the while statements in the braces are skipped, and execution begins after the closing brace of that block of code, the next code statement

We will use the same example for this exercise as we did in the while loop exercise. To avoid having to enter the code again we can copy and paste code as required.

1. Right click on the **com.gerrybyrne.module08** package
2. Choose **New**.
3. Choose **Class**.
4. Name the class **DoWhileIteration.java.**
5. Put a tick in the checkbox beside the public static void main(String[] args) box.
6. Click on the **Finish** button.
7. Amend the code to add the Scanner class and instantiate it inside the main() method:

```java
package com.gerrybyrne.module08;

import java.util.Scanner;

public class DoWhileIteration
{
    public static void main(String[] args)
    {
        Scanner myScanner = new Scanner(System.in);
```

```
    } // End of main method()
} // End of DoWhileIteration class
```

8. Amend the code to add the variables we will use in the code after the Scanner instantiation:

```
Scanner myScanner = new Scanner(System.in);

/*
    We will setup our variables that will be used in the quote application
    The details will be:
        - the repair shop unique id              (String)
        - the vehicle insurance policy number    (String)
        - the date of the claim                  (String)
        - the claim amount and                   (double)
*/
String repairShopID;
String vehiclePolicyNumber;
String claimDate;
double claimAmount;
int numberOfClaimsBeingMade;

/* This variable will be used to maintain a count for the number
   of claims that have been entered by the user
*/
int numberOfClaimsEntered =0;
```

9. Amend the code to request user input and assign the input value to the variable numberOfClaimsBeingMade:

```
/* This variable will be used to maintain a count for the number
   of claims that have been entered by the user
*/
int numberOfClaimsEntered =0;

/*
    Read the user input for the number of claims being made and convert
    the string value to an integer data type using the nextInt() method
*/
System.out.println("How many claims are we wishing to make?\n");
```

numberOfClaimsBeingMade = myScanner.nextInt();

10. Amend the code to add the do while loop:

   System.*out*.println("How many claims are we wishing to make?\n");
   numberOfClaimsBeingMade = myScanner.nextInt();

   /*
      Here we use the do iteration which means at least one iteration will be performed.
      The do iteration uses a Boolean test after iteration one to see if the number of claims
      entered by the user so far is less than the number of claims being made.
      If the comparison equates to true then the do loop block of code is executed again.
      If the comparison equates to false then the do loop block of code is not executed.
      As we are using a variable in the loop our code is flexible and can be used for any
      number of claims. An ideal situation and good code.
   */
   do
   {
   System.*out*.println("The current value of the counter is :" +
   numberOfClaimsEntered + "\n");

   /*
      Read the user input for the repair shop id and keep it as a string
   */
   System.*out*.println("What is our repair shop id?\n");
   repairShopID = myScanner.next();

   /*
      Read the user input for the vehicle policy number and keep it
      as a string */
   System.*out*.println("What is the vehicle policy number?\n");
   vehiclePolicyNumber = myScanner.next();

   /*
      Read the user input for the repair amount and convert it to
      a double
   */
   System.*out*.println("What is the amount being claimed for the repair?\n");
   claimAmount = myScanner.nextDouble();

   /*

Read the user input for the repair date leaving it as a String
*/

```java
System.out.println("What was the date of the repair?\n");
claimDate = myScanner.next();

System.out.println("The details entered for repair " + (numberOfClaimsEntered + 1) + " are");
System.out.println("Repair shop id:\t" + repairShopID);
System.out.println("Policy number:\t" + vehiclePolicyNumber);
System.out.println("Claim amount:\t" + claimAmount);
System.out.println("Claim date:\t" + claimDate);
    /*
    Increment the loop counter by 1
    */
    numberOfClaimsEntered++;
} while (numberOfClaimsEntered < numberOfClaimsBeingMade);

System.out.println("End of program?\n");
myScanner.close();

} // End of main() method
} // End of DoWhileIteration class
```

When the code is executed, the user will be asked to input the number of claims to be entered. We will enter **2** and the user will therefore be asked to input 2 sets of details as:

- the block of code is executed immediately, remember the statement associated with the do while loop, 'execute at least once'
- the counter in the do while loop will be the variable called numberOfClaimsEntered which will start at 0 as it enters the loop
- at the end of the block of code the variable called numberOfClaimsEntered is incremented and is now 1
- at the end of the do while loop the numberOfClaimsEntered is compared to the variable numberOfClaimsBeingEntered (which is 2)
- the comparison produces a true value and the block of code is executed
- in this example the block of code is executed

- next the numberOfClaimsEntered variable is incremented by 1 and is now 2
- at the end of the do while loop the numberOfClaimsEntered is compared to the variable numberOfClaimsBeingEntered (which is 2)
- the comparison produces a false value and the block of code is not executed

11. Click on the **File** menu.
12. Choose **Save All.**
13. Click on the green **Run** button at the top of the screen.

The console window will appear and ask the user to input the number of claims to be entered.

14. Type **2** and press the Enter key.

The console window will appear and ask the user to input the repair shop id.

15. Type **RS000001** and press the Enter key.

The console will now ask the user to input the vehicle policy number.

16. Type **VP000001** and press the Enter key.

The console will now ask the user to input the claim amount.

17. Type **1999.99** and press the Enter key.

The console will now ask the user to input the date of the repair

18. Type **01/10/2021** and press the Enter key.

```
Problems  @ Javadoc  Declaration  Console  X
DoWhileIteration [Java Application] C:\Users\gerardbyrne\.p2\pool\plu
How many claims are we wishing to make?

2
The current value of the counter is :0

What is our repair shop id?

RS000001
What is the vehicle policy number?

VP000001
What is the amount being claimed for the repair?

1999.99
What was the date of the repair?

01/10/2021
The details entered for repair 1 are
Repair shop id: RS000001
Policy number:  VP000001
Claim amount:   1999.99
Claim date:     01/10/2021
The current value of the counter is :1

What is our repair shop id?
```

Iteration one is now completed, the block of code has been executed and the counter has been incremented to 1. The comparison is made to see if the counter value is less than 2, and as it is the iterations continue.

The console window will now ask the user to input the repair shop id.

19. Type **RS000001** and press the Enter key.

The console will now ask the user to input the vehicle policy number.

20. Type **VP001234** and press the Enter key.

The console will now ask the user to input the claim amount.

21. Type **2500.99** and press the Enter key.

The console will now ask the user to input the date of the repair

22. Type **01/10/2021** and press the Enter key.

```
What is our repair shop id?

RS000001
What is the vehicle policy number?

VP001234
What is the amount being claimed for the repair?

2500.99
What was the date of the repair?

01/10/2021
The details entered for repair 2 are
Repair shop id: RS000001
Policy number:  VP001234
Claim amount:   2500.99
Claim date:     01/10/2021
End of program?
```

Iteration two is now completed, the block of code has been executed for the second time. The claims counter, numberOfClaimsEntered, will now be incremented by 1 and becomes a 2. The comparison is made to see if this value is less than 2 (the number of claims being made), and, as it is not the do while loop exits, and the iterations will end.

The code will now move to the next line after the Do While loop, which ends the program.

Break Statement

Control of the Do While loop is determined by the Boolean section as shown:

    do {
      <statements>
    } **while** (<Condition>)
        Boolean section

The Boolean section determines if the counter has reached its target. However, the control may be modified by using the **Break** statement, where the **break** statement forces a do while loop to exit immediately.

We will now add a break statement in the same way as we did with the for and while loop. We will create a variable called maximumNumberOfClaims and set its value to 0. Now we will check inside the while condition if the counter has reached the value set for the maximumNumberOfClaims i.e. 0. If the value of the counter has reached 0 the loop will be exited.

23. Amend the code to add a variable to hold the maximum number of claims:

    ```
    double claimAmount;
    int numberOfClaimsBeingMade;

    int maximumNumberOfClaims = 0;
    ```

24. Amend the code to implement this break statement within an if construct:

    ```
    do
    {
      System.out.println("The current value of the counter is :" + numberOfClaimsEntered + "\n");
      /*
          We will use the if statement to perform a boolean test and if the test
          produces a true value we will break out of the loop. If the boolean
          test produces a false value the loop simply continues executing the
          block of code
      */
      if (numberOfClaimsEntered == maximumNumberOfClaims)
      {
        /*
           We have reached the maximum number of claims allowed in one
           session so we will break out of the loop early
        */
        break;
      }
      /*
         Read the user input for the repair shop id and keep it as a string
      */
      System.out.println("What is our repair shop id?\n");
    ```

repairShopID = myScanner.next();

25. Click on the **File** menu.
26. Choose **Save All**.
27. Click on the green **Run** button at the top of the screen.
28. When the console window appears type **3** as the number of claims we wish to make (remember that we have set a variable that will stop the iteration when the counter is 0, so the number entered here will be irrelevant to the extent that the loop will definitely be entered and the break statement will be executed).
29. Press the **Enter** key.

The **break** statement has been executed and we are not asked any of the questions as the loop was exited.

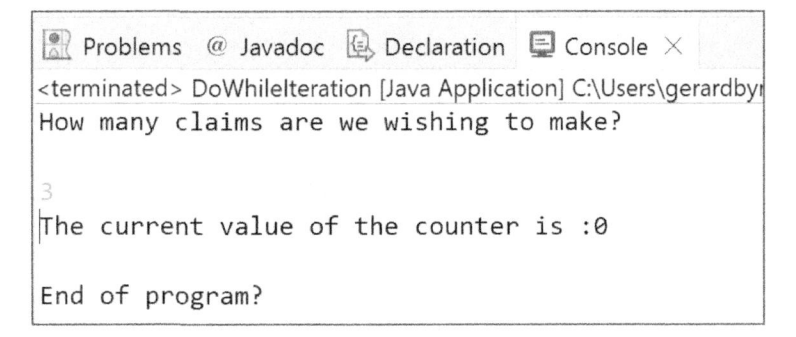

```
Problems  @ Javadoc  Declaration  Console  ×
<terminated> DoWhileIteration [Java Application] C:\Users\gerardby
How many claims are we wishing to make?

3
The current value of the counter is :0

End of program?
```

Continue Statement

Control of the do while loop may also be modified by using the **Continue** statement. The **continue** statement forces the code to move to the next iteration in the loop. So, the loop continues (skipping the rest of the code in the current iteration) unlike the break statement where the loop is exited with no more iterations taking place. This is exactly the same as we saw in the for and while loops. We will now add a continue statement in the same way as we did with the for loop.

We will use the same sample scenario as used in the for loop, where the number of claims to be entered is keyed in as 3.

30. Amend the code to implement this continue statement:

```
double claimAmount;
int numberOfClaimsBeingMade;
int maximumNumberOfClaims = 5;
```

31. Amend the code to implement this continue statement within an if construct:

    ```
    if (numberOfClaimsEntered == maximumNumberOfClaims)
    {
      /*
        We have reached the maximum number of claims allowed in one
        session so we will break out of the loop early
      */
      break;
    }
    /*
      We will use the if statement to perform a boolean test and if the test produces a true
      value we will continue with the loop but will skip out of this current iteration. In this
      example we will check if the value of the counter is even (when we divide by 2 the
      remainder is 0). If it is an even number we will skip the rest of this iteration by using
      the continue statement. There is no else part to the if statement so if the boolean test
      produces a false value the loop carries on executing the block of code */
    if (numberOfClaimsEntered % 2 == 0)
    {
      /* We have reached the maximum number of claims allowed in one
         session so we will break out of the loop early.
         Increment the loop counter by 1 */
      numberOfClaimsEntered++;
      continue;
    }

    /* Read the user input for the repair shop id and keep it as a string */
    System.out.println("What is our repair shop id?\n");
    repairShopID = myScanner.next();
    ```

32. Click on the **File** menu.
33. Choose **Save All**.
34. Click on the green **Run** button at the top of the screen.

The console window will appear and ask the user to input the number of claims to be made.

35. Type **3** and press the Enter key.

The console window will show that the current value of the claims counter is 0. The console window will immediately show that the current value of the claims counter is 1. This means no block of code was executed the first time, as the 0 value of the counter (numberOfClaimsEntered) was an even number and as such the continue statement was executed, putting the code to the next iteration, skipping the code in the current iteration.

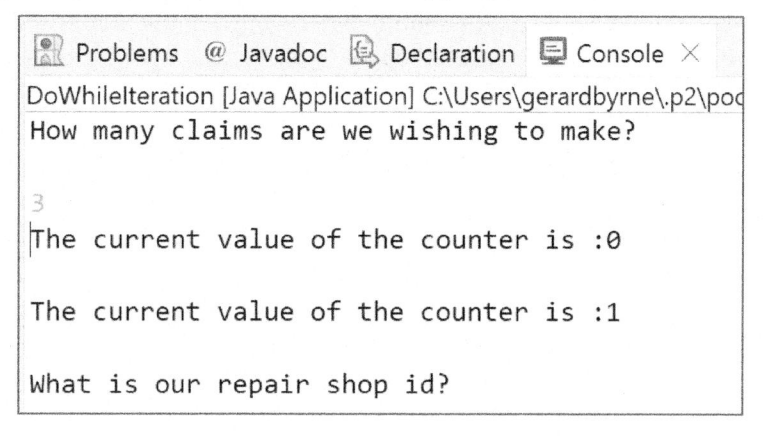

```
Problems  @ Javadoc  Declaration  Console  X
DoWhileIteration [Java Application] C:\Users\gerardbyrne\.p2\pod
How many claims are we wishing to make?

3
The current value of the counter is :0

The current value of the counter is :1

What is our repair shop id?
```

As the value of the counter is now 1 and this is not an even number the block of code in the current iteration is executed and consequently the questions are asked.

36. Type **RS000001** for the repair shop id and press the Enter key.

The console will now ask the user to input the vehicle policy number.

37. Type **VP000001** and press the Enter key.

The console will now ask the user to input the claim amount.

38. Type **1999.99** and press the Enter key.

The console will now ask the user to input the date of the repair

39. Type **01/10/2021** and press the Enter key.

```
What is our repair shop id?

RS000001
What is the vehicle policy number?

VP000001
What is the amount being claimed for the repair?

1999.99
What was the date of the repair?

01/10/2021
The details entered for repair 2 are
Repair shop id: RS000001
Policy number:  VP000001
Claim amount:   1999.99
Claim date:     01/10/2021
The current value of the counter is :2

End of program?
```

Iteration one is now completed, the block of code has been executed. The counter will now be incremented by 1 and becomes a 2. The counter value of 2 is an even number and as such the continue statement was executed, putting the code to the next iteration, skipping the code in the current iteration. The counter will now be incremented by 1 and becomes a 3 and as this is not less than the numberOfClaimsBeingMade the do while loop has completed and will be exited.

We will learn about the foreach statement when we study the next module on arrays.

Module summary

In this module we have learnt about a very important programming concept called iteration.

We have learnt that:

- iteration in Java can have different formats, including
    - the **for loop**
    - the **while loop**
    - the **do loop**
    - the **foreach loop** which will be covered more in the arrays module
    - the **break** statement
    - the **continue** statement
- we can have more than one class in a package

Yet another great achievement for us in our learning. Be proud of the learning to date.

Our dot just got bigger

Program Practically

Java

Module 09

Arrays

Data structure
'Collection'
Homogeneous data types
Fixed size
Declare and create an array

Gerry Byrne

Program Practically - Arrays

We learnt in module 8 that:

Iteration is a very important programming concept in all programming languages. To use iteration in our Java code we have a number of options and the best option to choose will depend on the particular task the code has to perform. The different formats for the iteration construct are the for construct, the while construct, the do while construct and the foreach loop. Within the constructs there are options to break out of the iterations completely or to break out of a particular iteration using the continue keyword. In terms of the project structure we once again used the ability to have multiple classes within a package where each class has to have a unique name.

Introduction to single dimensional array

An array is a list of data items all of the same type. We could also describe it as a **collection** of data items all of the same type. We could have an array which contains a:

- list of integers
- list of real numbers
- list of characters
- list of strings

If we think about a Java application (program) which is applicable to a business that sells food products it may contain arrays for:

- vegetables   -   this could be list of strings
- cheeses   -   this could be list of strings
- product codes -   this could be list of integers

If we think about a Java application (program) which is applicable to a business that sells insurance, it may contain arrays for:

- insurance types   -   this could be list of strings
- account numbers   -   this could be list of integers
- insurance costs   -   this could be list of doubles
- vehicle manufacturers -   this could be a list of strings
- vehicle models   -   this could be a list of strings

An array is therefore a list of related items that can be treated by Java as one **object**. We could equally say that an array is a number of variables which can be treated as one **object.** So, when we think of an array we should understand that we are dealing with individual items, but with the added advantage of them being organised for us in one object.

If we have the array object with the data items 'lumped' together into one object we are said to have what is called a **data structure**. In programming, data structures may be very complex or more simplistic, and will be in the form of a sequence of data items such as a data **record** or **array**. In a program for a playing card game, like solitaire, we might want to keep a record which holds information about a card i.e. the suit and the value. This really means we have two fields in the record. With the Java programming language, we have access to data structures which we can use to accommodate this record. Such structures in Java include an **Array** and an **ArrayList**.

When declaring an **array** in Java we must abide by some basic rules:
- the array must be assigned a **data type**
- after the data type will be an **open square bracket** followed by a **closing square bracket**
- the square brackets can come after the data type **or** after the array identifier name
- the array will have a single name which is called its **identifier**

- the array is **fixed size** and cannot be made bigger or smaller, so it is not a dynamic structure like an ArrayList, which we will look at later

When we initialise or populate the array we must ensure that each item in the array is of the same data type, the one identified by the data type assigned to the array so we say an array is **homogenous** (having similarity in structure)

When we wish to access an item in the array we must refer to the item by a **subscript** or **index** which gives its position within the array. In Java, arrays are **zero indexed** which simply means that the first element of the array has an index of zero. Arrays are common across nearly all programming languages and in each language they are used in a similar manner.

In Java there is support for the following array types:
- Single-dimensional arrays
- Multidimensional arrays
- Jagged arrays (also known as an array-of-arrays)

We will look at single dimensional arrays in more detail and will see how to
- declare the array
- initialise the array
- reference the members of the arra

We will see that there are different ways to declare and create arrays and different ways to initialise the arrays, so, it is important at the outset to understand that we will find our own preferred option from the various approaches. Each approach will have its advantages and disadvantages but as a developer we will usually have a preferred option. On the other hand, as a developer we will spend much of our time maintaining code rather than writing new code and often the code we maintain has not been written by us, so we need to understand all the approaches.

Single Dimensional Arrays

A single dimensional or one-dimensional array is a list of data items all of the same data type. It can be thought of a type of linear array. At the start of this module we read that a Java application for a business that sells insurance could contain arrays for:

- insurance types   -   this could be list of strings
- account numbers   -   this could be list of integers
- insurance costs   -   this could be list of doubles
- vehicle manufacturers   -   this could be a list of strings
- vehicle models   -   this could be a list of strings

Taking this theme a little further we could see that the arrays might contain data as shown:

- a list of insurancetypes (strings)

    {"Auto", "SUV 4x4", "Motorcycle", "Motorhome", "Snowmobile", "Boat"}

Another way to think of the single dimensional array is as a table with rows and columns. In the case of a single dimensional array there will only be a single row with the required number of columns.

Array name	[0]	[1]	[2]	[3]	[4]	[5]
insurancetypes	Auto	SUV 4x4	Motorcycle	Motorhome	Snowmobile	Boat

Now, based on what was stated earlier about the basic rules to be abided by when declaring an array, we could write the code for this example as:

```
String[]  insurancetypes = new String [6];
insurancetypes [0] = "Auto";
insurancetypes [1] = "SUV 4x4";
insurancetypes [2] = "Motorcycle";
insurancetypes [3] = "Motorhome";
insurancetypes [4] = "Snowmobile";
insurancetypes [5] = "Boat";
```

- a list of account numbers (integers)

{000001, 001122, 002233, 003344, 004455, 005566}

Thinking of this single dimensional array as a row with columns it could be represented as:

Array name	[0]	[1]	[2]	[3]	[4]	[5]
insurancetypes	000001	001122	002233	003344	004455	005566

Now, based on what was stated earlier about the basic rules to be abided by when declaring an array, we could write the code for this example as:

```
int[] accountnumber = new int [6];
accountnumber [0] = 000011;
accountnumber [1] = 001122;
accountnumber [2] = 002233;
accountnumber [3] = 003344;
accountnumber [4] = 004455;
accountnumber [5] = 005566;
```

- a list of insurance costs (doubles)

{104.99, 105.99, 106.99, 107.99, 108.99, 109.99}

Thinking of this single dimensional array as a row with columns it could be represented as:

Array name	[0]	[1]	[2]	[3]	[4]	[5]
insurancepremium	104.99	105.99	106.99	107.99	108.99	109.99

Now, based on what was stated earlier about the basic rules to be abided by when declaring an array, we could write the code for this example as:

double[] insurancepremium= new double[6];
insurancepremium [0] = 104.99;
insurancepremium [1] = 105.99;
insurancepremium [2] = 106.99;
insurancepremium [3] = 107.99;
insurancepremium [4] = 108.99;
insurancepremium [5] = 109.99;

Now that we have the concept of an array being a **collection**, a **container**, a **store**, for items of the same data type we can look at how to code the implementation of an array. Like many things in life, we have choice. So, Java gives us choices (different techniques) to setup and use arrays.

Choice 1:   **Declaring and creating an array in two stages**

Stage 1 – Declare

In Java the single dimensional arrays we have just considered can be **declared** as shown:

      string[] insurancetypes;   or   string insurancetypes[];

      int[] accountnumber;   or   int accountnumber[];

      double[] insurancepremium;   or   double insurancepremium[];

When we say that we are **declaring** an array in Java we are really saying that **we want to use an array which will consist of items of the data type stated**, but it will not exist yet.

Stage 2 – Create

Now, when an array has been declared it needs to be **created**. To create the array, it must be **instantiated,** and this can be achieved by using the **new** keyword syntax.

The single dimensional arrays we have just considered can be **created** as shown:

      string[] insurancetypes;   **declaration**
      insurancetypes   =   new string[6];   **creation**

      int[] accountnumber;   **declaration**
      accountnumber   =   new int[6];   **creation**

      double[] insurancepremium;   **declaration**
      insurancepremium   =   new double[6];   **creation**

Instantiating the array sets aside the required memory resources for the array of the specified size and data type.

Choice 2: Declaring and creating an array in one stage

The single dimensional arrays we have just considered can be **declared** and **created** (**instantiated**) in one stage as shown below:

declaration		creation
string[] insurancetypes	=	new string[6];
int[] accountnumber	=	new int[6];
double[] insurancepremium	=	new double[6];

In each line of code we are:

- declaring the data type of the array (string, int, double)
- stating that the array is single dimensional (this is the [ ] part)
- giving the array its name (insurancetype, accountnumber, insurancepremium)
- instantiating the array with the new keyword
- saying it will contain 6 elements

The statement

    string[] insurancetypes = **new** string[6];

creates an array that can hold 6 strings and sets the array name as insurancetypes.

The newly created array is automatically filled with nulls. In Java, a newly created array is filled with the default value of the designated data type, as shown in the table below.

Value type	Default value
boolean	false
byte	0
short	0
int	0
long	0L
float	0.0f
double	0.0d

char	'\0'
String (or any object)	null
decimal	0.0M

The statement

    int[] accountnumber = new int[6];

creates an array that can hold 6 integer values and sets the array name as accountnumber.

The newly created array is automatically filled with zeros.

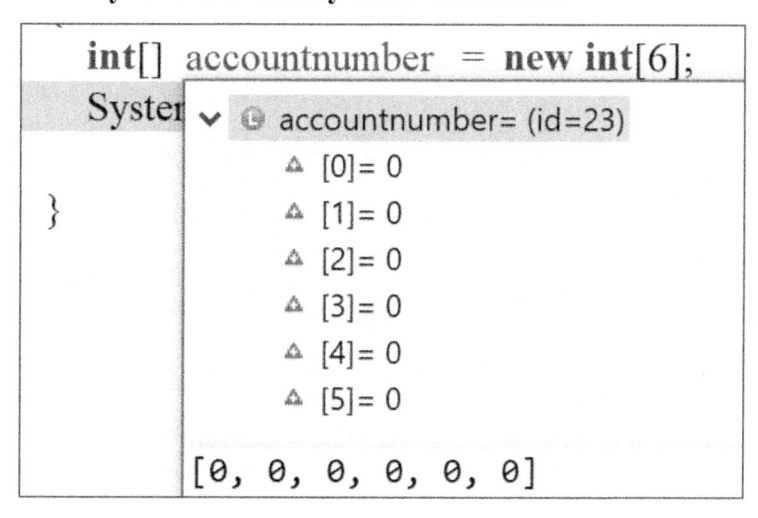

```
int[] accountnumber = new int[6];
System
   accountnumber= (id=23)
      [0]= 0
      [1]= 0
      [2]= 0
      [3]= 0
      [4]= 0
      [5]= 0
   [0, 0, 0, 0, 0, 0]
```

The statement   double[] insurancepremium = new double[6];

creates an array that can hold 6 double values and sets the array name as insurancepremium.

The newly created array of is automatically filled with 0.0 values.

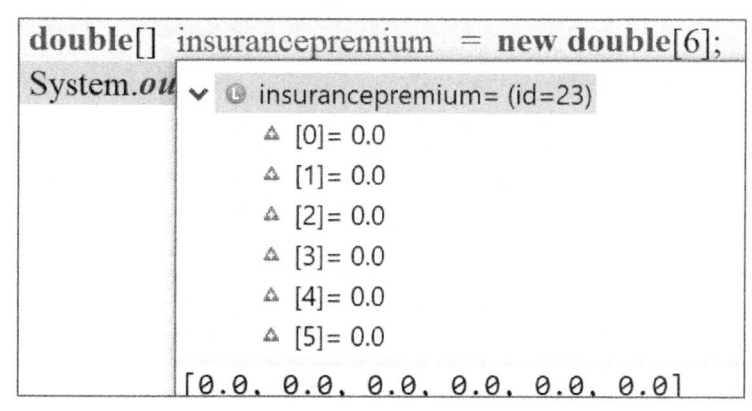

```
double[] insurancepremium = new double[6];
System.ou
   insurancepremium= (id=23)
      [0]= 0.0
      [1]= 0.0
      [2]= 0.0
      [3]= 0.0
      [4]= 0.0
      [5]= 0.0
   [0.0, 0.0, 0.0, 0.0, 0.0, 0.0]
```

Referencing the array elements

Now that we have declared, created and instantiated arrays we need to have a way to access the elements of the arrays so we can use them in our code as required. Java allows us to access array elements if two things are known:

- the **array name**
- the **numeric position** of the element we wish to access, remembering what was said earlier about Java using zero based referencing

    example   arrayname[position in array - 1]

                                  insurancetypes[2]

So, what are the names of the elements in the array, or put another way, what are the names of the variables in the array:

Insurance type single dimensional array

insurancetypes[0] = "Auto";	The first item in the array is indexed as 0
insurancetypes[1] = "SUV 4x4";	The second item in the array is indexed as 1
insurancetypes[2] = "Motorcycle";	The third item in the array is indexed as 2
insurancetypes[3] = "Motorhome";	The fourth item in the array is indexed as 3
insurancetypes[4] = "Snowmobile";	The fifth item in the array is indexed as 4
insurancetypes[5] = "Boat";	The sixth item in the array is indexed as 5

Account number single dimensional array

accountnumber [0] = 000011;	The first item in the array is indexed as 0
accountnumber [1] = 001122;	The second item in the array is indexed as 1
accountnumber [2] = 002233;	The third item in the array is indexed as 2
accountnumber [3] = 003344;	The fourth item in the array is indexed as 3
accountnumber [4] = 004455;	The fifth item in the array is indexed as 4
accountnumber [5] = 005566;	The sixth item in the array is indexed as 5

Insurance cost single dimensional array

insurancepremium [0] = 104.99;	The first item in the array is indexed as 0
insurancepremium [1] = 105.99;	The second item in the array is indexed as 1
insurancepremium [2] = 106.99;	The third item in the array is indexed as 2
insurancepremium [3] = 107.99;	The fourth item in the array is indexed as 3
insurancepremium [4] = 108.99;	The fifth item in the array is indexed as 4
insurancepremium [5] = 109.99;	The sixth item in the array is indexed as 5

Exercise One - Declare and create string arrays in 2 stages with no initialisation

1. Right click on the **src** folder.
2. Choose **New**.
3. Choose **Package**.
4. Name the package **com.gerrybyrne.module09**.
5. Click the **Finish** button.
6. Right click on the package icon.
7. Choose **New**.
8. Choose **Class**.
9. Name the class **Arrays**.
10. Put a tick in the checkbox beside the public static void main(String[] args) box.
11. Click on the **Finish** button.

The **Arrays** class code will appear in the editor window and will be similar to the following:

package com.gerrybyrne.module09;

public class Arrays
{
    public static void main(String[] args)
    {
        // TODO Auto-generated method stub
    } // End of main method()
} // End of DoWhileIteration class

As we have seen earlier and have coded as an example - when a vehicle is involved in an accident and has to be repaired, the repair shop has to supply specific details to the insurance company so they can be reimbursed for the costs. The details required are:

- the repair shop unique id   (String)
- the vehicle insurance policy number   (String)
- the claim amount and   (double)
- the date of the claim   (date)

When we coded this program as part of the last module on iteration, we were aware that any data entered was not stored by the program code. We were made aware that this 'flaw' would be rectified using an array. So, now the time has come to amend the last program so that the data entered by the repair shop will be stored, for the duration that the program runs.

To do this we will need to:

- **declare an array** – we need to decide what data type the array will hold

  Remember from the information at the start of this module, an array can only hold variables of the **same data type**, an array is **homogenous**. We have Strings, a double and a Date (as a String), so what data type will we us? Well, the answer is the String data type. This will mean that the double and the Date will have to be converted to a string value.

- use a name for the array. We will use **repairShopClaims** for the array name

- **create the array** – using the new keyword and stating the size of the array

  Remember from the information at the start of this module, an array has a fixed size and the compiler needs to know the size of the array at compile time.

- add the values to the array in correct position

Let's code some Java

1. Amend the code to create an instance of the Scanner class, so we can accept use input, calling the instance myScanner and importing the Scanner class.

   package com.gerrybyrne.module09;

   import java.util.Scanner;

   public class Arrays
   {
      public static void main(String[] args)
      {
         Scanner myScanner = **new** Scanner(System.*in*);

      } // End of main method()
   } // End of DoWhileIteration class

2. Amend the code to declare and create the array that will hold the 8 items of data input by the user:

   public static void main(String[] args)
   {
      Scanner myScanner = **new** Scanner(System.*in*);
   /*
      The array is going to hold the data for 2 claims. Each claim has
      four pieces of information. The number of data items is therefore
         2 multiplied by 4 = 8. So, we will make the array for this example
         of size 8. Not the best way to do things, but fine for now.
         */
      String[] repairShopClaims = **new** String[8];
      } // End of main method()
   } // End of DoWhileIteration class

3. Amend the code to add the variables to be used, some variables are initialised:

   String[] repairShopClaims = **new** String[8];

```
/*
    We will setup our variables that will be used in the quote application
    The details will be:
        - the repair shop unique id       (String)
        - the vehicle insurance policy number  (String)
        - the claim amount and  (double)
        - the date of the claim   (String)
*/
String repairShopID;
String vehiclePolicyNumber;
double claimAmount;
String claimDate;
int numberOfClaimsBeingMade;
int numberOfClaimsEntered = 0;
int arrayPositionCounter = 0;

    } // End of main method()
} // End of DoWhileIteration class
```

4. Amend the code to ask the user to input the number of claims being made, read the user input, convert it to an int and assign it to the variable numberOfClaimsBeingMade:

```
int numberOfClaimsBeingMade;
int numberOfClaimsEntered = 0;
int arrayPositionCounter = 0;

/*
    Read the user input for the number of claims being made and convert
    the string value to an integer data type
*/
System.out.println("How many claims are we wishing to make?\n");
numberOfClaimsBeingMade = myScanner.nextInt();

    } // End of main method()
} // End of DoWhileIteration class
```

5. Amend the code to include the start of a do-while loop which will iterate as many times as the user requested and display the current value of the counter for reference:

```
        System.out.println("How many claims are we wishing to make?\n");
        numberOfClaimsBeingMade = myScanner.nextInt();

        /*
        As we are using a variable in the loop our code is flexible and can be used
        for any number of claims. An ideal situation and good code.
        */
        do
        {
          System.out.println("The current value of the counter is :" + numberOfClaimsEntered + "\n");

        } // End of main method()
    } // End of DoWhileIteration class
```

6. Amend the code to ask the user to input the repair shop id, read the user input and assign the input to the variable repairShopID:

```
        do
        {
         System.out.println("The current value of the counter is :" +
         numberOfClaimsEntered + "\n");

         /*
           Read the user input for the repair shop id and keep it as a string
         */
         System.out.println("What is our repair shop id?\n");
         repairShopID = myScanner.next();
        } // End of main() method
    } // End of DoWhileIteration class
```

When the code is executed and the user has entered the details, we need to store these details in the array we have setup at position 0.

7. Amend the code to add the user input to the array in position 0 and then increment the counter, arrayPositionCounter, that is being used to track the positions at which the items go into the array:

```
System.out.println("What is our repair shop id?\n");
repairShopID = myScanner.next();

/*
Write the first input value to the array and then increment the
value of the arrayPositionCounter by 1.
*/

repairShopClaims[arrayPositionCounter] = repairShopID;
arrayPositionCounter++;

    } // End of main method()
} // End of DoWhileIteration class
```

8. Amend the code to ask the user to input the vehicle policy number, read the user input and assign the input to the variable vehiclePolicyNumber:

```
repairShopClaims[arrayPositionCounter] = repairShopID;
arrayPositionCounter++;

/*
Read the user input for the vehicle policy number and keep it
as a string
*/
System.out.println("What is the vehicle policy number?\n");
vehiclePolicyNumber = myScanner.next();

    } // End of main() method
} // End of DoWhileIteration class
```

When the code is executed and the user has entered the details, we need to store these details in the array we have setup at position 1.

9. Amend the code to add the user input to the array in position 1 and then increment the counter, arrayPositionCounter, that is being used to track the positions at which the items go into the array:

```
System.out.println("What is the vehicle policy number?\n");
vehiclePolicyNumber = myScanner.next();
```

```
/*
    Write the second input value to the array and then
    increment the value of the arrayPositionCounter by 1
*/
repairShopClaims[arrayPositionCounter] = vehiclePolicyNumber;
arrayPositionCounter++;

    } // End of main() method
} // End of DoWhileIteration class
```

10. Amend the code to ask the user to input the claim amount, read the user input, convert it to data type double and assign the input to the variable claimAmount:

```
repairShopClaims[arrayPositionCounter] = vehiclePolicyNumber;
arrayPositionCounter++;

/*
    Read the user input for the repair amount and convert it
    to a double and assign it to the variable claimAmount
*/
System.out.println("What is the amount being claimed for the repair?\n");
claimAmount = myScanner.nextDouble();

    } // End of main() method
} // End of DoWhileIteration class
```

When the code is executed and the user has entered the details, we need to store these details in the array we have setup at position 2.

11. Amend the code to add the user input to the array in position 2 and then increment the counter, arrayPositionCounter, that is being used to track the positions at which the items go into the array:

```
System.out.println("What is the amount being claimed for the repair?\n");
claimAmount = myScanner.nextDouble();

/*
    Write the third input value to the array and then increment the
```

value of the arrayPositionCounter by 1. The value read in from
the console is of data type double and the array holds Strings,
so a conversion from double to String must be done
*/

repairShopClaims[arrayPositionCounter] = Double.toString(claimAmount);
arrayPositionCounter++;

} // End of main() method
} // End of DoWhileIteration class

12. Amend the code to ask the user to input the date of the claim and then read the user input:

repairShopClaims[arrayPositionCounter] = Double.toString(claimAmount);
arrayPositionCounter++;

/*
Read the user input for the repair date leaving it as a String
*/
System.out.println("What was the date of the repair?\n");
claimDate = myScanner.next();

} // End of main() method
} // End of DoWhileIteration class

When the code is executed and the user has entered the details, we need to store these details in the array we have setup at position 3.

13. Amend the code to add the user input to the array in position 3 and then increment the counter, arrayPositionCounter, that is being used to track the positions at which the items go into the array:

System.out.println("What was the date of the repair?\n");
claimDate = myScanner.next();

/*
Write the fourth input value to the array and then increment the
value of the arrayPositionCounter by 1
*/

```
        repairShopClaims[arrayPositionCounter] = vehiclePolicyNumber;
        arrayPositionCounter++;
    } // End of main() method
} // End of DoWhileIteration class
```

Now we have accepted all the data required for the first claim. But before getting the details for the second claim we need to increment the numberOfClaimsEntered counter that is being used to hold the value of the number of claims that have been entered.

14. Amend the code to increment the counter that is being used to track the number of claims that have been entered, numberOfClaimsEntered.

```
        repairShopClaims[arrayPositionCounter] = vehiclePolicyNumber;
        arrayPositionCounter++;

        /* Increment the loop counter by 1 */
        numberOfClaimsEntered++;
    } // End of main() method
} // End of DoWhileIteration class
```

15. Amend the code to finish the do while loop by adding the Boolean condition to be tested.

```
        repairShopClaims[arrayPositionCounter] = vehiclePolicyNumber;
        arrayPositionCounter++;
        /* Increment the loop counter by 1 */
        numberOfClaimsEntered++;

    } while (numberOfClaimsEntered < numberOfClaimsBeingMade);

    } // End of main() method
} // End of DoWhileIteration class
```

Now, depending on the number of claims the user wishes to make, the do while loop will be executed again the required number of times. This is great but our only problem will be verifying that the details have been stored in the array. This now offers us a great opportunity to use the last type of iteration, **foreach**, that was mentioned in the last module.

foreach Loop

We can use a **foreach loop** as an efficient way to iterate through an array or any collection. Unlike the other iteration constructs we looked at in the previous module (for, while and do), there is no need for an index counter, as the foreach statement takes control and manages the required number of iterations. The foreach loop helps us as a developer by reducing the amount of code we need to write. On the other hand, we do not actually have a counter variable to work with if we wished to use it in a display line or for some other reason.

The format of the **foreach loop** is shown below:

```
for (datatype item : collection)
{
    <statements>
}
```

In the example:

- **datatype** represents the data type of the array or collection items
- **item** is a **variable** representing the member of the array, the item in the array, at the current position
- the name **item** is a variable name and we can call it whatever we like e.g. thememberofthearray
- **:** is used to represent to notion of **in** and must be used in this position
- **collection** represents the name of the array or collection we wish to iterate over

Applying this to the program we have coded above we would have the following iteration statement:

```
for (String itemInTheClaimsArray : repairShopClaims)
{
    System.out.println("The item in the array is:\t" +
    itemInTheClaimsArray + "\n");
}
```

Looking at this example:

- **String** represents the data type of the array or collection
- **item** has been replaced with the variable name **itemsInTheClaimsArray**
- **in** is represented by the : (colon)
- **repairShopClaims** represents the collection
- in the write line statement the variable **itemsInTheClaimsArray** has been displayed

We will now amend our code to iterate the array and display the items in the array as a way of confirming that the data entered by the user has been stored in the array.

16. Amend the code to add the foreach iteration and then close the Scanner instance:

    ```
    /* Increment the loop counter by 1 */
    numberOfClaimsEntered++;
    } while (numberOfClaimsEntered < numberOfClaimsBeingMade);

    for (String itemInTheClaimsArray: repairShopClaims)
    {
       System.out.println("The item in the array is:\t" +
       itemInTheClaimsArray + "\n");
    }
    myScanner.close();
    } // End of main() method
    } // End of DoWhileIteration class
    ```

17. Click on the **File** menu.
18. Choose **Save All**.
19. Click on the green **Run** button at the top of the screen.

The console window will appear and ask the user to input the number of claims to be made.

20. Type **2** and press the Enter key.

The console window will show that the current value of the claims counter is 0. The console window will immediately show that the current value of the claims counter is 1. This means no block of code was executed the first time as the 0 value of the numberOfClaimsEntered counter was an even number and as such the continue statement was executed, putting the code to the next iteration, skipping the code in the current iteration.

As the value of the counter is now 1 and this is not an even number the block of code in the current iteration is executed. So, the questions are asked.

21. Type **RS000001** for the repair shop id and press the Enter key.

The console will now ask the user to input the vehicle policy number.

22. Type **VP000001** and press the Enter key.

The console will now ask the user to input the claim amount.

23. Type **1999.99** and press the Enter key.

The console will now ask the user to input the date of the repair

24. Type **01/10/2021** and press the Enter key.

Iteration one is now completed, the block of code has been executed. The counter will now be incremented by 1 and becomes a 2. The questions are asked again for the second claim:

25. Type **RS000001** for the repair shop id and press the Enter key.
The console will now ask the user to input the vehicle policy number.

26. Type **VP000002** and press the Enter key.

The console will now ask the user to input the claim amount.

27. Type **2999.99** and press the Enter key.

The console will now ask the user to input the date of the repair

28. Type **01/10/2021** and press the Enter key.

The number of claims entered is 2 and this is all that the user requested, so, the do while loop is complete and the next lines of code are the foreach iteration. As a result of the foreach iteration the console will display all the items in the array as shown below:

```
Problems  @ Javadoc  Declaration  Console  ×
<terminated> Arrays [Java Application] C:\Users\gerardbyrne\.p2
01/10/2021
The item in the array is:      RS000001

The item in the array is:      VP000001

The item in the array is:      1999.99

The item in the array is:      VP000001

The item in the array is:      RS000001

The item in the array is:      VP000002

The item in the array is:      2500.99

The item in the array is:      VP000002
```

This shows that the array actually holds the data entered by the user. Our array is a single dimensional array holding items of data type String.

Now that we have the basics of an array, we can now explore arrays further and see some of the possible errors associated with them.

Exercise Two – Arrays and array errors

1. Right click on the **com.gerrybyrne.module09** package icon.
2. Choose **New**.
3. Choose **Class**.
4. In the name area type the name of the project – **ArrayErrors.java.**
5. Put a tick in the checkbox beside the public static void main(String[] args) box.
6. Click on the **Finish** button.

7. The **ArrayErrors** class code will appear in the editor window and will be similar to the following:

```
package com.gerrybyrne.module09;
public class ArrayErrors
{
    public static void main(String[] args)
    {
        // TODO Auto-generated method stub
    } // End of main method()
} // End of ArrayErrors class
```

We will now create a program that will declare and create an array whose size will be determined by the number of entries the user is making. Remember that the array size has to be known at compile time otherwise we will get an error. In this program we will keep the code simple and only ask the user for the vehicle policy number and the odometer reading.

8. Amend the code to declare and create the Scanner class instance and import the Scanner:

```
package com.gerrybyrne.module09;
import java.util.Scanner;

public class ArrayErrors
{
    public static void main(String[] args)
    {
        Scanner myScanner = new Scanner(System.in);
    } // End of main method()
} // End of ArrayErrors class
```

9. Amend the code to declare and create the array using a variable for the size of the array:

```
Scanner myScanner = new Scanner(System.in);
/*
    We will setup our variables that will be used in the application
    The number of entries being made will determine the size of the array
*/
```

```
int numberOfEntriesBeingMade;

/*
    The array is going to hold the data for a number of vehicles and
    their corresponding odometer readings. Each entry will be a
    vehicle policy number and the number of kilometres shown on the
    odometer. This means that the size of the array will be twice the
    number of entries being made by the repair shop.
*/
String[] odometerReadings = new String[numberOfEntriesBeingMade * 2];

    } // End of main method()
} // End of ArrayErrors class
```

We should take note that if we leave out the initialisation of the numberOfEntriesBeingMade variable, we will get an error.

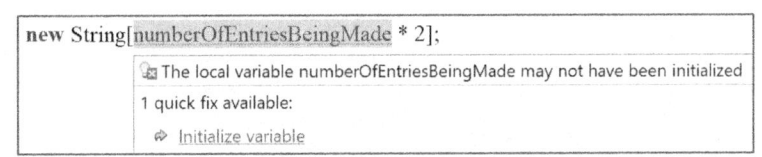

```
new String[numberOfEntriesBeingMade * 2];
    The local variable numberOfEntriesBeingMade may not have been initialized
    1 quick fix available:
        Initialize variable
```

The error message says we cannot use an unassigned variable for the array size. So we will simply add a line of code that will ask the user to input the number of entries they are going to make and assign this value to the variable. Now the program will be happy as it has a value for the variable, the variable is not unassigned. What we can see is that even though the actual value of the variable is not known, the program is happy as it will know the value before the array is created.

10. Amend the code to ask the user to input the number of entries being made, read this value from the console, convert it to data type int and assign the value to the variable called numberOfEntriesBeingMade. We will insert this code after the declaration of the array:

```
/*
    The array is going to hold the data for a number of vehicles and
    their corresponding odometer readings. Each entry will be a
    vehicle policy number and the number of kilometres shown on the
```

odometer. This means that the size of the array will be twice the
number of entries being made by the repair shop.
*/
String[] odometerReadings = **new** String[numberOfEntriesBeingMade * 2];

/*
Read the user input for the number of entries being made and convert
the string value to an integer data type
*/
System.out.println("How many entries are we wishing to make?\n");
numberOfEntriesBeingMade = myScanner.nextInt();
} // End of main() method
} // End of ArrayErrors class

We will still see a red underline under the variable numberOfEntriesBeingMade in the line String[] odometerReadings = new String[numberOfEntriesBeingMade * 2];

The reason is that the value read from the console is only known after the line of code that tries to declare and create the array. This is an error as the size needs to be known at compile time, **now**, not at runtime.

11. Amend the code to move the block of code we have just entered above the declaration statement as shown below:

   Scanner myScanner = **new** Scanner(System.in);
   /*
      We will setup our variables that will be used in the application
      The number of entries being made will determine the size of the array
   */
   int numberOfEntriesBeingMade;

   /*
      Read the user input for the number of entries being made and convert
      the string value to an integer data type
   */
   System.out.println("How many entries are we wishing to make?\n");
   numberOfEntriesBeingMade = myScanner.nextInt();

```
    /*
        The array is going to hold the data for a number of vehicles and their
        corresponding odometer readings. Each entry will be a vehicle policy
        number and the number of kilometres shown on the odometer. This means
        means that the size of the array will be twice the number of entries
        being made by the repair shop.
    */
    String[] odometerReadings = new String[numberOfEntriesBeingMade * 2];

    } // End of main() method
} // End of ArrayErrors class
```

Great, the red underline has disappeared, and the compiler is happy. **So, now we know that we must tell the compiler the size of the array to make it happy**. We can use a variable, but this must be known when the array is declared and created.

Now we will ask the user to input the value for the vehicle policy number followed by the odometer reading and this will be repeated the number of times requested by the user. For this we will use a do while loop. This code will be very similar to the code from the last example.

12. Amend the code to add the other variables we will use as shown below:

```
public static void main(String[] args)
{
    Scanner myScanner = new Scanner(System.in);
    /*
        We will setup our variables that will be used in the application
        The number of entries being made will determine the size of the array
    */
    int numberOfEntriesBeingMade;

    int numberOfEntriesEntered = 0;
    int arrayPositionCounter = 0;
    int odometerReadingForVehicle;
    String vehiclePolicyNumber;
```

13. Amend the code to add the loop and the questions within it as shown below:

```java
String[] odometerReadings = new String[numberOfEntriesBeingMade * 2];

/*
  As we are using a variable in the loop our code is flexible and can be
  used for any number of claims. An ideal situation and good code.
*/
do
{
   System.out.println("The current value of the counter is :" +
numberOfEntriesEntered + "\n");

   /*
     Read the user input for the vehicle policy number and keep it
     as a string
   */
   System.out.println("What is the vehicle policy number?\n");
   vehiclePolicyNumber = myScanner.next();

   /*
     Write this first input value to the array and then increment the
     value of the arrayPositionCounter by 1
   */
   odometerReadings[arrayPositionCounter] = vehiclePolicyNumber;
   arrayPositionCounter++;

   /* Read the user input for the odometer reading */
   System.out.println("What is the odometer reading?\n");
   odometerReadingForVehicle = myScanner.nextInt();

   /*
     Write the second input value to the array and then increment the
     value of the arrayPositionCounter by 1. The value read in from
     the console is of data type int and the array holds Strings, so
     a conversion from Integer to String must be done
   */
   odometerReadings[arrayPositionCounter] =
      Integer.toString(odometerReadingForVehicle);
   arrayPositionCounter++;

   /* Increment the loop counter by 1 */
```

```
        numberOfEntriesEntered++;
    } while (numberOfEntriesEntered < numberOfEntriesBeingMade);

    System.out.println("End of program?\n");
    myScanner.close();
    } // End of main() method
} // End of ArrayErrors class
```

14. Amend the code to add the iteration construct and display the array values as shown below:

```
    } while (numberOfEntriesEntered < numberOfEntriesBeingMade);

    for (String itemInTheodometerReadingsArray: odometerReadings)
    {
        System.out.println("The item in the array is:\t" +
        itemInTheodometerReadingsArray + "\n");
    }

    System.out.println("End of program?\n");
    myScanner.close();

    } // End of main() method
} // End of ArrayErrors class
```

15. Click on the **File** menu.
16. Choose **Save All.**
17. Click on the green **Run** button at the top of the screen.

The console window will appear and ask the user to input the number of claims to be made.

18. Type **2** for the number of entries to be made.
19. Press the **Enter** key.
20. Type **VP000001** for the vehicle policy number.
21. Press the Enter key.

The console will now ask the user to input the vehicle odometer reading.

22. Type **10000**.

23. Press the **Enter** key.

24. Type **VP000002** for the vehicle policy number.

25. Press the Enter key.

26. Type **20000**.

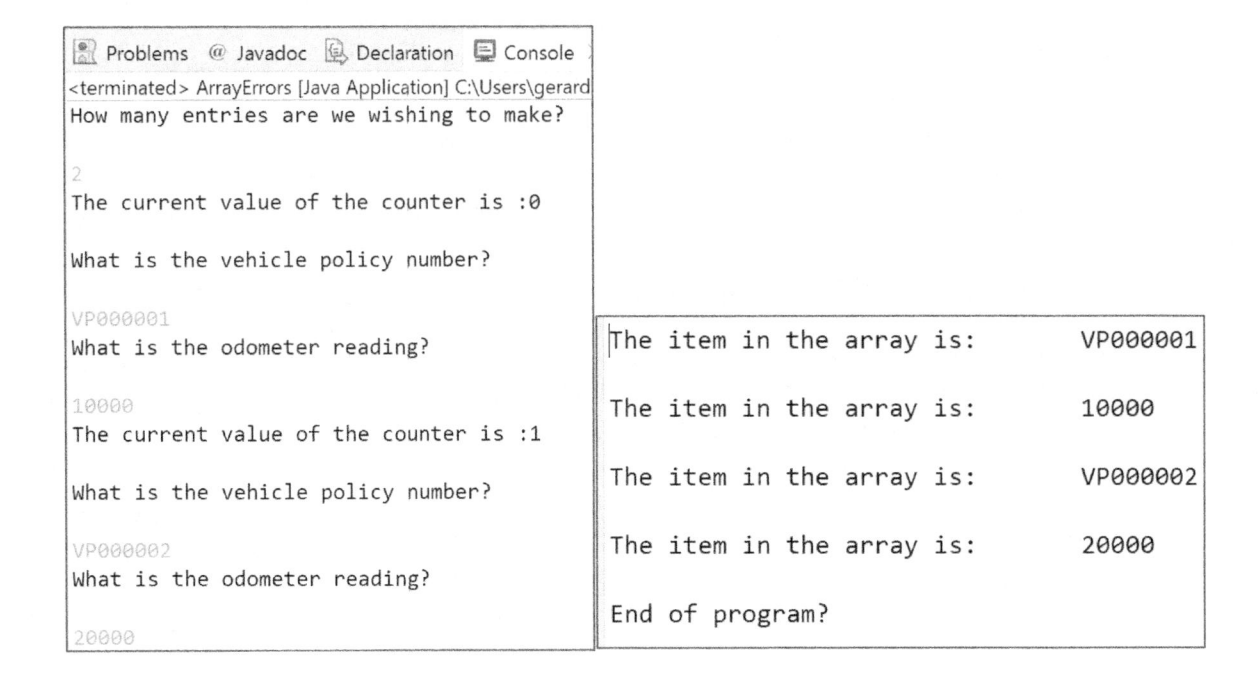

```
Problems  @ Javadoc  Declaration  Console
<terminated> ArrayErrors [Java Application] C:\Users\gerard
How many entries are we wishing to make?

2
The current value of the counter is :0

What is the vehicle policy number?

VP000001
What is the odometer reading?

10000
The current value of the counter is :1

What is the vehicle policy number?

VP000002
What is the odometer reading?

20000
```

```
The item in the array is:      VP000001

The item in the array is:      10000

The item in the array is:      VP000002

The item in the array is:      20000

End of program?
```

The array will therefore hold the string values as shown in the table below:

[0]	[1]	[2]	[3]
VP000001	10000	VP000002	20000

IndexOutOfBounds Exception

An array is fixed size and as such if we try to read or write a value which is outside the boundary of the array, we will be causing an exception. In Java the error is known as an **IndexOutOfBounds exception** because it happens when we have made the value of the index (counter) larger than the size of the array. Remember that the index starts at 0 not 1.

We will now make the iteration go one more than it currently does, by adding + 1 to the Boolean condition at the end of the do while construct.

27. Amend the code as shown below:

    ```
    } while (numberOfEntriesEntered < numberOfEntriesBeingMade + 1);

        for (String itemInTheodometerReadingsArray: odometerReadings)
        {
            System.out.println("The item in the array is:\t" +
            itemInTheodometerReadingsArray + "\n");
        }
    ```

28. Click on the **File** menu.
29. Choose **Save All**.
30. Click on the green **Run** button at the top of the screen.

The console window will appear and ask the user to input the number of claims to be made.

31. Type **2** for the number of entries to be made.
32. Press the **Enter** key.
33. Type **VP000001** for the vehicle policy number.
34. Press the **Enter** key.

The console will now ask the user to input the vehicle odometer reading.

35. Type **10000**.
36. Press the **Enter** key.
37. Type **VP000002** for the vehicle policy number.
38. Press the **Enter** key.
39. Type **20000**.
40. Type **VP000003** for the vehicle policy number.
41. Press the **Enter** key.

The exception is now in play and the application 'crashes' bringing us back to the code and showing the error as shown below:

```
20000
The current value of the counter is :2
What is the vehicle policy number?
VP000003
Exception in thread "main" java.lang.ArrayIndexOutOfBoundsException: Index 4 out of bounds for length 4
        at com.gerrybyrne.module09.ArrayErrors.main(ArrayErrors.java:59)
```

We will see that the value of the variable arrayPositionCounter is 4. Our array was made to have a size of:

    2 entries multiplied by the two values in each entry which equates to 4

This means that the positions available in the array are:
- odometerReadings[0]
- odometerReadings[1]
- odometerReadings[2]
- odometerReadings[3]

Our variable is 4 and we are therefore trying to write to position:
- odometerReadings[4]

and this means our index of 4 is out of bounds, as 3 is the maximum boundary limit. We will now change the test for the iteration back to its original value.

42. Amend the code as shown below to keep the array within bounds, removing the + 1:

```java
} while (numberOfEntriesEntered < numberOfEntriesBeingMade);
    for (String itemInTheodometerReadingsArray: odometerReadings)
    {
        System.out.println("The item in the array is:\t" +
        itemInTheodometerReadingsArray + "\n");
    }
```

43. Click on the **File** menu.
44. Choose **Save All.**

Module summary

In this module we have learnt about the particularly important programming concept called arrays. We have learnt that:

- arrays in Java are used to hold a collection of items all of the same data type
- a Java array is homogeneous and it is also of a fixed size, once we declare the size of the array its size cannot be altered
- arrays hold the data for the duration that the program runs
- there are single dimensional arrays which we have used in this module but there are also multi-dimensional arrays
- items in an array are referenced by their index (subscript)
- the indexes start at 0 not 1, arrays are zero indexed
- the for each loop is an ideal iterator to use with arrays, however it is not suitable if we need to reference a counter since no counter exists in the for each construct
- if we try to exceed the maximum index of the array we will get an IndexOutOfBounds Exception
- we can have more than one class in a package

Yet another great achievement for us in our learning. Be proud of the learning to date

Our dot just got bigger

Program Practically

Java

Module 10

Methods

Methods and modularisation

Void methods

Value methods

Parameter methods

Method overloading

User designed methods and Java class methods

Gerry Byrne

Program Practically - Methods

We learnt in module 9 that:

Arrays are a very important programming structure when we need to 'store' a collection of data, variables of the same data type. We saw that arrays in Java are of a fixed size and once we declare the size of the array its size cannot be altered. Each item in an array can be referenced using its index, which is also called its subscript and we can use the for each loop to iterate the array items. With the for each iteration, we do not need to use a counter as the for each construct handles the indexing for us. If we wish to reference an index in an iteration, we can use the more traditional for, while or do while iteration. We also learnt that we could cause an IndexOutOfBounds Exception if we are not careful in our coding.

Methods - concepts of methods and functions

Most commercial programs will involve large amounts of code and from a maintenance and testing perspective it is essential that the program has a good structure. Professionally written and organised programs allow those who maintain or test them to:
- follow the code and the flow of events easier
- find things quicker

Look at this image and think which side fits with a sense of being organised:

Would we say the right-hand image? There is a sense of organisation, there is space to see things and there is a sense of calm. The left-hand image gives a sense of confusion, clutter, and a sense of not caring. We do not want our code to look or feel like the left-hand image.

One way to help structure the program code is to break it into small functional parts - each part performing one task.

When we have a functional part, which **does one thing**, it may be possible for that functional part to be used by other parts of the program. These small functional parts can be thought of as **subprograms** or **methods** or **functions** or sometimes they are called **procedures**. The words function and method are often used interchangeably. If we think about functions in mathematics we can have mathematical functions such as square root, Sin, Cos and Tan.

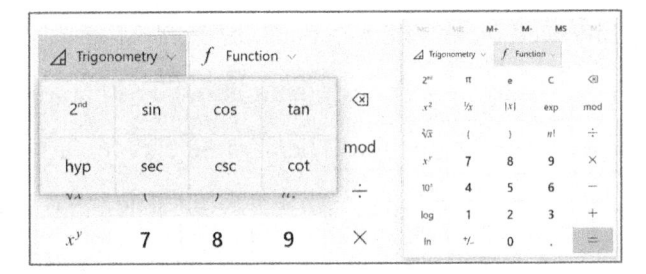

According to the Microsoft site:
> A method is a code block that contains a series of statements. A program causes the statements to be executed by calling the method and specifying any required method arguments.

In Java, every executed instruction is performed in the context of a method. The **main** method is the entry point for every Java application, and it is called when the program is started.

Some points regarding methods

- **a method begins with an access modifier**. The access modifier will determine the visibility of the method from another class. If we set the access modifier as:

- o **public** – the method is accessible inside the class we create it in and is available from outside this class
- o **private** - the method is only accessible inside the class we create it in

- a method access modifier is followed by the method **return type**. The return type means the data type of the variable that is being returned by the method. We can return any of the data types we have looked at e.g., **int, float, double, char, String, Boolean** but we could also return any data type that we create in our code. If the method will not return any value, the return type is said to be **void**.
- the return type is followed by the **method name**. The method name should follow good coding principles and let the reader know what the method is doing, simply by reading the name.
- the method name is followed by an opening and closing bracket ()
- inside the brackets () there may be a **list of parameters.** The parameters are variables that will hold any values passed to the method. The parameters are variables and will have a data type which is stated in front of the parameter name. The list of parameters is enclosed in parenthesis (). Not every method will accept parameters, they are optional in a method, so a method can contain no parameters.
- the parenthesis () are followed by an opening and closing curly brace {}. Inside the curly braces is where the business logic, code, goes.
- methods are coded outside the main method, if there is a main method, but inside the class.

General format for a method	Specific example of a method

access ret-type name (parameter-list)
{
         // body of method
}
	public void displayPremium()
	{
	    System.out.println(premiumAmount)
	}

Examples:

We will go into the structure more as we progress but for now we will look at three examples that fit the rules above:

1. **public void calculateCommission()**
    - here the access modifier is **public**
    - the method will not return a value, it is therefore declared as **void**
    - the method name is **calculateCommission**
    - the method accepts, takes in, **no parameters** (values, variables)

2. **private double calculateCommission()**
    - here the access modifier is **private**
    - the method will **return** a variable which is of data type **double**
    - the method name is **calculateCommission**
    - the method accepts, takes in, **no parameters** (values, variables)

3. **private double calculateCommission(double salesAmount, double commissionRate)**
    - here the access modifier is **private**
    - the method will **return** a variable which is of data type **double**
    - the method name is **calculateCommission**
    - the method accepts, takes in, **two parameters** (values, variables). The first parameter is called salesAmount which has a data type of double and the second parameter is called commissionRate which has a data type of double

Some other important points
- a method may contain one or more statements
- a method name can use any valid identifier that we want
- a method name should not use a Java keyword
- the method name is used to call the method and when we call the method we are asking the method to execute its code and then return to the code which made the call
- there is a very important method called **main( )** and it is **reserved** for the method that begins execution of our program

In the example shown in the diagram below method1 is called. The application code will look elsewhere in the code for a method with the name method1. When it finds method1 it executes the lines of code within it. Finally, the application code goes back to the code that called it.

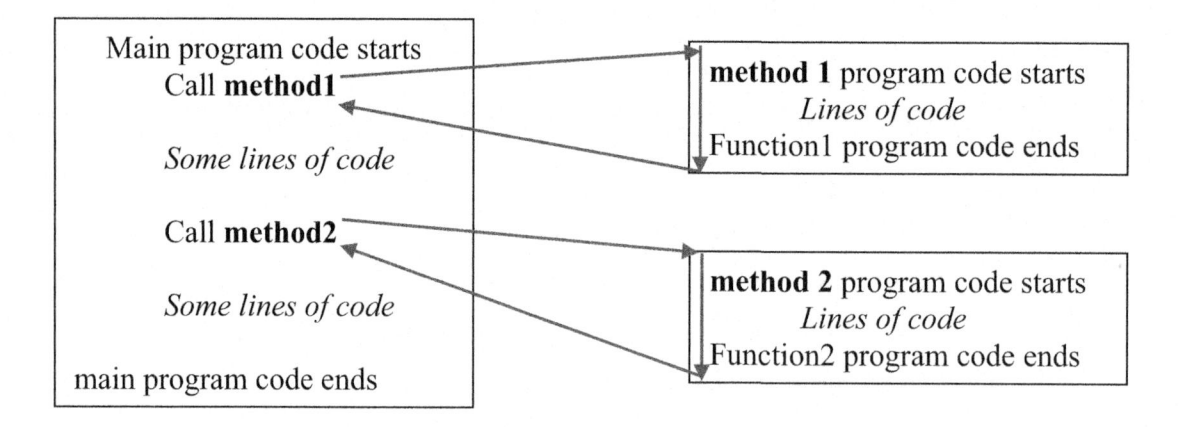

```
┌─────────────────────────────┐          ┌──────────────────────────────┐
│ Main program code starts    │          │ method 1 program code starts │
│   Call method1 ─────────────┼─────────▶│      Lines of code           │
│             ◀───────────────┼──────────│ Function1 program code ends  │
│                             │          └──────────────────────────────┘
│ Some lines of code          │
│                             │          ┌──────────────────────────────┐
│   Call method2 ─────────────┼─────────▶│ method 2 program code starts │
│             ◀───────────────┼──────────│      Lines of code           │
│ Some lines of code          │          │ Function2 program code ends  │
│                             │          └──────────────────────────────┘
│ main program code ends      │
└─────────────────────────────┘
```

After returning from method1 the next lines of code, indicated as some lines of code in the diagram, are executed until the second method, method2, is called. When method2 is called the application code will look elsewhere in the code for a method with the name method2. When it finds method2 it executes the lines of code within it. Finally, the application code goes back to the code that called it and continues executing the next lines of code.

Even looking at this simple flow diagram we get a sense that:

- methods can be kept separate from the main code and called when required
- methods are small blocks of code – modern programming style dictates that a method should do one thing and one thing only. Methods that do more than one thing should be split into further methods.

Now we will investigate the three types of method:

- **void method**

    we looked at this quickly earlier and saw that this type of method executed code and did not return any value, it is void. The format is:

    public void calculateCommission ()

- **value method**

    we looked at this earlier and saw that this type of method executed code and then returns a value. The value it returns is a variable and the variable must have a data type which matches the return type stated after the access modifier in the method signature. In the example we looked at, the return type was a double. The format is:

    private double calculateCommission()

- **parameter method**

    earlier we saw that this type of method accepted one or more parameters. The parameters are just variables, so they have a name and data type. The method executes code which will probably use the variable passed in as parameters, otherwise why would we accept the parameters? The method can also return a value, in which case it is also a value method, or it may not return a value in which case it is also a void method.

    In the example we looked at, the return type was a double, so the method was a value method and it accepted, took in, two values of data type double, so it is also a parameter method. The format is:

    private double calculateCommission(**double** salesAmount, **double** commissionRate)

    In the example below the return type is a void so the method is a void method and it accepts (takes in) two values of data type double, so it is also a parameter method. The format is:

    private void calculateCommission(**double** salesAmount, **double** commissionRate)

Void Method

When we call a method the lines of code within the method are implemented. In the diagram above we saw that when method1 was called the program looked for method1, the lines of code were executed and control of the program was returned to the main program.

When a method does not return a value it is said to be a **void method**. The declaration void indicates that the method returns no value to the caller. It is important to realise that every method declaration specifies a return type, even if it's void.

An example of a void method is:

```
public void odometerReading()
{
    // Ask the user to input the value on the odometer
    System.out.println("What is the odometer reading");

    // Read the value entered by the user
    odometerReadingEntered = Integer.toString(myScanner.next());
}
```

Code analysis:

- the method has an **access modifier** of **public** so the method will be available to all code inside the class or from outside the class
- the **return type** is **void** so the method will not return any value and we will therefore not see the last line of code in the method saying **return**
- the name of the method is **odometerReading**
- the open and close parenthesis follow the name and are empty indicating that the method accepts no parameters (variables)
- the open and close curly braces follow the parenthesis and it is between these braces that the business logic, code goes
- the business logic code is very simple as it displays a message to the user through the System.out.println() method and then it reads the user input from the console using the Integer.toString() method to convert the input String
- looking at the toString() method we can see that it accepts a parameter, a variable, which in this case is myScanner.next(), the next String entered into the console

The format for calling the method, using it, is by using the method name followed by the open and close parenthesis:

odometerReading();

Exercise One – Create and use void methods

1. Right click on the **src** folder.
2. Choose **New**.
3. Choose **Package**.
4. Name the package **com.gerrybyrne.module10**.
5. Click the **Finish** button.
6. Right click on the **com.gerrybyrne.module10** package icon.
7. Choose **New**.
8. Choose **Class**.
9. Name the class **MethodsVoid**.
10. Put a tick in the checkbox beside the public static void main(String[] args) box.
11. Click on the **Finish** button.

The **MethodsVoid** class code will appear in the editor window and will be similar to the following:

```
package gerrybyrne.module10;
public class MethodsVoid
{
        public static void main(String[] args)
        {
                // TODO Auto-generated method stub
        } // End of main method()
} // End of MethodsVoid class
```

We are now going to use the same code that we created for the Arrays1D program but we will make the code more maintainable by creating multiple methods. Shown below is the code that we will work with and the outlined rectangular shapes represent the methods we will create and then call as required.

DO NOT TYPE THE CODE BELOW, IT IS FOR REFERENCE ONLY AND IS THE SAME AS WE CODED IN THE LAST MODULE.

```java
package gerrybyrne.module09;
import java.util.Scanner;

public class Arrays
{
public static void main(String[] args)
{
        Scanner myScanner = new Scanner(System.in);

    /*
        The array is going to hold the data for 2 claims. Each claim has
        four pieces of information. The number of data items is therefore
        2 multiplied by 4 = 8. So we will make the array for this example
        of size 8.
        Not the best way to do things but fine for now.
    */
        String[] repairShopClaims = new String[8];

    /*
        We will setup our variables that will be used in the quote application
        The details will be:
            - the repair shop unique id                    (String)
            - the vehicle insurance policy number          (String)
            - the claim amount and                         (double)
            - the date of the claim                        (String)
    */

        String repairShopID;
        String vehiclePolicyNumber;
        double claimAmount;
        String claimDate;
        int numberOfClaimsBeingMade;
        int numberOfClaimsEntered = 0;
        int arrayPositionCounter = 0;


        /* Read the user input for the number of claims being made and convert
           the string value to an integer data type*/
        System.out.println("How many claims are we wishing to make?\n");
        numberOfClaimsBeingMade = myScanner.nextInt();
```

1

/* As we are using a variable in the loop our code is flexible and can be used
   for any number of claims. An ideal situation and good code.
*/
do
{

```
System.out.println("The current value of the counter is :" +
       numberOfClaimsEntered + "\n");
```
2

/*
Read the user input for the repair shop id and keep it as a string
*/

```
System.out.println("What is our repair shop id?\n");
repairShopID = myScanner.next();
```
3

/*
Write the first input value to the array and then increment the
value of the arrayPositionCounter by 1.
*/

```
repairShopClaims[arrayPositionCounter] = repairShopID;
arrayPositionCounter++;
```
4

/*
Read the user input for the vehicle policy number and keep it as a string
*/

```
System.out.println("What is the vehicle policy number?\n");
vehiclePolicyNumber = myScanner.next();
```
5

/*
Write the second input value to the array and then increment the
 * value of the arrayPositionCounter by 1
*/

```
repairShopClaims[arrayPositionCounter] = vehiclePolicyNumber;
arrayPositionCounter++;
```
6

/*
Read the user input for the repair amount and convert it to a double
*/

```java
System.out.println("What is the amount being claimed for the repair?\n");
claimAmount = myScanner.nextDouble();
```
7

/*
Write the third input value to the array and then increment the
value of the arrayPositionCounter by 1. The value read in from
the console is of data type double and the array holds Strings,
so a conversion from double to String must be done
*/

```java
repairShopClaims[arrayPositionCounter] = Double.toString(claimAmount);
arrayPositionCounter++;
```
8

/*
Read the user input for the repair date leaving it as a String
*/

```java
System.out.println("What was the date of the repair?\n");
claimDate = myScanner.next();
```
9

/*
Write the fourth input value to the array and then increment the
value of the arrayPositionCounter by 1
*/

```java
repairShopClaims[arrayPositionCounter] = vehiclePolicyNumber;
arrayPositionCounter++;
```
10

/*
Increment the loop counter by 1
*/
```java
numberOfClaimsEntered++;
    } while (numberOfClaimsEntered < numberOfClaimsBeingMade);

for (String itemInTheClaimsArray: repairShopClaims)
{
    System.out.println("The item in the array is:\t" + itemInTheClaimsArray + "\n");
}
```
11

```java
myScanner.close();
    }
}
```

- we will start by creating the variables we will use in the code. The variables will be created at the class level, inside the class and outside any methods
- in creating class level variables, we will use the keyword **static** before each variable data type
- in terms of the word static we will see more about it in the module on classes, but for now just accept that static means belonging to this class
- creating variables at the class level means that all the methods of the class will have access to them
- as we are on a module about creating and using methods, we will want to have easy access to the variables

Remember
We still have the code from the Arrays.java class so we can copy and paste the code into this MethodsVoid.java class, adding the static keyword when required.

1. Amend the code to import the Scanner class and create an instance of the Scanner class which we will use for reading user input as shown:

   package com.gerrybyrne.module10;
   import java.util.Scanner;

   public class MethodsVoid
   {
      static Scanner myScanner = **new** Scanner(System.in);
      } // End of main method()
   } // End of MethodsVoid class

2. Amend the code to create the array at the class level as shown:

   package com.gerrybyrne.module10;
   import java.util.Scanner;

   public class MethodsVoid
   {
      static Scanner *myScanner* = **new** Scanner(System.*in*);

```
/*
    The array is going to hold the data for 2 claims. Each claim has four
    pieces of information. The number of data items is therefore
    2 multiplied by 4 = 8. So, we will make the array for this example
    of size 8.

    Not the best way to do things but fine for now.
*/
    static String[] repairShopClaims = new String[8];

    public static void main(String[] args)
    {
    } // End of main method()
} // End of MethodsVoid class
```

3. Amend the code to create the variables at the class level as shown:

```
    static String[] repairShopClaims = new String[8];

    /*
        We will setup our variables that will be used in the quote application
        The details will be:
            - the repair shop unique id                    (String)
            - the vehicle insurance policy number          (String)
            - the claim amount and                         (double)
            - the date of the claim                        (String)
    */
    static String repairShopID;
    static String vehiclePolicyNumber;
    static double claimAmount;
    static String claimDate;
    static int numberOfClaimsBeingMade;
    static int numberOfClaimsEntered = 0;
    static int arrayPositionCounter = 0;

    public static void main(String[] args)
    {
    } // End of main method()
} // End of MethodsVoid class
```

Remember that methods are created outside the main() method but inside the class.
We can add the methods above the main() method or below it. Here we will add the methods below the main() method, so be careful and make sure to add the methods below the main method but still inside the class which is indicated by the last curly brace }.

4. Amend the code to create the first method that will hold the code for asking the user how many claims will be made and then collecting the user input from the console. The method will be called - **HowManyClaimsAreBeingMade()**.

   ```
   } //End of main() method

   /*
      All the methods will be located here.
      They are outside the main but inside the class
   */
   // Method 1
   public static void HowManyClaimsAreBeingMade()
   {
   /*
      Read the user input for the number of claims being made and convert
      the string value to an integer data type
   */
      System.out.println("How many claims are we wishing to make?\n");
      numberOfClaimsBeingMade = myScanner.nextInt();
   } // End of HowManyClaimsAreBeingMade() method
   } // End of MethodsVoid class
   ```

5. Amend the code to create the second method, after the first method, that will display the current value of the counter used to track how many entries have been made. The method will be called - **HowManyClaimsAreBeingMade()**.

   ```
      System.out.println("How many claims are we wishing to make?\n");
      numberOfClaimsBeingMade = myScanner.nextInt();
   } // End of HowManyClaimsAreBeingMade() method

   // Method 2
   public static void CurrentValueOfCounter()
   ```

```
{
System.out.println("The current value of the counter is :" +
numberOfClaimsEntered + "\n");
} // End of CurrentValueOfCounter() method
} // End of MethodsVoid class
```

6. Amend the code to create the third method, after the second method, which will ask the user what the id is for the repair shop and then collect the user input from the console. The method will be called - **ReadTheRepairShopId()**.

```
// Method 2
public static void CurrentValueOfCounter()
{
   Console.WriteLine("The current value of the counter is :" +
   numberOfClaimsEntered + "\n");
} // End of CurrentValueOfCounter() method

// Method 3
public static void ReadTheRepairShopId()
{
   /*
      Read the user input for the repair shop id and keep it
      as a string
   */
   System.out.println("What is our repair shop id?\n");
   repairShopID = myScanner.next();
} // End of ReadTheRepairShopId() method
} // End of MethodsVoid class
```

7. Amend the code to create the fourth method, after the third method, which writes the repair shop id into the array and then increments the value of the counter used to keep the position in the array. The method will be called - **WriteRepairShopIdToTheArray()**.

```
   System.out.println("What is our repair shop id?\n");
   repairShopID = Console.ReadLine();
} // End of ReadTheRepairShopId() method

// Method 4
public static void WriteRepairShopIdToTheArray()
```

{
/*
   Write the first input value to the array and then increment the
   value of the arrayPositionCounter by 1.
*/
   repairShopClaims[arrayPositionCounter] = repairShopID;
   arrayPositionCounter++;
} // End of WriteRepairShopIdToTheArray() method
} // End of MethodsVoid class

8. Amend the code to create the fifth method, after the fourth method, which will ask the user what the vehicle policy number is and then collect the user input from the console. The method will be called - **ReadTheVehiclePolicyNumber().**

   repairShopClaims[arrayPositionCounter] = repairShopID;
   arrayPositionCounter++;
} // End of WriteRepairShopIdToTheArray() method

// Method 5
public static void ReadTheVehiclePolicyNumber()
{
/*
   Read the user input for the vehicle policy number and keep it
   as a string
*/
System.out.println("What is the vehicle policy number?\n");
vehiclePolicyNumber = myScanner.next();
} // End of ReadTheVehiclePolicyNumber() method
} // End of MethodsVoid class

9. Amend the code to create the sixth method, after the fifth method, which writes the vehicle policy number into the array and then increment the value of the counter used to keep the position in the array. The method will be called - **WriteVehiclePolicyNumberToTheArray().**

   System.out.println("What is the vehicle policy number?\n");
   vehiclePolicyNumber = myScanner.next();

} // End of ReadTheVehiclePolicyNumber() method

// Method 6
public static void WriteVehiclePolicyNumberToTheArray()
{
/*
   Write the second input value to the array and then increment the
   value of the arrayPositionCounter by 1
*/
   repairShopClaims[arrayPositionCounter] = vehiclePolicyNumber;
   arrayPositionCounter++;
   } // End of WriteVehiclePolicyNumberToTheArray() method
} // End of MethodsVoid class

10. Amend the code to create the seventh, after the sixth method, method which will ask the user what the amount being claimed is, and then collect the user input from the console. The method will be called - **ReadTheAmountBeingClaimed().**

   repairShopClaims[arrayPositionCounter] = vehiclePolicyNumber;
   arrayPositionCounter++;
   } // End of WriteVehiclePolicyNumberToTheArray() method

// Method 7
public static void ReadTheAmountBeingClaimed()
{
/*
   Read the user input for the repair amount and convert it
   to a double
*/
   System.out.println("What is the amount being claimed for the repair?\n");
   claimAmount = myScanner.nextDouble();
   } // End of ReadTheAmountBeingClaimed() method
} // End of MethodsVoid class

11. Amend the code to create the eighth method, after the seventh method, which will write the claim amount into the array and then increment the value of the counter used to keep the position in the array. The method will be called - WriteClaimAmountToTheArray().
System.out.println("What is the amount being claimed for repair?\n");
    claimAmount = myScanner.nextDouble();

}// End of ReadTheAmountBeingClaimed() method

// Method 8
public static void WriteClaimAmountToTheArray()
{
  /*
    Write the third input value to the array and then increment the
    value of the arrayPositionCounter by 1
  */
  repairShopClaims[arrayPositionCounter] = String.valueOf(claimAmount);
  arrayPositionCounter++;
}// End of WriteClaimAmountToTheArray() method
} // End of MethodsVoid class

12. Amend the code to create the ninth method, after the eighth method, which will ask the user what the repair date is and then collect the user input from the console. The method will be called - **ReadTheRepairDate().**

   repairShopClaims[arrayPositionCounter] = String.valueOf(claimAmount);
   arrayPositionCounter++;
   }// End of WriteClaimAmountToTheArray() method

   // Method 9
   public static void ReadTheRepairDate()
   {
     /*
       Read the user input for the repair date leaving it
       as a String
     */
     System.out.println("What was the date of the repair?\n");
     claimDate = myScanner.next();
   } // End of ReadTheRepairDate() method
   } // End of MethodsVoid class

13. Amend the code to create the tenth method, after the ninth method, which will write the repair date which has been entered into the array and then increment the value of the counter used to keep the position in the array. The method will be called - **WriteRepairDateToTheArray().**

```
        System.out.println("What was the date of the repair?\n");
        claimDate = myScanner.next();
    }// End of ReadTheRepairDate() method

    // Method 10
    public static void WriteRepairDateToTheArray()
    {
        /*
          Write the fourth input value to the array and then increment the
          value of the arrayPositionCounter by 1
        */
        repairShopClaims[arrayPositionCounter] = claimDate;
        arrayPositionCounter++;
    }// End of WriteRepairDateToTheArray() method
} // End of MethodsVoid class
```

14. Amend the code to create the eleventh method, after the tenth method, which will iterate the array and display each item in the array. The method will be called - **DisplayAllItemsInTheArray().**

```
        repairShopClaims[arrayPositionCounter] = claimDate;
        arrayPositionCounter++;
    }// End of method WriteRepairDateToTheArray()

    // Method 11
    public static void DisplayAllItemsInTheArray()
    {
        for (String itemInTheClaimsArray: repairShopClaims)
        {
            System.out.println("The item in the array is:\t" + itemInTheClaimsArray + "\n");
        }
    } // End of DisplayAllItemsInTheArray() method
} // End of MethodsVoid class
```

Now we have created the methods, each executing a small amount of code, we can call any method at any time from within the main method in the program class or indeed from any method.

15. Amend the main method by adding the code that will call the methods as required:

```java
public static void main(String[] args)
{
    // Call the method that asks how many claims will be entered
    HowManyClaimsAreBeingMade();

    /*
        As we are using a variable in the loop our code is flexible and can be used
        for any number of claims. An ideal situation and good code.
    */
    do {
        // Call the methods as required
        CurrentValueOfCounter();
        ReadTheRepairShopId();
        WriteRepairShopIdToTheArray();
        ReadTheVehiclePolicyNumber();
        WriteVehiclePolicyNumberToTheArray();
        ReadTheAmountBeingClaimed();
        WriteClaimAmountToTheArray();
        ReadTheRepairDate();
        WriteRepairDateToTheArray();

        /* Increment the loop counter by 1 */
        numberOfClaimsEntered++;
    } while (numberOfClaimsEntered < numberOfClaimsBeingMade);

    DisplayAllItemsInTheArray();
} // End of main() method
```

16. Click on the **File** menu.
17. Choose **Save All**.
18. Click on the green **Run** button at the top of the screen.

The console window will appear and ask the user to input the number of claims to be made.

19. Type **2** and press the Enter key.

The console window will show that the current value of the claims counter is 0.

20. Type **RS000001** for the repair shop id and press the Enter key.

The console will now ask the user to input the vehicle policy number.

21. Type **VP000001** and press the Enter key.

The console will now ask the user to input the claim amount.

22. Type **1999.99** and press the Enter key.

The console will now ask the user to input the date of the repair

23. Type **01/10/2021** and press the Enter key.

Iteration one is now completed, the block of code has been executed. The counter will now be incremented by 1 and becomes a 1. The questions are asked again for the second claim:

24. Type **RS000001** for the repair shop id and press the Enter key.

The console will now ask the user to input the vehicle policy number.

25. Type **VP000002** and press the Enter key.

The console will now ask the user to input the claim amount.

26. Type **2999.99** and press the Enter key.

The console will now ask the user to input the date of the repair.

27. Type **01/10/2021** and press the Enter key.

The number of claims entered is 2 and this is all that the user requested so the do while loop is complete and the next lines of code are the foreach iteration. As a result of the for each iteration the console will display all the items in the array as shown below:

```
Problems  @ Javadoc  Declaration  Console  X
<terminated> MethodsVoid [Java Application] C:\Users\gerardbyrne\
01/10/2021
The item in the array is:      RS000001

The item in the array is:      VP000001

The item in the array is:      1999.99

The item in the array is:      01/10/2021

The item in the array is:      RS000001

The item in the array is:      VP000002

The item in the array is:      2999.99

The item in the array is:      01/10/2021
```

This shows that the array holds the data entered by the user. Our array is a single dimensional array holding items of data type String.

So, now we have refactored our original code and created **methods** that have small amounts of code. The code is much neater as all we have in the main() method are a series of calls to the methods. The methods sit outside the main() method, but still inside the class. This is now a good example of modern programming where methods are an essential feature of maintainable code, it is **modularisation**. With the code being decomposed into small methods it is a relatively easy process to test these small code blocks. We could improve the code, but this is a great starting point for modularised code.

Value Method

In the previous example when we called a method, the lines of code within the method were implemented and then control of the program was returned to the main program (to the calling statement). When a method is required to return a value to the calling statement it is said to be a **value method**. When we return a value, we have learnt from the start of our programming that all variables have a **data type** e.g. int, double, String and that data types are part of the Java programming language. In the last module we looked at arrays and the arrays we created hold objects with a data type. So, a value method could return a built-in data type such as int, double and String or it could return our own data type such as an array that we have created. In looking at void methods we used void in the method signature e.g.

>public **void** GetScoreDetails()

but when we have a value method that returns a variable of a specific data type, we must state the data type in the method signature:

>public **int** GetScoreDetails()
>public **double** GetScoreDetails()
>public **String** GetScoreDetails()

Every method declaration specifies a return type, even if it's void.

An example of a value method is:

>public **int** GetScoreDetails ()   ← return type declared as int
>{
>   // Ask the user to input the Score for Game One
>   System.out.println("What is the Score for Game One");
>
>   // Read the Score for Game One
>   scoreInGameOne = myScanner.nextInt();
>
>   return scoreInGameOne;   ← The return variable is of type int
>}

Code analysis:

- the method has an **access modifier** of **public** so the method will be available to all code inside the class or from outside the class
- the **return type** is **int** so the method will return a variable which must be of data type int and the last line of code in the method will say **return** followed by the variable name
- the name of the method is **GetScoreDetails**

- the open and close parenthesis () following the name are empty indicating that the method accepts no parameters
- the open and close curly braces follow the parenthesis and it is between these braces that the business logic goes
- the code simply uses the System.out.println() method to display a message for the user and then reads the user input from the console using the nextInt() method. The nextInt() methods is obtained from the myScanner instance of the Scanner class and converts the String value to an int.
- in the final line of code, the variable is returned and it is of data type int

The format for calling the method is by using the method name followed by the open and close parenthesis:

    GetScoreDetails();

Now, before we start coding an example of a value method, we will pause to think about the difference between a void method and value method.

	Void method	Value method
Signature	will contain the keyword **void**	will contain the keyword belonging to the **data type** being returned
Code	will **not contain a return keyword** on the last line of code	will contain a **return** keyword on the last line of code

Exercise One – Create and use value methods

First, we will create a copy of the class we have just finished coding. To make things easier we will simply use the existing methods and make amendments to some of them so that the method will no longer be a void method but a value method.

1. In the **com.gerrybyrne.module10** package right click on the **MethodsVoid**.java class.
2. Choose **Copy**.
3. Right click on the **com.gerrybyrne.module10** package.

4. Choose **Paste**.
5. Name the class **MethodsValue**.
6. Click on the **OK** button.
7. Double click on the **MethodsValue.java** class in the Package Explorer panel to open it in the Editor panel.

We will now amend the code using some ordered steps:
- in the method change the keyword void to the data type that is to be returned
- in the method add a return statement as the last line of the method followed by the variable name being returned

We should be aware that if a method returns a value to a calling statement, then the returned value should be used for something. In other words, what use would this line of code be if we called the method and it returned a value of 2:

> HowManyClaimsAreBeingMade();

No use at all, we will need to assign the returned value to a variable and we will do this from within the main() method where the call is made

8. Amend method 1, HowManyClaimsAreBeingMade(), as shown below:

```java
// Method 1
public static int HowManyClaimsAreBeingMade()
{
    /*
    Read the user input for the number of claims being made and convert
    the string value to an integer data type
    */
    System.out.println("How many claims are we wishing to make?\n");
    numberOfClaimsBeingMade = myScanner.nextInt();
    return numberOfClaimsBeingMade;
} // End of HowManyClaimsAreBeingMade() method
```

9. Amend the calling statement in the main() method to assign it to a variable as shown:

   public static void main(String[] args)
   {
   // Call the method that asks how many claims will be entered
   numberOfClaimsBeingMade = HowManyClaimsAreBeingMade();

Looking at this line we will see that numberOfClaimsBeingMade is the class level variable and we are assigning it the value returned from the HowManyClaimsAreBeingMade() method. Now, in the HowManyClaimsAreBeingMade() method we have also used the numberOfClaimsBeingMade class level variable and assigned it the value entered by the user. We could make the method code better by simply returning the value read in from the console as entered by the user.

10. Amend the method 1 code as shown by commenting the assignment code line and simply returning the value read in from the console:

```
// Method 1
public static int HowManyClaimsAreBeingMade()
{
/*
   Read the user input for the number of claims being made and convert
   the string value to an integer data type
*/
    System.out.println("How many claims are we wishing to make?\n");

    // numberOfClaimsBeingMade = myScanner.nextInt();

    return myScanner.nextInt();
} // End of HowManyClaimsAreBeingMade() method
```

The original line of code has been commented out, but it could be completely removed as shown below (remember YAGNI - You Aint Going to Need It, it's all part of the clean code ethos).

```
// Method 1
public static int HowManyClaimsAreBeingMade()
{
/*
   Read the user input for the number of claims being made and convert
   the string value to an integer data type
*/
    System.out.println("How many claims are we wishing to make?\n");

    return myScanner.nextInt();
} // End of HowManyClaimsAreBeingMade() method
```

This is a good example of making our code better, **refactoring**. We will do the same for the other methods, removing the line of code in each method that is not required.

No changes to method 2 as it simply displays a message.

11. Amend method 3, ReadTheRepairShopId() to return the user input as shown below:

```
// Method 3
public static String ReadTheRepairShopId()
{
    /*
     Read the user input for the repair shop id and keep it as a string
    */
    System.out.println("What is our repair shop id?\n");
    return myScanner.next();
} // End of ReadTheRepairShopId() method
```

12. Amend the calling statement in the do while iteration within the main() method as shown:

```
do {
    // Call the methods as required
    CurrentValueOfCounter();

    repairShopID = ReadTheRepairShopId();
```

13. Amend method 5, ReadTheVehiclePolicyNumber (), to return the user input as shown below:

    ```
    // Method 5
    public static String ReadTheVehiclePolicyNumber()
    {
        /* Read the user input for the vehicle policy number and keep it as a string */
        System.out.println("What is the vehicle policy number?\n");
        return myScanner.next();
    } // End of ReadTheVehiclePolicyNumber() method
    ```

14. Amend the calling statement in the do while iteration as shown:

    ```
    do {
        // Call the methods as required
        CurrentValueOfCounter();
        repairShopID = ReadTheRepairShopId();
        WriteRepairShopIdToTheArray();

        vehiclePolicyNumber = ReadTheVehiclePolicyNumber();
    ```

15. Amend method 7 in a slightly different way as we will be using the variable read from the user in another method which will be passed this value.

    ```
    // Method 7
    public static double ReadTheAmountBeingClaimed()
    {
        /*
          Read the user input for the repair amount and convert
          it to a double
        */
        System.out.println("What is the amount being claimed for the repair?\n");
        double claimAmountFromUser = myScanner.nextDouble();
        return claimAmountFromUser;

    } // End of ReadTheAmountBeingClaimed() method
    ```

16. Amend the calling statement in the do while iteration as shown:

```
do {
    // Call the methods as required
    CurrentValueOfCounter();
    repairShopID = ReadTheRepairShopId();
    WriteRepairShopIdToTheArray();
    vehiclePolicyNumber = ReadTheVehiclePolicyNumber();
    WriteVehiclePolicyNumberToTheArray();

    claimAmount = ReadTheAmountBeingClaimed();
```

17. Amend method 9, ReadTheRepairDate(), to return the user input value as shown below:

```
// Method 9
public static String ReadTheRepairDate()
{
    /*
       Read the user input for the repair date leaving
       it as a String
    */
    System.out.println("What was the date of the repair?\n");
    return myScanner.next();
}// End of ReadTheRepairDate() method
```

18. Amend the calling statement in the do while iteration as shown:

```
do {
    // Call the methods as required
    CurrentValueOfCounter();
    repairShopID = ReadTheRepairShopId();
    WriteRepairShopIdToTheArray();
    vehiclePolicyNumber = ReadTheVehiclePolicyNumber();
    WriteVehiclePolicyNumberToTheArray();
    claimAmount = ReadTheAmountBeingClaimed();
    WriteClaimAmountToTheArray();

    claimDate = ReadTheRepairDate();
```

19. Click on the **File** menu.
20. Choose **Save All.**

21. Click on the green **Run** button at the top of the screen.

The console window will appear and ask the user to input the number of claims to be made.

22. Type **2** and press the Enter key.

The console window will show that the current value of the claims counter is 0.

23. Type **RS000001** for the repair shop id and press the Enter key.

The console will now ask the user to input the vehicle policy number.

24. Type **VP000001** and press the Enter key.

The console will now ask the user to input the claim amount.

25. Type **1999.99** and press the Enter key.

The console will now ask the user to input the date of the repair.

26. Type **01/10/2021** and press the Enter key.

Iteration one is now completed, the block of code has been executed. The counter will now be incremented by 1 and becomes a 1. The questions are asked again for the second claim:

27. Type **RS000001** for the repair shop id and press the Enter key.

The console will now ask the user to input the vehicle policy number.

28. Type **VP000002** and press the Enter key.

The console will now ask the user to input the claim amount.

29. Type **2999.99** and press the Enter key.

The console will now ask the user to input the date of the repair.

30. Type **01/10/2021** and press the Enter key.

```
The item in the array is:      RS000001

The item in the array is:      VP000001

The item in the array is:      1999.99

The item in the array is:      01/10/2021

The item in the array is:      RS000001

The item in the array is:      VP000002

The item in the array is:      2999.99

The item in the array is:      01/10/2021
```

The number of claims entered is 2 and this is all that the user requested so, the do while loop is complete, and the next lines of code are the for each iteration. As a result of the for each iteration the console will display all the items in the array as shown below:

So now we have changed some of the methods to make them **value methods**. A value method means a value, which has a data type, is returned by or from the method. When creating a value method, the method signature must contain the data type being returned. This data type appears before the method name.

We now have void and value methods within our code.

Parameters Method

It is possible to have our methods accept a value or multiple values and then use these values within the body of the method as part of the business logic, processing. We could have a method that accepts two integer values and uses them in a multiplication.

In using a parameter method, we pass it actual values, as arguments. In creating the parameter method, the parameters and their data type, are enclosed as part of the method signature. When the **arguments (actual values)** are passed to the method, the method accepts these **arguments** and they are referred to as **parameters** in the accepting method.

A parameter is a variable in a method declaration and should be thought of as a placeholder that will hold the actual value when it passed to the method. An argument is the actual value passed to the method which accepts the value. Think of the A of arguments as actual values. We can say that the method defines the parameters and accepts the arguments.

In using parameter methods, we are using one of the principles of programming which expects us as developers to limit the accessibility of variables. To develop the black box idea for a method that accepts values we would have:

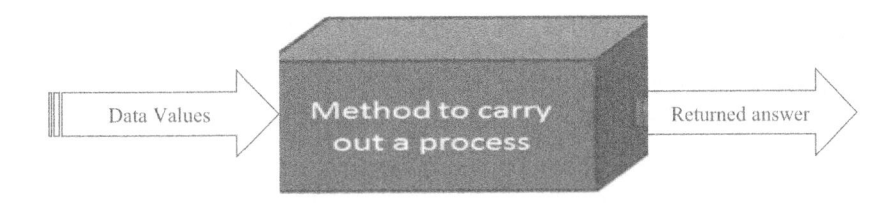

Data Values → Method to carry out a process → Returned answer

By providing the required input data the method produces the required answer. To obtain the correct answer we must ensure that the correct input data is provided i.e.:

- the right number of input data items.

- the correct type of input data.

Example

By setting up the input data as:
- number of items and

- the cost per item

the result of a multiplication can be produced. The method will have used the input data, performed its calculations and produced the result.

The values passed into the method are known as **arguments**. The method is said to take them as its **parameters**.

[Diagram: Call the method, providing the values. 3, 50 → Number of items = 3, Cost per item = 50 → Total Cost = 150. Method returns a value from the multiplication. Method uses the received values and carries out the calculation.]

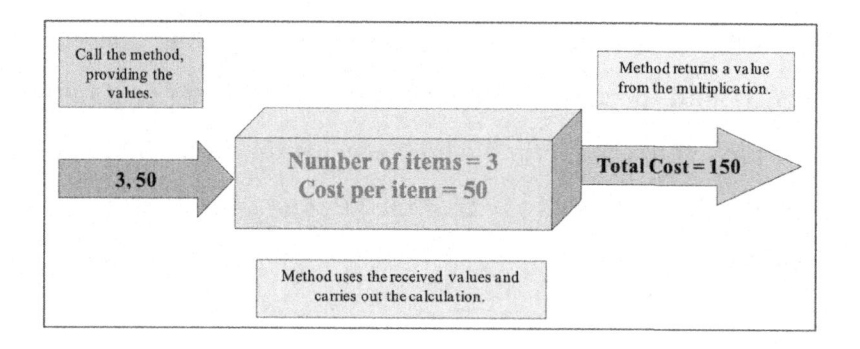

An example of a value method is:

```
public double AccumulateClaimAmount (double claimamount)
{
        totalofallclaims = totalofallclaims + claimamount;
        return totalofallclaims;     Return variable of type double
}
```

Code analysis:

- the method has an **access modifier** of **public** so the method will be available to all code inside the class or from outside the class
- the **return type** is **double** so the method will return a variable which must be of data type double and therefore the last line of code in the method will be the keyword **return** followed by the variable name
- the name of the method is **GetScoreDetails**
- the open and close parenthesis () follow the name and hold a local variable, claimamount, of data type double and the method accepts one argument as a parameter
- the open and close curly braces follow the parenthesis and it is between these braces that the business logic goes
- the business logic uses the variable value that has been passed in and the value is added to the variable called totalofallclaims which keeps the accumulated claims total
- in the final line of code the totalofallclaims variable is returned and it is of data type double

The format for calling the method is by using the method name followed by the open and close parenthesis:

AccumulateClaimAmount(1000);

Now before we start coding an example of a parameter method, pause to think about how a parameter method is associated with a void method and a value method.

	parameter method	
Signature	may contain the keyword **void**	may contain the keyword belonging to the **data type** being returned
Code	**may not contain a return keyword** on the last line of code	may contain a **return** keyword on the last line of code
Arguments	Will contain one or more arguments, local variables	

We will now add some parameter methods to the existing code where:
- the parameter method that accepts one argument, a parameter of type double
- the value passed in will be the value of the claim being made
- the method will use the value passed into it and total of all the claims being made
- we will create a method that accepts the accumulated total of the claims and works out how much of the accumulated total is Value Added Tax (VAT)
- the VAT amount will be included in the accumulated total and the formula for the calculation will be:

    vatamount = accumulated total passed in / 1.20

31. Amend the code to add a parameter method called **AccumulateClaimAmount** which has a parameter called **claimamount** which is of data type double (we will sort the errors that occur when we enter this code in the next step):

    ```
    for (String itemInTheClaimsArray: repairShopClaims)
    {
        System.out.println("The item in the array is:\t" +
    ```

```
            itemInTheClaimsArray + "\n");
        }
    } // End of DisplayAllItemsInTheArray() method

    // Method 12
    public static double AccumulateClaimAmount(double claimamountpassedin)
    {
        totalofallclaims = totalofallclaims + claimamountpassedin;
        return totalofallclaims;
    }
} // End of MethodsValue class
```

The method accumulates the total of all repair claims being added so we also need to create the variable to hold this total. Here we have named the variable **totalofallclaims**. We will declare this as a class level variable.

32. Amend the code to include this class level variable:

    ```
    public class MethodsValue
    {
        static Scanner myScanner = new Scanner(System.in);

        static double totalofallclaims;
    ```

We already have a method that accepts the value of the repair(s) so, all we need to do is to call the AccumulateClaimAmount method which we have just created and pass it the repair value which has been entered. This method simply adds the value to the existing total value of all claims.

33. Amend the code to call the method as shown:

    ```
    // Method 7
    public static double ReadTheAmountBeingClaimed()
    {
        /*
        Read the user input for the repair amount and convert
        it to a double
    ```

```
*/
    System.out.println("What is the amount being claimed for the repair?\n");
    double claimAmountFromUser = myScanner.nextDouble();

    AccumulateClaimAmount(claimAmountFromUser);

    return claimAmountFromUser;
} // End of ReadTheAmountBeingClaimed() method
```

Now we need to create

- a value method that accepts the total of all claims as a parameter and calculates the VAT based on this value
- a class level variable to hold the VAT value
- a void method that accepts the total of all claims and the VAT amount and displays a confirmation invoice showing the:
    - total of the claims without VAT
    - the total amount of VAT
    - the total of the claims including the vat.

34. Amend the code to include this class level variable:

```
public class MethodsValue
{
    static Scanner myScanner = new Scanner(System.in);
    static double totalofallclaims;

    static double vatamount;
```

35. Amend the code to add the new value method as shown:

```
// Method 12
public static double AccumulateClaimAmount(double claimamountpassedin)
{
    totalofallclaims = totalofallclaims + claimamountpassedin;
    return totalofallclaims;
}
```

```
// Method 13
public static double CalculateVATAmount(double totalvalueofclaimspassedin)
{
vatamount = totalvalueofclaimspassedin - (totalvalueofclaimspassedin/1.20);
return vatamount;
}
} // End of MethodsValue class
```

36. Amend the code in the main() method to call the VAT method as shown:

```
/* Increment the loop counter by 1 */
    numberOfClaimsEntered++;
} while (numberOfClaimsEntered < numberOfClaimsBeingMade);

vatamount = CalculateVATAmount(totalofallclaims);
```

37. Amend the code in the main() method to display the total of all claims:

```
} while (numberOfClaimsEntered < numberOfClaimsBeingMade);

vatamount = CalculateVATAmount(totalofallclaims);

DisplayAllItemsInTheArray();

System.out.println("The total amount claimed is:\t" + totalofallclaims);
} // End of main() method
```

Now we can create the void method that accepts the total of all claims and the VAT amount and displays the invoice receipt.

38. Amend the code to add the new void method which accepts the two arguments, (it's a parameter method), as shown:

```
// Method 13
public static double CalculateVATAmount(double totalvalueofclaimspassedin)
{
vatamount = totalvalueofclaimspassedin - (totalvalueofclaimspassedin/1.20);
return vatamount;
}
```

```
// Method 14
public static void DisplayInvoiceReceipt(double totalvalueofclaimspassedin, double
 vatPassedIn)
{
System.out.println("\nInvoice for vehicle repairs\n");
System.out.println("Nett claim\t" + (totalofallclaims - vatamount) + "\n");
System.out.println("VAT amount\t" +  vatamount + "\n");
System.out.println("Total amount\t" + totalofallclaims + "\n");
}
} // End of MethodsValue class
```

39. Amend the main() method code to call the method as shown:

```
vatamount = CalculateVATAmount(totalofallclaims);
DisplayAllItemsInTheArray();
System.out.println("The total amount claimed is:\t" + totalofallclaims);

DisplayInvoiceReceipt(totalofallclaims, vatamount);
} // End of main() method
```

Now we will run the code and use claim values that will make it easy to test if the code works properly. If we make two claim values as shown below, we can check that our output matches:

	Nett amount	VAT Amount	Total Amount
	1000	200	1200
	3000	600	3600
Totals	**4000**	**800**	**4800**

40. Click on the **File** menu.
41. Choose **Save All**.
42. Click on the green **Run** button at the top of the screen.

The console window will appear and ask the user to input the number of claims to be made.

43. Type **2** and press the Enter key.

The console window will show that the current value of the claims counter is 0.

44. Type **RS000001** for the repair shop id and press the Enter key.

The console will now ask the user to input the vehicle policy number.

45. Type **VP000001** and press the Enter key.

The console will now ask the user to input the claim amount.

46. Type **1200** and press the Enter key.

The console will now ask the user to input the date of the repair.

47. Type **01/10/2021** and press the Enter key.

The questions are asked again for the second claim:

48. Type **RS000001** for the repair shop id and press the Enter key.

The console will now ask the user to input the vehicle policy number.

49. Type **VP000002** and press the Enter key.

The console will now ask the user to input the claim amount.

50. Type **3600** and press the Enter key.

The console will now ask the user to input the date of the repair.

51. Type **01/10/2021** and press the Enter key.

The invoice receipt will be displayed as shown below:

```
Invoice for vehicle repairs

Nett claim      4000.0

VAT amount      800.0

Total amount    4800.0
```

So, now we have added parameter methods. Some of the parameter methods (methods 12 and 13) are also value methods because they return a value, but method 14 is a void method.

We now have void, value and parameter methods within our code.

Method Overloading

In Java we can have **more than one method with the same name** if we follow a few essential rules:

1. the number of arguments must be different

    e.g.   vatAmount(double claimamount, double vatRate)
           vatAmount(double claimamount, double vatRate, **String vatCode**)

2. the type of arguments are different

    e.g.   vatAmount(double claimamount, **double** vatRate)
           vatAmount(double claimamount, **float** vatRate)

3. the order of arguments are different

    e.g.   vatAmount(**double claimamount, double vatRate**)
           vatAmount(**double vatRate**, double claimamount)

Method overloading is a form of **Polymorphism** (different forms of the same object).

We will now code a new overloaded method to display a different invoice receipt.

52. Amend the code to add a new void method (method 15) which accepts the three arguments, (it is a parameter method), as shown. It is almost the same as the last display method (method 14) but it has the third argument:

    ```
    // Method 14
    public static void DisplayInvoiceReceipt(double totalvalueofclaimspassedin,
      double vatPassedIn)
    {
    ```

```java
        System.out.println("\nInvoice for vehicle repairs\n");
        System.out.println("Nett claim\t" + (totalofallclaims - vatamount) + "\n");
        System.out.println("VAT amount\t" + vatamount + "\n");
        System.out.println("Total amount\t" + totalofallclaims + "\n");
    }

    // Method 15
    public static void DisplayInvoiceReceipt(double totalvalueofclaimspassedin,
        double vatPassedIn, String messagePassedIn)
    {
        System.out.println("*****************************************");
        System.out.println("\nInvoice for vehicle repairs\n");
        System.out.println("Nett claim\t" + (totalofallclaims-vatamount) + "\n");
        System.out.println("VAT amount\t" + vatamount + "\n");
        System.out.println("Total amount\t" + totalofallclaims + "\n");

        System.out.println(messagePassedIn);

        System.out.println("*****************************************");
    }
} // End of MethodsValue class
```

53. Amend the main() method code to call the method as shown:

    ```java
    vatamount = CalculateVATAmount(totalofallclaims);

    DisplayAllItemsInTheArray();
    System.out.println("The total amount claimed is:\t" + totalofallclaims);

    DisplayInvoiceReceipt(totalofallclaims, vatamount);

    DisplayInvoiceReceipt(totalofallclaims, vatamount, "\tThank you for your
        claims\n\tthey will be processed today");

    } // End of main() method
    ```

54. Click on the **File** menu.

55. Choose **Save All**.

56. Click on the green **Run** button at the top of the screen.

The console window will appear and ask the user to input the number of claims to be made.

57. Type **2** and press the Enter key.

The console window will show that the current value of the claims counter is 0.

58. Type **RS000001** for the repair shop id and press the Enter key.

The console will now ask the user to input the vehicle policy number.

59. Type **VP000001** and press the Enter key.

The console will now ask the user to input the claim amount.

60. Type **1200** and press the Enter key.

The console will now ask the user to input the date of the repair.

61. Type **01/10/2021** and press the Enter key.

The questions are asked again for the second claim:

62. Type **RS000001** for the repair shop id and press the Enter key.

The console will now ask the user to input the vehicle policy number.

63. Type **VP000002** and press the Enter key.

The console will now ask the user to input the claim amount.

64. Type **3600** and press the Enter key.

The console will now ask the user to input the date of the repair.

65. Type **01/10/2021** and press the Enter key.

The first and second invoice receipt will be displayed as shown below where we can see the second receipt has a message:

```
Invoice for vehicle repairs

Nett claim      4000.0

VAT amount      800.0

Total amount    4800.0
```

```
*******************************************
Invoice for vehicle repairs

Nett claim      4000.0

VAT amount      800.0

Total amount    4800.0

      Thank you for your claims
      they will be processed today
*******************************************
```

So, now we have added an overloaded method (method 15).

It is overloaded because:

- it has the same name as the DisplayInvoiceReceipt method (method 14)
- it has 3 arguments whereas the first DisplayInvoiceReceipt method (method 14) has two arguments

Module Summary

So, finishing this module on methods we now have coded our own:
- void methods
- value methods
- parameter methods
- overloaded methods

However, we have also used methods in this code that we did not write. In fact, we have been using methods that we did not write from the first program we wrote in this course. The first real line of code we entered was:

println();

println() is a method. In this example there is no text in the () bracket so no text is written to the console, but a new line is taken. So, the println() method will move to a new line once it prints its content. How does it work? Well, we do not have to worry because we did not write the code and will not have to maintain the method code, it is part of the Java framework.

When we go to answer the question, How does it work? simply answer it like this – **don't know, don't care**. What this really means is, as developers we should not get involved with methods that are developed to help us and have been tested and proved reliable. They work, we just use them to build our application code.

Other examples of methods that we have used in our code that we did not write include:

print()	does not move to a new line once it prints its content
nextInt()	accepts no arguments
next()	accepts no arguments
nextDouble()	accepts no arguments
toString(claimAmount)	a parameter method that accepts one argument

Now, thinking about the methods we have created and the methods we have not created, but have used, they all have one thing in common and this commonality will lead us into the next module.

The common thing about them all is that they all live inside a class, they are part of a class.

When we code an example like this:

public class MethodsValue
{

}

this says that the code contained between the opening curly brace { and the closing curly brace } is within the class. All our code is inside the class apart from the package name and the import statements.

So, a takeaway from this module is that **a class contains**:
- **methods** that we create and
- **variables**, later we will call them a different name but for now variables is fine

Another great achievement for us in our learning.

Our dot just got bigger

Program Practically

Java

Module 11

Classes and objects

Classes as data structures

Classes as a template for objects

Classes and the main() method

Class methods and properties (fields, members)

Class constructors

Classes getters and setters

Gerry Byrne

Program Practically - Classes and Objects

We learnt in module 10 that:

Methods belong inside classes and classes consist of variables and methods. We saw that there are a number of different method types that can be used in our code. The method types we can create or use are:

- void methods that return no value and they simply execute code
- value methods that return a value of a specific data type having executed code
- parameter methods that accept actual values as their parameters and which may or may not return a value of a specific data type having executed code
- overloaded methods which are methods with the same name but different parameters.

There are many methods used in our code which are not written by us, examples include println(), print(), nextInt(), next(), nextDouble, toString().

The methods we have created and the methods we have not created, but have used, all have one thing in common:

They all live inside a class, they are part of a class.

It is the commonality of classes that this module will be concentrating on.

The crucial takeaway from the last module and a vital thing to remember in this module is that a class contains:
- **methods** and
- **variables**

As we have just seen in the methods module, all of what we have achieved so far in our code has used our own class, where we created our own variables (properties) and methods. We have also used methods that are provided as part of the Java Framework or through the imports and this has saved us much coding and effort.

When we create our classes, they act in the same way as the classes in the Java Framework or any other classes, in that they can be reused by creating instances (copies) of them to create one or more objects.

A Class is a data structure

In the software development world, there are many programming languages and many different types of program. Some are what can be called legacy programs such as those written in COBOL, whilst others use the popular and latest methods found in object-oriented programming languages. With traditional languages like COBOL, developers may simply have coded the programs as a set of instructions that followed a sequence and hence it was called sequential programming. With object-oriented programming (OOP) there is now a focus on structuring the code more. This is achieved by organising or capturing the code in logically related methods and data items called classes. This process of organising or capturing the data and methods is called **encapsulation**[1].

Our classes will contain members (variables, fields) which can be of different types:
- **data members** – that store data associated with the class or data associated with an instance of the class (the object), we can simply think of them as a variable
- **function members** – that are used to execute code, they are the **methods** we use to hold our code

In a class we can have the types:

1. **fields (sometimes called variables or members)**

    A field is a variable of any data type that is declared directly in our class. A field will usually store data that needs to be accessible to more than one class method and must be

---

[1] **Encapsulation** is the concept of making packages that hold all the things we need. In object oriented programming we can create classes that store all the variables and methods. The methods will be used to manipulate the data we have stored.

stored for longer than the lifetime of any single method. In relation to some of the examples we have used so far, we have had:

- a class called QuoteArithmetic that held details about an insurance quote and had fields in the class that represented the:
  - age of the vehicle in terms of years (it was called vehicleAgeInYears)
  - current mileage of the vehicle (it was called vehicleCurrentMileage)

    ```
    public class QuoteArithmetic
    {
        public int vehicleAgeInYears;
        public int vehicleCurrentMileage;
    }
    ```

- a class called MethodsVoid that held details about an insurance claim and had fields in the class that represented the
  - id of the repair shop making the claim (it was called repairShopID)
  - claim amount (it was called claimAmount)

    ```
    public class MethodsVoid
    {
        private String repairShopID;
        private double claimAmount;
    }
    ```

When we declare these fields at the class level, they can be used by more than one method of our class. The variables are said to have **'global' scope** within the class.

On the other hand, when the field variable will be used only by one method within the class, we should ensure that the variable is declared inside the method and therefore its scope is limited, it is only available inside the method, it is a local variable having local scope.

A field is declared within the class block by identifying:

- the **access level** of the field e.g. public, private, void

- o   the **type** of the field e.g. double, String
- o   the **name** of the field e.g. calculateQuote

Example code snippets

Example 1	Explanation

`public class QuoteArithmetic`
`{`
   `public int vehicleAgeInYears;`
   `public int vehicleCurrentMileage;`
`}`
	• field access modifier is public
	• field type is int
	• field name is vehicleAgeInYears

Example 2	Explanation

`public class MethodsVoid`
`{`
   `private String repairShopID;`
   `private double claimAmount;`
`}`
	• field access modifier is private
	• field type is String
	• field name is repairShopID

2. **constants**

The value of a variable can change throughout the lifetime of the application. In Java when a 'variable' is declared using the **final** keyword the value cannot be modified. In essence it is a **constant** value. A constant value therefore will not change during the lifetime of the application and is always known to the compiler at runtime.

A constant is declared within the class block by:

- o   identifying the **access level** of the field e.g. public, private
- o   adding the **final** modifier
- o   identifying the **type** of the field e.g. double, String
- o   identifying the **name** of the field, in Java the naming convention would be to use capital letters for the name of a constant e.g. BASEINSURANCEAMOUNT
- o   setting its fixed value

Example code snippets

Example 1

Code
```
public class QuoteArithmetic
{
    public final int MAXIMUMDRIVERAGE = 100;




    public final int VEHICLEAGEINYEARS;
    public final int VEHICLECURRENTMILEAGE;
}
```

Explanation
- constant access modifier is public
- modifier final makes it a constant value
- constant type is int
- constant name is maxDriverAge
- constant value is fixed to 100

Example 2

Code
```
public class MethodsVoid
{
    private final double MINIMUMQUOTE = 100.00;




    private final String REPAIRSHOPID;
    private final double CLAIMAMOUNT;
}
```

Explanation
- constant access modifier is private
- modifier final makes it a constant value
- constant type is double
- constant name is minimumQuote
- constant value is fixed at 100.00

3. **methods**

Methods form a large part of the Java language. Our Java application will start its execution from within the **main()** method, so, in our code the main method will exist in one of our classes and forms the entry point for the application being developed. As developers we use methods to modularise our code and make it easier to maintain. More importantly, methods form the basis for the crucially important concept of Test Driven Development (TDD) where the idea is to test a unit of code (a method). In Test Driven Development we write tests first before we write our classes and methods, yes that is strange. With Test Driven Development the tests themselves are methods which are inside a class, called the test class. So, once again we see the importance of classes with methods and variables.

When we create methods we are developing blocks of code that perform an action and we can say that methods hold our business logic.

A method is declared within the class block by:
- identifying the **access level** of the method
- identifying optional modifiers such as abstract or sealed
- identifying the **return type** of the method
- identifying the **name** of the method
- identifying any parameters that are passed into the method

Example code snippet

```
// Method 1
public static void HowManyClaimsAreBeingMade()
{
   /*
   Read the user input for the number of claims being made and convert the
   string value to an integer data type
   */
   System.out.println("How many claims are we wishing to make?\n");
   numberOfClaimsBeingMade = myScanner.nextInt();

} // End of HowManyClaimsAreBeingMade() method
```

Analysis of method 1 code

- the **access level** of the method is **public**

- o the **static** modifier has been applied to the method (more of static in this module)
- o the **return type** of the method is **void** (does not return anything)
- o the **name** of the method is **HowManyClaimsAreBeingMade**
- o no parameters are passed into the method

4. Accessors – also called getters and setters

As we saw when we talked about fields, it is possible to set the field access modifier as public or private. The reason for setting the field as private is to ensure that the field cannot be accessed directly from outside the class, from another class. We may therefore wonder how we can read the value of a field or write a value to a field, from outside its class, if it is set as private. Well, the answer is by using an accessor.

Within a class the accessor is a 'tool' that can read or write and compute the value of a private field. This 'magic' tool is really a method and we will have two types of accessor method, the **getter method** and the **setter method**. Accessors offer a way to get and set a field if we have a private field.

The **getter 'magic' tool** is a **read only method** and is described below:

- o **getter (read only)**

  a **getter** is a method used to read the value of a private field. The method is used to communicate with outside classes and the method will have the following features:

    - it must be created as **public**
    - it must return the same type of value as the field (variable) it represents
    - the name starts with **get** followed by the name of the field (variable) with the first letter of the field being transformed to upper case
    - it does not have any parameters
    - it returns the field (variable) it represents

    Example code snippet for getter

    ```
    // This is the private field (variable)
    private String repairShopID;
    ```

```
/*
    This getter has its access modifier set to public and the returned
    variable or value data type must be a String.
    The name of the getter starts with the word get followed by the name
    of the field (variable) where the first letter of the field is capitalised
*/
public static String getRepairShopID()
{
    return repairShopID; // repairShopID is the field (variable)
}
```

Example code snippet for getter

```
// This is the private field (variable)
private double claimAmount;

/*
    This getter has its access modifier set to public and the returned
    variable or value data type must be a double.
    The name of the getter starts with the word get followed by the name
    of the field (variable) where the first letter of the field is capitalised
*/
public static double getClaimAmount()
{
    return claimAmount; // claimAmount is the field (variable)
}
```

- In essence the getter method gets the value of a field (variable) and returns the value to the calling statement.

The **setter 'magic' tool** is a **write only method** and is described below:

o **setter (write only)**

a **setter** method is used to write to and change the value of a private field. The method is used to communicate with outside classes and the method will have the following features:

- it must be created as **public**
- it must be a **void** method as it does not return a value

- the name starts with **set** followed by the name of the field (variable) with the first letter of the field being transformed to upper case
- it has a parameter of the same data type as the field and with the same name as the field

Example code snippet for setter

```
// This is the private field (variable)
private String repairShopID;

/*
  This setter has its access modifier set to public and there is no returned
  variable so the data type in the signature must be void.
  The name of the setter starts with the word set followed by the name
  of the field (variable) where the first letter of the field is capitalised.
  The setter method must be passed a value (argument) and this is accepted as the
  parameter of the setter method. The value passed in must be of the same
  data type as the variable, in this case a String.
*/
public static void setRepairShopID(String repairShopID)
{
   // repairShopID is the field (variable)
   this.repairShopID = repairShopID;
}
```

Example code snippet for setter

```
// This is the private field (variable)
private double claimAmount;

/*
  This setter has its access modifier set to public and there is no returned
  variable so the data type in the signature must be void.
  The name of the setter starts with the word set followed by the name
  of the field (variable) where the first letter of the field is capitalised.
  The setter method must be passed a value (argument) and this is accepted as the
  parameter of the setter method. The value passed in must be of the same
  data type as the variable, in this case a double.
*/
```

```
    public static void setClaimAmount(double claimAmount)
    {
        // claimAmount is the field (variable)
        this.claimAmount = claimAmount;

    }
```

In essence the setter method sets the value of a field (variable).

5. constructor

We now know that fields with an access modifier of private can have their value amended using a setter. There is also a very special method that can exist in a class which can be used for the sole purpose of initialising the values of the fields. This special method is called a **constructor** and will be created by us as the developer.

If we do not want to initialise the fields, they will have the default value for the data type of the particular field e.g. the int data type has a default of 0, the double data type has a default of 0.00.

When we choose not to develop a constructor and therefore leave the default values for the fields, there is still a constructor in the class, it is called a **default constructor** and it will not be visible. Once we create our own constructor method the default constructor no longer exists.

Example constructor:

```
package com.gerrybyrne.module11;
public class MethodsVoid
{
    String repairShopID;
    double claimAmount;

    /*
    This constructor accepts two values the first is given the name
    repairShopID and the second is given the name claimAmount.
    The value of repairShopID (a variable) is assigned to the class level
    field (variable) called repairShopID. As the class level variable has
```

the same name as the local variable in the parameters we can avoid any confusion by using the Java keyword this followed by a period (.) in front of the class level variable.
*/
public MethodsVoid(String repairShopID, **double** claimAmount)
{
    this.repairShopID = repairShopID;

    this.claimAmount = claimAmount;
} // End of constructor

} // End of class

The **constructor** 'method' is used to initialise the value of the fields in the class. It may be used to initialise all the fields or just some of them. A constructor has the following features:

- it must have the **same name as the class**, which is MethodsVoid in this example
- it must have an access modifier of **public**
- it has **no return type**, not even void
- it has parameters and they are of the same type as the fields that are to be initialised

The **constructor** (method) is 'activated' when the class is used. We will see more about this as we code the examples in this module. The way a class is 'activated' is by creating an **instance of the class**. An **instance** of the class is a **copy** of the class.

The reason we use an instance (copy) of the class is because the class itself is a **template** and should not be used directly.

We have used the keyword **this** to refer to the field of the class rather that the parameter of the method.

Example code snippet to activate the default constructor:

```
public class Test
{
public static void main(String[] args)
{
    MethodsVoid myInstanceOfMethodsVoid = new MethodsVoid();
}

} // End of class
```

← calls the default constructor

Analysis of the constructor code

- here we create an instance of the class MethodsVoid, we are instantiating the class
- this instantiation passes in no values (arguments) to the class called MethodsVoid as there are no values between the open and close brackets ()
- this means that the default constructor has been used and the fields of the class will have the default value for their data type

Example code snippet to activate a custom constructor made by us as developers:

```
public class Test
{
public static void main(String[] args)
{
    MethodsVoid myInstanceOfMethodsVoid = new MethodsVoid("RS1234", 2999.50);
} // End of main() method

} // End of class
```

← calls our created constructor

Analysis of the constructor code

- this instantiation passes in two values (arguments) to the constructor of the MethodsVoid class
- as we can see from the two values between the open and close brackets () we are passing in one String and one double value to the class called MethodsVoid

- the values (arguments) are passed to the constructor, which we will have been created and the constructor accepts these arguments as its parameters
- the values are of type String and double in this particular order
- remember, the default constructor accepts no values
- once we as the developer create a constructor it automatically 'overwrites' the default constructor

The class code to go with this instantiation could be:

```java
package com.gerrybyrne.module11;
public class MethodsVoid
{
    String repairShopID;
    double claimAmount;
    /*
    The default constructor is being overwritten as we are creating our
    own constructor which accepts two values, the first is of type String
    and the second is of type double.

    The constructors sole purpose is to assign values to the class level
    variables (properties). To differentiate the class level variables
    (properties) we use the Java keyword this followed by a period and
    then the property name
    */
    public MethodsVoid(String repairShopID, double claimAmount)
    {
        this.repairShopID = repairShopID;

        this.claimAmount = claimAmount;
    } // End of constructor
} // End of class
```

Analysis of the constructor code

- when the class is instantiated the first argument is the value, "RS1234"
- this argument is accepted by the repairID as a parameter and the default value of the repairID field is overwritten and becomes "RS1234"
- when the class is instantiated the second argument is the value, 2999.50

- this argument is accepted by the claimAmount parameter and the default value of the claimAmount field is overwritten and becomes 2999.50
- the constructor therefore uses the parameters to initialise the fields
- this.repairShopID refers to the repairShopID field of the class (object)
- this.repairShopID is therefore assigned the value "RS1234"
- this.claimAmount refers to the claimAmount field of the class (object)
- this.claimAmount is therefore assigned the value 2999.50

Since there is a constructor 'method' in this example it means that the default constructor no longer exists, it has been overwritten.

Constructor Overloading

As we discussed in the methods module, Java allows us to use **overloading.** The concept of overloading can be applied to constructors in the same way as method overloading.

Overloading means that it is possible for us to have constructors with the same name, but which take a different set of input parameters.

Our last class could therefore take the format as shown below:

```
package com.gerrybyrne.module11;
public class MethodsVoid
{
    String repairShopID;
    double claimAmount;

    /*
    The default constructor is being overwritten as we are creating our
    own constructor which accepts two values, the first is of type String
    and the second is of type double.

    The constructors sole purpose is to assign values to the class level variables
    (properties). To differentiate the class level variables (properties) we use the Java
    keyword this followed by a period and then the property name
    */
```

```java
    public MethodsVoid(String repairShopID, double claimAmount)
    {
        this.repairShopID = repairShopID;

        this.claimAmount = claimAmount;
    }
```
← Constructor with two arguments of type String to initialise the field repairShopID and double to initialise the field claimAmount

```
/*
The default constructor is being overwritten as we are creating
another constructor which accepts only value which is of type
String.

This constructors sole purpose is to assign a value to the class
level variable (properties) called repairShopID. The other class
level variable called claimAmount will just be assigned its default
value which in this case is 0.00 as it is of data type double.
*/
```

```java
    public MethodsVoid(String repairShopID)
    {
        this.repairShopID = repairShopID;
    } // End of constructor
```
← Constructor with one argument of type String to initialise the field repairShopID

```
/*
The default constructor is being overwritten as we are creating
another constructor which accepts only one value which is of type
double.

This constructors sole purpose is to assign a value to the class
level variable (properties) called claimAmount. The other class
level variable called repairShopID will just be assigned its
default value which in this case is null as it is of data type
String.
*/
```

```java
    public MethodsVoid(double claimAmount)
    {
        this.claimAmount = claimAmount;
    } // End of constructor

} // End of class
```
← Use a constructor we have created

As we read earlier many commercial programs will involve large amounts of code and from a maintenance and testing perspective it is essential that the program has a good structure. Well written and organised programs allow those who maintain or test them to:
- follow the code and the flow of events easier
- find things quicker

Recapping what we have seen in the methods module:

To structure the program code better we could break the code into small functional parts, each part performing one task. When we have a functional part, which does one thing, it may be possible for that functional part to be used by other parts of the program. We created methods that performed one task and then the methods could be called as required. Well, this section will develop this concept even further.

Suppose we have developed a program with the following methods:
- agentCommission()
- customerPersonalDetails()
- customerVehicleDetails()
- agentBonus()

Suppose all the methods are inside a class but outside the main() method. Now, this would be fine, and the code could work, but looking closely at the method names we might suggest that they **relate to 2 distinct groups, an Agent** and **a Customer**.

Now we should think, would it not be better if each method was placed inside a class that related to these groupings. This would mean that our code would now look something like this with 3 classes:

Class 1 - which will be used to start the program as it has the main() method

```
public class Insurance
{
    public static void main(String[] args)
```

```
    {
        //Some code to call the methods in the other class(es)
    }
} // End of class
```

Class 2 - will have methods and properties (variables, fields) associated with an Agent

```
public class Agent
{
    public static void agentCommission()
    {
        //Some code to calculate the commission
    } // End of method

    public static void agentBonus()
    {
        //Some code to calculate the bonus
    } // End of method
} // End of class
```

Class 3 - will have methods and properties (variables, fields) associated with a Customer

```
public class Customer
{
    public static void customerPersonalDetails()
    {
        // Some code to read in the customer personal details
    } // End of method

    public static void customerVehicleDetails()
    {
        // Some code to read in the customers vehicle details
    } // End of method
} // End of class
```

Our code is now organised into classes and into methods within the classes and importantly the distinct classes hold methods that have a similar purpose. The classes could also have properties (variables, fields) and we will see this as we code our examples.

Whilst coding the examples in each of the modules completed so far we have used methods that belong to different classes.

Example code snippet:

    return *myScanner*.nextInt();

Here we used the method called nextInt() which belongs to the class called **myScanner**, which is our instance of the Scanner class.

- when this line of code is entered into the Integrated Development Environment (IDE) and the full stop is typed after the word myScanner, a pop-up appears
- the pop-up window displays the methods and fields that are part of the Scanner class
- the methods have the () after their name.
- the fields do not have the (), just their name

In the diagram below we can see the methods, and in particular the nextInt() method that does not accept an argument.

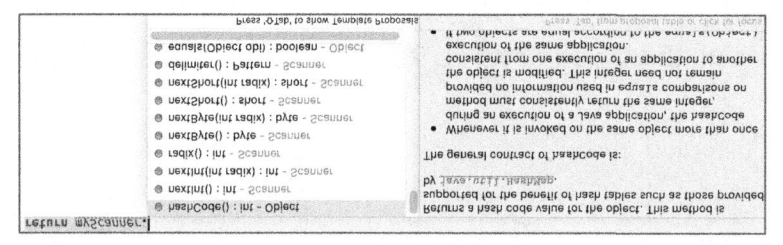

Example code snippet:

    Double answer = Math.*sqrt*(9.0);

Here we have used the method called sqrt() which belongs the class called **Math**.

- as this example code is entered into the Integrated Development Environment (IDE) and the full stop is typed after the word Math, a pop-up appears
- the pop-up window displays the methods and fields that are part of the Math class
- the methods have the () after their name
- the fields do not have the (), just their name

In the diagram below we can see the methods and in particular the sqrt() method that accepts a double as an argument.

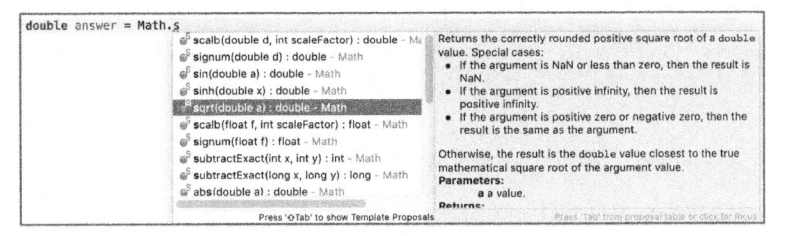

Great, so now we can think of methods that come with the Java framework and from the imports, not just being coded in one class but in numerous classes. With these classes there is a high degree of code separation, we call it **separation of concerns (SoC)**, where associated methods are kept together and this is what we can do, and have done, in the methods module. Think about separation of concerns using these examples:

- in a school there are different roles
    - the head teacher
    - the senior teachers
    - the teachers
    - the administration staff
    - the facilities staff
    - the canteen staff

All roles have separate concerns, but all serve one purpose, to keep the school working.

- in a hospital there are different roles
    - the consultants
    - the doctors
    - the nurses
    - the care assistants
    - the administration staff
    - the facilities staff
    - the catering staff

All roles have separate concerns, but all serve one purpose, to keep the hospital functioning.

Let's code some Java

Now it is time for us to code some classes with methods and show the separation of concern working in our application. We will be programming the same application that we have just completed in the methods module, so we can choose to copy and paste as required, but the instructions below assume that we are starting again with no code.

Exercise One – Create a class without a main() method

1. Right click on the **src** folder.
2. Choose **New**.
3. Choose **Package**.
4. Name the package **com.gerrybyrne.module11**.
5. Click the **Finish** button.
6. Right click on the **com.gerrybyrne.module11** package icon.
7. Choose **New**.
8. Choose **Class**.
9. Name the class **ClaimApplication**.
10. Put a tick in the checkbox beside the public static void main(String[] args) box.
11. Click on the Finish button.

The **ClaimApplication** class code will appear in the editor window and will be similar to the following:

package com.gerrybyrne.module11;

public class ClaimApplication
{
 public static void main(String[] args)
 {
 // TODO Auto-generated method stub
 } // End of main method()
} // End of ClaimApplication class

12. Right click on the **com.gerrybyrne.module11** package icon.
13. Choose **New**.
14. Choose **Class**.
15. Name the class **ClaimDetails**.
16. **DO NOT** put a tick in the checkbox beside the public static void main(String[] args) box.
17. Click on the Finish button.

The **ClaimDetails** class code will appear in the editor window and will be similar to the following:

package com.gerrybyrne.module11;

public class ClaimDetails
{
} // End of ClaimDetails class

We are now going to use the same code, with some small changes, that we created for the MethodsValue program, but the methods will be contained within the ClaimDetails class and will be called from within the ClaimApplication class which contains the main() method. This will now ensure that we have some degree of separation.

Remember that the methods in the MethodsValue program were numbered, so the instructions below will reference the methods by their number. We will then add further classes to enforce the concept of classes and objects.

18. Amend the ClaimDetails code to add an instance of the Scanner class so input can be read from the keyboard:

    package com.gerrybyrne.module11;
    import java.util.Scanner;

    public class ClaimDetails
    {
       Scanner myScanner = **new** Scanner(System.in);
    } // End of ClaimDetails class

19. Amend the code to add the required class level variables, these were in **Method1** in the MethodsValue application:

```
package com.gerrybyrne.module11;
import java.util.Scanner;

public class ClaimDetails
{
    Scanner myScanner = new Scanner(System.in);

    int numberOfClaimsBeingMade;
```

20. Amend the code to add **Method1**:

```
    // Method 1
    public int HowManyClaimsAreBeingMade()
    {
        /*
            Read the user input for the number of claims being made and
            convert the string value to an integer data type
        */
        System.out.println("How many claims are we wishing to make?\n");

        // numberOfClaimsBeingMade = myScanner.nextInt();
        return myScanner.nextInt();
    } // End of HowManyClaimsAreBeingMade() method
} // End of ClaimDetails class
```

21. Click on the **File** menu.
22. Choose **Save All**.

Now we have the method we should be able to refer to it from the other class. We should take note that the full name of the method contains the class name:

>ClaimDetails.HowManyClaimsAreBeingMade();

To use the ClaimDetails class we make a copy of it. We do not use the original class as it is the template. We will therefore make a copy, an instance, of the class from within the main() method of the ClaimApplication class.

23. Amend the **ClaimApplication** class as shown to make an instance of the ClaimDetails class:

    package com.gerrybyrne.module11;

    public class ClaimApplication
    {
        public static void main(String[] args)
        {
            /*
            Create an instance (copy) of the ClaimDetails class calling
            it myClaimDetailsInstance. When we use the new keyword with
            the ClaimDetails() we are calling the constructor method and
            in this case we have no values between the brackets () so we
            are not passing any values to the constructor. Obviously then
            the constructor is the default constructor or the programmer
            developed constructor is expecting no parameters
            */
            ClaimDetails myClaimDetailsInstance = **new** ClaimDetails();
        } // End of main method()
    } // End of ClaimApplication class

24. Amend the main() method code to call (Method1) HowManyClaimsAreBeingMade() and assign it to the variable numberOfClaimsBeingMade:

    ClaimDetails myClaimDetailsInstance = **new** ClaimDetails();

    int numberOfClaimsBeingMade =
    myClaimDetailsInstance.HowManyClaimsAreBeingMade();
        } // End of main method()
    } // End of ClaimApplication class

This code clearly shows the concept of classes and shows that:

- a class without a main() method has been created to hold methods and fields
- from another class, which has a main() method, an instance of the class containing the methods is created
- using the instance of the class we have access to the methods and fields of the class that have the public access modifier
- adding the full stop after the instance name means those methods and fields that are accessible will be displayed, this is called the dot notation

This means that we could create as many methods as we like in the class and create as many classes as we like. This idea of separating our code into methods and our methods into classes is exactly what a Java application should look like when it is being coded.

Now check that the method is being read correctly.

25. Click on the **File** menu.
26. Choose **Save All.**
27. Click on the green **Run** button at the top of the screen.

The console window will appear and ask the user to input the number of claims to be made.

28. Type **2** and press the Enter key.

The console window will accept our value and then exit the program.

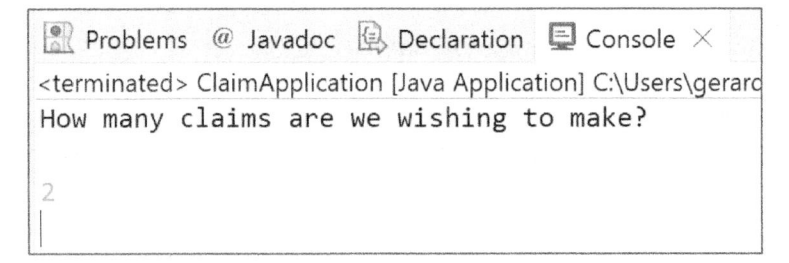

```
Problems  @ Javadoc  Declaration  Console  X
<terminated> ClaimApplication [Java Application] C:\Users\gerard
How many claims are we wishing to make?

2
```

This is excellent, our method has been called from another class. We will now add another of the methods.

29. Add the rest of the fields we will need to the **ClaimDetails** class (these are in the MethodsValue application):

```java
package com.gerrybyrne.module11;
import java.util.Scanner;

public class ClaimDetails
{
    Scanner myScanner = new Scanner(System.in);
    static int numberOfClaimsBeingMade;

    /*
    We will setup our variables that will be used in the quote application
    The details will be:
    - the repair shop unique id (String)
    - the vehicle insurance policy number (String)
    - the claim amount and (double)
    - the date of the claim (String)
    */

    String repairShopID;
    String vehiclePolicyNumber;
    double claimAmount;
    String claimDate;

    /*
    The array is going to hold the data for 2 claims. Each claim has
    four pieces of information. The number of data items is therefore
            2 multiplied by 4 = 8
    So, we will make the array for this example of size 8.
    Not the best way to do things but fine for now. */
    String[] repairShopClaims = new String[8];
    double totalofallclaims;
    double vatamount;
    int numberOfClaimsEntered = 0;
    int arrayPositionCounter = 0;

    // Method 1
    public int HowManyClaimsAreBeingMade()
    {
```

30. Add the code for **Method2** after the end of Method1:

    ```
    // Method 2
    public void CurrentValueOfCounter()
    {
        System.out.println("The current value of the counter is :" +
                            numberOfClaimsEntered + "\n");
    } // End of CurrentValueOfCounter() method

    } // End of ClaimDetails class
    ```

31. Add the code for **Method3** after the end of Method2:

    ```
    // Method 3
    public String ReadTheRepairShopId()
    {
        // Read the user input for the repair shop id and keep it as a string
        System.out.println("What is our repair shop id?\n");
        repairShopID = myScanner.next();
        return repairShopID;

    } // End of ReadTheReparShopId() method
    } // End of ClaimDetails class
    ```

32. Add the code that was in **Method4** after the end of Method3:

    ```
    // Method 4
    public void WriteRepairShopIdToTheArray()
    {
        /*
        Write the first input value to the array and then increment the
        value of the arrayPositionCounter by 1.
        */
        repairShopClaims[arrayPositionCounter] = repairShopID;

        arrayPositionCounter++;
    } // End of WriteRepairShopIdToTheArray() method

    } // End of ClaimDetails class
    ```

33. Add the code that was in **Method5** after the end of Method4:

    // Method 5
    public String ReadTheVehiclePolicyNumber()
    {
    /*
    Read the user input for the vehicle policy number and keep it
    as a string
    */
    System.out.println("What is the vehicle policy number?\n");
    vehiclePolicyNumber = myScanner.next();
    return vehiclePolicyNumber;
    } // End of ReadTheVehiclePolicyNumber() method

    } // End of ClaimDetails class

34. Add the code that was in **Method6** after the end of Method5:

    // Method 6
    public void WriteVehiclePolicyNumberToTheArray()
    {
    /*
    Write the second input value to the array and then increment the
    value of the arrayPositionCounter by 1
    */
    repairShopClaims[arrayPositionCounter] = vehiclePolicyNumber;

    arrayPositionCounter++;
    } // End of WriteVehiclePolicyNumberToTheArray() method

    } // End of ClaimDetails class

35. Add the code that was in **Method7** after the end of Method6:

    // Method 7
    public double ReadTheAmountBeingClaimed()
    {
    /*
    Read the user input for the repair amount and convert it to a double

```
*/
System.out.println("What is the amount being claimed for the repair?\n");

claimAmount = myScanner.nextDouble();

AccumulateClaimAmount(claimAmount);

return claimAmount;
} // End of ReadTheAmountBeingClaimed() method

} // End of ClaimDetails class
```

Do not worry about the error in relation to the AccumulateClaimAmount() method, as we have not created this method yet. We will create it shortly.

36. Add the code that was in **Method8** after the end of Method7:

```
// Method 8
public void WriteClaimAmountToTheArray()
{
/*
  Write the third input value to the array and then increment the
  value of the arrayPositionCounter by 1. The value read in from
  the console is of data type double and the array holds Strings,
  so a conversion from double to String must be done
*/
repairShopClaims[arrayPositionCounter] = Double.toString(claimAmount);

arrayPositionCounter++;
} // End of WriteClaimAmountToTheArray() method

} // End of ClaimDetails class
```

37. Add the code that was in **Method9** after the end of Method8:

```
// Method 9
public String ReadTheRepairDate()
{
  /*
```

```
        Read the user input for the repair date leaving it as a String
      */
      System.out.println("What was the date of the repair?\n");
      claimDate = myScanner.next();

      return claimDate;
      }// End of ReadTheRepairDate() method

} // End of ClaimDetails class
```

38. Add the code that was in **Method10** after the end of Method9:

```
    // Method 10
    public void WriteRepairDateToTheArray()
    {
      /*
        Write the fourth input value to the array and then increment the
        value of the arrayPositionCounter by 1
      */
      repairShopClaims[arrayPositionCounter] = claimDate;

      arrayPositionCounter++;
      }// End of WriteRepairDateToTheArray() method

} // End of ClaimDetails class
```

39. Add the code that was in **Method11** after the end of Method10:

```
    // Method 11
    public void DisplayAllItemsInTheArray()
    {
      for (String itemInTheClaimsArray: repairShopClaims)
      {
        System.out.println("The item in the array is:\t" +
                    itemInTheClaimsArray + "\n");
      }
    } // End of DisplayAllItemsInTheArray() method

} // End of ClaimDetails class
```

40. Add the code that was in **Method12** after the end of Method11:

    // Method 12
    public double AccumulateClaimAmount(**double** claimamountpassedin)
    {
        totalofallclaims = totalofallclaims + claimamountpassedin;
        return totalofallclaims;
    } // End of AccumulateClaimAmount method

    } // End of ClaimDetails class

41. Add the code that was in **Method13** after the end of Method12:

    // Method 13
    public double CalculateVATAmount(**double** totalvalueofclaimspassedin)
    {
    vatamount = totalvalueofclaimspassedin - (totalvalueofclaimspassedin/1.20);
     return vatamount;
    } // End of CalculateVATAmount method

    } // End of ClaimDetails class

42. Add the code that was in **Method14** after the end of Method13:

    // Method 14
    public void DisplayInvoiceReceipt(**double** totalvalueofclaimspassedin, **double** vatPassedIn)
    {
    System.out.println("\nInvoice for vehicle repairs\n");
    System.out.println("Nett claim\t" + (totalofallclaims-vatamount) + "\n");
    System.out.println("VAT amount\t" + vatamount + "\n");
    System.out.println("Total amount\t" + totalofallclaims + "\n");
    } // End of DisplayInvoiceReceipt method

    } // End of ClaimDetails class

43. Add the code that was in **Method15** after the end of Method14:

// Method 15
public void DisplayInvoiceReceipt(**double** totalvalueofclaimspassedin,
            double vatPassedIn, String messagePassedIn)
{
System.out.println("***");
System.out.println("\nInvoice for vehicle repairs\n");
System.out.println("Nett claim\t" + (totalofallclaims-vatamount) + "\n");
System.out.println("VAT amount\t" + vatamount + "\n");
System.out.println("Total amount\t" + totalofallclaims + "\n");
System.out.println(messagePassedIn);
System.out.println("***");
} // End of DisplayInvoiceReceipt method
} // End of ClaimDetails class

Code analysis

Now, let's stop and think what we have just done:
- we have created a new class without a main() method – it is called ClaimDetails
- we have added the fields that we will use in the methods of the class or in the class itself
- we have added the original methods we had in the MethodsValue class
- we have created a class with a main() method – it is called ClaimApplication
- in the main() method we have:
  - created an instance of the ClaimDetails class, our copy of the class
  - accessed the method called HowManyClaimsAreBeingMade() by using the name of the instance class we created, followed by a full stop (dot notation) and then selecting the method

We will now continue with the code in the ClaimApplication class.

44. Amend the code in the **ClaimApplication** class to add the rest of the fields we will need in this class:

    package com.gerrybyrne.module11;
    public class ClaimApplication
    {

```
static int numberOfClaimsBeingMade;
public static void main(String[] args)
{
  int numberOfClaimsEntered = 0;
  double vatamount;

  /*Create an instance (copy) of the ClaimDetails class calling
     it myClaimDetailsInstance. When we use the new keyword with
     the ClaimDetails() we are calling the constructor method and
     in this case we have no values between the brackets () so we
     are not passing any values to the constructor. Obviously then
     the constructor is the default constructor or the programmer
     developed constructor is expecting no parameters */
  ClaimDetails myClaimDetailsInstance = new ClaimDetails();

  numberOfClaimsBeingMade =
          myClaimDetailsInstance.HowManyClaimsAreBeingMade();
```

45. Now add the do-while loop as shown:

```
  ClaimDetails myClaimDetailsInstance = new ClaimDetails();

  int numberOfClaimsBeingMade =
  myClaimDetailsInstance.HowManyClaimsAreBeingMade();

  /*
  As we are using a variable in the loop our code is flexible and can
  be used for any number of claims.
  An ideal situation and good code.
  */
  do
  {

  } while (numberOfClaimsEntered < numberOfClaimsBeingMade);

  } // End of main method()
} // End of ClaimApplication class
```

Now we will call the method that will read the repair shop id, remembering that the method does not exist in the class we are in. We will need to call it using the instance of the class that we created, myClaimDetailsInstance.

Remember, after we enter the instance name and type the . (dot), the list of fields and methods of the class will appear, so we should select the method rather than typing it.

If the list of fields and methods of the class do not appear then there is something wrong with the code, go back and check it.

46. Add the following code in the **ClaimApplication** class to call the method which will read the repair shop id:

    ```
    do {
        // Call the methods as required
        myClaimDetailsInstance.ReadTheRepairShopId();
    ```

This once again clearly shows the concept of classes. Using the instance of the class, we have access to the methods and fields of the class that have the public access modifier. The dot notation, a full stop after the instance of the class name, shows us those methods and fields that are accessible.

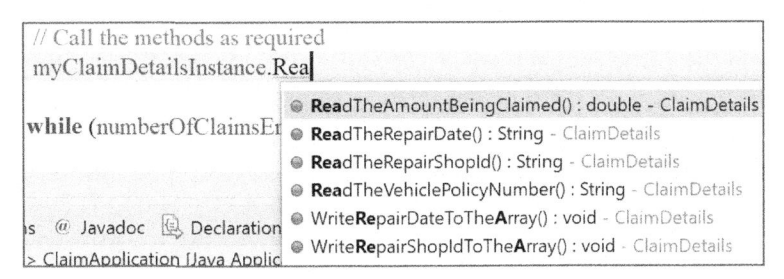

47. Add the following code to call the method which will write the repair shop id to the array:

    ```
    do
    {
        // Call the methods as required
        myClaimDetailsInstance.ReadTheRepairShopId();
        myClaimDetailsInstance.WriteRepairShopIdToTheArray();
    ```

We will now repeat the same two actions, read and write, for the vehicle policy number.

48. Add the following code to call the method which will read the vehicle policy number:

    ```
    do {
        // Call the methods as required
        myClaimDetailsInstance.ReadTheRepairShopId();
        myClaimDetailsInstance.WriteRepairShopIdToTheArray();

        myClaimDetailsInstance.ReadTheVehiclePolicyNumber();
    ```

49. Add the following code to call the method which will write the vehicle policy number to the array:

    ```
    do {
        // Call the methods as required
        myClaimDetailsInstance.ReadTheRepairShopId();
        myClaimDetailsInstance.WriteRepairShopIdToTheArray();
        myClaimDetailsInstance.ReadTheVehiclePolicyNumber();

        myClaimDetailsInstance.WriteVehiclePolicyNumberToTheArray();
    ```

We will now repeat the same two actions, read and write, for the claim amount.

50. Add the following code to call the method which will read the claim amount

    ```
    do {
        // Call the methods as required
        myClaimDetailsInstance.ReadTheRepairShopId();
        myClaimDetailsInstance.WriteRepairShopIdToTheArray();
        myClaimDetailsInstance.ReadTheVehiclePolicyNumber();
        myClaimDetailsInstance.WriteVehiclePolicyNumberToTheArray();

        myClaimDetailsInstance.ReadTheAmountBeingClaimed();
    ```

51. Add the following code to call the method which will write the claim amount to the array:

    ```
    do {
    ```

// Call the methods as required
myClaimDetailsInstance.WriteRepairShopIdToTheArray();
myClaimDetailsInstance.ReadTheVehiclePolicyNumber();
myClaimDetailsInstance.WriteVehiclePolicyNumberToTheArray();
myClaimDetailsInstance.ReadTheAmountBeingClaimed();

myClaimDetailsInstance.WriteClaimAmountToTheArray();

We will now repeat the same two actions, read and write, for the claim date.

52. Add the following code to call the method which will read the claim date

    do {
    // Call the methods as required
    myClaimDetailsInstance.WriteRepairShopIdToTheArray();
    myClaimDetailsInstance.ReadTheVehiclePolicyNumber();
    myClaimDetailsInstance.WriteVehiclePolicyNumberToTheArray();
    myClaimDetailsInstance.ReadTheAmountBeingClaimed();
    myClaimDetailsInstance.WriteClaimAmountToTheArray();

    myClaimDetailsInstance.ReadTheRepairDate();

53. Add the following code to call the method which will write the claim date to the array:

    myClaimDetailsInstance.WriteRepairShopIdToTheArray();
    myClaimDetailsInstance.ReadTheVehiclePolicyNumber();
    myClaimDetailsInstance.WriteVehiclePolicyNumberToTheArray();
    myClaimDetailsInstance.ReadTheAmountBeingClaimed();
    myClaimDetailsInstance.WriteClaimAmountToTheArray();
    myClaimDetailsInstance.ReadTheRepairDate();

    myClaimDetailsInstance.WriteRepairDateToTheArray();

54. Add the following code to increment the number of claims that have been entered by one:

    myClaimDetailsInstance.ReadTheRepairDate();
    myClaimDetailsInstance.WriteRepairDateToTheArray();

```
/* Increment the loop counter by 1 */
numberOfClaimsEntered++;
} while (numberOfClaimsEntered < numberOfClaimsBeingMade);
```

Now we have the bulk of the work done because we have our methods in a class and we have called the methods to get the user input and stored the details in an array. Now we need to add a few more things so that the invoice receipt can be displayed.

Remember when we referenced a method in the other class we referred to it using the instance name followed by a . followed by the method name.

In this next part we are going to refer to a method and a field in the external class ClaimDetails. We will therefore use the instance name followed by a . followed by the field name when accessing a field.

55. Add the following code to call the method which will calculate the amount of VAT based on the total of the claims:

```
} while (numberOfClaimsEntered < numberOfClaimsBeingMade);

vatamount = myClaimDetailsInstance.CalculateVATAmount(myClaimDetailsInstance.totalofallclaims);
    } // End of main method()
} // End of ClaimApplication class
```

Note that

- the method name is preceded by myClaimDetailsInstance

and
- the field name is preceded by myClaimDetailsInstance.

myClaimDetailsInstance is, as it says, our instance of the ClaimDetails class. It gives us access to the methods and fields of the class.

Now we have the VAT and all the other details for the claims we can call the method that will display the invoice receipt. As there are two methods in the code that will do the display, we need to be specific about which one to call.

The two methods have the same name, DisplayInvoiceReceipt, but have different parameters and this is referred to as method overloading. In this example we will call the method that has three parameters.

56. Add the following code to call the method which will display the invoice receipt based on the total of the claims, the VAT amount and the message string:

```
        numberOfClaimsEntered++;
    } while (numberOfClaimsEntered < numberOfClaimsBeingMade);

    vatamount = myClaimDetailsInstance.CalculateVATAmount(myClaimDetailsInstance.totalofallclaims);

    myClaimDetailsInstance.DisplayInvoiceReceipt(myClaimDetailsInstance.totalofallclaims, vatamount, "\tThank you for your claims \n\tthey will be processed today");

    } // End of main() method
}// End of ClaimApplication class
```

57. Click on the **File** menu.
58. Choose **Save All**.
59. Click on the green **Run** button at the top of the screen.
60. Click in the Console window at the bottom of the screen.

The console window will appear and ask the user to input the number of claims to be made.

61. Type **2** and press the Enter key.

The console window will appear and ask the user to input the repair shop id.

62. Type **RS000001** for the repair shop id and press the Enter key.

The console will now ask the user to input the vehicle policy number.

63. Type **VP000001** and press the Enter key.

The console will now ask the user to input the claim amount.

64. Type **1200** and press the Enter key.

The console will now ask the user to input the date of the repair

65. Type **01/10/2021** and press the Enter key.

The questions are asked again for the second claim:

66. Type **RS000001** for the repair shop id and press the Enter key.

The console will now ask the user to input the vehicle policy number.

67. Type **VP000002** and press the Enter key.

The console will now ask the user to input the claim amount.

68. Type **3600** and press the Enter key.

The console will now ask the user to input the date of the repair

69. Type **01/10/2021** and press the Enter key.

The invoice receipt will be displayed as shown below:

```
*******************************************
Invoice for vehicle repairs

Nett claim       4000.0

VAT amount       800.0

Total amount     4800.0

         Thank you for your claims
         they will be processed today
*******************************************
```

This is the same application as MethodsValue and the same invoice receipt. The big difference is the separation of the methods from the class that contains the main() method.

This is just an example to show how classes work, it certainly is not a 'polished' application and it can be improved upon, but the important things to take away from what we have done so far are:

- a class contains **fields**, also called members, variables, properties
- a class contains **methods**
- to use a class from within another class we need to create an instance of it, this is called **instantiation**
- the instantiated class gives us access to the fields and methods of the class

Constructor

In the ClaimApplication class we made an instance of the ClaimDetails class so we could access the fields and methods of the class. The code line was:

ClaimDetails myClaimDetailsInstance = **new** ClaimDetails();

The **new ClaimDetails()** section of the code means we are not passing in any parameters to the class, this is why there are no values between the brackets (). What we are doing is calling the **default constructor**.

We read earlier that the **constructor** 'method' is used to initialise the value of the fields in the class. It may be used to initialise all the fields or some of them, or in the case of a default constructor, none of the fields are initialised, they just have their default values.

Refreshing what we read earlier, a constructor has the following features:

- it must have the same name as the class, we will therefore use the name ClaimDetails
- it must have an access modifier of public
- it does not have a return type, not even void
- it takes in arguments of the same type as the fields that are to be initialised

Next

- we will create a constructor that will set the date field which is of data type String
- the new constructor will therefore overwrite the default constructor
- by setting the date field to the date read from the computer, we will not need to have the method that asks the user to input the date of the claim, (method 9), so this method will not be called from the main metho
- for now, we will leave the method in the ClaimDetails class.

70. In the **ClaimDetails** amend the code to add a constructor that will set the date field to the current computer date.

```
static String[] repairShopClaims = new String[8];
static double totalofallclaims;
static double vatamount;
static int numberOfClaimsEntered = 0;
static int arrayPositionCounter = 0;

/*
  This is a constructor that accepts one String argument
  The value that is passed to the constructor is used to
  set the value of the field called claimDate.
  The constructor has the same name as the class, it has
  an access modifier of public, it takes an argument of
  data type String as this is the same data type as the
  field, claimDate, that is being initialised, and it does
  not return a value so there is no return type
*/
public ClaimDetails(String claimDate)
{
  this.claimDate = claimDate;
}

// Method 1
public int HowManyClaimsAreBeingMade()
{
```

Now that we have created the constructor we can use it when creating the instance of the class from within the main() method. If we look in the ClaimApplication class we will now see that there is an error in the line that instantiates the class. This is because there is no default constructor and the new constructor expects a String value to be passed to it. This can be seen in the 3 quick fixes shown below, it is the first fix we could use but we will do this 'manually' so do not click on the first fix.

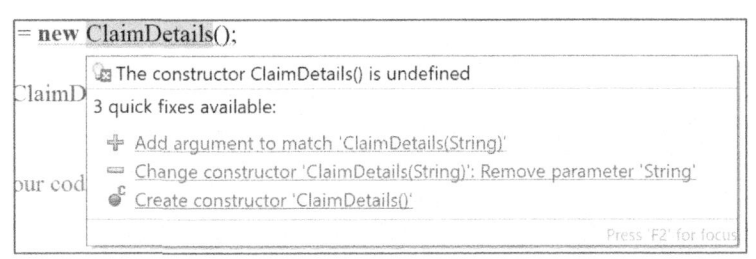

```
= new ClaimDetails();
    The constructor ClaimDetails() is undefined
ClaimD
    3 quick fixes available:
       Add argument to match 'ClaimDetails(String)'
       Change constructor 'ClaimDetails(String)': Remove parameter 'String'
ur cod
       Create constructor 'ClaimDetails()'
                                                    Press 'F2' for focus
```

71. Amend the ClaimApplication code to read the date from the computer:

    ```
    public static void main(String[] args)
    {
        int numberOfClaimsEntered = 0;
        int numberOfClaimsBeingMade = 0;
        double vatamount;

        // Read the date from the computer clock
        LocalDate localDate = LocalDate.now();
    ```

72. Add the code to import the LocalDate class:

    package com.gerrybyrne.module11;

    import java.time.LocalDate;

73. Add the code to convert the date to a String:

    ```
    // Read the date from the computer clock
    LocalDate localDate = LocalDate.now();

    String myDateString = localDate.toString();
    ```

74. Amend the ClaimApplication code so that the instantiation we have now passes the string version of the date to the constructor:

```
// Read the date from the computer clock
LocalDate localDate = LocalDate.now();

String myDateString = localDate.toString();

/*
Create an instance (copy) of the ClaimDetails class calling
it myClaimDetailsInstance. When we use the new keyword with
the ClaimDetails() we are calling the constructor method and
in this case we have no values between the brackets () so we
are not passing any values to the constructor. Obviously then
the constructor is the default constructor or the programmer
developed constructor is expecting no parameters
*/
ClaimDetails myClaimDetailsInstance = new ClaimDetails(myDateString);
```

75. As we now have the date, we do not need to ask the user to input the date. The method call can be removed or commented out so it is not used:

```
do
{
    // Call the methods as required
    myClaimDetailsInstance.ReadTheRepairShopId();
    myClaimDetailsInstance.WriteRepairShopIdToTheArray();
    myClaimDetailsInstance.ReadTheVehiclePolicyNumber();
    myClaimDetailsInstance.WriteVehiclePolicyNumberToTheArray();
    myClaimDetailsInstance.ReadTheAmountBeingClaimed();
    myClaimDetailsInstance.WriteClaimAmountToTheArray();

    // myClaimDetailsInstance.ReadTheRepairDate();

    myClaimDetailsInstance.WriteRepairDateToTheArray();

    /* Increment the loop counter by 1 */
    numberOfClaimsEntered++;
```

} **while** (numberOfClaimsEntered < numberOfClaimsBeingMade);

In order to see the date being displayed we need to iterate the array and display the items within it.

76. Add the for each loop after the do while loop:

```
   numberOfClaimsEntered++;
 } while (numberOfClaimsEntered < numberOfClaimsBeingMade);

 for(String item:myClaimDetailsInstance.repairShopClaims)
 {
      System.out.println(item);
 }
```

vatamount = myClaimDetailsInstance.
    CalculateVATAmount(myClaimDetailsInstance.totalofallclaims);

Now we can test the code to ensure the constructor works. If it does, the array will be populated with the current date.

77. Click on the **File** menu.
78. Choose **Save All**.
79. Click on the green **Run** button at the top of the screen.
80. Click in the Console window at the bottom of the screen.

The console window will appear and ask the user to input the number of claims to be made.

81. Type **2** and press the Enter key.

The console window will appear and ask the user to input the repair shop id.

82. Type **RS000001** for the repair shop id and press the Enter key.

The console will now ask the user to input the vehicle policy number.

83. Type **VP000001** and press the Enter key.

The console will now ask the user to input the claim amount.

84. Type **1200** and press the Enter key.

We have removed the call to the method that asks the user to input the date of the repair so we will not be asked for the date of the repair.

The questions are asked again for the second claim:

85. Type **RS000001** for the repair shop id and press the Enter key.

The console will now ask the user to input the vehicle policy number.

86. Type **VP000002** and press the Enter key.

The console will now ask the user to input the claim amount.

87. Type **3600** and press the Enter key.

The array and the invoice receipt will be displayed as shown below:

```
RS000001
VP000001
1200.0
2021-05-23
RS000001
VP000002
3600.0
2021-05-23
*******************************************

Invoice for vehicle repairs

Nett claim      4000.0

VAT amount      800.0

Total amount    4800.0

        Thank you for your claims
        they will be processed today
*******************************************
```

Another Constructor

We will now create a second constructor that will set the date field which is of data type String and a message field which is also of data type String. This new constructor will therefore be different from the first constructor, as it has two arguments as opposed to one, this is constructor overloading. We will need to create an additional field called message of data type String.

1. Amend the code to add an additional field called message:

   ```
   String repairShopID;
   String vehiclePolicyNumber;
   double claimAmount;
   String claimDate;
   String message ="";
   ```

2. Amend the ClaimDetails code to add the second constructor that will set the date field to the current computer date and the message field to whatever message, String, is passed in when the ClaimDetails class is instantiated:

   ```
   public ClaimDetails(String claimDate)
   {
      this.claimDate = claimDate;
   }

   /*
      This is a second constructor that accepts two String
      arguments and the values that are passed to the constructor
      are used to set the value of the field called claimDate and
      the field called message.

      The constructor has the same name as the class, it has an
      access modifier of public, it takes two arguments of data
      type String as these are the same data types as the fields,
      claimDate and message, that are being initialised, and it
      does not return a value so there is no return type.
      As the constructor has two arguments it is different from
      the first constructor
   */
   ```

```
public ClaimDetails(String claimDate, String message)
{
  this.claimDate = claimDate;
  this.message = message;
}
```

Now look back at the call to the **DisplayInvoiceReceipt()** method in the ClaimApplication class:

myClaimDetailsInstance.DisplayInvoiceReceipt(myClaimDetailsInstance.totalofallclaims, vatamount, "\tThank you for your claims \n\tthey will be processed today");

} // End of main() method

Here we have passed in a message to the method and then the method uses this value to display the message. But, as we have now created a constructor that accepts a message string, we could pass the message at the time we instantiate the class. If we do this we could:

- remove method 15, DisplayInvoiceReceipt(**double** totalvalueofclaimspassedin, **double** vatPassedIn, String messagePassedIn)

- call method 14, DisplayInvoiceReceipt(**double** totalvalueofclaimspassedin, **double** vatPassedIn) from in the ClaimApplication class

- add an extra line to method 14 to display the message

As the message is initialised to an empty string if there is no message created by our constructor, a blank will be written for the message. What this means is, if we left the original instantiation which uses the first constructor, no message is passed in so the message will use the value assigned to it, "", null (empty).

3. Amend the code to remove method 15, simply comment the method code:

   // Method 15
   // public void DisplayInvoiceReceipt(double totalvalueofclaimspassedin,

```
//                 double vatPassedIn, String messagePassedIn)
// {
// System.out.println("**\*\***\*\***\*\***\***\*\***\***\*\***");
// System.out.println("\nInvoice for vehicle repairs\n");
// System.out.println("Nett claim\t"+(totalofallclaims-vatamount)+"\n");
// System.out.println("VAT amount\t" + vatamount + "\n");
// System.out.println("Total amount\t" + totalofallclaims + "\n");
// System.out.println(messagePassedIn);
// System.out.println("**\*\***\*\***\*\***\***\*\***\***\*\***");
// }

} // End of ClaimDetails class
```

We will now see that the ClaimApplication class has an error as it is trying to use the DisplayInvoiceReceipt () method which has 3 arguments.

4. Amend the code in the ClaimApplication class to remove string message:

   Change the method call from this

   myClaimDetailsInstance.DisplayInvoiceReceipt(myClaimDetailsInstance.totalofallclaims, vatamount, ~~"\tThank we for our claims \n\tthey will be processed today")~~;

   To this

   myClaimDetailsInstance.DisplayInvoiceReceipt(myClaimDetailsInstance.totalofallclaims, vatamount);

   The error is corrected.

5. Now amend the instantiation code line, in the ClaimApplication class, to pass the two values to the new constructor:

   ```
   // Read the date from the computer clock
   LocalDate localDate = LocalDate.now();
   String myDateString = localDate.toString();
   ClaimDetails myClaimDetailsInstance = new ClaimDetails(myDateString,
   "\tThank you for our claims \n\tthey will be processed today");
   ```

numberOfClaimsBeingMade =
    myClaimDetailsInstance.HowManyClaimsAreBeingMade();

6. Amend the DisplayInvoiceReceipt () method in the ClaimDetails class to add the new line which will print the message line:

```
// Method 14
public void DisplayInvoiceReceipt(double totalvalueofclaimspassedin,
double vatPassedIn)
{
System.out.println("\nInvoice for vehicle repairs\n");
System.out.println("Nett claim\t" + (totalofallclaims - vatamount) + "\n");
System.out.println("VAT amount\t" + vatamount + "\n");
System.out.println("Total amount\t" + totalofallclaims + "\n");

System.out.println(message);
} // End of DisplayInvoiceReceipt method
```

7. Open the **ClaimApplication** class.
8. Click on the **File** menu.
9. Choose **Save All**.
10. Click on the green **Run** button at the top of the screen.
11. Click in the Console window at the bottom of the screen.

The console window will appear and ask the user to input the number of claims to be made.

12. Type **2** and press the Enter key.

The console window will appear and ask the user to input the repair shop id.

13. Type **RS000001** for the repair shop id and press the Enter key.

The console will now ask the user to input the vehicle policy number.

14. Type **VP000001** and press the Enter key.

The console will now ask the user to input the claim amount.

15. Type **1200** and press the Enter key.

We have removed the call to the method that asks the user to input the date of the repair so we will not be asked for the date of the repair.

The questions are asked again for the second claim:

16. Type **RS000001** for the repair shop id and press the Enter key.

The console will now ask the user to input the vehicle policy number.

17. Type **VP000002** and press the Enter key.

The console will now ask the user to input the claim amount.

18. Type **3600** and press the Enter key.

The invoice receipt will be displayed as shown below:

```
Invoice for vehicle repairs

Nett claim        4000.0

VAT amount        800.0

Total amount      4800.0

        Thank you for our claims
        they will be processed today
```

19. Now amend the instantiation code line to pass only the one value, the date string, to the constructor. This means the first constructor will be used and hence the message field will not be changed, it will have the default "". Comment the other instantiation statement:

/*ClaimDetails myClaimDetailsInstance = new ClaimDetails(myDateString,
"\tThank you for your claims \n\tthey will be processed today");*/

```
ClaimDetails myClaimDetailsInstance = new ClaimDetails(myDateString);

int numberOfClaimsBeingMade =
        myClaimDetailsInstance.HowManyClaimsAreBeingMade();
```

20. Click on the **File** menu.
21. Choose **Save All**.
22. Click on the green **Run** button at the top of the screen.
23. Click in the Console window at the bottom of the screen.

The console window will appear and ask the user to input the number of claims to be made.

24. Type **2** and press the Enter key.

The console window will appear and ask the user to input the repair shop id.

25. Type **RS000001** for the repair shop id and press the Enter key.

The console will now ask the user to input the vehicle policy number.

26. Type **VP000001** and press the Enter key.

The console will now ask the user to input the claim amount.

27. Type **1200** and press the Enter key.

We have removed the call to the method that asks the user to input the date of the repair so we will not be asked for the date of the repair.

The questions are asked again for the second claim:

28. Type **RS000001** for the repair shop id and press the Enter key.

The console will now ask the user to input the vehicle policy number.

29. Type **VP000002** and press the Enter key.

The console will now ask the user to input the claim amount.

30. Type **3600** and press the Enter key.

The invoice receipt will be displayed as shown below:

```
Invoice for vehicle repairs

Nett claim        4000.0

VAT amount         800.0

Total amount      4800.0
```

Additional Example for classes and objects

Now we will consolidate what we have learnt in the previous section regarding classes. Here we will take another example and create a class with methods and properties and call them from another class with a main method. The example we will use will involve some mathematical formulae and be related to shapes.

Exercise Two – Shapes and circle shapes formulae

1. Right click on the **src** folder.
2. Choose **New**.
3. Choose **Package**.
4. Name the package **com.gerrybyrne.shapes**.
5. Click the **Finish** button.
6. Right click on the **com.gerrybyrne.shapes** package icon.
7. Choose **New**.
8. Choose **Class**.
9. Name the class **ShapesCalculator**.
10. Put a tick in the checkbox beside the public static void main(String[] args) box.
11. Click on the **Finish** button.

The **ShapesCalculator** class code will appear in the editor window and will be similar to the following:

package com.gerrybyrne.shapes;

public class ShapesCalculator
{
    public static void main(String[] args)
    {
        // TODO Auto-generated method stub

    } // End of main method()
} // End of ShapesCalculator class

12. Right click on the **com.gerrybyrne.shapes** package icon.
13. Choose **New**.
14. Choose **Class**.
15. Name the class **CircleFormulae**.
16. **DO NOT** put a tick in the checkbox beside the public static void main(String[] args) box.
17. Click on the **Finish** button.

The **CircleFormulae** class code will appear in the editor window and will be similar to the following:

package com.gerrybyrne.shapes;

public class CircleFormulae
{

} // End of CircleFormulae class

- we will create a method for the area of a circle:
    - the formula for the area of a circle is PI multiplied by the Radius multiplied by the Radius
    - the formula can also be stated as 'PI R squared' (where R represents the radius)
    - the formula will therefore be our business logic
- to calculate the area of the circle we will ask the user to input the radius they require. In doing this we will need to create a Scanner instance

18. Amend the code to create an instance of the Scanner class and import the Scanner class.

    package com.gerrybyrne.shapes;
    import java.util.Scanner;

    public class CircleFormulae
    {
        Scanner myScanner = **new** Scanner(System.*in*);
    } // End of CircleFormulae class

19. Amend the code to add the method that will calculate the area of the circle.

    package com.gerrybyrne.shapes;

    import java.util.Scanner;

    public class CircleFormulae
    {
        Scanner myScanner = **new** Scanner(System.*in*);

        /*
            This is a method that will ask the user to input the length of
            the radius of the circle, calculate the area of the circle and
            display the area of the circle in the console window
        */
        public void areaOfCircle()
        {

        } //End of areaOfCircle method

    } // End of CircleFormulae class

20. Amend the new method code to create variables to hold the radius and the area of the circle, setting their initial value to be 0.

    public class CircleFormulae
    {
        Scanner myScanner = **new** Scanner(System.*in*);

        /*
            This is a method that will ask the user to input the length of
            the radius of the circle, calculate the area of the circle and
            display the area of the circle in the console window
        */
        public void areaOfCircle()
        {
            /*
                Create two variables of data type double to hold the value of the
                radius input by the user and the calculated area of the circle
            */

```
        // Initialise the two variables to zero
        double radiusLength = 0;

        double areaOfCircle = 0;
    } //End of areaOfCircle method

} // End of CircleFormulae class
```

21. Amend the code to ask the user to input the radius of the circle and then read this value using the Scanner instance.

```
        // Initialise the two variables to zero
        double radiusLength = 0;

        double areaOfCircle = 0;

        // Read the user input for the size of the radius
        System.out.println("What is the length of the radius of the circle?\n");

        radiusLength = myScanner.nextDouble();

    } //End of areaOfCircle method

} // End of CircleFormulae class
```

22. Now add the code that will calculate the area of the circle.

```
        // Read the user input for the size of the radius
        System.out.println("What is the length of the radius of the circle?\n");

        radiusLength = myScanner.nextDouble();

        // Calculate the area of the circle with the formula
        areaOfCircle =Math.PI * radiusLength * radiusLength;

    } //End of areaOfCircle method

} // End of CircleFormulae class
```

23. Now add the code that will display the details of the area and radius of the circle.

```
        // Calculate the area of the circle with the formula
        areaOfCircle =Math.PI * radiusLength * radiusLength;

        // Display the answer
        System.out.printf("\nA circle with radius %.2f has an area of %.2f",
        radiusLength, areaOfCircle);

    } //End of areaOfCircle method

} // End of CircleFormulae class
```

Now we have created a class with a method in it, we will be able to call the method from the main() method in the ShapesCalculator class.

24. Open the **ShapesCalculator** class and create an instance of the ShapesFormulae class. Remember, we do not use the ShapesFormulae class directly, we make an instance of it.

```
package com.gerrybyrne.shapes;

public class ShapesCalculator
{
    public static void main(String[] args)
    {
        CircleFormulae myCircleFormulae = new CircleFormulae();
    } // End of main method()
} // End of ShapesCalculator class
```

25. Now add the code to call the areaOfCircle() method of our new instance class.

```
package com.gerrybyrne.shapes;

public class ShapesCalculator
{
    public static void main(String[] args)
    {
        CircleFormulae myCircleFormulae = new CircleFormulae();
```

```
        myCircleFormulae.areaOfCircle();
    } // End of main method()
} // End of ShapesCalculator class
```

Now check that the method is working correctly.

26. Click on the **File** menu.
27. Choose **Save All**.
28. Click on the green **Run** button at the top of the screen.

The console window will appear and ask the user to input the radius of the circle.

29. Type **10** and press the Enter key.

The console window will show the area of the circle.

```
Problems  @ Javadoc  Declaration  Console ×
<terminated> ShapesCalculator [Java Application] C:\Users\gerardbyrne\.
What is the length of the radius of the circle?

10

A circle with radius 10.00 has an area of 314.16
```

This is excellent, our method has been called from another class. We will now add another method in the CircleFormulae class.

30. Amend the code in the **CircleFormulae** class to add the method that will calculate the **circumference** of the circle. This new method will be added just after the method areaOfCircle and inside the class.

```
} //End of areaOfCircle method
    /*
    This is a method that will accept the value of the radius
    passed to it. The radius has been obtained in the
    areaOfCircle method and then the areaOfCircle() method
    will call this new circumferenceOfCircle() method passing
    it the value of the radius. This method will then calculate
    the circumference and display the value in the console window
    */
```

```
public void circumferenceOfCircle(double radiusOfCirclePassedIn)
{

} // End of circumferenceOfCircle method

} // End of CircleFormulae class
```

31. Amend the new method code to create a variable to hold the circumference of the circle.

```
public void circumferenceOfCircle(double radiusOfCirclePassedIn)
{
  /*
    Create a variable of data type double to hold the value calculated
    for the circumference of the circle. Initialise the variable to zero.
    We have the radius as it is passed into this method
  */
  double circumferenceOfCircle = 0;

} // End of circumferenceOfCircle method

} // End of CircleFormulae class
```

32. Now add the code that will calculate the circumference of the circle.

```
public void circumferenceOfCircle(double radiusOfCirclePassedIn)
{
  /*
    Create a variable of data type double to hold the value calculated
    for the circumference of the circle. Initialise the variable to zero.
    We have the radius as it is passed into this method
  */
  double circumferenceOfCircle = 0;

  // Calculate the circumference of the circle with the formula
  circumferenceOfCircle = 2 * Math.PI * radiusOfCirclePassedIn;

} // End of circumferenceOfCircle method

} // End of CircleFormulae class
```

33. Now add the code to display the circumference of the circle.

    // Calculate the circumference of the circle with the formula
    circumferenceOfCircle = 2 * Math.*PI* * radiusOfCirclePassedIn;

    // Display the answer
    System.*out*.printf("\nA circle with radius %.2f has a circumference of %.2f",radiusOfCirclePassedIn, circumferenceOfCircle);

    } // End of circumferenceOfCircle method

} // End of CircleFormulae class

Now that we have created the second method we will call it from the first method, **areaOfCircle**, passing it the radius that has been input by the user.

34. Add the code in the areaOfCircle() method to call the circumferenceOfCircle() method:

    // Calculate the area of the circle with the formula
    areaOfCircle = Math.*PI* * radiusLength * radiusLength;

    // Display the answer
    System.*out*.printf("\nA circle with radius %.2f has an area of %.2f", radiusLength, areaOfCircle);

    /*
      Now call the method which calculates the circumference of the circle
      using the radius the user has input.
      We call the method and pass the radius as a parameter.
    */
    circumferenceOfCircle(radiusLength);

    } //End of areaOfCircle method

Now check that the method is working correctly.

35. Click on the **File** menu.
36. Choose **Save All**.

37. Click on the green **Run** button at the top of the screen.

The console window will appear and ask the user to input the radius of the circle.

38. Type **10** and press the Enter key.

The console window will show the area and circumference of the circle.

```
Problems  @ Javadoc  Declaration  Console  ×
<terminated> ShapesCalculator [Java Application] C:\Users\gerardbyrne\.p2\poc
What is the length of the radius of the circle?

10

A circle with radius 10.00 has an area of 314.16
A circle with radius 10.00 has a circumference of 62.83
```

This is excellent, our two methods which contain the business logic and the formulae are created in a class and have been called from another class.

We can see that we have used the principle of 'separation of concern', where we have kept our circle formulae separate from the class with the main method. We will now reinforce the principle of 'separation of concern' by creating another class that will be related to a rectangle and will hold any formula related to a rectangle.

Exercise Three – Shapes and rectangle shapes formulae

1. Right click on the **com.gerrybyrne.shapes** package icon.
2. Choose **New**.
3. Choose **Class**.
4. Name the class **RectangleFormulae**.
5. **DO NOT** put a tick in the checkbox beside the public static void main(String[] args) box.
6. Click on the **Finish** button.

The **RectangleFormulae** class code will appear in the editor window and will be similar to the following:

```
package com.gerrybyrne.shapes;

public class RectangleFormulae
{
} // End of RectangleFormulae class
```

We will create a method for the area of a rectangle. The formula for the area of a rectangle is the length multiplied by the breadth (width). This formula will therefore be our business logic. To calculate the area of the rectangle we will ask the user to input the length and breadth of the rectangle they require. In doing this we will need to create a Scanner instance.

7. Amend the code to create an instance of the Scanner class and import the Scanner class

    ```
    package com.gerrybyrne.shapes;

    import java.util.Scanner;

    public class RectangleFormulae
    {
        Scanner myScanner = new Scanner(System.in);
    } // End of RectangleFormulae class
    ```

8. Amend the code to add the method that will calculate the area of the rectangle.

    ```
    public class RectangleFormulae
    {
        Scanner myScanner = new Scanner(System.in);
        /*
        This is a method that will ask the user to input the length of the
        rectangle, then ask them for the breadth of the rectangle, calculate
        the area of the rectangle and display the area of the rectangle in
        the console window
        */
        public void areaOfRectangle()
        {
        } // End of areaOfRectangle method
    } // End of RectangleFormulae class
    ```

9. Amend the code to create variables to hold the length and breadth of the rectangle and the area of the rectangle.

```
public void areaOfRectangle()
{
/*
Create three variables of data type double to hold the value of the length and
breadth as input by the user and the calculated area of the rectangle.
Initialise the three variables to zero.
*/
double lengthOfRectangle = 0;

double breadthOfRectangle = 0;

double areaOfRectangle = 0;
} // End of areaOfRectangle method
} // End of RectangleFormulae class
```

10. Amend the code to ask the user to input the length and breadth of the rectangle and then read these values using the Scanner instance.

```
public void areaOfRectangle()
{
/*
Create three variables of data type double to hold the value of the length and
breadth as input by the user and the calculated area of the rectangle.
Initialise the three variables to zero.
*/
double lengthOfRectangle = 0;

double breadthOfRectangle = 0;

double areaOfRectangle = 0;

// Read the user input for the size of the sides
System.out.println("\nWhat is the length of the rectangle?\n");

lengthOfRectangle = myScanner.nextDouble();

System.out.println("\nWhat is the breadth of the rectangle?\n");
```

breadthOfRectangle = myScanner.nextDouble();

 } // End of areaOfRectangle method
} // End of RectangleFormulae class

11. Now add the code that will calculate the area of the rectangle.

 System.*out*.println("\nWhat is the breadth of the rectangle?\n");

 breadthOfRectangle = myScanner.nextDouble();

 // Calculate the area of the rectangle with the formula
 areaOfRectangle = lengthOfRectangle * breadthOfRectangle;

 } // End of areaOfRectangle method
} // End of RectangleFormulae class

12. Now add the code that will display the details of the area, length and breadth.

 System.*out*.println("\nWhat is the breadth of the rectangle?\n");

 breadthOfRectangle = myScanner.nextDouble();

 // Calculate the area of the rectangle with the formula
 areaOfRectangle = lengthOfRectangle * breadthOfRectangle;

 // Display the answer
 System.*out*.printf("\nA rectangle with length of %.2f and breadth of %.2f has an area of %.2f",lengthOfRectangle, breadthOfRectangle, areaOfRectangle);

 } // End of areaOfRectangle method
} // End of RectangleFormulae class

Now that we have created another class with a method in it we will be able to call the method from the main() method in the ShapesCalculator class.

13. Open the ShapesCalculator class and create an instance of the RectangleFormulae class. Remember, we do not use the RectangleFormulae class directly, make an instance of it.

```
package com.gerrybyrne.shapes;

public class ShapesCalculator
{
    public static void main(String[] args)
    {
        CircleFormulae myCircleFormulae = new CircleFormulae();
        myCircleFormulae.areaOfCircle();

        RectangleFormulae myRectangleFormulae = new RectangleFormulae();

    } // End of main method()
} // End of ShapesCalculator class
```

14. Now add the code to call the areaOfRectangle () method of our new instance class.

```
package com.gerrybyrne.shapes;

public class ShapesCalculator
{
    public static void main(String[] args)
    {
        CircleFormulae myCircleFormulae = new CircleFormulae();
        myCircleFormulae.areaOfCircle();

        RectangleFormulae myRectangleFormulae = new RectangleFormulae();
        myRectangleFormulae.areaOfRectangle();

    } // End of main method()
} // End of ShapesCalculator class
```

Now check that the method is working correctly.

15. Click on the **File** menu.
16. Choose **Save All**.
17. Click on the green **Run** button at the top of the screen.

The console window will appear and ask the user to input the radius of the circle.

18. Type **10** and press the Enter key.

The console window will ask the user to input the length of the rectangle.

19. Type **12** and press the Enter key.

The console window will ask the user to input the breadth of the rectangle.

20. Type **20** and press the Enter key.

The console window will show the area of the circle and the area of the rectangle.

```
Problems  @ Javadoc  Declaration  Console ×
<terminated> ShapesCalculator [Java Application] C:\Users\gerardbyrne\.p2\pool\plugins\org.eclipse.justj.op
What is the length of the radius of the circle?

10

A circle with radius 10.00 has an area of 314.16
A circle with radius 10.00 has a circumference of 62.83
What is the length of the rectangle?

12

What is the breadth of the rectangle?

20

A rectangle with length of 12.00 and breadth of 20.00 has an area of 240.00
```

This is excellent, our method for the rectangle area has been called from another class. Now we will extend of formulae class by adding another method.

39. Amend the code in the RectangleFormulae class to add the method that will calculate the perimeter of the rectangle. This new method will be added just after the method areaOfRectangle and inside the class.

> } // End of areaOfRectangle method
>
> /*
> This is a method that will accept the values of the length and breadth passed to it. Both values have been obtained in the areaOfRectangle method and then the areaOfRectangle() method will call this new perimeterOfRectangle() method passing it the values of the length and breadth. This method will then calculate the perimeter and display the value in the console window

```
*/
public void perimeterOfRectangle(double lengthPassedIn, double breadthPassedIn)
{
} // End of perimeterOfRectangle method

} // End of RectangleFormulae class
```

40. Amend the code to create a variable to hold the perimeter of the rectangle.

```
public void perimeterOfRectangle(double lengthPassedIn, double breadthPassedIn)
{
    /*
    Create a variable of data type double to hold the value calculated for
    the perimeter of the rectangle.
    Initialise the variable to zero.
    We have the length and breadth as they are passed into this method
    */
    double perimeterOfRectangle = 0;

} // End of perimeterOfRectangle method

} // End of RectangleFormulae class
```

41. Now add the code that will calculate the perimeter of the rectangle.

```
public void perimeterOfRectangle(double lengthPassedIn, double breadthPassedIn)
{
    /*
    Create a variable of data type double to hold the value calculated for
    the perimeter of the rectangle.
    Initialise the variable to zero.
    We have the length and breadth as they are passed into this method
    */
    double perimeterOfRectangle = 0;

    // Calculate the perimeter of the rectangle with the formula
    perimeterOfRectangle = 2 * (lengthPassedIn + breadthPassedIn);

} // End of perimeterOfRectangle method
```

42. Now add the code to display the perimeter of the rectangle.

```
double perimeterOfRectangle = 0;

// Calculate the perimeter of the rectangle with the formula
perimeterOfRectangle = 2 * (lengthPassedIn + breadthPassedIn);

// Display the answer
   System.out.printf("\nA rectangle with length %.2f and breadth  %.2f has a perimeter of %.2f",lengthPassedIn, breadthPassedIn, perimeterOfRectangle);

  } // End of perimeterOfRectangle method
} // End of RectangleFormulae class
```

Now we have created the second method for the rectangle formula we will call it from the first method, areaOfRectangle, passing it the length and breadth that input by the user.

43. Add the code in the areaOfRectangle() method to call the perimeterOfRectangle() method of our instance class.

```
// Display the answer
   System.out.printf("\nA rectangle with length of %.2f and breadth of %.2f has an area of %.2f",lengthOfRectangle, breadthOfRectangle, areaOfRectangle);

  /*
   Now call the method which calculates the perimeter of the rectangle
   using the length and breadth the user has input.
   We call the method and pass the radius as a parameter
  */
   perimeterOfRectangle(lengthOfRectangle, breadthOfRectangle);
 } // End of areaOfRectangle method
```

Now check that the method is working correctly.

44. Click on the **File** menu.
45. Choose **Save All**.
46. Open the **ShapesCalculator** class.

47. Click on the green **Run** button at the top of the screen.

The console window will appear and ask the user to input the radius of the circle.

48. Type **10** and press the Enter key.

The console window will ask the user to input the length of the rectangle.

49. Type **12** and press the Enter key.

The console window will ask the user to input the breadth of the rectangle.

50. Type **20** and press the Enter key.

The console window will show the area and circumference of the circle and the area and perimeter of the rectangle.

```
Problems  @ Javadoc  Declaration  Console ×
<terminated> ShapesCalculator [Java Application] C:\Users\gerardbyrne\.p2\pool\plugins\org.eclipse.justj.ope
What is the length of the radius of the circle?

10

A circle with radius 10.00 has an area of 314.16
A circle with radius 10.00 has a circumference of 62.83
What is the length of the rectangle?

12

What is the breadth of the rectangle?

20

A rectangle with length of 12.00 and breadth of 20.00 has an area of 240.00
A rectangle with length 12.00 and breadth  20.00 has a perimeter of 64.00
```

This is excellent, our formulae methods have been called from another class.

Module summary

So, finishing this module on classes we should remember what we covered in the module on methods because the two concepts are highly connected. Classes contain methods and variables (fields, members).

We have created classes to hold methods and variables and we have created separate classes when necessary, so that each class represents related items. We can access classes from the main() method of another class and in doing this we need to create a copy of the class. We call the copy an instance of the class. The instance of the class gives us access to the methods and properties of the class.

We have come a long way from module 1 and getting to this stage where we can create and use classes is a really great achievement for us in our learning. We should be very proud of the learning to date.

Another great achievement for us in our learning.

Our dot just got bigger

Program Practically

Java

Module 12

String Handling

String literal
Strings as immutable objects
Strings and the new keyword
String methods

Gerry Byrne

Program Practically - String Handling

We learnt from all previous modules about the core constructs of a Java program including the structure of a Java program with the concept of a class containing methods and properties and inherent in this was the concept of data types for the properties. We learnt how to structure code in the form of methods within classes and the importance of the main() method to start the programming running. We looked at the important constructs of selection to make choices, iteration to repeat blocks of code and we saw how to temporarily store data in a data structure called an Array. Now we will take a closer look at Strings which have been part of many of our code examples.

String Handling

Throughout our modules we used Strings and in many of our coding examples we saw how we could concatenate a String to another String or to a non-String data type which has been converted to a String. When we look back to the data types module we can see that String is not one of the primitive data types whereas char is. So, we know that String as a data type is special, just look at the fact that we use a capital S when coding it. The capital S might then suggest to us that it is a class, as classes by convention start with a capital letter. Indeed, we are correct in this assumption and we would say that String is a class.

We said that a character is represented by the char primitive data type, but a String is a sequence of characters or a character array, char[], and it can be used for the purpose of representing a character sequence in a convenient way. We read in a previous module that:

> One important thing to note is the capital letter of the 'data type'. When we see the capital letter, we are not using a data type the way we did when we were defining a variable, we are using **an object, a class**. A **Wrapper class** is the fancy name for it.

However, this comment applied to the primitive data types and String is not a primitive data type. So, let us be clear, the String class is not a wrapper class. To reinforce this the table below shows the Java wrapper classes.

Primitive Data Type	Wrapper Class
byte	Byte
short	Short
int	Integer
long	Long
float	Float
double	Double
boolean	Boolean
char	Character

As we have said a **String** is a sequence of characters e.g. "Home Insurance" is a string of 14 characters. A String in Java is an **immutable object,** it is constant and therefore cannot be changed once it has been created. The String class offers us many String methods and properties that we can use to manipulate our Strings and we will now look at arrange of these.

Creating a String

We can create a String in one of two ways in Java

1. as a **String literal.**
2. using the **new** keyword.

String literal

Create a new package
1. Right click on the **src** folder.
2. Choose **New**.
3. Choose **Package**.
4. Name the package as **com.gerrybyrne.module12.**
5. Choose the **Finish** button.
6. Right click on the **com.gerrybyrne.module12** package.

7. Choose **New**.

8. Choose **Class**.

9. Enter the new name for the file, we will call it **Strings**.

10. Put a tick in the checkbox beside the public static void main(String[] args) box.

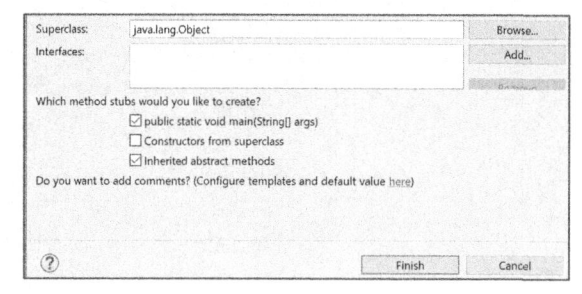

11. Click on the **Finish** button.

The Strings class code will appear in the editor window and will be similar to the following:

package com.gerrybyrne.module12;

public class Strings
{
    public static void main(String[] args)
    {
        // **TODO** Auto-generated method stub
    } // End of main method()
} // End of Strings class

12. Amend the code to create three string literals, 2 of which will have the same content:

package com.gerrybyrne.module12;

public class Strings
{
  public static void main(String[] args)
  {
    /*
    A String is an object in Java and when we created classes we saw that we instantiated the class we used the new keyword. Here we have not created any string object using the new keyword. However the compiler will perform the task for us and it will create a String object from the String literal.

>   In this example Home Insurance is only created once and even
>   though we have 2 string instances there is only one string object.
>   */
>   String myVehicleInsurance = "Vehicle Insurance";
>   String myHomeInsurance = "Home Insurance";
>   String myInsurance = "Home Insurance";
>   } // End of main method()
> } // End of Strings class

In this code example the String object Home Insurance is only created once, and even though we have two string instances, they point to the same String object.

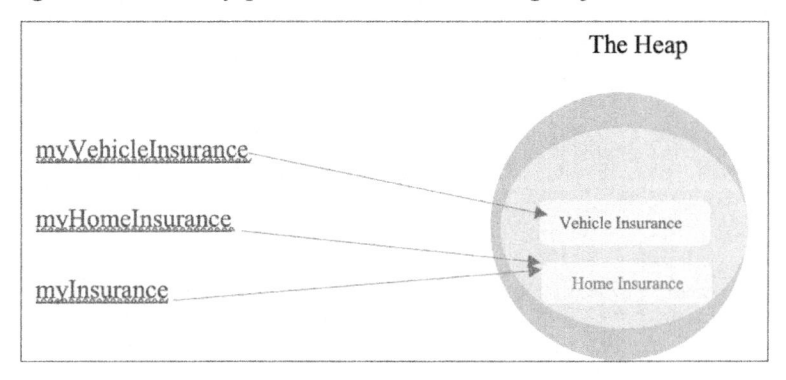

Using New Keyword

Now, using the String literal is fine but we may equally wish to have separate objects for the same String and we can do this using the **new keyword**. Let us now recreate the last example but using the new keyword.

13. Amend the code to create another three new String objects, two of which will have the same content:

    ```
    String myVehicleInsurance = "Vehicle Insurance";
    String myHomeInsurance = "Home Insurance";
    String myInsurance = "Home Insurance";
    ```

    > /*
    > Let us now recreate the same example but using the new keyword. We will need
    > to use different variable names. Using the new keyword causes the compiler to
    > create two different objects in memory, each object having the same string saying
    > Home Insurance.

```
        */
        String myVehicleInsuranceNew = new String("Vehicle Insurance");
        String myHomeInsuranceNew = new String("Home Insurance");
        String myInsuranceNew = new String("Home Insurance");
    } // End of main method()
} // End of Strings class
```

In the second part of this code example the String object Home Insurance is created twice and we have 2 string instances and 2 String objects.

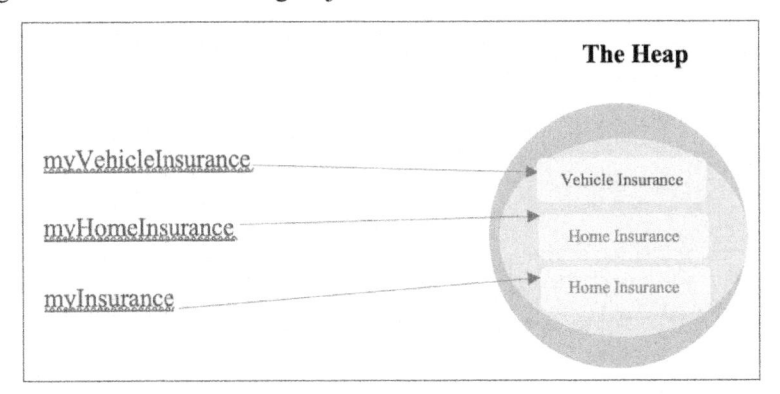

[Diagram: The Heap containing Vehicle Insurance, Home Insurance, Home Insurance objects, with myVehicleInsurance, myHomeInsurance, and myInsurance references pointing to them.]

Remember that the String we create is an object and will have associated methods and properties which we will now look at.

String Methods

Our insurance application might need to find a character at a specific position in the vehicle registration so we could use the **charAt()** method of the String class.

charAt(int index) which will return the char value at the specified index. We will need to specify the object, String, we are using and then when we type the dot (.) the list of methods and properties will appear, verifying that String is a class.

14. Amend the code to create a new String object to hold a vehicle registration number:

```
String myVehicleInsuranceNew = new String("Vehicle Insurance");
String myHomeInsuranceNew = new String("Home Insurance");
```

String myInsuranceNew = **new** String("Home Insurance");

String myVehicleRegistration = **new** String("ZER 7890");

} // End of main method()
} // End of Strings class

15. Amend the code to find the character at position 0 of the String object called myVehicleRegistration:

    String myVehicleRegistration = **new** String("ZER 7890");

    ```
    /*
    Use the charAt() method from the String class to find
    which character is at a specific position
    */
    ```
    System.*out*.println("The first character is: " + myVehicleRegistration.charAt(0));

    } // End of main method()
    } // End of Strings class

16. Click on the **File** menu
17. Choose **Save All.**
18. Click on the green **Run** button at the top of the screen or click on the Run menu and choose the Run option.
19. Look in the Console window at the bottom of the screen and you should see the output from the charAt() method call on the myVehicleRegistration String object.

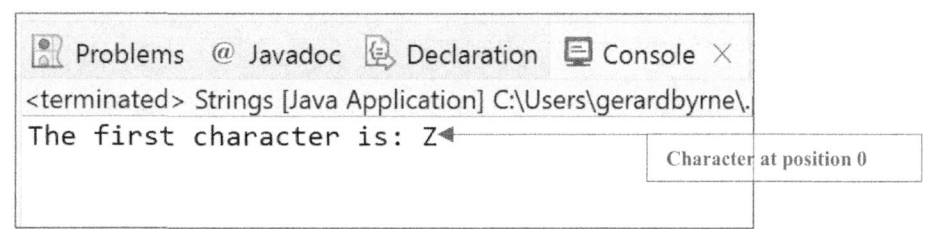

    ```
    Problems  @ Javadoc  Declaration  Console  ×
    <terminated> Strings [Java Application] C:\Users\gerardbyrne\.
    The first character is: Z     ← Character at position 0
    ```

Our insurance application might need to find the first or last part of a vehicle registration so we could use the **substring()** method of the String class.

substring(startIndex, endIndex) which will return the char values starting with the char at the start index and ending with the char at the end index minus 1. In other words, substring is inclusive of the char at the first position but exclusive of the char at the end position. We will need to specify the object, String, we are using and then when we type the dot (.) the list of methods and properties will appear and we will see substring().

20. Amend the code to find the characters from position 0 to position 2, the first three characters, of the String object called myVehicleRegistration:

    ```
    /*
    Use the charAt() method from the String class to find
    which character is at a specific position
    */
    System.out.println("The first character is: " + myVehicleRegistration.charAt(0));

    /*
    Use the substring() method from the String class to find the
    first 3 characters of the myVehicleRegistration object.
    Remember substring is inclusive of the char at the first
    position but exclusive of the char at the end position
    */

    System.out.println("The first 3 characters are: "+myVehicleRegistration.substring(0, 3));

        } // End of main method()
    } // End of Strings class
    ```

21. Click on the **File** menu.
22. Choose **Save All.**
23. Click on the green **Run** button at the top of the screen or click on the Run menu and choose the Run option.
24. Look in the Console window at the bottom of the screen and you should see the output from the substring() method call on the myVehicleRegistration String object.

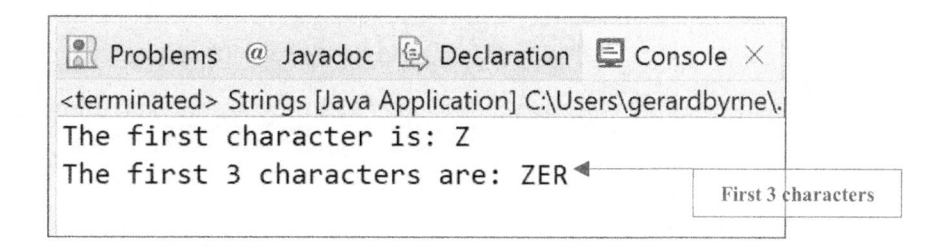

```
Problems  @ Javadoc  Declaration  Console  X
<terminated> Strings [Java Application] C:\Users\gerardbyrne\.
The first character is: Z
The first 3 characters are: ZER     ← First 3 characters
```

25. Amend the code to find the characters from position 5 to position 8, the last four characters, of the String object called myVehicleRegistration:

    System.*out*.println("The first 3 characters are: "+myVehicleRegistration.substring(0, 3));

    /*
    Use the substring() method from the String class to find the
    last 4 characters of the myVehicleRegistration object.
    */
    System.*out*.println("The last 4 characters are: "+myVehicleRegistration.substring(4, 8));

    　} // End of main method()
    } // End of Strings class

26. Click on the **File** menu.
27. Choose **Save All.**
28. Click on the green **Run** button at the top of the screen or click on the Run menu and choose the Run option
29. Look in the Console window at the bottom of the screen and you should see the output from the substring() method call on the myVehicleRegistration String object.

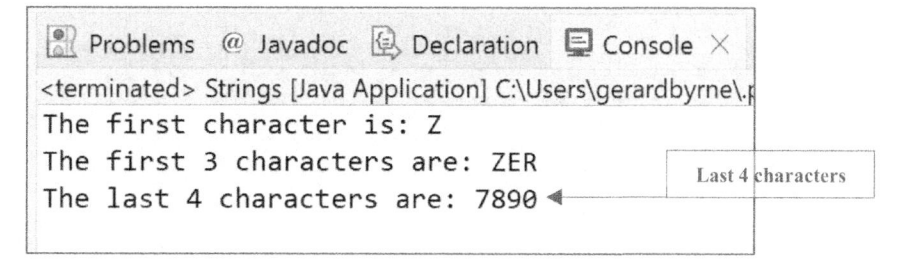

```
Problems  @ Javadoc  Declaration  Console  X
<terminated> Strings [Java Application] C:\Users\gerardbyrne\.
The first character is: Z
The first 3 characters are: ZER
The last 4 characters are: 7890     ← Last 4 characters
```

Our insurance application might need to find the length of a vehicle registration to ensure the correct number of characters have been entered so we could use the substring() method of the String class.

length() which will return an integer that represents the number of char values in the String object. The method will count spaces in the object as they are also characters.

30. Amend the code to find the number of characters in the String object called myVehicleRegistration:

    System.*out*.println("The last 4 characters are: " +myVehicleRegistration.substring(4, 8));

    ```
    /*
    Use the length() method from the String class to find the
    number of characters in the myVehicleRegistration object.
    */
    ```
    System.*out*.println("The number of characters is: " +myVehicleRegistration.length());

    } // End of main method()
    } // End of Strings class

31. Click on the **File** menu.
32. Choose **Save All.**
33. Click on the green **Run** button at the top of the screen or click on the Run menu and choose the Run option
34. Look in the Console window at the bottom of the screen and you should see the output from the length() method call on the myVehicleRegistration String object.

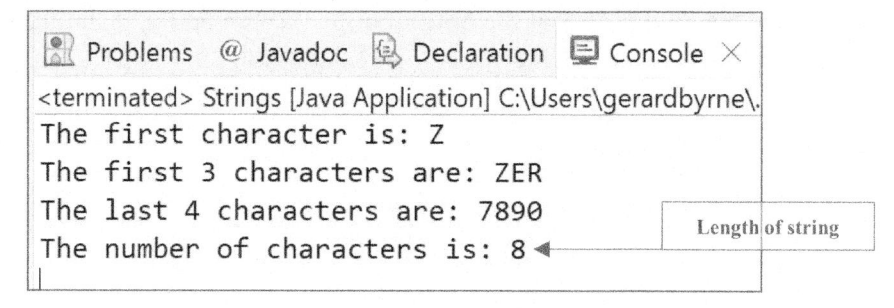

    ```
    Problems  @ Javadoc  Declaration  Console ×
    <terminated> Strings [Java Application] C:\Users\gerardbyrne\.
    The first character is: Z
    The first 3 characters are: ZER
    The last 4 characters are: 7890          Length of string
    The number of characters is: 8
    ```

Let us add more vehicle registrations and then we can use some different methods on them.

35. Amend the code to add an array of String objects:

    System.*out*.println("The number of characters is: " +myVehicleRegistration.length());
    // Create an array of String objects

```
String[] myVehicleRegistrations =new String[] {"ZER 7890","ZAC 7124", "ARC 3330"};
    } // End of main method()
} // End of Strings class
```

Our insurance application might need to find a specific character or characters in a vehicle registration because of an accident where a vehicle with the specific character(s) was involved. For this situation we could use the startsWith() method of the String class. There are two forms of this method that we will use (method overloading).

startsWith(char) which will return a boolean value of true or false depending on whether the String object begins with the specific letter or letters. The methods starts at character 0.

36. Amend the code to iterate and display those String objects from the array that start with (startWith()) the letter Z:

```
// Create an array of String objects
String[] myVehicleRegistrations =new String[] {"ZER 7890","ZAC 7124", "ARC 3330"};

    for(String registration: myVehicleRegistrations)
    {
      if(registration.startsWith("Z"))
      {
      System.out.printf("The registration %s starts with the letter Z %n", registration);
      }
      else
      {
      System.out.printf("The registration %s does not start with the letter Z %n", registration);
      }
    } // End of for each iteration
  } // End of main method()
} // End of Strings class
```
Here we have checked if the registration object returned in each iteration, starts with the letter Z. If it does start with the letter Z then the startsWith() method returns a boolean **true** value

and the first part of the if construct is executed, this is the true part of the if construct. If the String object does not start with the letter Z then the startsWith() method returns a boolean **false** value and the second part of the if construct is executed, this is the false part of the if construct.

37. Click on the **File** menu.
38. Choose **Save All.**
39. Click on the green **Run** button at the top of the screen or click on the Run menu and choose the Run option
40. Look in the Console window at the bottom of the screen and you should see the output from the startsWith() method call on the myVehicleRegistration String object.

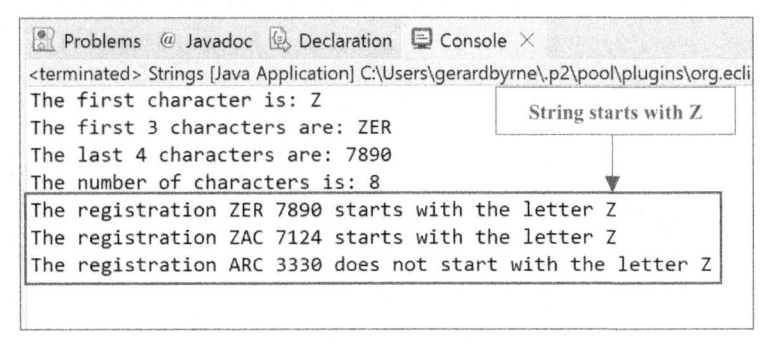

```
<terminated> Strings [Java Application] C:\Users\gerardbyrne\.p2\pool\plugins\org.ecli
The first character is: Z
The first 3 characters are: ZER
The last 4 characters are: 7890
The number of characters is: 8
The registration ZER 7890 starts with the letter Z
The registration ZAC 7124 starts with the letter Z
The registration ARC 3330 does not start with the letter Z
```

String starts with Z

startsWith(char, startIndex) which will return a boolean value of true or false depending on whether the String object, starting at the specified index beginning, starts with the specific letter or letters.

41. Amend the code to iterate and display those String objects from the array that start with (startWith()) the letter C at index 2:

// Create an array of String objects
String[] myVehicleRegistrations =**new** String[] {"ZER 7890","ZAC 7124", "ARC 3330"};

   for(String registration: myVehicleRegistrations)
   {
    if(registration.startsWith("C",2))
    {

//System.out.printf("The registration %s starts with the letter Z %n", registration);
System.*out*.printf("The registration %s has the letter C at position 3 %n", registration);
  }
  else
  {
System.*out*.printf("The registration %s does not have the letter C at position 3 %n", registration);
}
  } // End of for each iteration
 } // End of main method()
} // End of Strings class

42. Click on the **File** menu.
43. Choose **Save All.**
44. Click on the green **Run** button at the top of the screen or click on the Run menu and choose the Run option
45. Look in the Console window at the bottom of the screen and you should see the output from the startsWith(char, startIndex) method call on the myVehicleRegistration String object.

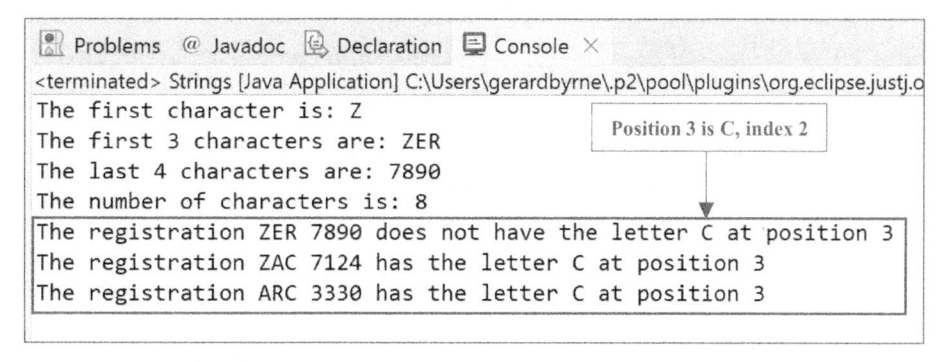

```
Problems  @ Javadoc  Declaration  Console  X
<terminated> Strings [Java Application] C:\Users\gerardbyrne\.p2\pool\plugins\org.eclipse.justj.o
The first character is: Z
The first 3 characters are: ZER        Position 3 is C, index 2
The last 4 characters are: 7890
The number of characters is: 8
The registration ZER 7890 does not have the letter C at position 3
The registration ZAC 7124 has the letter C at position 3
The registration ARC 3330 has the letter C at position 3
```

Our insurance application might need to split the String object which is in a particular format. In our example the vehicle registration is in two parts separated by a space. To split the object we use the split() method of the String class.

split (expression)   which will return an array of strings after it has split the string object at the specified expression.

46. Amend the code to split the String objects at the space and put the two parts of the split result into the newly created array called splitRegistration:

```
else
{
System.out.printf("The registration %s does not have the letter C at position 3 %n",
registration);
}
} // End of for each iteration

    // Iterate the array and split the items as they are read
    for(String registration: myVehicleRegistrations)
       {
            // Create an array to hold the 2 parts of the vehicle registration
            String[] splitRegistration = new String[2];

            // Split the array at the space
            splitRegistration = registration.split(" ");

            System.out.printf("Part 0 is %s  %n", splitRegistration[0]);
            System.out.printf("Part 1 is %s  %n", splitRegistration[1]);

       } // End of for each iteration for splitting at the space character

  } // End of main method()
} // End of Strings class
```

47. Click on the **File** menu.

48. Choose **Save All.**

49. Click on the green **Run** button at the top of the screen or click on the Run menu and choose the Run option

50. Look in the Console window at the bottom of the screen and you should see the output from the array which held the output from the split(" ") method call on the myVehicleRegistration String object.

```
Problems  @ Javadoc  Declaration  Console ×
<terminated> Strings [Java Application] C:\Users\gerardbyrne\.p2\pool\plugins\org.eclipse.justj
The first character is: Z
The first 3 characters are: ZER
The last 4 characters are: 7890
The number of characters is: 8
The registration ZER 7890 does not have the letter C at position 3
The registration ZAC 7124 has the letter C at position 3
The registration ARC 3330 has the letter C at position 3
Part 0 is ZER
Part 1 is 7890
Part 0 is ZAC           Array items have
Part 1 is 7124          been split at the space
Part 0 is ARC           character
Part 1 is 3330
```

We can also split on multiple characters (delimiters or regular expressions).

51. Amend the code to add a new array, just before the end of the main() method, called myMixedVehicleRegistrations:

    System.*out*.printf("Part 0 is %s %n", splitRegistration[0]);
    System.*out*.printf("Part 1 is %s %n", splitRegistration[1]);

    } // End of for each iteration for splitting at the space character

    // Create a new array of String objects
    String[] myMixedVehicleRegistrations = **new** String[] {"ZER 7890","ZAC_7124", "ARC,3330"};
    } // End of main method()
    } // End of Strings class

52. Amend the code to iterate the new array and split each String object at the underscore, space or comma and put the result into the newly created array called:

    // Create a new array of String objects
    String[] myMixedVehicleRegistrations =**new** String[] {"ZER 7890","ZAC_7124", "ARC,3330"};

    // Iterate the array and split the items as they are read
    for(String mixedRegistrationPart:myMixedVehicleRegistrations)
    {
        // Create an array to hold the 2 parts of the vehicle registration
        String[] splitMixedRegistration = **new** String[2];

```
        // Split the array at the underscore, space or ,
        splitMixedRegistration = mixedRegistrationPart.split("[_ ,]");
    } // End of for each iteration for splitting at the underscore, space or , character
} // End of main method()
} // End of Strings class
```

53. Amend the code to display the elements of the split String objects within the iteration. Add the new code, just before the end of the main() method:

```
        // Split the array at the underscore, space or ,
        splitMixedRegistration = mixedRegistrationPart.split("[_ ,]");

        System.out.printf("Part 0 is %s %n", splitMixedRegistration[0]);
        System.out.printf("Part 1 is %s %n", splitMixedRegistration[1]);

    } // End of for each iteration for splitting at the underscore, space or , character
} // End of main method()
} // End of Strings class
```

54. Click on the **File** menu.
55. Choose **Save All.**
56. Click on the green **Run** button at the top of the screen or click on the Run menu and choose the Run option
57. Look in the Console window at the bottom of the screen and you should see the output from the array which held the output from the split() method call on each of the String objects in the myMixedVehicleRegistrations String array.

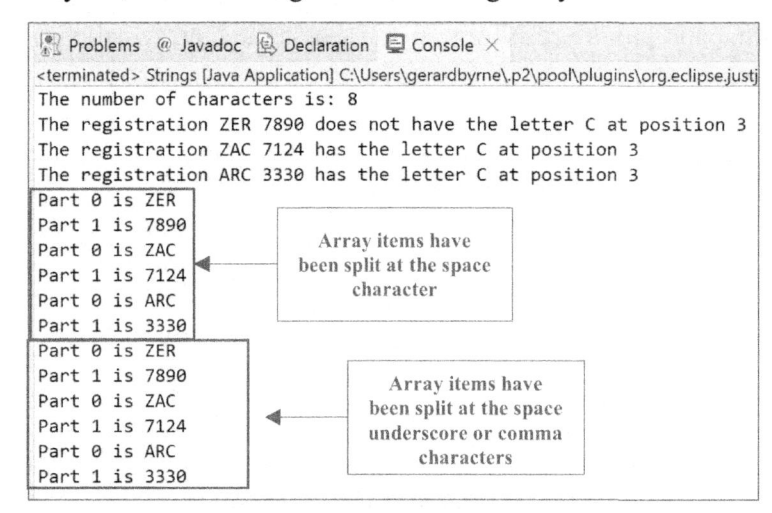

```
Problems  @ Javadoc  Declaration  Console ×
<terminated> Strings [Java Application] C:\Users\gerardbyrne\.p2\pool\plugins\org.eclipse.justj
The number of characters is: 8
The registration ZER 7890 does not have the letter C at position 3
The registration ZAC 7124 has the letter C at position 3
The registration ARC 3330 has the letter C at position 3
Part 0 is ZER
Part 1 is 7890
Part 0 is ZAC            ← Array items have
Part 1 is 7124             been split at the space
Part 0 is ARC              character
Part 1 is 3330
Part 0 is ZER
Part 1 is 7890
Part 0 is ZAC            ← Array items have
Part 1 is 7124             been split at the space
Part 0 is ARC              underscore or comma
Part 1 is 3330             characters
```

Our insurance application might need to compare String objects and to do this we use the compareTo() method of the String class.

compareTo() will return an integer value of 0 if the two string objects are lexicographically equal. If they are not equal then the compareTo() method will return a positive integer if the first String is greater than the otherwise it returns a negative integer value.

58. Amend the code to add another new array with additional String objects called myDuplicateVehicleRegistrations. Add the new code, just before the end of the main() method:

    ```
    } // End of for each iteration for splitting at the underscore, space or , character

    // Create a new array of String objects
    String[] myDuplicateVehicleRegistrations =new String[] {"ZER 7890","ZAC_7124", "ARC,3330", "ZER 7890", "ARC,3330", "zer 7890"," zac_7124"};

    } // End of main method()
    } // End of Strings class
    ```

59. Add the code to iterate the new array and compare each String object with each of the other String objects and output a message to say that the Strings are the same. This will require an inner iteration.

    ```
    // Create a new array of String objects
    String[] myDuplicateVehicleRegistrations =new String[] {"ZER 7890","ZAC_7124", "ARC,3330", "ZER 7890", "ARC,3330", "zer 7890"," zac_7124"};

    // Iterate the array and split the items as they are read
    for(int counter =0; counter < myDuplicateVehicleRegistrations.length; counter++)
    {
      for(int innercounter =counter + 1; innercounter <
          myDuplicateVehicleRegistrations.length; innercounter++)
      {
    ```

```
if(myDuplicateVehicleRegistrations[counter].compareTo(myDuplicateVehicleRegistrations[innercounter]) == 0)
    {
    System.out.printf("%s is the same String as array index %d %s %n",
        myDuplicateVehicleRegistrations[counter], innercounter,
            myDuplicateVehicleRegistrations[innercounter]);
    }
} // End of for iteration inner loop
} // End of for each iteration outer loop

} // End of main method()
} // End of Strings class
```

60. Click on the **File** menu.
61. Choose **Save All.**
62. Click on the green **Run** button at the top of the screen or click on the Run menu and choose the Run option
63. Look in the Console window at the bottom of the screen and you should see the output from the compareTo() method call on each of the String objects in the myDuplicateVehicleRegistrations String array.

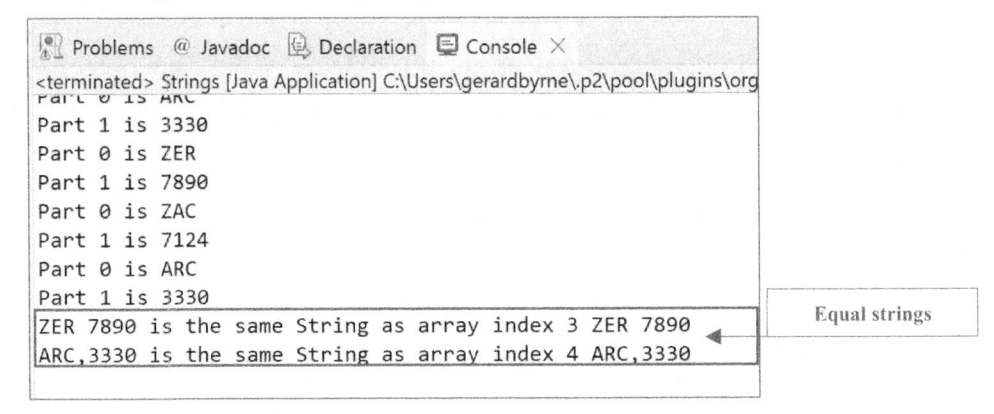

```
Problems  @ Javadoc  Declaration  Console ×
<terminated> Strings [Java Application] C:\Users\gerardbyrne\.p2\pool\plugins\org
Part 0 is ARC
Part 1 is 3330
Part 0 is ZER
Part 1 is 7890
Part 0 is ZAC
Part 1 is 7124
Part 0 is ARC
Part 1 is 3330
ZER 7890 is the same String as array index 3 ZER 7890     ◄── Equal strings
ARC,3330 is the same String as array index 4 ARC,3330
```

We will now amend the code to use the ignore case version of the compare to method which is compareToIgnoreCase().

compareToIgnoreCase() will return an integer value of 0 if the two string objects are lexicographically equal with the caveat that the case of the characters are ignored. If they are not equal then the compareTo() method will return a positive integer if the first String is greater than the otherwise it returns a negative integer value.

64. Amend the code to iterate the new array and compare each String object with each of the other String objects ignoring the case of the characters. Add the new code, just before the end of the main() method:

    } // End of for iteration inner loop
    } // End of for each iteration outer loop

    // Iterate the array and compare the items, ignoring the case, as they are read
    for(int counter =0; counter < myDuplicateVehicleRegistrations.length; counter++)
    {
      for(int innercounter =counter + 1; innercounter <
          myDuplicateVehicleRegistrations.length; innercounter++)
      {

        if(myDuplicateVehicleRegistrations[counter].compareToIgnoreCase(myDuplicateVehicleRegistrations[innercounter]) == 0)
        {
            System.*out*.printf("Ignoring case %s at index %d is the same String as array index %d %s %n", myDuplicateVehicleRegistrations[counter], counter, innercounter,
                myDuplicateVehicleRegistrations[innercounter]);
        }
      } // End of for iteration inner loop
    } // End of for each iteration outer loop

    } // End of main method()
    } // End of Strings class

65. Click on the **File** menu.
66. Choose **Save All.**
67. Click on the green **Run** button at the top of the screen or click on the Run menu and choose the Run option
68. Look in the Console window at the bottom of the screen and you should see the output from the compareToIgnoreCase() method call.

```
Console  Problems  Debug Shell
<terminated> Strings [Java Application] C:\Users\gerardbyrne\.p2\pool\plugins\org.eclipse.justj.openjdk.hotspot.jre\f
Part 0 is ARC                                                    Equal strings ignoring case
Part 1 is 3330
ZER 7890 is the same String as array index 3 ZER 7890
ARC,3330 is the same String as array index 4 ARC,3330
Ignoring case ZER 7890 at index 0 is the same String as array index 3 ZER 7890
Ignoring case ZER 7890 at index 0 is the same String as array index 5 zer 7890
Ignoring case ARC,3330 at index 2 is the same String as array index 4 ARC,3330
Ignoring case ZER 7890 at index 3 is the same String as array index 5 zer 7890
```

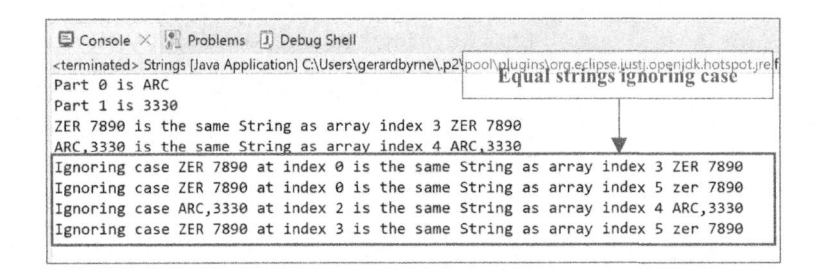

Instead of using the ignore case we could have turned each String object to upper case using the toUpperCase() method of the String class.

toUpperCase() will convert the characters of the String object into upper case characters.

There is also an overloaded method, toUpperCase(Locale locale) which converts the characters of the String to upper case based on the rules defined by Locale (the locations settings of the JVM/our computer).

69. Add the code to convert the String objects to upper case when we are comparing the, the original array objects remain the same.

```
    } // End of for iteration inner loop
} // End of for each iteration outer loop

// Iterate the array and convert the items to upper case as they are read
for(int counter =0; counter < myDuplicateVehicleRegistrations.length; counter++)
{
    for(int innercounter =counter + 1; innercounter <
                myDuplicateVehicleRegistrations.length; innercounter++)
    {
        if(myDuplicateVehicleRegistrations[counter]
.toUpperCase().compareTo(myDuplicateVehicleRegistrations[innercounter].toUpperCase()) == 0)
        {
            System.out.printf("With Upper Case %s at index %d is the same String as array index %d %s %n", myDuplicateVehicleRegistrations[counter], counter, innercounter,
                myDuplicateVehicleRegistrations[innercounter]);
        }
    } // End of for iteration inner loop
```

```
        } // End of for each iteration outer loop

    } // End of main method()
} // End of Strings class
```

70. Click on the **File** menu.
71. Choose **Save All.**
72. Click on the green **Run** button at the top of the screen or click on the Run menu and choose the Run option
73. Look in the Console window at the bottom of the screen and you should see the output from the compareTo () method call after the objects have been converted to upper case.

```
Ignoring case ZER 7890 at index 0 is the same String as array index 3 ZER 7890
Ignoring case ZER 7890 at index 0 is the same String as array index 5 zer 7890
Ignoring case ARC,3330 at index 2 is the same String as array index 4 ARC,3330
Ignoring case ZER 7890 at index 3 is the same String as array index 5 zer 7890
With Upper Case ZER 7890 at index 0 is the same String as array index 3 ZER 7890
With Upper Case ZER 7890 at index 0 is the same String as array index 5 zer 7890
With Upper Case ARC,3330 at index 2 is the same String as array index 4 ARC,3330
With Upper Case ZER 7890 at index 3 is the same String as array index 5 zer 7890
```
Equal strings using upper case

Instead of using the toUpperCase() method of the String class we could also have used the **toLowerCase()** method.

Sometimes we may need to concatenate more than one String to form a new String and we can achieve this using the concat() method.

concat().   will concatenate (join) multiple strings by appending the specified Strings to the initial String object. The concat() method returns the newly combined String of characters.

74. Amend the code to create two new String objects and then concatenate these String objects and the myVehicleInsuranceNew String object we created earlier in this module. Note the space before Gerry and the space after the ". "

```
        } // End of for iteration inner loop
    } // End of for each iteration outer loop

    String myInsuredPerson = new String(" Gerry Byrne,");
    String myWelcome = new String("thank you for taking out insurance with us.");
```

439

```
    String myOfferDetails = myInsuredPerson.concat(" ").concat(myWelcome).concat("
You now have full ").concat(myVehicleInsuranceNew).concat(". ");
        System.out.printf("%s", myOfferDetails);

    } // End of main method()
} // End of Strings class
```

75. Click on the **File** menu.
76. Choose **Save All.**
77. Click on the green **Run** button at the top of the screen or click on the Run menu and choose the Run option
78. Look in the Console window at the bottom of the screen and you should see the output from the concat() methods.

```
With Upper Case ZER 7890 at index 0 is the same String as array index 3 ZER 7890
With Upper Case ZER 7890 at index 0 is the same String as array index 5 zer 7890
With Upper Case ARC,3330 at index 2 is the same String as array index 4 ARC,3330
With Upper Case ZER 7890 at index 3 is the same String as array index 5 zer 7890
 Gerry Byrne, thank you for taking out insurance with us. You now have full Vehicle Insurance.
```
Concatenated strings

As you can see, we have a space before the message and a space after it. We will use another method, trim(), to remove these.

trim().   will remove any leading (at the start) and trailing (at the end) spaces from the String object. The method will leave spaces that exist inside the String.

79. Amend the code to use the trim() method and then display the new String. Create two new String objects and concatenate these String objects and the myVehicleInsuranceNew String object we created earlier in this module.

```
    String myInsuredPerson = new String(" Gerry Byrne,");
    String myWelcome = new String("thank you for taking out insurance with us.");
    String myOfferDetails = myInsuredPerson.concat(" ").concat(myWelcome).concat("
You now have full ").concat(myVehicleInsuranceNew).concat(". ");
    System.out.printf("%s", myOfferDetails);

    String trimmedMyOfferDetails = myOfferDetails.trim();
    System.out.printf("%n%s", trimmedMyOfferDetails);
    } // End of main method()
} // End of Strings class
```

80. Click on the **File** menu.
81. Choose **Save All.**
82. Click on the green **Run** button at the top of the screen or click on the Run menu and choose the Run option.
83. Look in the Console window at the bottom of the screen and you should see the output from the trim() method.

Trimmed string →
```
With Upper Case ZER 7890 at index 0 is the same String as array index 3 ZER 7890
With Upper Case ZER 7890 at index 0 is the same String as array index 5 zer 7890
With Upper Case ARC,3330 at index 2 is the same String as array index 4 ARC,3330
With Upper Case ZER 7890 at index 3 is the same String as array index 5 zer 7890
 Gerry Byrne, thank you for taking out insurance with us. You now have full Vehicle Insurance.
Gerry Byrne, thank you for taking out insurance with us. You now have full Vehicle Insurance.
```

In an application we may need to replace a character or characters with different characters and this can be achieved using the replace() method.

replace(old char, new char) will replace all occurrences of the old character with the new character.

replaceFirst(regex, new string) will replace the first substring that matches the regular expression with the new string.

replaceAll(regex, new string) will replace all substrings that match the regular expression with the new string.

The subtle difference between the replace() and replaceAll() methods is that the replace() method replaces all occurrences of a **character** whereas the replaceAll() method replaces all occurrences of a **string of characters** (multiple characters). Basically replace() works with replacing chars whereas replaceAll() works with replacing part of strings.

84. Amend the code to use the replace() method and then display the new String. Add the new code just before the end of the main() method:

    String trimmedMyOfferDetails = myOfferDetails.trim();
    System.*out*.printf("%n%s", trimmedMyOfferDetails);

    String name = **new** String("Gerry Byrne");

```
String newNameReplace = name.replace('e', 'E');
System.out.printf("%n%s", newNameReplace);

    } // End of main method()
} // End of Strings class
```

85. Click on the **File** menu.

86. Choose **Save All.**

87. Click on the green **Run** button at the top of the screen or click on the Run menu and choose the Run option

88. Look in the Console window at the bottom of the screen and you should see the output from the replace() method.

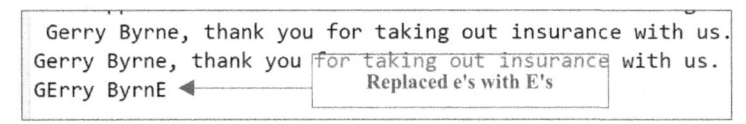

```
Gerry Byrne, thank you for taking out insurance with us.
Gerry Byrne, thank you for taking out insurance with us.
GErry ByrnE          Replaced e's with E's
```

89. Amend the code to use the replaceAll() method which works with strings (so we use double quotes "") and then display the new String. Add the new code just before the end of the main() method:

```
String name = new String("Gerry Byrne");
String newNameReplace = name.replace('e', 'E');
System.out.printf("%n%s", newNameReplace);

String newNameReplaceAll = name.replaceAll("e", "ER");
System.out.printf("%n%s", newNameReplaceAll);

    } // End of main method()
} // End of Strings class
```

90. Click on the **File** menu.

91. Choose **Save All.**

92. Click on the green **Run** button at the top of the screen or click on the Run menu and choose the Run option

93. Look in the Console window at the bottom of the screen and you should see the output from the replaceAll() method.

```
Gerry Byrne, thank you for taking out insurance with us.
Gerry Byrne, thank you for taking out insurance with us.
GErry ByrnE
GERrry ByrnER
```
⟵ Replaced all er's with ER's

94. Amend the code to use the replaceFirst() method which works with strings (so we use double quotes "") and then display the new String. Add the new code just before the end of the main() method:

    String newNameReplaceAll = name.replaceAll("e", "ER");
    System.*out*.printf("%n%s", newNameReplaceAll);

    String newNameReplaceFirst = name.replaceFirst("e", "E");
    System.*out*.printf("%n%s", newNameReplaceFirst);

    } // End of main method()
    } // End of Strings class

95. Click on the **File** menu.
96. Choose **Save All.**
97. Click on the green **Run** button at the top of the screen or click on the Run menu and choose the Run option
98. Look in the Console window at the bottom of the screen and you should see the output from the replaceFirst() method.

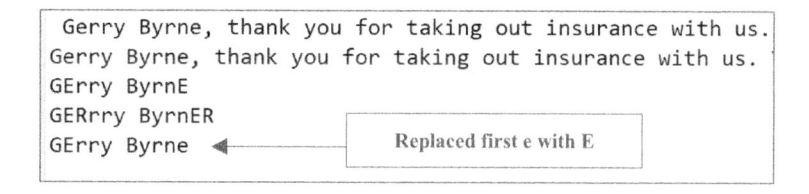

```
Gerry Byrne, thank you for taking out insurance with us.
Gerry Byrne, thank you for taking out insurance with us.
GErry ByrnE
GERrry ByrnER
GErry Byrne
```
⟵ Replaced first e with E

Module summary

So, finishing this module on String handling we should remember that a String is not one of the Java primitive data types. String is a class and therefore it has methods and properties just like any other class. We have completed a module on classes and objects where we saw that when we typed the name of the instantiated class into our Eclipse editor and typed the . (period) the name of the methods and properties appeared. In this module we saw some of the methods of the String class e.g. trim(), toUpperCase(), split() and charAt(). Whilst we have covered some of the methods, we have not covered them all and we could investigate many more of the methods and their use.

We should be very proud of the learning to date.

Another great achievement for us in our learning.

Our dot just got bigger

Program Practically

Java

Module 13

File Handling

File streaming with Java I/O class

Write to a text file, FileWriter and BufferedWriter

Read from a text file, FileReader and BufferedReader

Try catch exception handling when using File Handling

Gerry Byrne

Program Practically - File Handling

We learnt throughout all the previous modules about the core constructs of a Java program and saw how we can write data to an Array. We also read that an array is used to temporarily store data in a data structure. Now we will look at how to store the data in the more permanent form of a text file. Once we have seen how to write to a text file, we should easily be capable of writing the data to a database, but for this course we will not get into the setting up of a database.

It is common for developers to need to interact with files within their applications. Within the Java framework we are provided with many interfaces, classes and methods to help us interact with the file system. Files provide a means by which our programs can store and access data. Within Java the file I/O is a subset of Java's overall I/O system. The core of Java's I/O system is packaged in java.io.

An Overview of File Handling

In Java, file handling is taken care of by file I/O which is just part of Java's overall I/O system. Key points in respect of the I/O system are:

- the Java I/O system is built on interrelated classes which are organised in a hierarchy
- the most important classes are abstract classes that define much of the basic functionality shared by all specific concrete subclasses
- the stream concept ties together the file system because all I/O operations occur through a stream

Streaming – Old Java versus New Java

When we discuss file handling, we will inevitably come across the term **streaming** and we need to be sure what streaming in Java means. In versions of Java before 1.7 we had streams and they were associated with I/O (input and output). Streams were therefore used to read the contents of a file or to write the contents of a file.

Then came Java 1.8 and we met the Stream, yes, the same name, but used for a completely different purpose than the traditional, read or write the contents of a file. The modern Stream is used to **manipulate** a collection of data, a data structure. A Stream does not store data and, in that sense, is not a data structure, and it will never alter the underlying data source.

So, we have streams and Streams, the old and still used stream to read or to write the contents of a file and the new Streams that are used to manipulate a collection of data.

Writing to a file

Create a new package

1. Right click on the **src** folder.
2. Choose **New**.
3. Choose **Package**.
4. Name the package as **com.gerrybyrne.module13**.
5. Choose the **Finish** button.
6. Right click on the **com.gerrybyrne.module13** package.
7. Choose **New**.
8. Choose **Class**.
9. Enter the new name for the file, we will call it **WriteFile**.
10. Put a tick in the checkbox beside the public static void main(String[] args) box.
11. Click on the **Finish** button.

The WriteFile class code will appear in the editor window and will be similar to the following:

```
package com.gerrybyrne.module13;
public class WriteFile
{
    public static void main(String[] args)
    {
        // TODO Auto-generated method stub
    } // End of main method()
} // End of WriteFile class
```

12. Amend the code to add the required imports:

```
package com.gerrybyrne.module13;

import java.io.BufferedWriter;
import java.io.FileWriter;
import java.io.IOException;

public class WriteFile
{
    public static void main(String[] args)
    {
            // TODO Auto-generated method stub
    } // End of main method()
} // End of WriteFile class
```

13. Amend the code to add a String variable that will hold the pathname of the text file:

```
public static void main(String[] args)
{
  // Assign the name of the file to be used to a variable.
  String filePath = "txtOutputFile.txt";

} // End of main method()
} // End of WriteFile class
```

This sets up a variable to hold the file path and name of the text file that is to be written. The text file will be created in the same directory as the bin folder and therefore we can simply type in the file name. If the file was to be stored in a directory above the bin folder the pathname would be set to "../txtOutputFile.txt".

14. Amend the code to add an instance of the FileWriter class, inside a try catch construct, passing it the name of the file which we have already set up in a variable called filePath. Do not worry about any error messages, the code is incomplete:

```
  // Assign the name of the file to be used to a variable.
  String filePath = "txtOutputFile.txt";
```

```
// Enclose the code in a try catch to handle errors
try
{
    /*
        Create an instance of the FileWriter and call it fileWriter
        FileWriter is used to write text files in the default encoding.
    */
    FileWriter fileWriter = new FileWriter(filePath);

    } // End of main method()
} // End of WriteFile class
```

Do not worry about the error message, we will sort this as we progress with more code.

15. Amend the code to add an instance of the BufferedWriter class passing it the name of the file writer which we have just setup:

```
FileWriter fileWriter = new FileWriter(filePath);

/*
    Create an instance of the BufferedWriter and call it bufferedWriter
    we should always wrap a FileWriter in a BufferedWriter
*/
BufferedWriter bufferedWriter = new BufferedWriter(fileWriter);

    } // End of main method()
} // End of WriteFile class
```

16. Amend the code to add lines of text to the text file using the write() method of the BufferedWriter class:

```
BufferedWriter bufferedWriter = new BufferedWriter(fileWriter);

    /*
        Write text to the file using the write() method.
        In Java the write method will not automatically use a newline character
        so we will use the newLine() method to add the new line.
    */
    bufferedWriter.write("Welcome to Java File handling");
```

```
        bufferedWriter.newLine();
        bufferedWriter.write("We can write text to files and databases");
        bufferedWriter.newLine();
        bufferedWriter.write("We can read text from files and databases");

    } // End of main method()
} // End of WriteFile class
```

17. Amend the code to close the FileWriter and BufferedWriter we have opened and end the try block with a closing curly brace:

```
        bufferedWriter.newLine();
        bufferedWriter.write("We can read text from files and databases");

        // Close the BufferedWriter.
        bufferedWriter.close();

        // Close the FileWriter.
        fileWriter.close();
    } // End of the try section of the error handling

    } // End of main method()
} // End of WriteFile class
```

18. Amend the code to add the catch block of the error handling:

```
        // Close the BufferedWriter.
        bufferedWriter.close();

        // Close the FileWriter.
        fileWriter.close();
    } // End of the try section of the error handling

    catch(IOException ex)
    {
        System.out.println("Error writing file '" + filePath + "'");
    } // End of the catch section of the error handling

    } // End of main method()
} // End of WriteFile class
```

19. Click on the **File** menu.

20. Choose **Save All.**

21. Click on the green **Run** button at the top of the screen or click on the Run menu and choose the Run option.

22. Look in the Package Explorer window and you should see the text file that was created. You may need to right click on the JavaExamples folder and choose Refresh.

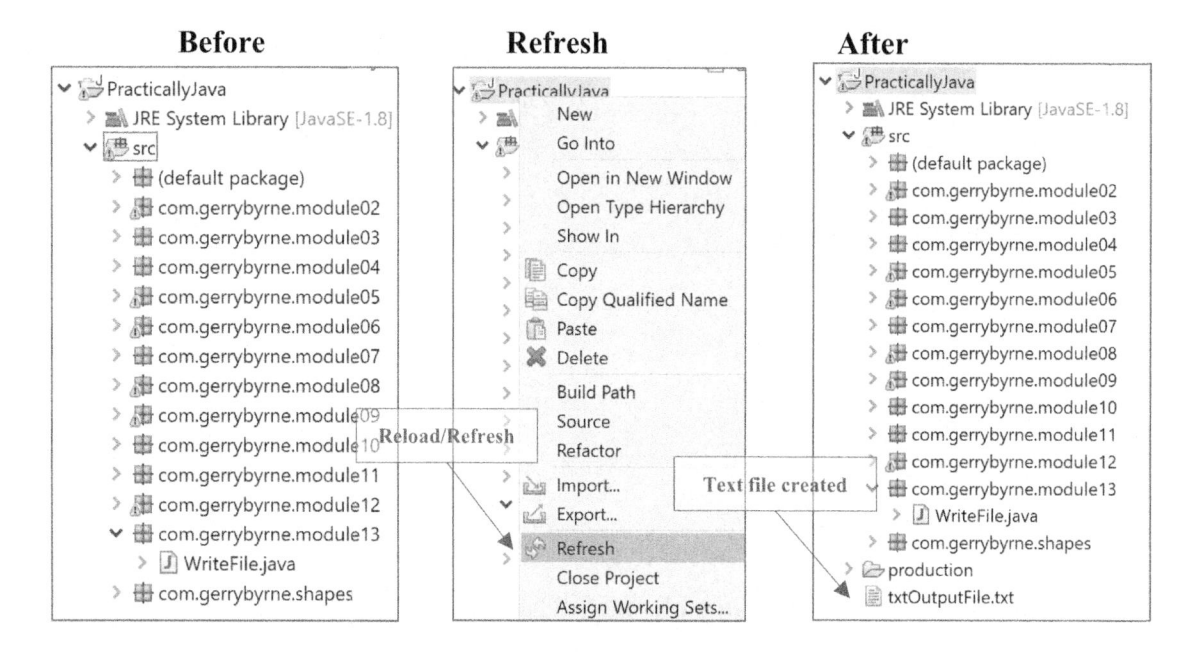

23. Double click on the **txtOutPutFile.txt** to open it in the Editor window:

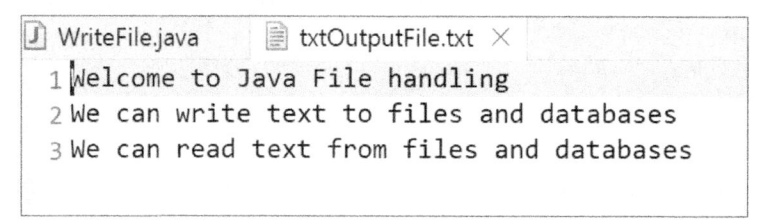

```
1 Welcome to Java File handling
2 We can write text to files and databases
3 We can read text from files and databases
```

Reading from a file

1. Right click on the **com.gerrybyrne.module13** package.
2. Choose **New**.
3. Choose **Class**.
4. Enter the new name for the file, we will call it **ReadFile**.
5. Put a tick in the checkbox beside the public static void main(String[] args) box.
6. Click on the **Finish** button.

The ReadFile class code will appear in the editor window and will be similar to the following:

```java
package com.gerrybyrne.module13;

public class ReadFile
{
    public static void main(String[] args)
    {
        // TODO Auto-generated method stub
    } // End of main method()
} // End of ReadFile class
```

7. Amend the code to add the required imports:

```java
package com.gerrybyrne.module13;

import java.io.*;

public class ReadFile
{
```

8. Amend the code to add a String variable that will hold the pathname of the text file:

```java
    public static void main(String[] args)
    {
        // Assign the name of the file to be used to a variable.
        String filePath = "txtOutputFile.txt";
    } // End of main method()
} // End of ReadFile class
```

This sets up a variable to hold the file path and name. The text file has been created in the same directory as the bin folder and therefore we can simply type in the file name. If the file was stored in a directory above the bin folder the pathname would be set to "../txtOutputFile.txt".

9. Amend the code to add a String variable that will hold the data read back from the text file. We will initialise the String as null:

```java
// Assign the name of the file to be used to a variable.
String filePath = "txtOutputFile.txt";

// Set up a string variable to hold the lines read
String line = null;
    } // End of main method()
} // End of ReadFile class
```

We also have set up a string variable called line that will hold the data read from the file and set it to have a null value initially

10. Amend the code to add an instance of the FileReader class passing it the name of the file which we setup in the variable called filePath. Don't worry about any error messages, the code is incomplete:

```java
String line = null;

// Enclose the code in a try catch to handle errors
try
{
    /*
    Create an instance of the FileReader and call it fileReader
    FileReader is used to read text files in the default encoding.
    */
    FileReader fileReader= new FileReader(filePath);   ◄──── Source Data
    } // End of main method()
} // End of ReadFile class
```

11. Amend the code to add an instance of the BufferedReader class passing it the name of the file writer which we have just setup:

    FileReader fileReader= new FileReader(filePath);

    /*
      Create an instance of the BufferedReader and call it bufferedReader
      we should always wrap a FileReader in a BufferedReader
    */
    BufferedReader bufferedReader = new BufferedReader(fileReader);
    } // End of main method()
    } // End of ReadFile class

12. Amend the code to use an iteration to read the lines of text from the text file using the readLine() method of the BufferedReader class:

    BufferedReader bufferedReader = new BufferedReader(fileReader);

    /* Iterate the buffer and read one line at a time and display it */
    while((line = bufferedReader.readLine()) != null)
    {
       System.out.println(line);
    }   // End of while iteration
    } // End of main method()
    } // End of ReadFile class

13. Amend the code to close the FileReader and BufferedReader we have opened and end the try block with a closing curly brace:

    while((line = bufferedReader.readLine()) != null)
    {
       System.out.println(line);
    } // End of while iteration

    // Close the bufferedReader
    bufferedReader.close();

    // Close the fileReader
    fileReader.close();

```
        } // End of try section of the error handling
      } // End of main method()
    } // End of ReadFile class
```

14. Amend the code to add the catch block of the error handling:

```
          // Close the fileReader
          fileReader.close();
        } // End of try section of the error handling

        catch(IOException ex)
        {
           System.out.println("Error reading file '" + filePath + "'");
        } // End of the catch section of the error handling
      } // End of main method()
    } // End of ReadFile class
```

15. Click on the **File** menu.

16. Choose **Save All.**

17. Click on the green **Run** button at the top of the screen or click on the Run menu and choose the Run option.

18. Look in the Console window at the bottom of the screen and you should see the output from the text file.

```
Problems  @ Javadoc  Declaration  Console  ×
<terminated> ReadFile [Java Application] C:\Users\gerardbyrne\.p2\
Welcome to Java File handling
We can write text to files and databases
We can read text from files and databases
```

Module summary

So, finishing this module on File handling we should be aware that Java file handling is taken care of by file I/O which is just part of Java's overall I/O system. We have used the FileWriter and BufferedWriter within a try catch code block to write the data to a text file and have used the FileReader and BufferedReader within a try catch code block to read the data from a text file. It is great to be able to read and write to a text file and we could in the future apply a similar concept to reading and writing to a database.

We can really code Java now with all the foundational concepts and have extended our knowledge and skills with file handling. We should be immensely proud of the learning to date.

We should be very proud of the learning to date.

Another great achievement for us in our learning.

Our dot just got bigger

Program Practically

Java

Module 14

Serialisation of an object (class entity)

Serialisation
Deserialisation
Transient keyword

Gerry Byrne

Program Practically - Serialisation

In a previous module we gained knowledge of classes and objects. This module will extend our knowledge and explain how we can save an object so it can be recreated when required. The processes we will investigate are called serialisation and deserialisation.

Serialisation

Serialisation is a process to convert an object into a stream of bytes so that the bytes can be written into a file. We will normally do this so the serialised data can be used to store the data in a database or for sending it across a network e.g. to a message queue to form part of a transaction process. The byte stream created is platform independent, it is an object serialised on one platform that can be deserialised on a different platform.

A class must implement the **java.io.Serializable** interface to be able to serialise data. The Java Serialisation API provides the features to perform serialisation ad de-serialisation.

Example

```
public class Customer implements java.io.Serializable
{
}
```

De-serialisation

De-serialisation is the process of taking the serialised data (file) and returning it to an object as defined by the class.

Access modifier - transient

The keyword **transient** is a variable modifier which can be used in serialisation. When we serialise, there may be some values we do not want to save to the file. These values may contain sensitive data or data that can be calculated again. Changing the variable modifier to transient means that during the serialisation process the Java Virtual Machine (JVM) will ignore the transient variable value and save the default value of the variable data type. The transient keyword assists us with the important role of meeting security constraints when we do not want to save private data in a file. It is important to use the transient keyword with private confidential fields (members) of a class during serialisation.

Let's code some Java

Serialisation is about objects and an object, as we know, is an instance of a class. So, let's create the class first with its properties, methods, constructor, getters and setters. The class will be called **Customer**.

1. Right click on the **src** folder.
2. Choose **New**.
3. Choose **Package**.
4. Name the package as **com.gerrybyrne.module14**.
5. Choose the **Finish** button.
6. Right click on the **com.gerrybyrne.module14** package.
7. Choose **New**.
8. Choose **Class**.
9. Enter the new name for the file, we will call it **Customer**.
10. **Do not put a tick in the checkbox** beside the public static void main(String[] args) box.
11. Click on the **Finish** button.

The Customer class code will appear in the editor window and will be similar to the following:

package com.gerrybyrne.module14;

public class Customer
{

} // End of Customer class

12. Amend the code so that the class implements java.io.Serializable:

```java
package com.gerrybyrne.module14;

public class Customer implements java.io.Serializable
{
} // End of Customer class
```

13. Amend the code to add the class properties (members, fields, variables):

```java
package com.gerrybyrne.module14;

public class Customer implements java.io.Serializable
{
/***************************************************************
transient is a variable modifier which can be used in serialization.
When we need to serialise there may be some values we do not want to save to
the file. These may be sensitive data or data that can be calculated again.
Changing the variable modifier to transient means that during the serialisation
process the Java Virtual Machine (JVM) will ignore the transient variable value
and save the default value of the variable data type.

The transient keyword assists us with the important role of meeting security
constraints e.g. when we do not want to save private data   in file. It is important
to use the transient keyword with private confidential fields (members) of a class
during serialization.
***************************************************************/
    private int        customerAccountNumber;
    private int        customerAge;
    private String     customerName;
    private String     customerAddress;
    private int        customerYearsWithCompany;

} // End of Customer class
```

14. Amend the code to add a constructor for the class:

```
private  String     customerName;
private  String     customerAddress;
private  int        customerYearsWithCompany;
```

```
/*****************************************************************
Create a constructor for the Customer class. The constructor will over-write the
default constructor. The constructor is used to accept the value passed into it from
the code used to instantiate the class. The values passed into the constructor are used
to initialise the values of fields (members, variables!). The keyword this is used in
front of the field (member, variable!) names.
******************************************************************/
    public Customer(int accountNumberPassedIn, int agePassedIn, String namePassedIn,
      String addressPassedIn, int yearsPassedIn) {
      this.customerAccountNumber = accountNumberPassedIn;
      this.customerAge = agePassedIn;
      this.customerName = namePassedIn;
      this.customerAddress = addressPassedIn;
      this.customerYearsWithCompany = yearsPassedIn;
    } // End of constructor
} // End of Customer class
```

15. Amend the code to add a getters and setters for the private properties:

```
    } // End of constructor

/*****************************************************************
As the fields (members, variables!) are marked as private they are not accessible
from outside the class. To enable the fields to be accessed from outside the class
we use a getter method to get the value and a setter method to set the value of
field. We do not need to have a getter and setter for all fields but we normally will.

This is what we have done below.
******************************************************************/
    public int getCustomerAccountNumber() {
      return customerAccountNumber;
    }
    public void setCustomerAccountNumber(int customerAccountNumber) {
      this.customerAccountNumber = customerAccountNumber;
    }
    public int getCustomerAge() {
      return customerAge;
    }
    public void setCustomerAge(int customerAge) {
      this.customerAge = customerAge;
    }
```

```java
        public String getCustomerName() {
            return customerName;
        }
        public void setCustomerName(String customerName) {
            this.customerName = customerName;
        }
        public String getCustomerAddress() {
            return customerAddress;
        }
        public void setCustomerAddress(String customerAddress) {
            this.customerAddress = customerAddress;
        }
        public int getCustomerYearsWithCompany() {
            return customerYearsWithCompany;
        }
        public void setCustomerYearsWithCompany(int customerYearsWithCompany) {
            this.customerYearsWithCompany = customerYearsWithCompany;
        }
} // End of Customer class
```

Serialising the object

Now we have the class that is to be serialised we will create a class that will perform the serialisation on the instance of the class, the object. So, let's create the class called SerialiseCustomer and add the required code.

1. Right click on the **com.gerrybyrne.module14** package.
2. Choose **New**.
3. Choose **Class**.
4. Enter the new name for the file, we will call it **SerialiseCustomer**.
5. **Put a tick in the checkbox** beside the public static void main(String[] args) box.
6. Click on the **Finish** button.

The SerialiseCustomer class code will appear in the editor window and will be similar to the following:

```java
package com.gerrybyrne.module14;
```

```
public class SeraliseCustomer
{
    public static void main(String[] args)
    {
        // TODO Auto-generated method stub
    } // End of main() method
} // End of SerialiseCustomer class
```

7. Amend the code to add the required imports:

```
package com.gerrybyrne.module14;

import java.io.FileOutputStream;
import java.io.ObjectOutputStream;
import java.io.IOException;

public class SerialiseCustomer
{
    public static void main(String[] args)
    {
        // TODO Auto-generated method stub
    } // End of main() method
} // End of SerialiseCustomer class
```

8. Amend the code to add some comments about Serialisation, you may choose to leave these out and go to the next step:

```
import java.io.FileOutputStream;
package com.gerrybyrne.module14;

import java.io.FileOutputStream;
import java.io.ObjectOutputStream;
import java.io.IOException;

/*****************************************************************
Serialisation is a process to convert an object into a stream of bytes so that the bytes can be written into a file. Usually we do this so the file can be used in the storing of the data to a database or for sending across a network e.g. to a message queue to form part of a transaction process.
```

De-serialisation is the process of taking the serialised data (file) and returning it to an object as defined by the class.
The Java Serialisation API provides the features to perform serialisation and de-serialisation but the class must implement the java.io.Serializable interface to be able to serialise data.
**/

public class SeraliseCustomer
{

9. Amend the code to create an instance of the Customer class (the object) passing to the constructor the initial values for the properties:

public class SerialiseCustomer
{
  public static void main(String[] args)
  {
  /**
    Create an instance of the Customer class passing in the initial values that will be used to set the values of the fields (members) in the Customer object being created.

    As a matter of best practice, when we use Java Serialization, the file name should have .ser extension.
    **/
    Customer myCustomerObject = **new** Customer(123456, 45, "Gerry", "1 Any Street, Belfast, BT1 ANY", 10);

  } // End of main() method
} // End of SerialiseCustomer class

10. Amend the code to create a FileOutputStream, which will hold the serialised data. The serialised data will be in the file called CustomerSerialisedData.ser. We enclose the code in a try catch block:

Customer myCustomerObject = **new** Customer(123456, 45, "Gerry", "1 Any Street, Belfast, BT1 ANY", 10);

  try {
    // A file output stream is an output stream for writing data to a File

```
        FileOutputStream fileOutputStreamForData = new
        FileOutputStream("CustomerSerialisedData.ser");

    } // End of main() method
} // End of SerialiseCustomer class
```

11. To the end of the code add the code as shown below to create an ObjectOutputStream, which will write the serialised data to an Output Stream.

```
try {
    // A file output stream is an output stream for writing data to a File
    FileOutputStream fileOutputStreamForData = new
            FileOutputStream("CustomerSerialisedData.ser");

    // An ObjectOutputStream writes primitive data types of Java objects to an OutputStream
    ObjectOutputStream objectOutputStreamForData = new
        ObjectOutputStream(fileOutputStreamForData);

    } // End of main() method
} // End of SerialiseCustomer class
```

12. To the end of the code add the code as shown below to use the writeObject() method to write the Customer object to the ObjectOutputStream.

```
    // An ObjectOutputStream writes primitive data types of Java objects to an
    OutputStream
    ObjectOutputStream objectOutputStreamForData = new
    ObjectOutputStream(fileOutputStreamForData);

    objectOutputStreamForData.writeObject(myCustomerObject);

    } // End of main() method
} // End of SerialiseCustomer class
```

13. To the end of the code add the code as shown below to close the opened ObjectOutputStream and FileOutputStream and end the try block.

```
        objectOutputStreamForData.writeObject(myCustomerObject);
```

objectOutputStreamForData.close();

fileOutputStreamForData.close();

System.out.println("The serialisation has been completed");
} // End of try block

   } // End of main() method
} // End of SerialiseCustomer class

14. Add the code as shown below to add the catch block of the error handling.

System.*out*.println("The serialisation has been completed");
} // End of try block

catch(IOException exceptionGenerated)
{
   System.*out*.println(exceptionGenerated);
} // End of catch block

   } // End of main() method
} // End of SerialiseCustomer class

24. Click on the **File** menu.
25. Choose **Save All.**
26. Click on the green **Run** button at the top of the screen or click on the Run menu and choose the Run option
27. Look in the console window and check that the message appears to say that the process was successful.

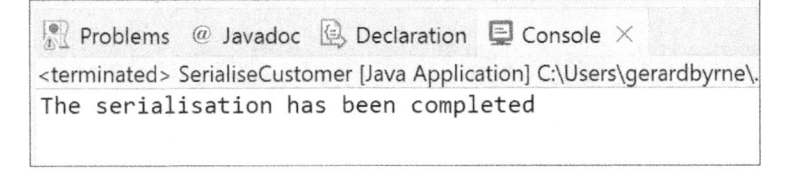

```
Problems  @ Javadoc  Declaration  Console  ×
<terminated> SerialiseCustomer [Java Application] C:\Users\gerardbyrne\.
The serialisation has been completed
```

28. Look in the Package Explorer window and you should see the serialised (.ser) file that was created. You may need to right click on the JavaExamples folder and choose Refresh.

Before   **After**

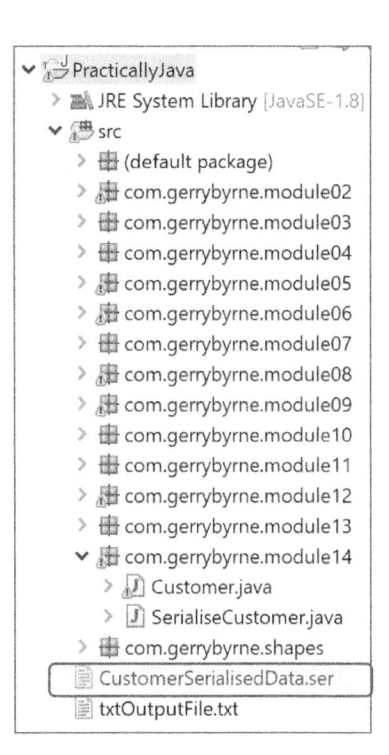

De-serialising the serialised the file back to an instance of the class

The code below has been commented to help you understand it better. You do not need to add the comments when you are keying in the code.

1. Right click on the **com.gerrybyrne.module14** package.
2. Choose **New**.
3. Choose **Class**.
4. Enter the new name for the file, we will call it **DeserialiseFileToCustomerObject**.
5. **Put a tick in the checkbox** beside the public static void main(String[] args) box.
6. Click on the **Finish** button.

The DeserialiseFileToCustomerObject class code will appear in the editor window and will be similar to the following:

```
package com.gerrybyrne.module14;

public class DeserialiseFileToCustomerObject
{
    public static void main(String[] args)
```

```
        {
                // TODO Auto-generated method stub
        } // End of main() method
} // End of SerialiseCustomer class
```

7. Amend the code to add the required imports:

```
package com.gerrybyrne.module14;

import java.io.FileInputStream;
import java.io.ObjectInputStream;

public class DeserialiseFileToCustomerObject
{
```

8. Amend the code to add some comments about Serialisation, you may choose to leave these out and go to the next step:

```
import java.io.FileInputStream;
import java.io.ObjectInputStream;

/*******************************************************************
Serialisation is a process to convert an object into a stream of bytes so that the bytes
can be written into a file. Usually we do this so the file can be used in the storing of
the data to a database or for sending across a network e.g. to a message queue to
form part of a transaction process. De-serialisation is the process of taking the
serialised data (file) and returning it to an object as defined by the class.
The Java Serialisation API provides the features to perform de-serialisation and
serialisation and a class must implement java.io.Serializable interface to be able
to serialise data.
*******************************************************************/

public class DeserialiseFileToCustomerObject
{
  public static void main(String[] args)
  {
```

9. Amend the code to create an instance of the Customer class within a try catch construct.

```
    public static void main(String[] args)
    {
```

```
    try
    {
        /* Create a Customer object */
        Customer myCustomer = null;
    } // End of main() method
} // End of SerialiseCustomer class
```

10. Amend the code to create a FileInputStream, to hold the data from the serialised file. The serialised data is in the file called CustomerSerialisedData.ser. We enclose the code in a try catch block, do not worry about errors yet, the code is incomplete.

```
    try
    {
        /* Create a Customer object */
        Customer myCustomer = null;

        /*
         FileInputStream allows us to read the contents
         of a file as a stream of bytes
        */
        FileInputStream fileInputStreamForData = new
      FileInputStream("CustomerSerialisedData.ser");
    } // End of main() method
} // End of SerialiseCustomer class
```

11. Add the code as shown below to create an ObjectInputStream, which will deserialise data written using an Object Output Stream.

```
/*
  FileInputStream allows us to read the contents of a file as a stream of bytes
*/
FileInputStream fileInputStreamForData = new
FileInputStream("CustomerSerialisedData.ser");

/* An ObjectInputStream deserializes primitive data and objects written using an
ObjectOutputStream */
ObjectInputStream objectInputStreamForData = new ObjectInputStream
(fileInputStreamForData);
    } // End of main() method
} // End of SerialiseCustomer class
```

12. Add the code as shown below to use the readObject() method to read the object and cast it as a Customer object.

    ```
    ObjectInputStream objectInputStreamForData = new ObjectInputStream (fileInputStreamForData);

        /*
           The serialised file has been read and we use the readObject() method to get the
           object, we then cast the object to a Customer object
        */
        myCustomer = (Customer) objectInputStreamForData.readObject();
      } // End of main() method
    } // End of SerialiseCustomer class
    ```

13. Add the code as shown below to display the de-serialised data:

    ```
        /*
           The serialised file has been read and we use the readObject() method to get the
           object, we then cast the object to a Customer object
        */
        myCustomer = (Customer) objectInputStreamForData.readObject();

        System.out.println("Customer Details");
        System.out.println("Customer Name: " + myCustomer.getCustomerName());
        System.out.println("Customer Age: " + myCustomer.getCustomerAge());
        System.out.println("Customer Account No:" + myCustomer.getCustomerAccountNumber());
        System.out.println("Customer Address:" + myCustomer.getCustomerAddress());
        System.out.println("Customer Years a Customer:  " + myCustomer.getCustomerYearsWithCompany());
      } // End of main() method
    } // End of SerialiseCustomer class
    ```

14. To the end of the code add the code as shown below to close the opened ObjectInputStream and FileInputStream and end the try block.

    ```
    System.out.println("Customer Address:" + myCustomer.getCustomerAddress());
    System.out.println("Customer Years a Customer:  " + myCustomer.getCustomerYearsWithCompany());
    ```

objectInputStreamForData.close();

fileInputStreamForData.close();
} // End of try block

} // End of main() method
} // End of SerialiseCustomer class

15. Add the code as shown below to add the catch block of the error handling.

objectInputStreamForData.close();

fileInputStreamForData.close();
} // End of try block

catch(Exception exceptionGenerated)
{
   System.*out*.println(exceptionGenerated);
} // End of catch block

} // End of main() method
} // End of SerialiseCustomer class

16. Click on the **File** menu.
17. Choose **Save All**.
18. Click on the green **Run** button at the top of the screen or click on the Run menu and choose the Run option
19. Look in the console window and check that the display of the object properties have been displayed successfully.

```
Problems  @ Javadoc  Declaration  Console  X
<terminated> DeserialiseFileToCustomerObject [Java Application] C:\Users\ger
Customer Details
Customer Name: Gerry
Customer Age: 45
Customer Account No:123456
Customer Address:1 Any Street, Belfast, BT1 ANY
Customer Years a Customer:  10
```

Customer.toString()
Deserialised data

Access modifier - transient

The variable modifier **transient** can be used in serialisation which means that during the serialisation process the Java Virtual Machine (JVM) will ignore the transient variable value and save the default value of the variable data type.

1. Open the **Customer** file.
2. Amend the code to make **customerAge** property of type transient:

```
private int            customerAccountNumber;    transient keyword
private transient int  customerAge;
private String         customerName;
private String         customerAddress;
private int            customerYearsWithCompany;
```

3. Click on the **File** menu.
4. Choose **Save All**.
5. Open the **SerialiseCustomer** file.
6. Click on the green **Run** button at the top of the screen or click on the Run menu and choose the Run option to run the **SerialiseCustomer** file.
7. Look in the console window and check that the message appears to say that the process was successful.

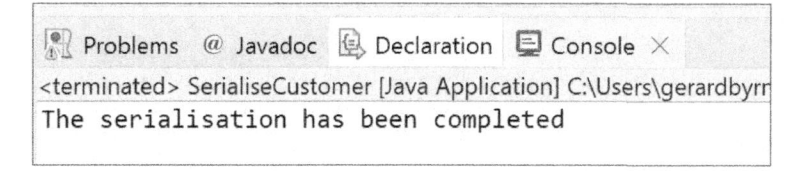

```
Problems  @ Javadoc  Declaration  Console  X
<terminated> SerialiseCustomer [Java Application] C:\Users\gerardbyrr
The serialisation has been completed
```

8. Open the **DeserialiseFileToCustomerObject** file.
9. Click on the green **Run** button at the top of the screen or click on the Run menu and choose the Run option to run the **DeserialiseFileToCustomerObject** file.
10. Look in the console window and check that the display of the object properties is correct with the default value for the age.

Using Transient modifier

```
Problems  @ Javadoc  Declaration  Console ×
<terminated> DeserialiseFileToCustomerObject [Java Application] C:\Users\
Customer Details
Customer Name: Gerry
Customer Age: 0     ◄────  Transient means
Customer Account No:123456        default value
Customer Address:1 Any Street, Belfast, BT1 ANY
Customer Years a Customer:  10
```

Without Transient modifier

```
Problems  @ Javadoc  Declaration  Console ×
<terminated> DeserialiseFileToCustomerObject [Java Application] C:\Users\ger
Customer Details
Customer Name: Gerry              Not Transient so
Customer Age: 45    ◄────           actual value
Customer Account No:123456
Customer Address:1 Any Street, Belfast, BT1 ANY
Customer Years a Customer:  10
```

Module summary

So, finishing this module on object serialisation and deserialisation we should be familiar with the use of a class and the instantiation of the class to create an object. We realise that our object (instantiated class) will be treated like all the other objects we have in our code when the application is closed. When the Java Virtual Machine (JVM) stops, our object, and every other object will not be accessible. We saw in the file handling module that we could persist data by writing it to a text file which is accessible to us after the JVM stops. So, we can now think of serialisation as a method to write the object with its real data to a file so we can reuse it at a later stage. We may also want to transfer the object to another computer over the network or internet.

We also saw that deserialisation allows us to reverse the process carried out by serialisation, which means converting our serialised byte stream back to our object.

Wow, what an achievement, this is not basic coding, we are doing some wonderful things with our Java code.

We should be immensely proud of the learning to date.

Our dot just got bigger

Program Practically

Java

Module 15

Common programming routines

Gerry Byrne

Program Practically - Applying your knowledge to some common theoretical routines

Linear search

A Linear search is used to search a series of elements in a data structure for a specified a key element. Whilst a linear search can be used successfully it will generally be slower than a binary search. It can be thought of as a 'brute-force' algorithm as it simply compares each item in the data structure with the element being searched for. It does not need to change the state of the data structure before it begins e.g. it does not need to sort the elements to have them in a chronological or alphabetic order. We can think of a linear search as undertaking the steps below or following the algorithm:

- navigate through the data structure one element at a time
- check if the element being searched for matches the current element of the data structure
- if there is a match, the element is found and we return the index (position) of the current data structure element
- if there is no match, the element has not been found and we return the value -1

Let's create an application that will implement a linear search.

1. Right click on the **src** folder.
2. Choose **New**.
3. Choose **Package**.
4. Name the package as **com.gerrybyrne.module15**.
5. Choose the **Finish** button.
6. Right click on the **com.gerrybyrne.module15** package.
7. Choose **New**.
8. Choose **Class**.
9. Enter the new name for the file, we will call it **LinearSearch**.
10. Put a tick in the checkbox beside the public static void main(String[] args) box.
11. Click on the **Finish** button.

The LinearSearch code will appear in the editor window and will be similar to the following:

```java
package com.gerrybyrne.module15;

public class LinearSearch
{
    public static void main(String[] args)
    {
        // TODO Auto-generated method stub
    } // End of main() method
} // End of LinearSearch class
```

12. Amend the code to add a comment block, create an array and initialise the values:

```java
package com.gerrybyrne.module15;

/*
A Linear search is a simple searching algorithm that searches for an
element in a list in sequential order. The linear search starts at the start
of the list and checks every element until the desired element is not found.
*/
public class LinearSearch
{
    public static void main(String[] args)
    {
    // Declare and create the array of claim values
        int claimValues[] = {6000, 9000, 3000, 4000, 8000, 1000, 2000, 5000, 7000};

    } // End of main() method
} // End of LinearSearch class
```

13. Amend the code to create the variable that will hold the value to be found, the key:

```java
public static void main(String[] args)
{
// Declare and create the array of claim values
    int claimValues[] = {6000, 9000, 3000, 4000, 8000, 1000, 2000, 5000, 7000};

    // Value to be located using linear search
    int valueToBeLocated = 1000;
} // End of main() method
} // End of LinearSearch class
```

14. Amend the code to call a method that will display the array:

    ```
    // Value to be located using linear search
    int valueToBeLocated = 1000;

    // Display the elements of the array
    displayArrayElements(claimValues);

    } // End of main() method
    } // End of LinearSearch class
    ```

15. Amend the code to call a method that will do a linear search of the array for the specified value and assign the returned value to a variable:

    ```
    // Display the elements of the array
    displayArrayElements(claimValues);

    /*
      Call the linear search method passing it the array and the
      value to be located and store the returned value in a variable
      called returnedValue
    */
    int returnedValue = searchForTheValue(claimValues, valueToBeLocated);
    } // End of main() method
    } // End of LinearSearch class
    ```

16. Amend the code to perform a selection that will display one message if the value is -1 and another message if the value is not -1. The -1 value means no match was found.

    ```
    int returnedValue = searchForTheValue(claimValues, valueToBeLocated);

    // Display the appropriate message (located or not)
    if ( returnedValue == -1)
    {
       System.out.println("The value is not present in array");
    } // End of if section
    else
    {
    ```

System.*out*.printf("The value was located at index %d (position %d)",
returnedValue,
   returnedValue + 1);
   } // End of else section

 } // End of main() method
} // End of LinearSearch class

17. Amend the code to create the method that will search the array for the required value. This method is created outside the main() method:

   } // End of else section
   } // End of main() method

   public static int searchForTheValue(int claimValuesPassedIn[],
      int valueToBeLocatedPassedIn)
   {
    for (int counter = 0; counter < claimValuesPassedIn.length; counter++)
    {
    // This line is used to display the values being compared, remove when completed
    System.*out*.println("Comparing " + claimValuesPassedIn[counter] + " and " +
       valueToBeLocatedPassedIn);
    if (claimValuesPassedIn[counter] == valueToBeLocatedPassedIn)
    {
     return counter;
    }
    }
    return -1;
   } // End of searchForTheValue() method

 } // End of LinearSearch class

18. Amend the code to create the method that will display the array values. This method is created outside the main() method:

   }
   return -1;

   } // End of searchForTheValue() method

```
/* Prints the array */
static void displayArrayElements(int claimValuesPassedIn[])
{
  for (int counter = 0; counter<claimValuesPassedIn.length; ++counter)
  {
      System.out.println(claimValuesPassedIn[counter] + " ");
  }
} // End of displayArrayElements

} // End of LinearSearch class
```

19. Click on the **File** menu.
20. Choose **Save All**.
21. Click on the green **Run** button at the top of the screen or click on the Run menu and choose the Run option
22. Look in the console window and check that the object properties have been displayed successfully.

Output

```
Problems  @ Javadoc  Declaration  Console  X
<terminated> LinearSearch [Java Application] C:\Users\gerardbyrne\.p2
6000
9000
3000
4000
8000
1000
2000
5000
7000
Comparing 6000 and 1000
Comparing 9000 and 1000
Comparing 3000 and 1000
Comparing 4000 and 1000
Comparing 8000 and 1000
Comparing 1000 and 1000
The value was located at index 5 (position 6)
```

1000 found

Binary search (Iterative Binary Search)

A Binary search is used to search a series of elements (the data structure) for a specified a key. Unlike the linear search the binary search only works when the array is sorted. The binary search starts with the whole sorted array and checks if the value of our search key is less than the item in the middle of the array and if it:

- is, the search is narrowed to the lower (left) half of the array
- is not, then we use the upper (right) half and we repeat the process until the value is found or there are no elements to half

1. Right click on the **com.gerrybyrne.module15** package.
2. Choose **New**.
3. Choose **Class**.
4. Enter the new name for the file, we will call it **BinarySearch**.
5. Put a tick in the checkbox beside the public static void main(String[] args) box.
6. Click on the **Finish** button.

The BinarySearch code will appear in the editor window and will be similar to the following:

package com.gerrybyrne.module15;

public class BinarySearch
{
   public static void main(String[] args)
   {
      // TODO Auto-generated method stub
   } // End of main() method

} // End of BinarySearch class

7. Amend the code to add a comment block, create an array and initialise the values:

package com.gerrybyrne.module15;

/*
With a binary search we must first ensure the array is sorted.
The binary search starts with the whole array and checks if the

value of our search key is less than the item in the middle of the array.
If it is, the search is narrowed to the lower (left) half of the array.
If it is not, then we use the upper (right) half.
We repeat this process until the value is found or the there are elements left to half.
*/

public class BinarySearch
{
   public static void main(String[] args)
   {
     int claimValues[] = {6000, 9000, 3000, 4000, 8000, 1000, 2000, 5000, 7000};
   } // End of main() method

} // End of BinarySearch class

8. Amend the code to create the variable that will hold the value to be found, the key:

   public static void main(String[] args)
   {
     int claimValues[] = {6000, 9000, 3000, 4000, 8000, 1000, 2000, 5000, 7000};

     // Value to be located using linear search
     int valueToBeLocated = 6000;

   } // End of main() method

} // End of BinarySearch class

9. Amend the code to sort the array as a binary search requires this for it to work:

     // Value to be located using linear search
     int valueToBeLocated = 6000;

     // Sort the array as this is essential for a Binary search
     Arrays.*sort*(claimValues);

   } // End of main() method

} // End of BinarySearch class

10. Amend the code to add the import for the Arrays:

    package com.gerrybyrne.module15;

    import java.util.Arrays;

11. Amend the code to call a method that will display the array:

    ```
    // Sort the array as this is essential for a Binary search
    Arrays.sort(claimValues);

    // Display the elements of the array
    displayArrayElements(claimValues);
    } // End of main() method
    } // End of BinarySearch class
    ```

12. Amend the code to call a method that will perform a binary search of the array for the specified value and assign the returned value to a variable:

    ```
    // Display the elements of the array
    displayArrayElements(claimValues);

    /*
    Call the binary search method passing it the array and the
    value to be located and store the returned value in a variable
    called returnedValue
    */
    int returnedValue = performBinarySearch(claimValues, valueToBeLocated);
    } // End of main() method
    } // End of BinarySearch class
    ```

13. Amend the code to perform a selection that will display one message if the value is -1 and another message if the values is not -1. The -1 value means no match was found.

    ```
    int returnedValue = performBinarySearch(claimValues, valueToBeLocated);

    // Display the appropriate message (located or not)
    if ( returnedValue == -1)
    {
    ```

```
            System.out.println("The value is not present in array");
        } // End of if section
        else
        {
        System.out.printf("The value %d was located at index %d (position %d)",
valueToBeLocated, returnedValue, returnedValue + 1 );
        } // End of else section

    } // End of main() method

} // End of BinarySearch class
```

14. Amend the code to create the method that will search the array for the required value. This method is created outside the main() method:

```
        } // End of else section

    } // End of main() method

    public static int performBinarySearch(int[] arrayPassedIn, int numberToBeFound)
    {
      int firstPosition = 0;
      int lastPosition = arrayPassedIn.length - 1;
      int middlePosition = (firstPosition + lastPosition) / 2;

      while (firstPosition <= lastPosition)
      {
        if (arrayPassedIn[middlePosition] < numberToBeFound)
        {
            firstPosition = middlePosition + 1;
        }
          else if (arrayPassedIn[middlePosition] == numberToBeFound)
          {
            break;
          }
                else
                {
                    lastPosition = middlePosition - 1;
                }
        middlePosition = (firstPosition + lastPosition) / 2;
```

```
        } // End of while iteration

        if (firstPosition > lastPosition)
        {
                middlePosition = -1;
        }
        return middlePosition;
    } // End of performBinarySearch() method

} // End of BinarySearch class
```

15. Amend the code to create the method that will display the array values. This method is created outside the main() method:

```
    return middlePosition;
    } // End of performBinarySearch() method

    /* Prints the array */
    static void displayArrayElements(int claimValuesPassedIn[])
    {
       for (int counter = 0; counter<claimValuesPassedIn.length; ++counter)
       {
           System.out.println(claimValuesPassedIn[counter] + " ");
       }
    } // End of displayArrayElements

} // End of BinarySearch class
```

16. Click on the **File** menu.
17. Choose **Save All**.
18. Click on the green **Run** button at the top of the screen or click on the Run menu and choose the Run option
19. Look in the console window and check that the object properties have been displayed successfully.

Output

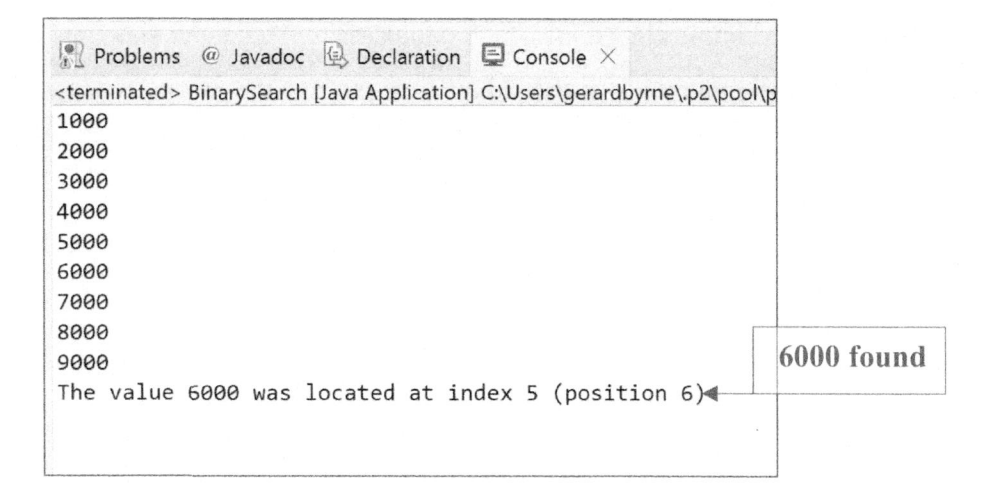

```
1000
2000
3000
4000
5000
6000
7000
8000
9000
The value 6000 was located at index 5 (position 6)
```

← 6000 found

Bubble sort

A Bubble sort is a simple algorithm which compares two adjacent elements of the array. If the first element is numerically greater than the next one, the elements are swapped. The process is then repeated to move across all the elements of the array.

1. Right click on the **com.gerrybyrne.module15** package.
2. Choose **New**.
3. Choose **Class**.
4. Enter the new name for the file, we will call it **BubbleSort**.
5. Put a tick in the checkbox beside the public static void main(String[] args) box.
6. Click on the **Finish** button.

The BubbleSort code will appear in the editor window and will be similar to the following:

```
package com.gerrybyrne.module15;

public class BubbleSort
{
    public static void main(String[] args)
    {
        // TODO Auto-generated method stub

    } // End of main() method

} // End of LinearSearch class
```

7. Amend the code to add a comment block, create an array and initialise the values:

```
package com.gerrybyrne.module15;

/*
A Bubble sort is a simple algorithm which compares two adjacent elements
of the array. If the first element is numerically greater than the next one, the
elements are swapped. The process is then repeated to move across all the
elements of the array.
*/
```

```java
public class BubbleSort
{
    public static void main(String[] args)
    {
        // Declare and create the array of claim values
        int claimValues[] = {6000, 9000, 3000, 4000, 8000, 1000, 2000, 5000, 7000};
    } // End of main() method

} // End of LinearSearch class
```

8. Amend the code to call a method that will sort the array:

```java
public static void main(String[] args)
{
    // Declare and create the array of claim values
    int claimValues[] = {6000, 9000, 3000, 4000, 8000, 1000, 2000, 5000, 7000};

    // Pass the array of claim values to the method bubbleSortTheArray()
    bubbleSortOfTheArray(claimValues);

} // End of main() method

} // End of LinearSearch class
```

9. Amend the code to call the method that will display the elements of the array:

```java
    // Pass the array of claim values to the method bubbleSortTheArray()
    bubbleSortOfTheArray(claimValues);

    System.out.println("The sorted array is");

    // Pass the sorted array to the method displayArrayElements()
    displayArrayElements(claimValues);

} // End of main() method

} // End of LinearSearch class
```

10. Amend the code to create the method that will sort the array for the required value. This method is created outside the main() method:

```
} // End of main() method

static void bubbleSortOfTheArray(int claimValuesPassedIn[])
{
  for (int outerCounter = 0; outerCounter < claimValuesPassedIn.length-1;
       outerCounter++)
  {
    for (int innerCounter = 0; innerCounter < claimValuesPassedIn.length-
         outerCounter-1; innerCounter++)
    {
      if (claimValuesPassedIn[innerCounter] >
      claimValuesPassedIn[innerCounter+1])
      {
        // Swap the two values
        int temporaryValue = claimValuesPassedIn[innerCounter];
        claimValuesPassedIn[innerCounter] = claimValuesPassedIn[innerCounter+1];
        claimValuesPassedIn[innerCounter+1] = temporaryValue;
        displayArrayElements(claimValuesPassedIn);
      } // End of if construct
    } // End of for iteration inner iteration
  } // End of for iteration inner iteration
} // End of bubbleSortTheArray

} // End of LinearSearch class
```

11. Amend the code to create the method that will display the array values. This method is created outside the main() method:

```
        displayArrayElements(claimValuesPassedIn);
      } // End of if construct
    } // End of for iteration inner iteration
  } // End of for iteration inner iteration
} // End of bubbleSortTheArray

/* Prints the array */
static void displayArrayElements(int claimValuesPassedIn[])
{
```

```
    for (int counter = 0; counter<claimValuesPassedIn.length; ++counter)
        System.out.print(claimValuesPassedIn[counter] + " ");
        System.out.println();
  } // End of displayArrayElements

} // End of LinearSearch class
```

Output

```
<terminated> BubbleSort [Java Application] C:\Users\gerardbyrne\.p2\
6000 3000 9000 4000 8000 1000 2000 5000 7000
6000 3000 4000 9000 8000 1000 2000 5000 7000
6000 3000 4000 8000 9000 1000 2000 5000 7000
6000 3000 4000 8000 1000 9000 2000 5000 7000
6000 3000 4000 8000 1000 2000 9000 5000 7000
6000 3000 4000 8000 1000 2000 5000 9000 7000
6000 3000 4000 8000 1000 2000 5000 7000 9000
3000 6000 4000 8000 1000 2000 5000 7000 9000
3000 4000 6000 8000 1000 2000 5000 7000 9000
3000 4000 6000 1000 8000 2000 5000 7000 9000
3000 4000 6000 1000 2000 8000 5000 7000 9000
3000 4000 6000 1000 2000 5000 8000 7000 9000
3000 4000 6000 1000 2000 5000 7000 8000 9000
3000 4000 1000 6000 2000 5000 7000 8000 9000
3000 4000 1000 2000 6000 5000 7000 8000 9000
3000 4000 1000 2000 5000 6000 7000 8000 9000
3000 1000 4000 2000 5000 6000 7000 8000 9000
3000 1000 2000 4000 5000 6000 7000 8000 9000
1000 3000 2000 4000 5000 6000 7000 8000 9000
1000 2000 3000 4000 5000 6000 7000 8000 9000
The sorted array is
1000 2000 3000 4000 5000 6000 7000 8000 9000
```

Insertion sort

An Insertion Sort is similar to a Bubble sort, however, it is a more efficient sort. We should think about using the Insertion sort when we have a small number of elements to sort. Larger data sets will take more time.

1. Right click on the **com.gerrybyrne.module15** package.
2. Choose **New**.
3. Choose **Class**.
4. Enter the new name for the file, we will call it **InsertionSort**.
5. Put a tick in the checkbox beside the public static void main(String[] args) box.
6. Click on the **Finish** button.

The InsertionSort code will appear in the editor window and will be similar to the following:

```
package com.gerrybyrne.module15;
public class InsertionSort
{
    public static void main(String[] args)
    {
        // TODO Auto-generated method stub
    } // End of main() method
} // End of InsertionSort class
```

7. Amend the code to add a comment block, create an array and initialise the values:

```
package com.gerrybyrne.module15;

/*
An Insertion Sort is similar to a Bubble sort, however, it is a more efficient
sort. We should think about using the Insertion sort when we have a small
number of elements to sort. Larger data sets will take more time.
*/

public class InsertionSort
{
```

```
public static void main(String[] args)
{
    // Declare and create the array of claim values
    int claimValues[] = {6000, 9000, 3000, 4000, 8000, 1000, 2000, 5000, 7000};

} // End of main() method
} // End of InsertionSort class
```

8. Amend the code to call a method that will sort the array:

```
public static void main(String[] args)
{
    // Declare and create the array of claim values
    int claimValues[] = {6000, 9000, 3000, 4000, 8000, 1000, 2000, 5000, 7000};

    insertionSortOfArray(claimValues);

} // End of main() method
} // End of InsertionSort class
```

9. Amend the code to call the method that will display the elements of the array:

```
    // Declare and create the array of claim values
    int claimValues[] = {6000, 9000, 3000, 4000, 8000, 1000, 2000, 5000, 7000};

    insertionSortOfArray(claimValues);

    displayArrayElements(claimValues);

} // End of main() method
} // End of InsertionSort class
```

10. Amend the code to create the method that will sort the array for the required value. This method is created outside the main() method:

```
} // End of main() method

/* Method to sort array using an insertion sort*/
static void insertionSortOfArray(int claimValuesPassedIn[])
{
```

```
        for (int counter = 1; counter < claimValuesPassedIn.length; ++counter)
        {
          int currentKeyValue = claimValuesPassedIn[counter];
          int previousValue = counter - 1;

          /* Move elements that are greater than the currentArrayValue
              to one position in front of their current position */
          while (previousValue >= 0 && claimValuesPassedIn[previousValue] > currentKeyValue) {
                System.out.println("Comparing " + claimValuesPassedIn[previousValue] + " and " + currentKeyValue);
                claimValuesPassedIn[previousValue + 1] = claimValuesPassedIn[previousValue];
                previousValue = previousValue - 1;
          }
          claimValuesPassedIn[previousValue + 1] = currentKeyValue;
          // This line is used to display the values being compared, remove when completed
          displayArrayElements(claimValuesPassedIn);
        } // End of iteration of the array
    } // End of insertionSortOfArray() method
} // End of InsertionSort class
```

11. Amend the code to create the method that will display the array values. This method is created outside the main() method:

```
          claimValuesPassedIn[previousValue + 1] = currentKeyValue;
          // This line is used to display the values being compared, remove when completed
          displayArrayElements(claimValuesPassedIn);
        } // End of iteration of the array
    } // End of insertionSortOfArray() method

    /* Prints the array */
    static void displayArrayElements(int claimValuesPassedIn[])
    {
       for (int counter = 0; counter<claimValuesPassedIn.length; ++counter)
          System.out.print(claimValuesPassedIn[counter] + " ");
          System.out.println();
    } // End of displayArrayElements
} // End of InsertionSort class
```

Original values

6000 9000 3000 4000 8000 1000 2000 5000 7000

Resulting iterations – highlighted values are the ones being compared

6000	9000	3000	4000	8000	1000	2000	5000	7000
6000	9000	3000	4000	8000	1000	2000	5000	7000
6000	3000	9000	4000	8000	1000	2000	5000	7000
3000	6000	9000	4000	8000	1000	2000	5000	7000
3000	6000	4000	9000	8000	1000	2000	5000	7000
3000	4000	6000	9000	8000	1000	2000	5000	7000
3000	4000	6000	8000	9000	1000	2000	5000	7000
3000	4000	6000	8000	1000	9000	2000	5000	7000
3000	4000	6000	1000	8000	9000	2000	5000	7000
3000	4000	1000	6000	8000	9000	2000	5000	7000
3000	1000	4000	6000	8000	9000	2000	5000	7000
1000	3000	4000	6000	8000	9000	2000	5000	7000
1000	3000	4000	6000	8000	2000	9000	5000	7000
1000	3000	4000	6000	2000	8000	9000	5000	7000
1000	3000	4000	2000	6000	8000	9000	5000	7000
1000	3000	2000	4000	6000	8000	9000	5000	7000
1000	2000	3000	4000	6000	8000	9000	5000	7000
1000	2000	3000	4000	6000	8000	5000	9000	7000
1000	2000	3000	4000	6000	5000	8000	9000	7000
1000	2000	3000	4000	5000	6000	8000	9000	7000
1000	2000	3000	4000	5000	6000	8000	7000	9000
1000	2000	3000	4000	5000	6000	7000	8000	9000

Output

```
6000 9000 3000 4000 8000 1000 2000 5000 7000
Comparing 9000 and 3000
Comparing 6000 and 3000
3000 6000 9000 4000 8000 1000 2000 5000 7000
Comparing 9000 and 4000
Comparing 6000 and 4000
3000 4000 6000 9000 8000 1000 2000 5000 7000
Comparing 9000 and 8000
3000 4000 6000 8000 9000 1000 2000 5000 7000
Comparing 9000 and 1000
Comparing 8000 and 1000
Comparing 6000 and 1000
Comparing 4000 and 1000
Comparing 3000 and 1000
1000 3000 4000 6000 8000 9000 2000 5000 7000
Comparing 9000 and 2000
Comparing 8000 and 2000
Comparing 6000 and 2000
Comparing 4000 and 2000
Comparing 3000 and 2000
1000 2000 3000 4000 6000 8000 9000 5000 7000
Comparing 9000 and 5000
Comparing 8000 and 5000
Comparing 6000 and 5000
1000 2000 3000 4000 5000 6000 8000 9000 7000
Comparing 9000 and 7000
Comparing 8000 and 7000
1000 2000 3000 4000 5000 6000 7000 8000 9000
1000 2000 3000 4000 5000 6000 7000 8000 9000
```

Program Practically

Java

Labs
It's time to reinforce our learning

Gerry Byrne

Program Practically - Module Labs

This is our opportunity to practise what we have learnt. We should complete the labs by referring to the book modules when we are unsure about how to do something, but more importantly we should look at the previous code we have written.

The code we have written should be an invaluable source of working code and it is important not to 'reinvent the wheel', use the code, copy, paste and amend it if required. Reuse the code, that is what the professional developer would do and is expected to do. Professional software developers are expected to create applications as fast and accurately as possible and reusing existing code is one technique they apply, so, why should we be any different.

If we really get stuck there are sample solutions following the labs and we can refer to these, but it is important we understand any code that we copy and paste.

It is important we enjoy the challenge of developing solutions for each lab. We will apply the things we have learnt in the modules but more importantly we will develop our own techniques and styles for coding, debugging and problem solving.

Think about the saying:

"Life begins at the edge of our comfort zone"

We will inevitably feel at the edge of our programming ability but every new thing we learn in completing each lab should make us feel better and encourage us to learn more. Whilst we may be 'frightened' and 'uncomfortable' completing the coding labs the process will lead us to grow and develop our coding skills. We might find it 'painful' at times but that is the reality of programming. We will find it exciting and challenging as we are stretched and brought to a place we have not been to before.

Module 2 Labs – Println()

Lab One

Write a Java console application, using the println() command, that will display the letter E using * to form the shape e.g. one line could be System.out.println("*******");

Lab Two

Write a Java console application, using the println() command, that will display the letter A using * to form the shape e.g. one line could be System.out.println("   *");

Lab Three

Write a Java console application that will display your name and address in a format that might look like a label for an envelope.

Lab Four

Using the same code that you developed for Lab Three, the name and address label, add a statement between each of the name and address lines that will require the user to press a key on the keyboard before the display moves to the next line.

Module 2 Labs – Possible solutions

Lab One

package labs.module02;
```
/*
Write a Java console application, using the println()
command, that will display the letter E using * to form
the shape e.g. one line could be System.out.println("*******");
*/
```
public class LabOne
{
   public static void main(String[] args)
   {
      System.*out*.println("*******");
      System.*out*.println("*");
      System.*out*.println("*");
      System.*out*.println("*******");
      System.*out*.println("*");
      System.*out*.println("*");
      System.*out*.println("*******");
   } // This is the end of the method
} // This is the end of the class

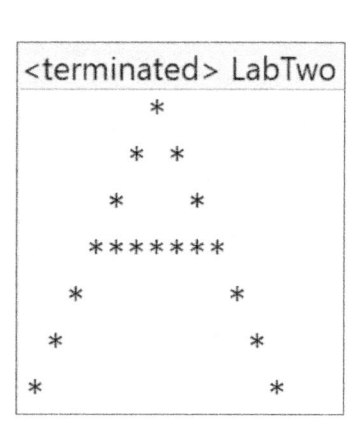

```
<terminated> LabOne [
*******
*
*
*******
*
*
*******
```

Lab Two

package labs.module02;
```
/*
Write a Java console application, using the println()
command, that will display the letter A using * to form
the shape e.g. one line could be System.out.println("    *");
*/
```
public class LabTwo
{
   public static void main(String[] args)
   {
   System.*out*.println("   *");
   System.*out*.println("   * *");
   System.*out*.println(" *   *");
   System.*out*.println(" *******");
   System.*out*.println(" *   *");
   System.*out*.println(" *   *");
   System.*out*.println("*   *");
   } // This is the end of the method
} // This is the end of the class

```
<terminated> LabTwo
      *
     * *
    *   *
   *******
  *       *
 *         *
*           *
```

Lab Three

package labs.module02;
/*
Write a Java console application that will display your name and address in a format that might look like a label for an envelope.
*/
public class LabThree
{
   public static void main(String[] args)
   {
    System.*out*.println("Mr Gerard Byrne");
    System.*out*.println("1 Any Street");
    System.*out*.println("Any Road");
    System.*out*.println("Belfast");
    System.*out*.println("BT1 1AN");
   } // This is the end of the method
} // This is the end of the class

```
<terminated> LabThree [
Mr Gerard Byrne
1 Any Street
Any Road
Belfast
BT1 1AN
```

Lab Four

package labs.module02;
import java.util.Scanner;
/* Using the same code that you developed for Lab Three, the name and address label, add a statement between of the name and address lines that will require the user to press a key on the keyboard before the display moves to the next line. */
public class LabFour
{
 static Scanner *myScanner* = **new** Scanner(System.*in*);
 public static void main(String[] args)
 {
  System.*out*.println("Mr Gerard Byrne");
  System.*out*.println("Press any key to continue");
  myScanner.nextLine();
  System.*out*.println("1 Any Street");
  System.*out*.println("Press any key to continue");
  myScanner.nextLine();
  System.*out*.println("Any Road");
  System.*out*.println("Press any key to continue");
  myScanner.nextLine();
  System.*out*.println("Belfast");
  System.*out*.println("Press any key to continue");
  myScanner.nextLine();
  System.*out*.println("BT1 1AN");
   } // This is the end of the method
} // This is the end of the class

```
<terminated> LabFour [Java Application]
Mr Gerard Byrne
Press any key to continue

1 Any Street
Press any key to continue

Any Road
Press any key to continue

Belfast
Press any key to continue

BT1 1AN
```

Module 4 Labs – Data types

Lab One

Write a Java console application that will calculate and display the area of a rectangle using a length of 20 and a breadth of 10. The formula for the area of a rectangle is length multiplied by breadth.

Lab Two

Write a Java console application that will calculate and display the area of a rectangle using the length and breadth that are input at the console by the user. The formula for the area of a rectangle is length multiplied by breadth.

Lab Three

Using the code from Lab Two write a Java console application that will calculate and display the volume of a cuboid using the length, breadth and height that are input at the console by the user. The formula for the volume of a cuboid is length multiplied by breadth multiplied by height.

Lab Four

Write a Java console application that will accept user input regarding the credit card details required for making an online purchase. The details required are:

- Credit card number — contain 16 digits and hyphens between each 4 digits
- Card expiry month — a number from 1 to 12 (Jan to Dec)
- Card expiry year — a two-digit number for the year e.g. 21
- Card issue number — a single digit number
- Three Digit Security Code — a three-digit number
- Card holder name on card — a String

The details read from the console input of the user should be displayed to the console.

Module 4 Labs – Possible solutions

Lab One - Possible Solution

```java
package labs.module04;
/*
 Write a Java console application that will calculate and display the area of a rectangle using
 the length and breadth that are input at the console by the user.
*/
public class LabOne
{
  public static void main(String[] args)
  {
     int length;
     int breadth;
     int area;

     length = 20;
     breadth = 10;

     area = length * breadth;

     System.out.println("");
     System.out.println("The area of the rectangle is " + area + " square centimetres");
     System.out.println("");

  } // This is the end of the method
} // This is the end of the class
```

Sample output

```
<terminated> LabOne (1) [Java Application] C:\Users\gerardbyrne\.p2\pod

The area of the rectangle is 200 square centimetres
```

Lab Two – Possible Solution

```java
package labs.module04;
import java.util.Scanner;
/*
Write a Java console application that will calculate
and display the area of a rectangle using the length
and breadth that are input at the console by the user.
*/
public class LabTwo
{
    public static void main(String[] args)
    {
        Scanner myScanner = new Scanner(System.in);

        int length;
        int breadth;
        int area;

        System.out.println("What is the length of the rectangle in centimteres");
        length = myScanner.nextInt();

        System.out.println("What is the breadth of the rectangle in centimteres");
        breadth = myScanner.nextInt();

        area = length * breadth;

        System.out.println("");
        System.out.println("The area of the rectangle is " + area + " square centimetres");
        System.out.println("");

        myScanner.close();
    } // This is the end of the method
} // This is the end of the class
```

Sample output

```
<terminated> LabTwo (1) [Java Application] C:\Users\gerardbyrne\.p2\poo
What is the length of the rectangle in centimteres
20
What is the breadth of the rectangle in centimteres
10

The area of the rectangle is 200 square centimetres
```

Lab Three – Possible Solution

```java
package labs.module04;
import java.util.Scanner;
/*
Using the code from Lab Two write a Java console application that will calculate and display
the volume of a cuboid using the length, breadth and height that are input at the console by
the user. The formula for the volume of a cuboid is length * breadth * height.
*/
public class LabThree
{
    public static void main(String[] args)
    {
    Scanner myScanner = new Scanner(System.in);
    int length;
    int breadth;
    int height;
    int volume;

    System.out.println("What is the length of the cuboid in centimteres");
    length = myScanner.nextInt();

    System.out.println("What is the breadth of the cuboid in centimteres");
    breadth = myScanner.nextInt();

    System.out.println("What is the height of the cuboid in centimteres");
    height = myScanner.nextInt();

    volume = length * breadth * height;

    System.out.println("");
    System.out.println("The volume of the cuboid is " + volume + " cubic centimetres");
    System.out.println("");
    myScanner.close();
    } // This is the end of the method
} // This is the end of the class
```

Sample output

```
<terminated> LabThree (1) [Java Application] C:\Users\gerardbyrne\.p2\
What is the length of the cuboid in centimteres
20
What is the breadth of the cuboid in centimteres
10
What is the height of the cuboid in centimteres
10

The volume of the cuboid is 2000 cubic centimetres
```

Lab Four – Possible Solution

package labs.module04;
import java.util.Scanner;
/*
The class holds variables (properties) and methods. In this example there will only be a main
method. This is where the application will start running.
*/
public class LabFour
{
    /*
    The main method is where we will add all our variables and write all our code.
    This is only suitable as we are learning to program but as we develop our skills we will
    modularise our code i.e. we will break the code up into small methods each method having
    only one role or function. We might not want to declare all our variables in the main
    method, we may want them to be declared inside the smaller methods (modules). This is
    where we will begin to understand about the scope of variables.
    */
    public static void main(String[] args)
    {
        Scanner myScanner = **new** Scanner(System.*in*);

        /*
        A credit card will have a 16-digit number on the front of the card. We may
        wish to include hyphens or spaces between each set of 4 digits. For this
        reason, we are making the data type string.
        */
        String creditCardNumber;

        /*
        The month in which the credit card will expire will be entered as a number
        which will be from 0-12 based on the calendar months. This means we can use a
        byte. The byte data type has a minimum value of 0 and a maximum value of 255.
        As a month cannot be a negative, we should use a byte data type.
        */
        byte expiryMonth;

        /*
        The year of expiry only requires the last two digits of the year, it will not
        require the two digits of the century. We should use a byte data type as 0 –
        255 will be an acceptable range for the year.
        */
        byte expiryYear;

        /*
        The card issue number is a one or two digit number on the front of the card.
        Some credit cards will not have an issue number. For this example we should

expect the user to enter a 0 if there is no issue number.
*/
byte issueNumber;

/*
A card verification code (CVC) is also known as the card verification value (CVV) and is a security feature used when the user is not present to make the payment and present the card. It is aimed at reducing fraud.
*/
int threeDigitSecurityCode;

/*
A credit card will have a name imprinted on it. This must be the exact name used when making a transaction. The name will be treated as a String input.
*/
String nameAsItAppearsOnCard;

// Enter the card holder name as it appears on the credit card
System.*out*.println("Enter your name as it appears on your Credit Card");
nameAsItAppearsOnCard = myScanner.nextLine();

/*
Ask the user to enter the 16-digit credit card number as it appears on the credit card and insert hyphens (-) between each set of 4 digits. Then use the nextLine() method to read the data input at the console as a String. The String input data needs no conversion as we are assigning the value to a variable we declared as data type String.
*/
System.*out*.println("Enter the 16 digit credit number");
System.*out*.println("Use hyphens as shown in this example to separate each ");
System.*out*.println("set of 4 digits   1234-5678-1234-7890");;
creditCardNumber = myScanner.nextLine();

/*
Ask the user to enter the value of the expiry month. Then use the nextByte() method to read the data input at the console. The input data will be a String but the method handles the conversion.
*/
System.*out*.println("Enter the expiry month number");
expiryMonth = myScanner.nextByte();

/*
Ask the user to enter the value of the expiry year. Then use the nextByte() method to read the data input at the console and convert it to a byte
*/
System.*out*.println("Enter the expiry year number");
expiryYear = myScanner.nextByte();

```java
/*
Ask the user to enter the value for the issue number. Then use the nextByte()
method to read the data input at the console. The input data will be a String
and the nextByte() methods does the conversion.
*/
System.out.println("Enter the value for the issue number (enter 0 if there is no issue number on our card)");
issueNumber = myScanner.nextByte();

/*
Ask the user to enter the value for the 3-digit security number as it appears
on the back of the card. Then use the nextInt() method to read the data input
at the console. The input data will be a String and the nextInt() methods
does the conversion.
*/
System.out.println("Enter the 3 digit security number from the back of the card");
threeDigitSecurityCode = myScanner.nextInt();

/*
Now we will display the data we have accepted from the user. We use the
println() method to display the data. The * information we have between the
brackets () of the println() is a concatenation of a String of text between
the double quotes "" and a variable. We have also used the escape sequence \n
(new line) and the \t (tab) in an attempt to format the display.
*/
System.out.println("*************************************************\n");
System.out.println("    We have entered the following details \n ");
System.out.println("*************************************************\n");
System.out.println("\nCardholder name:\t" + nameAsItAppearsOnCard);
System.out.println("\nCard number:\t\t" + creditCardNumber);
System.out.println("\nCard expiry month:\t" + expiryMonth);
System.out.println("\nCard expiry year:\t" + expiryYear);
System.out.println("\nCard issue number:\t" + issueNumber);
System.out.println("\nCard security code:\t" + threeDigitSecurityCode);
System.out.println("*************************************************\n");
System.out.println("*************************************************\n");
myScanner.next();

myScanner.close();
    } // This is the end of the method
} // This is the end of the class
```

Sample output

```
LabFour (1) [Java Application] C:\Users\gerardbyrne\.p2\pool\plugins\org.eclipse.justj.openjdk.hotspot.jre.full.win32.x86_64
Enter your name as it appears on your Credit Card
Mr G Byrne
Enter the 16 digit credit number
Use hyphens as shown in this example to separate each
set of 4 digits  1234-5678-1234-7890
1111-2222-3333-4444
Enter the expiry month number
6
Enter the expiry year number
23
Enter the value for the issue number (enter 0 if there is no issue number on our card)
0
Enter the 3 digit security number from the back of the card
098
**************************************************

        We have entered the following details

**************************************************


Cardholder name:        Mr G Byrne

Card number:            1111-2222-3333-4444

Card expiry month:      6

Card expiry year:       23

Card issue number:      0

Card security code:     98
**************************************************


**************************************************
```

Module 5 Labs – Data conversion and arithmetic

Lab One

Write a Java console application that will calculate and display the number of points accumulated by a sports team during their season. The program should ask the user to input the number of games won, the number of games drawn and the number of games lost. The program should total the number of games played and calculate the number of points won based on the facts that 3 points are given for a win, 1 point is given for a draw and 0 points are given for a lost game. Display the number of games played and the number of points accumulated.

Lab Two

Write a Java console application that will calculate and display:

- the total score for two tests that a student undertakes
- the average of the two scores
- the two scores will be input by the user at the console and will be **accepted as String values** by the program code (conversion will be needed)

Module 5 Labs – Possible solutions

Lab One - Possible Solution

```java
package labs.module05;

import java.util.Scanner;
/*
Write a Java console application that will calculate and display
the number of points accumulated by a sports team during their season.
The program should ask the user to input the number of games won,
the number of games drawn, and the number of games lost. The program
should total the number of games played and calculate the number of
points won based on the facts that 3 points are given for a win,
1 point is given for a draw and 0 points are given for a lost game.
Display the number of games played and the number of points accumulated.
*/
public class LabOne
{
    public static void main(String[] args)
    {
        Scanner myScanner = new Scanner(System.in);

        // Declare the variables
        int numberOfGamesWon, numberOfGamesDrawn, numberOfGamesLost;
        int numberOfGamesPlayed, numberOfPointsAccumulated;

        // Input - accept user input
        System.out.println("How many games were won this season? ");
        numberOfGamesWon = myScanner.nextInt();

        System.out.println("How many games were drawn this season? ");
        numberOfGamesDrawn = myScanner.nextInt();

        System.out.println("How many games were lost this season? ");
        numberOfGamesLost = myScanner.nextInt();

        // Process - total the number of games played
        numberOfGamesPlayed = numberOfGamesWon + numberOfGamesDrawn +
            numberOfGamesLost;

        // Calculate the number of points based on 3 points for a win
        // 1 point for a draw and 0 points for a lost game
        numberOfPointsAccumulated = (3 * numberOfGamesWon) + numberOfGamesDrawn;

        // Output the details
```

```java
            System.out.println("");
            System.out.printf("The number of games season was %d ", numberOfGamesPlayed);
            System.out.println("\n\n");
            System.out.printf("The number of points was %d", numberOfPointsAccumulated);

            myScanner.close();

    } // This is the end of the method
} // This is the end of the class
```

Sample output

```
<terminated> LabOne (2) [Java Application] C:\Users\ge
How many games were won this season?
12
How many games were drawn this season?
10
How many games were lost this season?
8

The number of games season was 30


The number of points was 46
```

Lab Two – Possible Solution

```java
package labs.module05;

import java.util.Scanner;
/* Write a Java console application that will calculate and display the total score for two tests
   that a student undertakes the average of the two scores the two scores will be input by the
   user at the console and will be accepted as String values by the program code. */
public class LabTwo
{
    public static void main(String[] args)
    {
        Scanner myScanner = new Scanner(System.in);
        // Declare the variables
        int scoreInTestOne , scoreInTestTwo , totalScoreForTwoTests ;
        double averageOfTheTwoScores ;

        // Input - accept user input for test score one
        System.out.println("What was the score for test one? ");
        scoreInTestOne = Integer.parseInt(myScanner.next());
        System.out.println("What was the score for test two? ");
        scoreInTestTwo = Integer.parseInt(myScanner.next());

        // Process - calculate the total the number of games played
        totalScoreForTwoTests = scoreInTestOne + scoreInTestTwo ;
        // Process - calculate the average the two scores
        averageOfTheTwoScores = totalScoreForTwoTests / 2.0 ;

        // Output the details
        System.out.println("");
        System.out.printf("The total of the two scores is %d " , totalScoreForTwoTests);
        System.out.println("\n\n");
        System.out.printf("The average mark for the two tests is %.2f",
            averageOfTheTwoScores);
        myScanner.close();
    } // This is the end of the method
} // This is the end of the class
```

Sample output

```
<terminated> LabTwo (2) [Java Application] C:\Users\gerardby
What was the score for test one?
60
What was the score for test two?
80

The total of the two scores is 140


The average mark for the two tests is 70.00
```

Module 6 Labs - Arithmetic

Lab One

Write a Java console application that will simulate a simple payroll program. The program should:

- allow a user to input the number of hours worked by an employee
- allow a user to input the rate per hour which the employee is paid
- calculate the gross wage (the hours worked times the rate per hour)
- calculate the amount of national insurance to be deducted when the rate of national insurance is 5% of the gross wage
- calculate the amount of tax to be deducted, after the national insurance has been deducted, when the rate of income tax is 20% of the wage
- display a simplified wages slip showing the gross wage, the deductions and the nett pay

Sample Output using test data

How many hours were worked? 40
What was the rate per hour? £   10.00

Payslip

Hours	40
Rate	£10.00
Gross	£400.00
National Insurance Deductions:	£20.00
Tax Deductions	£76.00
Net Pay	£304.00

Lab One – Possible Solution

```java
package labs.module06;
import java.util.Scanner;
/*
Write a Java console application that will simulate a simple payroll program.
The program should:

 • allow a user to input the number of hours worked by an employee
 • allow a user to input the rate per hour which the employee is paid
 • calculate the gross wage (the hours worked times the rate per hour)
 • calculate the amount of national insurance to be deducted when the
   rate of national insurance is 5% of the gross wage
 • calculate the amount of tax to be deducted when the rate of income
   tax is 20% of the wage after the national insurance has been deducted
 • display a simplified wages slip showing the gross wage, the deductions
   and the nett pay

Sample Output using test data
How many hours were worked? 40
What was the rate per hour? £ 10.00

Payslip
Hours                              40
Rate                               £10.00
Gross                              £400.00
National Insurance Deductions:     £20.00
Income Tax                         £76.00
Net Pay                            £304.00
*/

public class LabOne
{
// Define main() method
 public static void main(String[] args)
 {
    Scanner myScanner = new Scanner(System.in);

    // Declare variables required
    int hoursWorked;
    double  hourlyRate, nettPay, grossPay, nationalInsuranceDeductions,
    incomeTaxDeductions;
    double  nationalInsuranceRate =0.05, incomeTaxRate=0.2;

    // Input Hours Worked
    System.out.println("\n\nEnter Hours Worked: ");
    hoursWorked = myScanner.nextInt();
```

```java
// Input Hourly Rate
System.out.println("\n\nEnter Hourly Rate: ");
hourlyRate = myScanner.nextDouble();

// Process - calculate the nett pay
grossPay = hoursWorked * hourlyRate;

nationalInsuranceDeductions = grossPay * nationalInsuranceRate;

incomeTaxDeductions = (grossPay - nationalInsuranceDeductions) * incomeTaxRate;

nettPay = grossPay - nationalInsuranceDeductions - incomeTaxDeductions;

// Output simple payslip
System.out.println("\n\nPAYSLIP");
System.out.println("=======");
System.out.printf("\nHours Worked\t\t %d", hoursWorked);
System.out.printf("\nHourly Rate \t\t £%.2f", hourlyRate);
System.out.printf("\nGross Pay \t\t £%.2f", grossPay);
System.out.printf("\nNational Insurance \t £%.2f",  nationalInsuranceDeductions);
System.out.printf("\nIncome Tax \t\t £%.2f", incomeTaxDeductions);
System.out.println("\n\t\t\t =======");
System.out.printf("Nett Pay \t\t £%.2f", nettPay);
System.out.println("\n\t\t\t =======");

myScanner.close();
} // End of main() method
} // End of class definition
```

Sample output

```
Enter Hours Worked:
40


Enter Hourly Rate:
10
            PAYSLIP
=====================================
Hours Worked                      40
Hourly Rate                    10.00
Gross Pay                     400.00
National Insurance             20.00
Income Tax                     76.00
                             =======
Nett Pay                      304.00
                             =======
```

Module 7 Labs - Selection

Lab One

Write a Java console application that will ask the user to input a numeric value representing the month of the year (1-12) and the number of days in that month will be displayed. Use a Switch construct.

Lab Two

Write a Java console application that will ask the user to input an examination score, marks out of 100, and the grade will be displayed. The grade will be determined using the business logic:

- marks greater than or equal to 90 receive   Distinction
- marks greater than or equal to 75 receive   Pass
- marks greater less than 75 receive   Unsuccessful

Use an if-else construct.

Lab Three

Write a Java console application that will ask the user to input the name of one of the programming languages Java, Python or C# and a short description of the language will be displayed. Use an if-else construct and be careful when comparing the String values.

Lab One – Possible Solution

```java
package labs.module07;
import java.util.Scanner;
/*Write a Java console application that will ask the user to input a numeric value representing
the month the year (1-12) and the number of days in that month will be displayed.*/
public class LabOneDaysInTheMonth
{
    public static void main(String[] args)
    {
        Scanner myScanner = new Scanner(System.in);
        int month, numberOfDaysInMonth = 0;

        System.out.print("Enter the numeric number representing the month ");
        month = myScanner.nextInt();
        switch (month) {
        case 1:
        case 3:
        case 5:
        case 7:
        case 8:
        case 10:
        case 12:
            numberOfDaysInMonth = 31;
            break;
        case 4:
        case 6:
        case 9:
        case 11:
            numberOfDaysInMonth = 30;
            break;
        case 2:
            numberOfDaysInMonth = 28;
            break;
        default:
            System.out.println("Invalid month! ");
        }
        System.out.println("The number of days in this month is " + numberOfDaysInMonth);
        myScanner.close();
    } // End of main() method
} // End of class LabOneDaysInTheMonth
```

Sample output

```
<terminated> LabOneDaysInTheMonth [Java Application] C:\Users\gera
Enter the numeric number representing the month 6
The number of days in this month is 30
```

Lab Two – Possible Solution

```java
package labs.module07;
import java.util.Scanner;
/* Write a Java console application that will ask the user to input an examination score (out of
100) and the grade will be displayed. The grade will be determined using the business logic:
    • marks greater than or equal to 90 receive          Distinction
    • marks greater than or equal to 75 receive          Pass
    • marks greater less than 75 receive                 Unsuccessful */
public class LabTwoExaminationMarks
{
    public static void main(String[] args)
    {
        Scanner myScanner = new Scanner(System.in);
        String grade = null;
        System.out.print("Enter your examination mark: ");
        int mark = myScanner.nextInt();

        if (mark > 0 && mark <= 100)
        {
          if (mark >= 90)
          {
                grade = "Distinction";
          }
          else if (mark >= 75)
          {
                grade = "pass";
          }
          else
          {
                grade = "unsuccessful";
          }
          System.out.printf("Your mark of %d has given you a grade of '%s'", mark, grade);
        }
        else
        {
          System.out.println("Mark must be between 1 and 100");
        }
        myScanner.close();
    } // End of main() method
} // End of class LabTwoExaminationMarks
```

Sample output

```
<terminated> LabTwoExaminationMarks [Java Application] C:\Users
Enter your examination mark: 78
Your mark of 78 has given you a grade of 'pass'
```

Lab Three – Possible Solution

```java
package labs.module07;
import java.util.Scanner;
/*
Write a Java console application that will ask the user to input the name of a programming
 language (Java, Python or C#) and a short description of the language will be displayed.
Use an if-else construct and be careful when comparing the String values.
*/
public class LabThreeProgrammingLanguages
{
    public static void main(String[] args)
    {
        Scanner myScanner = new Scanner(System.in);
        String userInputLanguage = null;

        System.out.println("Enter the programming: ");
        userInputLanguage = myScanner.next();

        if (userInputLanguage.equalsIgnoreCase("Java"))
        {
            System.out.println("Java is a programming language and computing platform first "
            + "\n" + " released by Sun Microsystems in 1995. There are lots of applications "
            + "\n" + " and websites that will not work unless you have Java installed, and "
            + "\n" + " more are created every day.");
        }
            else if (userInputLanguage.equalsIgnoreCase("C#"))
            {
                System.out.println("C# pronounced as (See Sharp) is a modern, "
                + "\n" + "object-oriented, and type-safe programming language. "
                + "\n" + "C# enables developers to build many types of secure "
                + "\n" + "and robust applications that run in the .NET ecosystem.");
            }
            else if (userInputLanguage.equalsIgnoreCase("Python"))
            {
                System.out.println("Python is an interpreted, object-oriented, high-level "
                + "\n" + "programming language with dynamic semantics. ");
            }
        else
        {
            System.out.println("Sorry, this is not one of our programming languages");
        }
        myScanner.close();
    } // End of main() method
} // End of class LabThreeProgrammingLanguages
```

Sample Output

Upper and lower case

```
<terminated> LabThreeProgrammingLanguages [Java Application] C:\Users\gerardbyrne\.p2\pool\p
Enter the programming:
Java
Java is a programming language and computing platform first
 released by Sun Microsystems in 1995. There are lots of applications
 and websites that will not work unless you have Java installed, and
 more are created every day.
```

Lower case

```
<terminated> LabThreeProgrammingLanguages [Java Application] C:\Users\gerardbyrne\.p2\pool\p
Enter the programming:
java
Java is a programming language and computing platform first
 released by Sun Microsystems in 1995. There are lots of applications
 and websites that will not work unless you have Java installed, and
 more are created every day.
```

Upper case

```
<terminated> LabThreeProgrammingLanguages [Java Application] C:\Users\gerardbyrne\.p2\pool\
Enter the programming:
JAVA
Java is a programming language and computing platform first
 released by Sun Microsystems in 1995. There are lots of applications
 and websites that will not work unless you have Java installed, and
 more are created every day.
```

Module 8 Labs - Iteration

Lab One

Write a Java console application that will display a table showing a column with pound values (£) and a second column showing the equivalent amount in US dollars ($). The pound amounts should be from £1 to £10 and the exchange rate to be used is $1.40 for each £1.00

Sample Output

Pounds	Dollars
1	1.40
2	2.80
3	4.20
4	5.60
5	7.00

Lab Two

Write a Java console application that will display a table showing a column with pound values (£) and a second column showing the equivalent amount in US dollars ($). The application will ask the user to enter the number of pounds they wish to start their conversion table at and then ask them to enter the number of pounds they wish to stop their conversion table at display. The application will display a table showing a column with pound values (£), starting at the users start value and ending at the users end value and a second column showing the equivalent amount in US dollars ($). The exchange rate to be used is $1.40 for each £1.00

Sample Output

Pounds	Dollars
4	5.60
5	7.00
6	8.40
7	9.80
8	11.20
9	12.60
10	14.00

Lab Three

Write a Java console application that will continually ask the user to input the name of a programming language and the message "There are many programming languages including (the language input by the user)" will be displayed. The question will stop being asked when the user inputs X as the language. The message should not be displayed when X has been entered.

Example output:

There are many programming languages including Java

There are many programming languages including JavaScript

Lab Four

Write a Java console application that will ask the user to input how many new vehicle registration numbers they wish to input. The application will continually ask the user to input a vehicle registration number until the required number of registrations have been entered. When the vehicle registration number has been entered a message will display the number of entries that have been made.

Lab One – Possible Solution

```java
package labs.module08;
/*
Write a Java console application that will display a table showing a column with pound (£)
values and a second column showing the equivalent amount in US dollars ($). The pound
amounts should be from £1 to £10 and the exchange rate to be used is $1.40 for each £1.00.
*/

public class LabOnePoundsToDollars
{
    public static void main(String[] args)
    {
        // Create a variable to hold the dollar amount
        double dollarAmount = 0.00;

        // Create a constant to hold the exchange rate
        final double dollarsPerPoundRate = 1.40;

        // Display a heading for the columns
        System.out.println("Pounds \t\t Dollars");

        // Iterate 10 times to convert the pounds to dollars
        for (int poundAmount=1; poundAmount<11; poundAmount++)
        {
            // Convert pounds to dollars at the rate assigned
            dollarAmount = poundAmount * dollarsPerPoundRate;

            System.out.printf("%d \t\t %.2f \n", poundAmount, dollarAmount);
        }
    } // End of main() method
} // End of class LabOnePoundsToDollars
```

Sample Output

```
<terminated> LabOnePoundsToDollars
Pounds          Dollars
1               1.40
2               2.80
3               4.20
4               5.60
5               7.00
6               8.40
7               9.80
8               11.20
9               12.60
10              14.00
```

Lab Two – Possible Solution

```java
package labs.module08;

import java.util.Scanner;

/*
   Write a Java console application that will display a table showing a column with pound (£)
   values and a second column showing the equivalent amount in US dollars ($).
   The application will ask the user to enter the number of pounds they wish to start their
   conversion table at and then ask them to enter the number of pounds they wish to stop their
   conversion table at display.  The application will display a table showing a column with
   pound (£) values, starting at the users start value and ending at the users end value and a
   second column showing the equivalent amount in US dollars ($).
   The exchange rate to be used is $1.40 for each £1.00
*/

public class LabTwoPoundsToDollarsUserInput {

    public static void main(String[] args)
    {
        Scanner myScanner = new Scanner(System.in);

        // Create a variable to hold the dollar amount
        double dollarAmount = 0.00;

        // Create variables for the start and end values
        int startValue = 0, endValue = 0;
        // Create a constant to hold the exchange rate
        final double dollarsPerPoundRate = 1.40;

        // Ask the user to input the start value
        System.out.println("What value do you wish to start at?");
        startValue = myScanner.nextInt();

        // Ask the user to input the end value
        System.out.println("What value do you wish to end at?");
        endValue = myScanner.nextInt();

        // Display a heading for the columns
        System.out.println("Pounds \t\t Dollars");

        /* Iterate starting at the users start value and stopping at the
           users end value */
        for (int poundAmount=startValue; poundAmount<=endValue; poundAmount++)
        {
            // Convert pounds to dollars at the rate assigned
```

```
            dollarAmount = poundAmount * dollarsPerPoundRate;

            System.out.printf("%d \t\t %.2f \n", poundAmount, dollarAmount);
        }

        myScanner.close();
    } // End of main() method
} // End of class LabTwoPoundsToDollars
```

Sample Output

```
<terminated> LabTwoPoundsToDollarsUserInput [J
What value do you wish to start at?
10
What value do you wish to end at?
20
Pounds          Dollars
10              14.00
11              15.40
12              16.80
13              18.20
14              19.60
15              21.00
16              22.40
17              23.80
18              25.20
19              26.60
20              28.00
```

Lab Three – Possible Solution

```java
package labs.module08;
import java.util.Scanner;
/*
Write a Java console application that will continually ask the user to input the name of
a programming language and the message "There are many programming languages
including (the language input by the user)". The question will stop being asked when the user
inputs X as the language. The message should not be displayed when X has been entered.
*/
public class LabThreeProgrammingLanguageUserInput {
    public static void main(String[] args)
    {
        Scanner myScanner = new Scanner(System.in);
        // Create a variable to hold the user input
        String programmingLanguageInput = null;
        do
        {
            // Ask the user to input the programming language
            System.out.println("What is the programming language?");
            programmingLanguageInput = myScanner.next().toUpperCase();

            if(programmingLanguageInput.equals("X"))
            {
                // Display an end message
                System.out.println("Goodbye");
            }
            else
            {
                // Display a heading for the columns
                System.out.printf("\"There are many programming languages including %s\n", programmingLanguageInput);
            }
        } while (!"X".equals(programmingLanguageInput));

        myScanner.close();
    } // End of main() method
} // End of class Lab3ProgrammingLanguageUserInput
```

Sample Output

```
<terminated> LabThreeProgrammingLanguageUserInput [Java Application] C:\Users\
What is the programming language?
Java
"There are many programming languages including JAVA
What is the programming language?
javascript
"There are many programming languages including JAVASCRIPT
What is the programming language?
python
"There are many programming languages including PYTHON
What is the programming language?
x
Goodbye
```

Lab Four – Possible Solution

```java
package labs.module08;

import java.util.Scanner;
/*
 Write a Java console application that will ask the user to input how many new vehicle
 registration numbers they wish to input. Then continually ask the user to input a vehicle
 registration number until the required number of registrations have been entered.
 When the vehicle registration number has been entered a message will display the number
 of entries that have been made.
*/
public class LabFourRegistrationNumbers {
    public static void main(String[] args)
    {
        Scanner myScanner = new Scanner(System.in);

        // Create a variable to hold the number of entries
        int numberOfEntriesBeingMade = 0, numberOfEntriesCompleted = 0;

        // Ask the user to input the number of entries being made
        System.out.println("How many new vehicle registartions are you entering?");
        numberOfEntriesBeingMade = myScanner.nextInt();
        myScanner.nextLine();

        while (numberOfEntriesBeingMade > numberOfEntriesCompleted)
        {
            // Ask the user to input the vehicle registration number
            System.out.println("What is the vehicle registration number?");
            String vehicleRegistrationNumber = myScanner.nextLine();

            // Display a heading for the columns
            System.out.printf("\"You have entered %d vehicle registration number which was %s\n", numberOfEntriesCompleted+1, vehicleRegistrationNumber);
            numberOfEntriesCompleted++;
        }
        System.out.println("Goodbye");
        myScanner.close();
    } // End of main() method
} // End of class LabFourRegistrationNumbers
```

Sample Output

```
<terminated> LabFourRegistrationNumbers [Java Application] C:\Users\gerardbyrne\.p2\pool\p
How many new vehicle registartions are you entering?
2
What is the vehicle registration number?
FHZ 1122
"You have entered 1 vehicle registration number which was FHZ 1122
What is the vehicle registration number?
SHX 3434
"You have entered 2 vehicle registration number which was SHX 3434
Goodbye
```

Module 9 Labs - Arrays

Lab One

Write a Java console application that will use an array with the claim values, 1000.00, 4000.00, 3000.00, 2000.00. The application should calculate and display the total, average, minimum and maximum value of the claims.

Lab Two

Write a Java console application that will ask the user to enter four employee names, store them in an array and then iterate the array to display the employee name.

Lab Three

Write a Java console application that will read an array which contains a list of staff alongside their salary, increase the salary by 10% (1.10) and write the new details to a new array.

The original array should be:

{"Gerry Byrne", "20000.00", "Peter Johnston", "30000.00", "Ryan Jones", "50000.00"}

The new array will be:

{"Gerry Byrne", "22000.00", "Peter Johnston", "33000.00", "Ryan Jones", "55000.00"}

Once the new array has been written use an iteration to display each employee in column one and their new salary in column two.

Lab One – Possible Solution

package labs.module09;

/*
Write a Java console application that will use an array with the claim values, 1000.00, 4000.00, 3000.00, 2000.00. The application should calculate and display the total, average, minimum and maximum value of the claims. */
public class LabOneClaimValues {

  public static void main (String[] arguments)
  {
  // Declare the variables to be used **import** java.util.Scanner;
  double maximumValueOfClaims, minimumValueOfClaims;
  double totalValueOfClaims, averageValueOfClaims ;

  // Declare and initialise the array of claim values
  double [] claimValues = { 1000.00, 4000.00, 3000.00, 2000.00 };

  /* Set up a variable for the total of the claim values
    and initialise its value to 0; */
  totalValueOfClaims = 0 ;

  // Iterate the array and accumulate the claim values
  for (**int** counter = 0 ; counter < claimValues.length ; counter++)
  {
    totalValueOfClaims = totalValueOfClaims + claimValues[counter];
  }

  // Calculate the average using real arithmetic
  averageValueOfClaims = totalValueOfClaims /claimValues.length;

  // Display the total and average
  System.*out*.printf("The total of the claims is £%.2f\n", totalValueOfClaims) ;
  System.*out*.printf("The average claim value is £%.2f\n", averageValueOfClaims) ;

  // Find the maximum value - we assume first value is the maximum value
  maximumValueOfClaims = claimValues[0] ;

  // Compare all the other numbers to the maximum
  for (**int** counter = 1 ; counter < claimValues.length ; counter++)

```java
    {
        // If the next number is greater than the maximum, update the maximum
        if ( claimValues [ counter ] > maximumValueOfClaims )
        {
              maximumValueOfClaims = claimValues[counter];
        }
    }

    // Display the maximum claim value
    System.out.printf("The maximum claim value is £%.2f\n", maximumValueOfClaims ) ;

    // Find the minimum value- we assume the first number is the minimum value
    minimumValueOfClaims = claimValues [0] ;

    // Compare all the other numbers to the minimum
    for (int counter = 1 ; counter < claimValues.length ; counter++ )
    {
        // If the next number is smaller than the minimum, update the minimum
        if ( claimValues [ counter ] < minimumValueOfClaims )
        {
              minimumValueOfClaims = claimValues[counter];
        }
    }

    // Display the minimum claim value
    System.out.printf("The minimum claim value is £%.2f\n", minimumValueOfClaims ) ;
  } // End of main() method
} // End of class LabOneClaimValues
```

Sample Output

```
<terminated> LabOneClaimValues [Java Application]
The total of the claims is £10000.00
The average claim value is £2500.00
The maximum claim value is £4000.00
The minimum claim value is £1000.00
```

Lab Two – Possible Solution

```java
package labs.module09;
import java.util.Scanner;
/*
  Write a Java console application that will ask the user to enter four employee names, store
  them in an array and then iterate the array to display the employee name.
*/
public class LabTwoEmployeeNames
{
    public static void main(String[] args)
    {
        Scanner myScanner = new Scanner(System.in);

        String[] EmployeeNames = new String[4];

        for(int employeenumber=0; employeenumber<4; employeenumber++)
        {
            // Ask the user to input the employee name
            System.out.printf("What is the name of employee %d?", employeenumber+1);
            EmployeeNames[employeenumber] = myScanner.nextLine();
        }

        for(String name: EmployeeNames)
        {
            System.out.println(name);
        }
        myScanner.close();

    } // End of main() method
} // End of class LabTwoEmployeeNames
```

Sample Output

```
<terminated> LabTwoEmployeeNames [Java Application] C:\User
What is the name of employee 1?Gerry Byrne
What is the name of employee 2?Peter Johnston
What is the name of employee 3?Ryan Jones
What is the name of employee 4?May Anderson
Gerry Byrne
Peter Johnston
Ryan Jones
May Anderson
```

Lab Three – Possible Solution

```java
package labs.module09;

import java.text.DecimalFormat;

/*
Write a Java console application that will read an array which contains a list of
staff alongside their salary, increase the salary by 10% (1.10) and write the new
details to a new array.
The array is:
{"Gerry Byrne", "20000.00", "Peter Johnston", "30000.00", "Ryan Jones", "50000.00"}

The new array will be
{"Gerry Byrne", "22000.00", "Peter Johnston", "33000.00", "Ryan Jones", "55000.00"}

Once the new array has been written use an iteration to display each
employee in column one and their new salary in column two.
*/
public class LabThreeEmployeeSalaryIncrease
{

    public static void main ( String[] arguments )
    {
        DecimalFormat myDecimalFormat=new DecimalFormat("#.00");

        // Declare and initialise the array of employees and their salary
        String [] employeeAndSalary = {"Gerry Byrne", "20000.00", "Peter Johnston", "30000.00", "Ryan Jones", "50000.00"};

        // Declare an array of employees and their new salary
        String [] employeeAndSalaryWithIncrease = new String[employeeAndSalary.length];

        // Iterate the array and find every second value which is the salary
        for ( int counter = 0 ; counter < employeeAndSalary.length ; counter+=2 )
        {
            employeeAndSalaryWithIncrease[counter] = employeeAndSalary[counter];
            // Create a variable of type Double (wrapper class) not double
            Double newSalary = Double.parseDouble(employeeAndSalary[counter+1]) * 1.10;

            // Write the employee name to the new array
            employeeAndSalaryWithIncrease[counter] = employeeAndSalary[counter];

            // Write the Double number to the array comverting it to a String
            employeeAndSalaryWithIncrease[counter+1] =
                    myDecimalFormat.format(newSalary).toString();
        }
```

```java
        System.out.print("Employee name" + "\t\t" + "New Salary" + "\n");
        // Compare all the other numbers to the maximum
        for ( int counter = 0 ; counter < employeeAndSalaryWithIncrease.length ; counter+=2 )
        {
            // Display the Employee name and their new salary
            System.out.printf("%s \t\t %s\n", employeeAndSalaryWithIncrease[counter],
                    employeeAndSalaryWithIncrease[counter+1] ) ;
        }

    } // End of main() method
} // End of class LabThreeEmployeeSalaryIncrease
```

Sample Output

```
Problems  @ Javadoc  Declaration  Console  X
<terminated> LabThreeEmployeeSalaryIncrease [Java Application] C:\Us
Employee name              New Salary
Gerry Byrne                22000.00
Peter Johnston             33000.00
Ryan Jones                 55000.00
```

Module 10 Labs - Methods

Lab One

Write a Java console application that will use an array with the claim values, 1000.00, 4000.00, 3000.00, 2000.00. The application should use separate **VOID methods** to:

- calculate the total of the claim values (void method)
- calculate the average of the claim values (void method)
- calculate the minimum of the claim values (void method)
- calculate the maximum of the claim values(void method)
- display a message which states each of the calculated values (void method)

(Refer to Module 09 Lab One the code is the same, but it is sequential)

Lab Two

Use the code from Lab One above if you have completed it.

Write a Java console application that will use an array with the claim values, 1000.00, 4000.00, 3000.00, 2000.00. The application should use separate **VALUE methods** to:

- calculate the total of the claim values (value method, returns a double)
- calculate the average of the claim values (value method, returns a double)
- calculate the minimum of the claim values (value method, returns a double)
- calculate the maximum of the claim values (value method, returns a double)

and a **PARAMETER** method that accepts the four calculated values to:

- display a message which states each of the calculated values (void method)

The application should only use variables which are local to the methods we use. The declaration of the array can be at the class level.

Lab One – Possible Solution

package labs.module10;

```
/*
   Write a Java console application that will use an array with the
   claim values, 1000.00, 4000.00, 3000.00, 2000.00.
   The application should use separate VOID methods to:
      • calculate the total of the claim values
      • calculate the average of the claim values
      • calculate the minimum of the claim values
      • calculate the maximum of the claim values
      • display a message which states each of the calculated values
(Refer to Module 09 Lab One the code is the same but it is sequential)

*/
```

public class LabOneClaimValuesVoidMethods
{
   // Declare and initialise the array of claim values at the class level
   static double []   *claimValues* = { 1000.00, 4000.00, 3000.00, 2000.00 };

   ```
   /*
    Set up the variables at the class level.
   */
   ```
   static double *maximumValueOfClaims*, *minimumValueOfClaims*;
   static double *totalValueOfClaims*, *averageValueOfClaims* ;

   public static void main (String[] arguments)
   {
      totalOfClaimValues();
      averageOfClaimValues();
      maximumClaimValue();
      minimumClaimValue();
      displayTheCalculatedValues();
   } // End of main() method

   /***
            CREATE THE METHODS OUTSIDE THE MAIN METHOD
                     BUT INSIDE THE CLASS
   ***/
   public static void totalOfClaimValues()

```java
{
    // Iterate the array and accumulate the claim values
    for ( int counter = 0 ; counter < claimValues.length ; counter++ )
    {
        totalValueOfClaims = totalValueOfClaims + claimValues[counter];
    }
} // End of totalOfClaimValues() method

public static void  averageOfClaimValues()
{
    // Calculate the average using real arithmetic
    averageValueOfClaims = totalValueOfClaims /claimValues.length;
}

public static void maximumClaimValue()
{
    // Find the maximum value - we assume first value is the maximum value
    maximumValueOfClaims = claimValues[0] ;

    // Compare all the other numbers to the maximum
    for ( int counter = 1 ; counter < claimValues.length ; counter++ )
    {
        // If the next number is greater than the maximum, update the maximum
        if ( claimValues [ counter ] > maximumValueOfClaims )
        {
            maximumValueOfClaims = claimValues[counter];
        }
    }
} // End of maximumClaimValue() method

public static void minimumClaimValue()
{
    // Find the minimum value- we assume the first number is the minimum value
    minimumValueOfClaims = claimValues [0] ;

    // Compare all the other numbers to the minimum
    for (int counter = 1 ; counter < claimValues.length ; counter++ )
    {
        // If the next number is smaller than the minimum, update the minimum
        if ( claimValues [ counter ] < minimumValueOfClaims )
        {
```

```java
                minimumValueOfClaims = claimValues[counter];
            }
        }
    } // End of minimumClaimValue() method

    public static void displayTheCalculatedValues()
    {
        // Display the total of the claim values
        System.out.printf("The total of the claims is £%.2f\n", totalValueOfClaims ) ;

        // Display the average of the claim values
        System.out.printf("The average claim value is £%.2f\n", averageValueOfClaims ) ;

        // Display the maximum claim value
        System.out.printf("The maximum claim value is £%.2f\n", maximumValueOfClaims ) ;

        // Display the minimum claim value
        System.out.printf("The minimum claim value is £%.2f\n", minimumValueOfClaims ) ;
    }
} // End of class LabOneClaimValuesVoidMethods
```

Sample Output

```
<terminated> LabOneClaimValuesVoidMethods [Java
The total of the claims is £10000.00
The average claim value is £2500.00
The maximum claim value is £4000.00
The minimum claim value is £1000.00
```

Lab Two – Possible Solution

package labs.module10;
```
/*
    Use the code from Lab One if you have completed it.
    Write a Java console application that will use an array with
    the claim values, 1000.00, 4000.00, 3000.00, 2000.00.
    The application should use separate VALUE methods to:
    • calculate the total of the claim values (value method, returns a double)
    • calculate the average of the claim values (value method, returns a double)
    • calculate the minimum of the claim values (value method, returns a double)
    • calculate the maximum of the claim values (value method, returns a double)
    and a PARAMETER method that accepts the four calculated values to:
    • display a message which states each of the calculated values (void method)
    The application should only use variables which are local to the methods we use. The
    declaration of the array can be at the class level.
*/
```
public class LabTwoClaimValuesValueMethods
{
  // Declare and initialise the array of claim values at the class level
  static double []   *claimValues* = { 1000.00, 4000.00, 3000.00, 2000.00 } ;

  public static void main (String[] arguments)
  {
    /* Set up the variables at the class level.*/
    double maximumValueOfClaims, minimumValueOfClaims;
    double totalValueOfClaims, averageValueOfClaims ;

    totalValueOfClaims = *totalOfClaimValues*();
    averageValueOfClaims = *averageOfClaimValues*();
    maximumValueOfClaims = *maximumClaimValue*();
    minimumValueOfClaims = *minimumClaimValue*();

    displayTheCalculatedValues(totalValueOfClaims, averageValueOfClaims,
      maximumValueOfClaims, minimumValueOfClaims);
  } // End of main() method
  /***
       CREATE THE METHODS OUTSIDE THE MAIN METHOD
            BUT INSIDE THE CLASS
  ***/
  public static double totalOfClaimValues()

```java
{
    double totalOfClaims = 0.00;
    // Iterate the array and accumulate the claim values
    for ( int counter = 0 ; counter < claimValues.length ; counter++ )
    {
        totalOfClaims = totalOfClaims + claimValues[counter];
    }
    return totalOfClaims;
} // End of totalOfClaimValues() method

public static double averageOfClaimValues()
{
    double averageOfClaims = 0.00;
    // Calculate the average using real arithmetic
    averageOfClaims = totalOfClaimValues() /claimValues.length;
    return averageOfClaims;
}

public static double maximumClaimValue()
{
    // Find the maximum value - we assume first value is the maximum value
    double maximumOfClaims = claimValues[0] ;

    // Compare all the other numbers to the maximum
    for ( int counter = 1 ; counter < claimValues.length ; counter++ )
    {
        // If the next number is greater than the maximum, update the maximum
        if ( claimValues [ counter ] > maximumOfClaims )
        {
            maximumOfClaims = claimValues[counter];
        }
    }
    return maximumOfClaims;
} // End of maximumClaimValue() method

public static double minimumClaimValue()
{
    // Find the minimum value- we assume the first number is the minimum value
    double minimumOfClaims = claimValues [0] ;

    // Compare all the other numbers to the minimum
```

```java
        for (int counter = 1 ; counter < claimValues.length ; counter++ )
        {
            // If the next number is smaller than the minimum, update the minimum
            if ( claimValues [ counter ] < minimumOfClaims )
            {
                minimumOfClaims = claimValues[counter];
            }
        }
        return minimumOfClaims;
    } // End of minimumClaimValue() method

    public static void displayTheCalculatedValues(double totalValueOfClaimsPassedIn, double averageValueOfClaimsPassedIn, double maximumValueOfClaimsPassedIn, double minimumValueOfClaimsPassedIn)
    {
        // Display the total of the claim values
        System.out.printf("The total of the claims is £%.2f\n", totalValueOfClaimsPassedIn) ;

        // Display the average of the claim values
        System.out.printf("The average claim value is £%.2f\n", averageValueOfClaimsPassedIn) ;

        // Display the maximum claim value
        System.out.printf("The maximum claim value is £%.2f\n", maximumValueOfClaimsPassedIn) ;

        // Display the minimum claim value
        System.out.printf("The minimum claim value is £%.2f\n", minimumValueOfClaimsPassedIn) ;
    }
} // End of class ClaimValues
```

Sample Output

```
<terminated> LabTwoClaimValuesValueMethods [Jav
The total of the claims is £10000.00
The average claim value is £2500.00
The maximum claim value is £4000.00
The minimum claim value is £1000.00
```

Module 11 Labs - Classes

Lab One

Use the code from Module 10 Lab Two if you have completed it.

Write a Java console application that will have:

- a class called CalculatedValues and inside it:

    o declare an array with the claim values, 1000.00, 4000.00, 3000.00, 2000.00.
    o use separate **VALUE methods** to:
    - calculate the total of the claim values (value method, returns a double)
    - calculate the average of the claim values (value method, returns a double)
    - calculate the minimum of the claim values (value method, returns a double)
    - calculate the maximum of the claim values (value method, returns a double)

    o use a PARAMETER method that accepts the four calculated values to:
    - display a message which states each of the calculated values (void method)

- a class called ClaimCalculator and inside it:

    o instantiate the CalculatedValues class
    o call each of the four value methods and assign the return value to variables
    o pass the four variables to the parameter method, which will display the table of values

The application should only use variables which are local the method we use. The declaration of the array can be at the class level.

Lab Two

Write a Java console application for an insurance quote that will have:

- a class called QuoteCustomerDetails and inside it:

    o use separate **methods** to ask the user to input:
    - their name
    - the age of their vehicle
    - the engine size of their vehicle
    - calculate the quote value based on the formula:

        100 * (engine size/1000) * (10 / age of vehicle)

        Example test:

        Engine cc   1600

        Age of vehicle 2

        Quote value = 100 * (1600/1000) * (10/2) = 100 * 1.6 * 5 = 800

        Example test:

        Engine cc   3000

        Age of vehicle 10

        Quote value = 100 * (3000/1000) * (10/10) = 100 * 3 * 1 = 300

- a class called QuoteCalculator and inside it:

    o instantiate the QuoteCustomerDetails class
    o call each of the four value methods
    o display the quote amount

Lab One – Possible Solution

CalculatedValues

```java
package labs.module11;
/*Use the code from Module 10 Lab Two if you have completed it.
    Write a Java console application that will:
•   have a class called CalculatedValues and inside it:
    o declare an array with the claim values, 1000.00, 4000.00, 3000.00, 2000.00.
    o use separate VALUE methods to:
        o calculate the total of the claim values (value method, returns a double)
        o calculate the average of the claim values (value method, returns a double)
        o calculate the minimum of the claim values (value method, returns a double)
        o calculate the maximum of the claim values (value method, returns a double)
    o use a PARAMETER method that accepts the four calculated values to:
        o display a message which states each of the calculated values (void method)
*/
public class CalculatedValues
{
    // Declare and initialise the array of claim values at the class level
    static double []    claimValues  =  { 1000.00, 4000.00, 3000.00, 2000.00 } ;

    /******************************************************
            CREATE THE METHODS OUTSIDE THE MAIN METHOD
                BUT INSIDE THE CLASS
    ******************************************************/
    public double totalOfClaimValues()
    {
        double totalOfClaims = 0.00;
        // Iterate the array and accumulate the claim values
        for ( int counter = 0 ; counter < claimValues.length ; counter++ )
        {
            totalOfClaims = totalOfClaims + claimValues[counter];
        }

        return totalOfClaims;
    } // End of totalOfClaimValues() method

    public double averageOfClaimValues()
    {
        double averageOfClaims = 0.00;
```

```java
  // Calculate the average using real arithmetic
  averageOfClaims = totalOfClaimValues() /claimValues.length;

  return averageOfClaims;
}

public double maximumClaimValue()
{
  // Find the maximum value - we assume first value is the maximum value
  double maximumOfClaims = claimValues[0] ;

  // Compare all the other numbers to the maximum
  for ( int counter = 1 ; counter < claimValues.length ; counter++ )
  {
    // If the next number is greater than the maximum, update the maximum
    if ( claimValues [ counter ] > maximumOfClaims )
    {
        maximumOfClaims = claimValues[counter];
    }
  }

  return maximumOfClaims;
} // End of maximumClaimValue() method

public double minimumClaimValue()
{
  // Find the minimum value- we assume the first number is the minimum value
  double minimumOfClaims = claimValues [0] ;

  // Compare all the other numbers to the minimum
  for (int counter = 1 ; counter < claimValues.length ; counter++ )
  {
    // If the next number is smaller than the minimum, update the minimum
    if ( claimValues [ counter ] < minimumOfClaims )
    {
        minimumOfClaims = claimValues[counter];
    }
  }

  return minimumOfClaims;
} // End of minimumClaimValue() method
```

```java
public void displayTheCalculatedValues(double totalValueOfClaimsPassedIn, double averageValueOfClaimsPassedIn, double maximumValueOfClaimsPassedIn, double minimumValueOfClaimsPassedIn)
{
    // Display the total of the claim values
    System.out.printf("The total of the claims is £%.2f\n", totalValueOfClaimsPassedIn) ;

    // Display the average of the claim values
    System.out.printf("The average claim value is £%.2f\n", averageValueOfClaimsPassedIn) ;

    // Display the maximum claim value
    System.out.printf("The maximum claim value is £%.2f\n", maximumValueOfClaimsPassedIn) ;

    // Display the minimum claim value
    System.out.printf("The minimum claim value is £%.2f\n", minimumValueOfClaimsPassedIn) ;
    }
} // End of class CalculatedValues
```

ClaimCalculator

```java
package labs.module11;

/*
    Use the code from Module 10 Lab Two if you have completed it.
    Write a Java console application that will:
        o have a class called ClaimCalculator and inside it:
            o instantiate the CalculatedValues class
            o call each of the four value methods and assign them to variables
            o pass the four variables to the parameter method, which will display the table of values

*/
public class ClaimCalculator
{
    public  static void  main ( String[] arguments )
    {
        /*
```

Set up the variables at the class level.
*/
double maximumValueOfClaims, minimumValueOfClaims;
double totalValueOfClaims, averageValueOfClaims ;

// Instantiate the CalculatedValues class
CalculatedValues myCalculatedValues = **new** CalculatedValues();

// Call each method and assign each to a value
totalValueOfClaims = myCalculatedValues.totalOfClaimValues();
averageValueOfClaims = myCalculatedValues.averageOfClaimValues();
maximumValueOfClaims = myCalculatedValues.maximumClaimValue();
minimumValueOfClaims = myCalculatedValues.minimumClaimValue();

// Pass each value to the display method
myCalculatedValues.displayTheCalculatedValues(totalValueOfClaims, averageValueOfClaims, maximumValueOfClaims, minimumValueOfClaims);
  } // End of main() method
} // End of class ClaimCalculator

Sample Output

```
<terminated> ClaimCalculator [Java Application] C:\U
The total of the claims is £10000.00
The average claim value is £2500.00
The maximum claim value is £4000.00
The minimum claim value is £1000.00
```

Module 12 Labs – String Handling

Lab One

Write a Java console application that will:

- have a class called Registrations and inside it:
  - declare an array of strings with the following vehicle registrations, ABC 1000, FEA 2222, QWA 4444, FAC 9098, FEA 3344.
- use a separate method to:
  - find all vehicle registrations beginning with an F and display them in the console window.

Lab Two

Write a Java console application that will:

- have a class called ClaimsPerState and inside it:
  - declare an array of strings with the following claim details, 1000IL, 2000FL, 1500TX, 1200CA, 2000NC, 300FL

- use separate methods to:

  - display the full array of claim details in alphabetical order
  - check whether a given string ends with the contents of another string and if it does, write it to the console, in this example we will look for the string FL
  - read the claim values and find the total of the claim values given that the claim values are the first 4 numbers in the claim string

Lab One – Possible Solution

Registrations

```java
package labs.module12;

public class LabOneRegistrations
{
    static String[] vehicleRegistrations = {"ABC 1000", "FEA 2222", "QWA 4444", "FAC 9098", "FEA 3344"};

    public static void main(String[] args)
    {
        // Call the method that will find the registration starting with the letter F
        allRegistrationsBeginningWithSpecifiedLetter("F");

    } // End of main () method

    public static void allRegistrationsBeginningWithSpecifiedLetter(String letterInRegistration)
    {
        // Iterate the array
        for(int counter=0;counter<vehicleRegistrations.length; counter++)
        {
            // Check if the current element of the array starts with the letter passed to the method
            if(vehicleRegistrations[counter].startsWith(letterInRegistration))
            {
                System.out.println(vehicleRegistrations[counter]);
            }
        }
    } // End of allRegistrationsBeginningWithSpecifiedLetter() method

} // End of LabOneRegistrations class
```

Sample Output

```
<terminated> LabOneRegistrations
FEA 2222
FAC 9098
FEA 3344
```

Lab Two – Possible Solution

Claims per state

```java
package labs.module12;

import java.util.Arrays;

public class LabTwoClaimsPerState
{
  static String[] claimsWithStateAbbreviation = {"1000IL", "2000FL", "1500TX", "1200CA", "2000NC", "300FL"};

  public static void main(String[] args)
  {
    // Call the displayTheSortedClaims() method
    System.out.println("The sorted array elements are");
    displayTheSortedClaims();

    // Declare the state to be found
    String stateAbbreviationToFind = "FL";

    // Call the allClaimsInASpecificState() method passing it the string to be found
    System.out.printf("The claims for the state of %s are %n", stateAbbreviationToFind);
    allClaimsInASpecificState(stateAbbreviationToFind);

    // Call the findTheTotalOfAllClaimValues() method
    double totalOfAllClaims = findTheTotalOfAllClaimValues();
    System.out.printf("The total of the claim values is %.2f ", totalOfAllClaims);
  } // End of main () method

  public static void allClaimsInASpecificState(String stateAbbreviationToFind)
  {
    // Iterate the array
    for(int counter=0;counter<claimsWithStateAbbreviation.length; counter++)
    {
        // Check if the current element of the array ends with the letter passed to the method
        if(claimsWithStateAbbreviation[counter].endsWith(stateAbbreviationToFind))
        {
            System.out.println(claimsWithStateAbbreviation[counter]);
        }
    }
  } // End of allClaimsInASpecificState() method

  public static void displayTheSortedClaims()
  {
```

```java
    // Sort the claimsWithStateAbbreviation array
    Arrays.sort(claimsWithStateAbbreviation);
    // Iterate the sorted array using the foreach construct
    for(String claim:claimsWithStateAbbreviation)
    {
        System.out.println(claim);
    }
} // End of displayTheSortedClaims() method

public static double findTheTotalOfAllClaimValues()
{
    double currentTotalValue = 0.00;
    double claimValue = 0.00;
    String firstFourCharacters;

    // Iterate the array
    for(int counter=0;counter<claimsWithStateAbbreviation.length; counter++)
    {
        /*
          Read the first four characters of the array element, parse (convert) it
          to a double and add it to the current total
        */
        firstFourCharacters = claimsWithStateAbbreviation[counter].substring(0,4);
        claimValue = Double.parseDouble(firstFourCharacters);
        currentTotalValue += claimValue;
    }
    return currentTotalValue;
} // End of findTheTotalOfAllClaimValues() method

} // End of LabTwoClaimsPerState class
```

Sample Output

```
<terminated> LabTwoClaimsPerState [Java Application] C:
The sorted array elements are
1000IL
1200CA
1500TX
2000FL
2000NC
300FL
The claims for the state of FL are
2000FL
300FL
The total of the claim values is 8000.00
```

Module 13 Labs – File Handling

Lab One

Write a Java console application that will:

- have a class called WriteRegistrationsToFile
- ask a user to input 5 vehicle registrations with the format, 3 letters followed by a space followed by 4 numbers e.g. ABC 1234
- write each of the 5 vehicle registrations to a new line in a text file called vehicleregistrations.txt

Lab Two

Write a Java console application that will:

- have a class called ReadRegistrationsFromFile
- declare an array of strings called vehicleRegistrations
- read the 5 lines from the vehicleregistrations.txt created in Lab One and add them to the array.
- iterate the array and display each vehicle registration

Lab One – Possible Solution

Write Registrations To File

```java
package labs.module13;

import java.io.BufferedWriter;
import java.io.FileWriter;
import java.io.IOException;
import java.util.Scanner;

public class LabOneWriteRegistrationsToFile
{
    static Scanner myScanner = new Scanner(System.in);

    static String vehicleRegistration;

    // Assign the name of the file to be used to a variable.
    static String filePath = "vehicleregistrations.txt";

    public static void main(String[] args)
    {
        /*
           Create a loop to iterate 5 times asking the user
           to input a vehicle registration each time.
        */
        for(int counter = 1; counter <6; counter++)
        {
            System.out.println("Enter vehicle registration number  " + counter);
            vehicleRegistration = myScanner.nextLine();
            writeRegistrationToTextFile(vehicleRegistration);
        } // Enter of iteration

    } // End of main method()

    public static void writeRegistrationToTextFile(String vehicleRegistration)
    {
        // Enclose the code in a try catch to handle errors
        try
        {
            /*
               Create an instance of the FileWriter and call it fileWriter
               FileWriterr is used to write text files in the default encoding.
            */
            FileWriter fileWriter = new FileWriter(filePath, true);
```

```java
        /*
         Create an instance of the BufferedReader and call it bufferedReader
         we should always wrap a FileWriter in a BufferedWriter
        */
        BufferedWriter bufferedWriter = new BufferedWriter(fileWriter);

        /*
         Write text to the file using the write() method.
         In Java the write method will not automatically use a newline character
         so we will use the newLine() method to add the new line.
        */
        bufferedWriter.write(vehicleRegistration);
        bufferedWriter.newLine();

        // Close the files.
        bufferedWriter.close();
    } // End of the try section of the error handling

    catch(IOException ex)
    {
        System.out.println("Error writing file '" + filePath + "'");

    } // End of the catch section of the error handling
  }

} // End of LabOneWriteRegistrationsToFile class
```

Sample Output

```
<terminated> LabOneWriteRegistrationsToFile [Java
Enter vehicle registration number   1
FHZ 0011
Enter vehicle registration number   2
FHZ 0012
Enter vehicle registration number   3
FHZ 0013
Enter vehicle registration number   4
SHX 1111
Enter vehicle registration number   5
SHX 1112
```

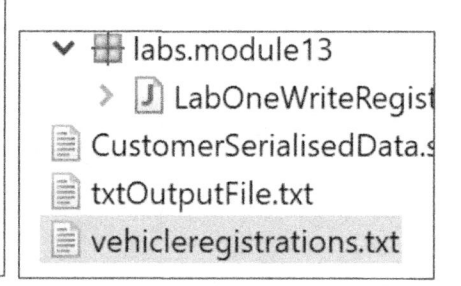

```
v  labs.module13
   >  J LabOneWriteRegist
   CustomerSerialisedData.s
   txtOutputFile.txt
   vehicleregistrations.txt
```

Lab Two – Possible Solution

Read Registrations From File

```java
package labs.module13;

import java.io.BufferedReader;
import java.io.FileReader;
import java.io.IOException;

public class LabTwoReadRegistrationsFromFile
{
   // Assign the name of the file to be used to a variable.
   static String filePath = "vehicleregistrations.txt";

   static String[] vehicleRegistrations = new String[5];

   public static void main(String[] args)
   {
      readRegistrationFromTextFile();
      displayArrayItems();
   } // End of main method()


   public static void readRegistrationFromTextFile()
   {
   // Set up a string variable to hold the lines read
   String line = null;

   int lineCountValue = 0;

   // Enclose the code in a try catch to handle errors
     try
     {
       /*
         Create an instance of the FileReader and call it fileReader
         FileReader is used to read text files in the default encoding.
       */
       FileReader fileReader= new FileReader(filePath);

       /*
          Create an instance of the BufferedReader and call it bufferedReader
          we should always wrap a FileReader in a BufferedReader
       */
       BufferedReader bufferedReader = new BufferedReader(fileReader);
```

```java
    /*
    Iterate the buffer and read one line at a time and display it
    */
    while((line = bufferedReader.readLine()) != null)
    {
        vehicleRegistrations[lineCountValue] = line;
        lineCountValue++;
    } // End of while iteration

    // Close the files.
    bufferedReader.close();
} // End of try section of the error handling

catch(IOException ex)
{
    System.out.println("Error reading file '" + filePath + "'");
} // End of the catch section of the error handling

} // End of readRegistrationFromTextFile() method

public static void displayArrayItems()
{
    // Iterate the sorted array using the foreach construct
    for(String vehicleRegistrations:vehicleRegistrations)
    {
        System.out.println(vehicleRegistrations);
    }
} // End of displayArrayItems() method
} // End of LabTwoReadRegistrationsFromFile class
```

Sample Output

<terminated> LabTwoReadRegistrationsFromFile
FHZ 0011
FHZ 0012
FHZ 0013
SHX 1111
SHX 1112

Module 14 Labs – Serialisation of a class

Lab One

Write a Java console application that will:

- have a class called Vehicle which implements Serializable
- the Vehicle class will have:
    - two private String properties called vehicleManufacturer and vehicleType
    - one private transient property called vehicleChasisNumber
    - a constructor using all three properties
    - getters and setters for the properties
    - a toString() method to return the three properties
- a class called VehicleSerialisation which will:
    - instantiate the Vehicle class and pass details of a vehicle to the constructor e.g. Vehicle myVehicle = **new** Vehicle("Ford", "Mondeo", "VIN 1234567890");
    - write the serialised data to a file called vehicleserialised.ser
    - read the serialised data file and display the vehicle details

Lab Two

Write a Java console application that will:

- have a class called AgentEntity which implements Serializable
    - the AgentEntity class will have:
        - the following private properties:
            - agentNumber which is of data type int
            - agentYearsOfService which is of data type int
            - agentFullName which is of data type String
        - the following private transient properties:
            - agentDOB which is of data type String
            - agentCapitalInvestment which is of data type double
        - a constructor using all the properties

- getters and setters for all the properties
- a toString() method to return the properties

- a class called AgentSerialisation which will:

  o instantiate the AgentEntity class and pass details of an Agent to the constructor e.g.

   AgentEntity myAgentEntity = new AgentEntity(190091, 25, "Gerry Byrne", "01/01/1970", 50000.00);

  o write the serialised data to a file called agentserialised.ser

- have a second class called AgentDeserialised which will deserialise the agentserialised.ser file and print the details of the AgentEntity that is returned

Lab One – Possible Solution

Vehicle serialisation and deserialization

Vehicle class (Entity)

```java
package labs.module14;

import java.io.Serializable;

public class Vehicle implements Serializable
{
    // Properties of the class. Transient properties are not serialised
    private String vehicleManufacturer;
    private String vehicleType;

    // Example for transient
    transient private String vehicleChasisNumber;

    public Vehicle(String vehicleManufacturer, String vehicleType, String vehicleChasisNumber) {
        this.vehicleManufacturer = vehicleManufacturer;
        this.vehicleType = vehicleType;
        this.vehicleChasisNumber = vehicleChasisNumber;
    }

    public String getVehicleManufacturer() {
        return vehicleManufacturer;
    }

    public void setVehicleManufacturer(String vehicleManufacturer) {
        this.vehicleManufacturer = vehicleManufacturer;
    }

    public String getVehicleType() {
        return vehicleType;
    }

    public void setVehicleType(String vehicleType) {
        this.vehicleType = vehicleType;
    }
    public String getVehicleChasisNumber() {
        return vehicleChasisNumber;
    }

    public void setVehicleChasisNumber(String vehicleChasisNumber) {
        this.vehicleChasisNumber = vehicleChasisNumber;
```

```java
    }

    @Override
    public String toString() {
        return "Vehicle [vehicleManufacturer=" + vehicleManufacturer + ", vehicleType=" + vehicleType
                + ", vehicleChasisNumber=" + vehicleChasisNumber + "]";
    }

} // End of Vehicle class
```

Vehicle Serialisation class

```java
package labs.module14;

import java.io.FileInputStream;
import java.io.FileOutputStream;
import java.io.ObjectInputStream;
import java.io.ObjectOutputStream;

public class VehicleSerialisation
{
    public static void main(String[] args)
    {
        String filename = "vehicleserialised.ser";

        /*****************************************************************
         Create an instance of the Vehicle class passing in the initial values
         that will be used to set the values of the properties (members, fields)
         in the Vehicle object being created.
         *****************************************************************/
        Vehicle myVehicle = new Vehicle("Ford", "Mondeo", "VIN 1234567890");

        // Save the myVehicle object to the file
        // The file output stream is an output stream for writing data to a File
        FileOutputStream fileOutputStreamForData = null;

        // An ObjectOutputStream writes primitive data types of Java objects to an OutputStream
        ObjectOutputStream objectOutputStreamForData = null;

        // Save the myVehicle object to the file
        try
        {
            fileOutputStreamForData = new FileOutputStream(filename);

            objectOutputStreamForData = new ObjectOutputStream(fileOutputStreamForData);
```

```java
      objectOutputStreamForData.writeObject(myVehicle);

      objectOutputStreamForData.close();

      fileOutputStreamForData.close();
   }
   catch (Exception ex)
   {
      ex.printStackTrace();
   }

   /*******************************************************************
      Read the object from file from the serialised file
      FileInputStream allows us to read the contents of a file as a stream of bytes
   *******************************************************************/
   FileInputStream fileInputStreamForData = null;

   /* An ObjectInputStream deserialises primitive data and objects written using an
       ObjectOutputStream */
   ObjectInputStream objectInputStreamForData = null;
   try
   {
      fileInputStreamForData = new FileInputStream(filename);

      /* An ObjectInputStream deserialises primitive data and objects written using an
          ObjectOutputStream */
      objectInputStreamForData = new ObjectInputStream (fileInputStreamForData);

      /*
         The serialised file has been read and we use the readObject() method to get the
         object, we then cast the object to a Vehicle object
      */
      myVehicle = (Vehicle) objectInputStreamForData.readObject();

      objectInputStreamForData.close();
   }
   catch (Exception ex)
   {
      ex.printStackTrace();
   }
   System.out.println(myVehicle);
 } // End of main() method
} // End of LabOneVehicleSerialisation class
```

Sample Output

```
<terminated> VehicleSerialisation [Java Application] C:\Users\gerardbyrne\.p2\pool\plugins\org.eclipse.justj.openj
Vehicle [vehicleManufacturer=Ford, vehicleType=Mondeo, vehicleChasisNumber=null]
```

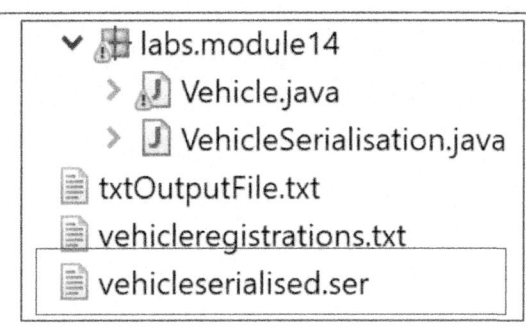

- ▾ labs.module14
  - › Vehicle.java
  - › VehicleSerialisation.java
- txtOutputFile.txt
- vehicleregistrations.txt
- vehicleserialised.ser

Lab Two – Possible Solution

AgentEntity class

```java
package labs.module14;
import java.io.Serializable;
public class AgentEntity implements Serializable
{
 /*
    Properties of the class are private as we have getters and setters and we have two transient
    properties as we do not want them to be serialised
  */
 private int agentNumber;
 private int agentYearsOfService;
 private String agentFullName;
 private transient String agentDOB;
 private transient double agentCapitalInvestment;
 /*
  * Create a constructor which will set the initial value for
  * properties when the AgentEntity class is being instantiated
  */
 /*******************************************************************
 Create a constructor for the AgentEntity class which will over-write the default constructor.
 The constructor is used to accept values passed into it from the code which instantiates the
 class. Values passed into the constructor are used to initialise the values of the properties
 (members, fields, variables!). The keyword this is used in front of the property names.
 *******************************************************************/
 public AgentEntity(int agentNumber, int agentYearsOfService, String agentFullName,
        String agentDOB, double agentCapitalInvestment)
 {
   this.agentNumber = agentNumber;
   this.agentYearsOfService = agentYearsOfService;
   this.agentFullName = agentFullName;
   this.agentDOB = agentDOB;
   this.agentCapitalInvestment = agentCapitalInvestment;
 } // End of constructor

 /*******************************************************************
 As the properties are marked private they are not accessible from outside the class and to
 enable the properties to be accessed from outside the class we use a getter method to get the
 value and a setter method to set the value of the property. We do not need to have a getter
 and setter for all fields but we normally will. This is what is done below.
 *******************************************************************/
 public int getAgentNumber() {
   return agentNumber;
 }
 public void setAgentNumber(int agentNumber) {
```

```java
    this.agentNumber = agentNumber;
  }

  public int getAgentYearsOfService() {
    return agentYearsOfService;
  }

  public void setAgentYearsOfService(int agentYearsOfService) {
    this.agentYearsOfService = agentYearsOfService;
  }

  public String getAgentFullName() {
    return agentFullName;
  }

  public void setAgentFullName(String agentFullName) {
    this.agentFullName = agentFullName;
  }

  public String getAgentDOB() {
    return agentDOB;
  }

  public void setAgentDOB(String agentDOB) {
    this.agentDOB = agentDOB;
  }

  public double getAgentCapitalInvestment() {
    return agentCapitalInvestment;
  }

  public void setAgentCapitalInvestment(double agentCapitalInvestment) {
    this.agentCapitalInvestment = agentCapitalInvestment;
  }

  @Override
  public String toString() {
    return "AgentEntity [agentNumber=" + agentNumber + ", agentYearsOfService=" + agentYearsOfService
        + ", agentFullName=" + agentFullName + ", agentDOB=" + agentDOB + ", agentCapitalInvestment=" + agentCapitalInvestment + "]";
  }
} // End of class
```

Agent serialisation

```java
package labs.module14;
import java.io.FileOutputStream;
import java.io.ObjectOutputStream;

public class AgentSerialisation
{
  public static void main(String[] args)
  {
    String filename = "agentserialised.ser";

    /*******************************************************************
    Create an instance of the AgentEntity class passing in the initial values that will be used
    to set the values of the properties in the AgentEntity object being created.
    *******************************************************************/
    AgentEntity myAgentEntity = new AgentEntity(190091, 25, "Gerry Byrne",
    "01/01/1970", 50000.00);

    // Save the myAgentEntity object to the file
    // The file output stream is an output stream for writing data to a File
    FileOutputStream fileOutputStreamForData = null;

    // An ObjectOutputStream writes primitive data types of Java objects to an OutputStream
    ObjectOutputStream objectOutputStreamForData = null;

    // Save the myAgentEntity object to the file
    try
    {
      fileOutputStreamForData = new FileOutputStream(filename);

      objectOutputStreamForData = new ObjectOutputStream(fileOutputStreamForData);

      objectOutputStreamForData.writeObject(myAgentEntity);

      objectOutputStreamForData.close();

      fileOutputStreamForData.close();
    }
    catch (Exception ex)
    {
      ex.printStackTrace();
    }
  } // End of main() method
} // End of AgentSerialisation class
```

Agent deserialization

```java
package labs.module14;
import java.io.FileInputStream;
import java.io.ObjectInputStream;

public class AgentDeserialised {
  public static void main(String[] args)
  {
    String filename = "agentserialised.ser";

    /* Create a Customer object */
    AgentEntity myAgentEntity = null;
    /*********************************************************************
      Read the object from file from the serialised file
      FileInputStream allows us to read the contents of a file as a stream of bytes
    *********************************************************************/
    FileInputStream fileInputStreamForData = null;

    /* An ObjectInputStream deserialises primitive data and objects written using an
       ObjectOutputStream */
    ObjectInputStream objectInputStreamForData = null;

    try {
      fileInputStreamForData = new FileInputStream(filename);

      /* An ObjectInputStream deserialises primitive data and objects written using an
         ObjectOutputStream */
      objectInputStreamForData = new ObjectInputStream (fileInputStreamForData);

      /*
        The serialised file has been read and we use the readObject() method to get the
        object, we then cast the object to a Vehicle object
      */
      myAgentEntity = (AgentEntity) objectInputStreamForData.readObject();

      objectInputStreamForData.close();
    }
    catch (Exception ex) {
      ex.printStackTrace();
    }

    System.out.println(myAgentEntity);
  } // End of main() method
} // End of AgentDeserialised class
```

Sample Output

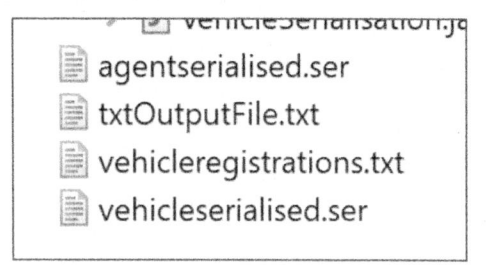

- agentserialised.ser
- txtOutputFile.txt
- vehicleregistrations.txt
- vehicleserialised.ser

```
<terminated> AgentDeserialised [Java Application] C:\Users\gerardbyrne\.p2\pool\plugins\org.eclipse.justj.openjdk.hot
AgentEntity [agentNumber=190091, agentYearsOfService=25, agentFullName=Gerry Byrne,
\plugins\org.eclipse.justj.openjdk.hotspot.jre.full.win32.x86_64
 agentDOB=null, agentCapitalInvestment=0.0]
```

Printed in Great Britain
by Amazon